ACCA

PAPER F8

AUDIT AND ASSURANCE
(INTERNATIONAL)

PRACTICE & REVISION KIT

In this June 2007 new edition

- We discuss the **best strategies** for revising and taking your ACCA exams

- We show you how to be well prepared for the **December 2007 exam**

- We give you **lots of great guidance** on tackling questions

- We include **genuine student answers** with BPP commentary

- We show you how you can **build your own exams**

- We provide you with **three** mock exams including the **Pilot paper**

- We provide the **ACCA examiner's answers** as well as our own to key exam questions and the Pilot Paper as an additional revision aid

Our **i-Pass** product also supports this paper.

FOR EXAMS IN DECEMBER 2007

LEARNING MEDIA

First edition June 2007

ISBN 9780 7517 3365 5

British Library Cataloguing-in-Publication Data
A catalogue record for this book
is available from the British Library

Published by

BPP Learning Media Ltd
BPP House, Aldine Place
London W12 8AA

www.bpp.com/learningmedia

Printed in Great Britain by
Polestar Wheatons
Exeter

Your learning materials, published by BPP Learning
Media Ltd, are printed on paper sourced from
sustainable, managed forests.

We are grateful to the Association of Chartered
Certified Accountants for permission to reproduce past
examination questions. The answers to past
examination questions have been prepared by BPP
Learning Media Ltd.

Contents

Review form & free prize draw

Question index

The headings in this checklist/index indicate the main topics of questions, but questions often cover several different topics.

Questions set under the old syllabus *Audit and Internal Review* (AIR) paper are included because their style and content are similar to those which appear in the F8 exam. The questions have been amended to reflect the current exam format.

Mock exam 1

Mock exam 2

Mock exam 3 (Pilot paper)

Planning your question practice

Our guidance from page 37 shows you how to organise your question practice, either by attempting questions from each syllabus area or **by building your own exams** – tackling questions as a series of practice exams.

Topic index

Listed below are the key Paper F8 syllabus topics and the numbers of the questions in this Kit covering those topics.

If you need to concentrate your practice and revision on certain topics or if you want to attempt all available questions that refer to a particular subject, you will find this index useful.

Syllabus topic	Question numbers
Analytical procedures	18, 23, 38, Mock 2 Q3
Assurance	65
Audit appointment	Mock 1 Q1, Mock 3 Q2
Audit evidence	23, 49, 56, Mock 3 Q2
Audit judgements	1
Audit planning	18, 19, 59
Audit regulation	4
Audit reporting	58, 61, 62, 63, 64, 65, Mock 2 Q5, Mock 3 Q5
Audit risk	12, 16, 17, 20, 21, 22, 28, 31, 37, Mock 2 Q3
Audit sampling	57
Auditing standards	5
CAATs	24, 25, 57, Mock 3 Q1
Cash and bank	46, 47
Confidentiality	11
Corporate governance	6, 7, 8, Mock 3 Q3
Estimates	45
Ethics	9, 10, 11, 12, 22, Mock 1 Q3, Mock 1 Q3, Mock 1 Q5, Mock 3 Q3
External audit	2
Fraud	3, 21, Mock 2 Q2
Going concern	20, 61, 63
Independence	3, Mock 1 Q3
Internal audit	7, 13, 14, 15, 21, Mock 1 Q3, Mock 2 Q1
Internal controls	16, 29, 30, 33, 35, 47, Mock 1 Q4, Mock 3 Q4
Inventory	40, 41, 42, 43, 50, 55, Mock 2 Q2
Management representations	51, 55, Mock 1 Q2
Materiality	36
Non-current assets	37, 38, 39, 50
Not for profit organisations	28, 35
Payables	48, Mock 3 Q1
Provisions	48, 50, Mock 1 Q5
Purchases systems	33

Syllabus topic	Question numbers
Receivables	30, 31, 44, 45, 55, 57
Removal from office	58
Report to management	29, 33, 42
Review reports	65
Sales systems	31, 32, 39
Subsequent events	50, 59, 60, 64, Mock 2 Q4, Mock 3 Q5
Wages systems	34, 49, Mock 1 Q4, Mock 3 Q4

Using your BPP Practice and Revision Kit

Tackling revision and the exam

You can significantly improve your chances of passing by tackling revision and the exam in the right ways. Our advice is based on recent feedback from ACCA examiners.

- We look at the dos and don'ts of revising for, and taking, ACCA exams
- We focus on Paper F8; we discuss revising the syllabus, what to do (and what not to do) in the exam, how to approach different types of question and ways of obtaining easy marks

Selecting questions

We provide signposts to help you plan your revision.

- A full **question index**
- A **topic index** listing all the questions that cover key topics, so that you can locate the questions that provide practice on these topics, and see the different ways in which they might be examined
- **BPP's question plan** highlighting the most important questions and explaining why you should attempt them
- **Build your own exams**, showing how you can practise questions in a series of exams

Making the most of question practice

At BPP we realise that you need more than just questions and model answers to get the most from your question practice.

- Our **Top tips** provide essential advice on tackling questions, presenting answers and the key points that answers need to include
- We show you how you can pick up **Easy marks** on questions, as we know that picking up all readily available marks often can make the difference between passing and failing
- We summarise **Examiner's comments**
- We include **marking guides** to show you what the examiner rewards
- We refer to the **BPP 2007 Study Text** for detailed coverage of the topics covered in each question
- A number of questions include **Analysis** and **Helping hands** attached to show you how to approach them if you are struggling
- We include **annotated student answers** to some questions to highlight how these questions can be tackled and ways answers can be improved.
- In a bank at the end of this Kit we include the **examiner's answers** to the Pilot paper and other questions. Used in conjunction with our answers they provide an indication of all possible points that could be made, issues that could be covered and approaches to adopt.

Attempting mock exams

There are three mock exams that provide practice at coping with the pressures of the exam day. We strongly recommend that you attempt them under exam conditions. **Mock exams 1 and 2** reflect the question styles and syllabus coverage of the exam; **Mock exam 3** is the Pilot paper. To help you get the most out of doing these exams, we not only provide help with each answer, but also guidance on how you should have approached the whole exam.

Passing ACCA exams

Revising and taking ACCA exams

To maximise your chances of passing your ACCA exams, you must make best use of your time, both before the exam during your revision, and when you are actually doing the exam.

- Making the most of your revision time can make a big, big difference to how well-prepared you are for the exam

- Time management is a core skill in the exam hall; all the work you've done can be wasted if you don't make the most of the three hours you have to attempt the exam

In this section we simply show you what to do and what not to do during your revision, and how to increase and decrease your prospects of passing your exams when you take them. Our advice is grounded in feedback we've had from ACCA examiners. You may be surprised to know that much examiner advice is the same whatever the exam, and the reasons why many students fail don't vary much between subjects and exam levels. So if you follow the advice we give you over the next few pages, you will **significantly** enhance your chances of passing **all** your ACCA exams.

How to revise

☑ Plan your revision

At the start of your revision period, you should draw up a **timetable** to plan how long you will spend on each subject and how you will revise each area. You need to consider the total time you have available and also the time that will be required to revise for other exams you're taking.

☑ Practise Practise Practise

The **more exam-standard questions** you do, the **more likely you are to pass** the exam. Practising full questions will mean that you'll get used to the time pressure of the exam. When the time is up, you should note where you've got to and then try to complete the question, giving yourself practice at everything the question tests.

☑ Revise enough

Make sure that your revision covers the breadth of the syllabus, as all topics could be examined in a compulsory question. However it is true that some topics are **key** – they are likely to appear often or are a particular interest of the examiner – and you need to spend sufficient time revising these. Make sure you also know the **basics** – the fundamental calculations, proformas and report layouts.

☑ Deal with your difficulties

Difficult areas are topics you find dull and pointless, or subjects that you found problematic when you were studying them. You mustn't become negative about these topics; instead you should build up your knowledge by reading the **Passcards** and using the **Quick Quiz** questions in the Study Text to test yourself. When practising questions in the Kit, go back to the Text if you're struggling.

☑ Learn from your mistakes

Having completed a question you must try to look at your answer critically. Always read the **Top tips guidance** in the answers; it's there to help you. Look at **Easy marks** to see how you could have quickly gained credit on the questions that you've done. As you go through the Kit, it's worth noting any traps you've fallen into, and key points in the **Top tips** or **Examiner's comments** sections, and referring to these notes in the days before the exam. Aim to learn at least one new point from each question you attempt, a technical point perhaps or a point on style or approach.

☑ Read the examiners' guidance

We refer throughout this Kit to **Examiner's comments**. As well as highlighting weaknesses, Examiner's comments often provide clues to future questions, as many examiners will test areas that are likely to cause students problems. ACCA's website also contains articles by examiners which you **must** read, as they may form the basis of questions on any paper after they've been published.

Read through the examiner's answers to key exam questions and the Pilot paper included at the back of the Kit. In general these are far longer and more comprehensive than any answer you could hope to produce in the exam, but used in conjunction with our more realistic solutions, they provide a useful revision tool, covering all possible points and approaches.

☑ Complete all three mock exams

You should attempt the **Mock exams** at the end of the Kit under **strict exam conditions**, to gain experience of selecting questions, managing your time and producing answers.

How NOT to revise

☒ Revise selectively

Examiners are well aware that some students try to forecast the contents of exams, and only revise those areas that they think will be examined. Examiners try to prevent this by doing the unexpected, for example setting the same topic in successive sittings.

☒ Spend all the revision period reading

You cannot pass the exam just by learning the contents of Passcards, Course Notes or Study Texts. You have to develop your **application skills** by practising questions.

☒ Audit the answers

This means reading the answers and guidance without having attempted the questions. Auditing the answers gives you **false reassurance** that you would have tackled the questions in the best way and made the points that our answers do. The feedback we give in our answers will mean more to you if you've attempted the questions and thought through the issues.

☒ Practise some types of question, but not others

Although you may find the numerical parts of certain papers challenging, you shouldn't just practise calculations. These papers will also contain written elements, and you therefore need to spend time practising written question parts.

☒ Get bogged down

Don't spend a lot of time worrying about all the minute detail of certain topic areas, and leave yourself insufficient time to cover the rest of the syllabus. Remember that a key skill in the exam is the ability to **concentrate on what's important** and this applies to your revision as well.

☒ Overdo studying

Studying for too long without interruption will mean your studying becomes less effective. A five minute break each hour will help. You should also make sure that you are leading a **healthy lifestyle** (proper meals, good sleep and some times when you're not studying).

How to PASS your exams

☑ Prepare for the day

Make sure you set at least one alarm (or get an alarm call), and allow plenty of time to get to the exam hall. You should have your route planned in advance and should listen on the radio for potential travel problems. You should check the night before to see that you have pens, pencils, erasers, watch, calculator with spare batteries, also exam documentation and evidence of identity.

☑ Select the right questions

You should select the optional questions you feel you can answer **best**, basing your selection on the topics covered, the requirements of the question, how easy it will be to apply the requirements and the availability of easy marks.

☑ Plan your three hours

You need to make sure that you will be answering the correct number of questions, and that you spend the right length of time on each question – this will be determined by the number of marks available. Each mark carries with it a **time allocation** of **1.8 minutes**. A 25 mark question therefore should be selected, completed and checked in 45 minutes. With some papers, it's better to do certain types of question first or last.

☑ Read the questions carefully

To score well, you must follow the requirements of the question, understanding what aspects of the subject area are being covered, and the tasks you will have to carry out. The requirements will also determine what information and examples you should provide. Reading the question scenarios carefully will help you decide what **issues** to discuss, **techniques** to use, **information** and **examples** to include and how to **organise** your answer.

☑ Plan your answers

Five minutes of planning plus twenty-five minutes of writing is certain to earn you more marks than thirty minutes of writing. Consider when you're planning how your answer should be **structured, w**hat the **format** should be and **how long** each part should take.

Confirm before you start writing that your plan makes **sense,** covers **all relevant points** and does not include **irrelevant material.**

☑ Show evidence of judgement

Remember that examiners aren't just looking for a display of knowledge; they want to see how well you can **apply** the knowledge you have. Evidence of application and judgement will include writing answers that only contain **relevant** material, using the material in scenarios to **support** what you say, **criticising** the **limitations** and **assumptions** of the techniques you use and making **reasonable recommendations** that follow from your discussion.

☑ Stay until the end of the exam

Use any spare time to **check and recheck** your script. This includes checking you have filled out the candidate details correctly, you have labelled question parts and workings clearly, you have used headers and underlining effectively and spelling, grammar and arithmetic are correct.

How to FAIL your exams

☒ Don't do enough questions

If you don't attempt sufficient questions on the paper, you are making it harder for yourself to pass the questions that you do attempt. If for example you don't do a 20 mark question, then you will have to score 50 marks out of 80 marks on the rest of the paper, and therefore have to obtain 63% of the marks on the questions you do attempt. Failing to attempt all of the paper is symptomatic of poor time management or poor question selection.

☒ Include irrelevant material

Markers are given detailed mark guides and will not give credit for irrelevant content. Therefore you should **NOT** braindump all you know about a broad subject area; the markers will only give credit for what is **relevant**, and you will also be showing that you lack the ability to **judge what's important.** Similarly forcing irrelevant theory into every answer won't gain you marks, nor will providing uncalled for features such as situation analyses, executive summaries and background information.

☒ Fail to use the details in the scenario

General answers or reproductions of Kit answers that don't refer to what is in the scenario in **this** question won't score enough marks to pass.

☒ Copy out the scenario details

Examiners see **selective** use of the right information as a key skill. If you copy out chunks of the scenario which aren't relevant to the question, or don't use the information to support your own judgements, you won't achieve good marks.

☒ Don't do what the question asks

Failing to provide all the examiner asks for will limit the marks you score. You will also decrease your chances by not providing an answer with enough **depth** – producing a single line bullet point list when the examiner asks for a discussion.

☒ Present your work poorly

Markers will only be able to give you credit if they can read your writing. There are also plenty of other things that will make it more difficult for markers to reward you. Examples include:

- Not using black or blue ink
- Not showing clearly which question you're attempting
- Scattering question parts from the same question throughout your answer booklet
- Not showing clearly workings or the results of your calculations

Paragraphs that are too long or which lack headers also won't help markers and hence won't help you.

Using your BPP products

This Kit gives you the question practice and guidance you need in the exam. Our other products can also help you pass:

- **Learning to Learn Accountancy** gives further valuable advice on revision

- **Passcards** provide you with clear topic summaries and exam tips

- **Success CDs** help you revise on the move

- **i-Pass CDs** offer tests of knowledge against the clock

- **Learn Online** is an e-learning resource delivered via the Internet, offering comprehensive tutor support and featuring areas such as study, practice, email service, revision and useful resources

You can purchase these products by visiting www.bpp.com/mybpp.

Visit our website www.bpp.com/acca/learnonline to sample aspects of Learn Online free of charge. Learn Online is hosted by BPP Professional Education.

Passing F8

Revising F8

Topics to revise

Alan Lewin has identified the key areas for the exam in his examiner's approach to F8.

The F8 paper consists of five compulsory questions which can cover all areas of the syllabus. The purpose of this paper is to develop knowledge and understanding of the audit and assurance engagement process and its application in the context of the relevant regulatory framework.

The F8 paper assumes knowledge of Paper F3 *Financial Accounting* and Paper F4 *Corporate and Business Law*. It is important, therefore, that candidates can apply the knowledge they have gained in these papers to the audit and assurance context of paper F8.

In his approach, the examiner has stressed that all questions will require a written response but there may be questions requiring the calculation and interpretation of some basic ratios in the context of audit planning or review.

The following table summarises the examiner's view of the expected format of the F8 exam.

Question	Format/indicative subject area	Marks available
1	This will always be a question on audit procedures and their application to a specific scenario.	30
2	Short factual questions based on ISAs and other key areas of the Study Guide.	10
3	Risk and audit approach.	20
4	More specialised audit areas.	20
5	Collection of audit evidence, closedown, reporting.	20

In short, remember that **all** the questions in this paper are compulsory. Therefore, we **strongly advise** that you do not selectively revise certain topics – any topic from the syllabus could be examined. Selective revision will limit the number of questions you can answer and hence reduce your chances of passing this paper.

Question practice

Question practice under timed conditions is essential, so that you can get used to the pressures of answering exam questions in **limited time** and practise not only the key techniques but allocating your time between different requirements in each question. Our list of recommended questions includes a range of 20 and 30 mark questions.

The key to success in this paper is question practice. It is essential that you attempt as many questions as you can in full. It is not enough to read the question, jot down some key points, then read through the solution in the Kit. Having completed a question you must try to look at your answer critically. Try to learn at least one new point from each one you attempt. This might be a technical point or a point on style or approach. You may like to keep a record of these for future reference. This will help your answers to improve over time.

Passing the F8 exam

Displaying the right qualities and avoiding weaknesses

In order to pass this paper it is important that you get some of the basics right. These include the following:

(a)   Reading time

You have 15 minutes of reading time – make sure you use it wisely.

Consider the following:

- Speed read through the question paper, jotting down any ideas that come to you about any of the questions

- Decide the order in which you would prefer to tackle questions

- Spend the reminder of the reading time reading the question(s) you'll do first in detail, analysing scenarios, jotting down plans

- When you can start writing, get straight on with the questions you've planned in detail

(b)   Read the question

Again this sounds obvious but is absolutely critical. When you are reading the question think about the following:

- Which technical area is being tested?

    This should let you identify the relevant areas of technical knowledge to draw on.

- What am I being asked to do?

    (We will take a more detailed look at the wording of requirements later.)

- Are there any key dates?

    This is important in questions on inventory. If the inventory count takes place at a time other than the year-end you need to be aware of this.

- What is the status of your client?

    For example is it large or small, is it a new or existing client? This might affect issues such as risk.

- What is the nature of the business?

    This is particularly relevant in planning questions as it will have an impact on risk areas.

- How many marks are allocated to each part of the question so approximately how many points do I need to make?

    When you think about the number of points you need to achieve you need to consider this in relation to the requirement. If you are asked for explanation it is likely that you will score more marks per point than if you are simply asked for a list of points.

You also need to think about the order in which you read information in the question. If the question is scenario based it is important that you read the requirement first so that as you read through the rest of the information you are aware of the key matters/issues which you are looking out for. For example if you are asked for risks in a scenario you can try to identify as many risk factors as possible as you read the detailed information.

You should also try to read the question as 'actively' as possible. Underline key words, annotate the question and link related points together. These points can often serve as the basis for an outline plan.

(c)   Understand the requirements

It is important that you can understand and differentiate between the requirements that the examiner typically uses. Here are some examples:

Requirement	Meaning
Explain	Make a point clear, develop basic point, justify a point of view
Discuss	Critically examine an issue
List	Normally punchier points than 'explain' or 'discuss'
Illustrate	Explain by using examples
Audit procedures/audit tests	Actions
Enquiries	Questions
Evidence	Source (eg document) and what it proves

(d)   Think and plan

No matter how well prepared you are you are going to have to do some thinking in the exam. Obviously you will be under time pressure, but if used effectively thinking and planning time should not be seen as a waste of time.

Generating ideas can often be a problem at this stage. Remember that your knowledge of key ISAs can serve as a good starting point.

In audit evidence questions you may think about the financial statement assertions (completeness, accuracy, valuation etc). You could also think about the different types of procedures listed in ISA 500 (inspection, observation, inquiry, confirmation, recalculation/reperformance and analytical procedures).

In risk questions it might be helpful to think about the different elements of risk (inherent risk, control risk, detection risk).

Repeating this knowledge will not be sufficient in most cases to pass the question but these ideas can form a very sound basis for developing a good answer.

One particular issue you need to consider at this stage is the problem of repetition. In many auditing questions it is possible that the same point may be relevant in more than one part of the answer. The examiner has stated that candidates will only get credit once so repeating the same point several times is a waste of time. Decide where you want to make the point, make it once and move on.

Keep going back to the requirement and make sure that you really are answering the question. One of the most common errors in auditing papers is identifying the correct point but using it in the wrong way. Make sure that your answer is focused on the requirements. It may be tempting to write everything you know about a particular point but this will not help you to pass the exam. This 'scattergun' approach will attract few, if any, marks.

(e)   Producing your answer

Although much of the hard work has been done by the time you get to this stage you need to think carefully about how you put down each point on paper. The way you make the point can make a difference to the number of marks scored. The main criticism from the examiner in the previous syllabus was the lack of clarity and precision. This is particularly the case regarding questions on audit evidence. For example lists of tests stating 'check this' and 'check that' without explaining what is being checked and why is likely to score few marks. If you find it difficult to gauge the right level of detail try to imagine that you are explaining the procedure to a junior member of staff. Would they be able to perform the procedure based on your description?

Think about your style. A well structured answer with clearly identifiable points is generally preferable to long paragraphs of text. However, do not fall into the trap of producing note-form answers. This is rarely sufficiently detailed to score marks.

Gaining the easy marks

All questions in this paper are compulsory so you need to attempt them all in order to improve your chances of passing. Easier marks are available in Question2, a 10 mark question based on factual elements of the syllabus. Such knowledge-based requirements could also feature in parts of the scenario questions in this paper. However, do not be tempted to write down everything you know about a particular topic – stick to the time allocation and answer the question set.

Tackling questions

In summary, you'll improve your chances by following a step-by-step approach along the following lines.

Step 1 **Read the requirement**

Identify the knowledge areas being tested and see precisely what the examiner wants you to do. This will help you focus on what's important in the scenario.

Step 2 **Check the mark allocation**

This shows the depth of answer anticipated and helps you allocate time.

Step 3 **Read the scenario/preamble**

Identify which information is relevant to which part. There are lots of clues in the scenario so make sure you identify those that you should use in your answer.

Step 4 **Plan your answer**

Consider the formats you'll use and discussion points you'll make.

Step 5 **Write your answer**

Stick carefully to the time allocation for each question, and for each part of each question.

Exam information

Format of the paper

	Number of Marks
5 compulsory questions	<u>100</u>
	<u>100</u>

Time allowed: 3 hours

Question 1 will comprise a 30 mark case-study style question, perhaps including one knowledge-based part. Question 2 will be a 10 mark knowledge-based question from across the syllabus. The remaining three questions will be 20 mark scenario-based questions.

Pilot paper

1   Substantive procedures on trade payables and purchases, and use of CAATs
2   Engagement letter, audit evidence audit reports
3   Threats to independence, corporate governance and audit committees
4   Weaknesses in wages system, fraud, use of an external consultant
5   Events after the balance sheet date and impact on audit report

The Pilot paper is Mock exam 3 in this Kit.

Examinable documents

Knowledge of new examinable regulations will not be assessed until at least six calendar months after the last day of the month in which the document was issued, or the legislation passed. The relevant last day for issue for the June examinations is 30 November of the previous year, and for the December examinations, it is 31 May of the same year.

The study guide offers more detailed guidance on the depth and level at which the examinable documents should be examined. The study guide should therefore be read in conjunction with the examinable documents list.

The accounting knowledge that is assumed for Paper F8 is the same as that examined in Paper F3. Therefore, candidates studying for Paper F8 should refer to the Accounting Standards listed under Paper F3.

	Title
	International Standards on Auditing (ISAs)
	Glossary of terms
	International Framework for Assurance Assignments
	Preface to International Standards on Quality Control, Auditing, Assurance and Related Services
ISA 200	Objective and general principles governing an audit of financial statements
ISA 210	Terms of audit engagements
ISA 220	Quality control for audits of historical financial information
ISA 230	Audit documentation
ISA 240	The auditor's responsibility to consider fraud in an audit of financial statements
ISA 250	Consideration of laws and regulations in an audit of financial statements
ISA 260	Communication of audit matters with those charged with governance
ISA 300	Planning an audit of financial statements

	Title
ISA 315	Understanding the entity and its environment and assessing the risks of material misstatement
ISA 320	Audit materiality
ISA 330	The auditor's procedures in response to assessed risks
ISA 402	Audit considerations relating to entities using service organisations
ISA 500	Audit evidence
ISA 501	Audit evidence – additional considerations for specific items
ISA 505	External confirmations
ISA 510	Initial engagements – opening balances
ISA 520	Analytical procedures
ISA 530	Audit sampling and other means of testing
ISA 540	Audit of accounting estimates
ISA 560	Subsequent events
ISA 570	Going concern
ISA 580	Management representations
ISA 610	Considering the work of internal auditing
ISA 620	Using the work of an expert
ISA 700	The independent auditor's report on a complete set of general purpose financial statements
ISA 701	Modifications to the independent auditor's report
ISA 710	Comparatives
	International Auditing Practice Statements (IAPSs)
ISPS 1000	Inter-bank confirmation procedures
IAPS 1013	Electronic commerce: Effect on the audit of financial statements
IAPS 1014	Reporting by auditors on compliance with international financial reporting standards
	International standards on assurance engagements (ISAEs)
ISAE 3000	Assurance engagements other than audits or reviews of historical financial information
	International standards on review engagements (ISREs)
ISRE 2400	Engagements to review financial statements
	Other documents
	ACCA's 'Code of Ethics and Conduct'
	The Combined Code (of the Committee on Corporate Governance) as an example of a code of best practice.

Useful websites

The websites below provide additional sources of information of relevance to your studies for *Audit and Assurance*.

* www.bpp.com

   Our website provides information about BPP products and services, with a link to the ACCA website.

* www.accaglobal.com

   ACCA's website. Includes student section.

* www.ifac.org

   This website provides information on international accounting and auditing issues.

* www.ft.com

   This website provides information about current international business.

Recent articles

This section includes recent articles relevant to 2.6. The following articles include one by Alan Lewin, the F8 examiner, on the audit of manual and computerised systems published in *student accountant* in June 2006. We also include an article on audit working papers from February 2007.

Auditing manual and computerised systems

This article explains how the wording of audit tests differs with regard to manual and computerised systems. It also shows how – within a sales system – manual and computer-based audit tests are similar, but are explained differently.

The sales system

To state the obvious, a company's sales system is designed to record all of a company's sales. The first few stages in such a system are normally as follows:

1   Customer orders are received and recorded in the system.

2   The order is processed, eventually leading to goods being dispatched to the customer (following credit checks – which are not considered in this article).

3   The dispatch of goods results in a sales invoice being raised, with a copy of the invoice being sent to the customer.

4   Sales invoices are recorded in the sales day book.

Within this system, as in any other system in a company, controls will be established to ensure that the system is working correctly. For example, sales invoices will almost certainly be pre-numbered, and this numbering will be shown in the sales day book. Pre-numbering and other accounting controls can then be used to test the completeness of the recording of sales invoices. For example, controls will include a review of the sales day book and a check that the numeric sequence of sales invoices in complete.

The auditor will record the accounting systems and controls within a company, and then devise tests to ensure that there are no errors in the company's systems or financial records. In audit terminology, the auditor is checking that various audit assertions have been met. In the income statement, for example, there is an assertion that all sales are recorded – the 'completeness' assertion. To verify that this assertion is correct, the auditor can carry out:

1   substantive tests – to re-perform the activity undertaken by the company

2   compliance tests – to check the effectiveness of any internal controls that the company has implemented.

When testing the completeness of recording of sales invoices, the auditor could:

1   review the sales day book to ensure that the numeric sequence of sales invoices is complete

2   ensure that the sales day book has been signed by a responsible officer at the end of each month, confirming that the numeric sequence has been checked.

Similar compliance and substantive tests will be devised to check the rest of the sales system. From the point of view of auditing a system, audit tests will focus on satisfying the audit assertions. It makes no difference whether the system is manual or computerised because test objectives are the same for both systems. However, the explanation of the tests in an examination answer will be different depending on the system being audited.

The main testing differences for a computer-based system are as follows:

•   Substantive tests focus on the computer and on access to specific computer files.

•   Additional substantive tests use computer-assisted auditing techniques (CAATs).

•   Compliance tests almost certainly require the use of CAATs, as many of the controls are 'inside' the computer.

When making these points in an examination answer, candidates must clearly show that the system being audited is computerised. As usual, an example of a system under audit will be provided in the question. The candidate's job is to identify and explain the audit tests required.

Example tests

The remainder of this article provides example tests that aim to satisfy the completeness assertion in an order/dispatch system. Each of the following three sections initially explains what the system does, and is followed by examples of audit tests for both manual and computerised systems.

Recording customer orders

All orders must be recorded. In this system, assume that customers either telephone the company with their order (manual system), or order using the website (computerised system).

Manual system	**Computerised system**
Substantive test	**Substantive test**
Place an order by telephone and ensure that the order has been recorded by obtaining the relevant customer order document produced within the company	Place an order using the website and ensure that it is recorded in the company's system by viewing the orders on screen.
Compliance test	**Substantive test (using CAATs)**
Observe staff in the company to ensure that orders are recorded on order documentation as customers phone in their orders.	Place orders on the website using test data.
Compliance test	**Compliance test**
Review customer complaint files for examples of orders not being fulfilled.	Review customer complaint files for examples of orders not being fulfilled.

The completeness of the recording of orders is quite difficult to test. The substantive tests above all use 'dummy' orders, sent to the company and then deleted from the system after the test. However, the actual test performed is very similar for both manual and the computerised systems. The wording is obviously different, reflecting the use of the computer, but both manual and computer-based tests focus on the input of 'dummy' orders.

Goods dispatched

All orders are dispatched, and in this system, the customer order has a goods dispatched note (GDN) number entered on it.

Manual system	**Computerised system**
Substantive test	**Substantive test**
Obtain a sample of customer orders and record the GDN numbers. Obtain the relevant GDNs to confirm the GDN number on each order is valid.	View a sample of customer orders on screen and record the GDN numbers. Open the GDN file and view relevant GDNs to ensure each order was raised.
Compliance test	**Substantive test (using CAATs)**
Ensure that each order is signed by a responsible officer confirming goods have been dispatched.	Programme audit software to select a sample of customer orders, obtain the GDN number from each order, and verify that each GDN number exists in the GDN file.
Compliance test	
Ensure that the GDN has been attached to the customer order.	

Again, the manual and computerised system tests are very similar, as both focus on obtaining the customer order and ensuring that a GDN has been raised. The words used show the difference between the two systems. The manual test assumes a paper document while the computer test explicitly states using the computer.

Invoice raised

An invoice is raised for each GDN and, in this system, the invoice number is entered on the GDN. Sales invoices are also pre-numbered, although the GDN and sales invoice number sequences are different.

Manual system	**Computerised system**
Substantive test	**Substantive test**
Obtain a sample of GDNs and record the invoice numbers. Obtain the relevant invoices to confirm that the GDN number on each invoice is valid.	View a sample of GDNs on screen and record the invoice numbers. Open the invoice file and view each invoice to ensure it was raised.
Compliance test	**Substantive test (using CAATs)**
Programme audit software to select a sample of GDNs, obtain the invoice numbers from each order and verify that each invoice number exists in the invoice file.	Ensure that each GDN is signed by responsible officer confirming the a invoice has been raised.

Again, the tests are similar. It is the wording that clearly shows the type of system being audited. The list of tests provided above is not exhaustive, but instead illustrates the type of test that could be included in an audit programme. Therefore, if an auditing question includes a computer-based system, this is not a cause for panic or concern. The computer system will differ from a manual system, but that does not mean it cannot be audited, or that a candidate with limited auditing experience cannot obtain a pass standard. Focusing the answer on the computer system itself, and showing that the system has been understood by detailing computer-based tests, will help candidates gain marks and hopefully achieve a pass standard.

Summary

- Manual and computer-based systems use the same audit assertions.

- The explanation of the audit test shows that the candidate has understood that a computer system is being audited.

- Examination questions may ask for computer-based substantive and/or compliance tests

BPP
LEARNING MEDIA

Effective audit service

This article is about audit working papers. Auditors should prepare and organise their working papers in a manner that helps the auditor carry out an appropriate audit service. The auditor should avoid preparing or accumulating unnecessary working papers, and should therefore avoid making extensive copies of the client's accounting records. It is worth noting at this stage that it is neither necessary nor practicable for the auditor to document every matter considered during the audit.

Audit documentation needs to be understood for both Papers F8 and P7.

The auditing standards

ISA 230, *Audit Documentation* (Revised)[1] contains the set of standards that deal with working papers. These standards are as follows:

The auditor should prepare, on a timely basis, audit documentation that provides:

(a)   A sufficient appropriate record of the basis for the auditor's report, and

(b)   Evidence that the audit was performed in accordance with ISAs and applicable legal and regulatory requirements.

The auditor should prepare the audit documentation so as to enable an experienced auditor, having no previous connection with the audit, to understand:

(a)   The nature, timing, and extent of the audit procedures performed to comply with ISAs and applicable legal and regulatory requirements

(b)   The results of the audit procedures and the audit evidence obtained, and

(c)   Significant matters arising during the audit and the conclusions reached.

In documenting the nature, timing, and extent of audit procedures performed, the auditor should record the identifying characteristics of the specific items or matters being tested.

The auditor should document discussions of significant matters with management and others on a timely basis.

If the auditor has identified information that contradicts or is inconsistent with the auditor's final conclusion regarding a significant matter, the auditor should document how the auditor addressed the contradictions or inconsistency in forming the final conclusion.

Where, in exceptional circumstances, the auditor judges it necessary to depart from a basic principle or an essential procedure that is relevant in the circumstances of the audit, the auditor should document how the alternative audit procedures performed achieve the objective of the audit, and, unless otherwise clear, the reasons for the departure.

In documenting the nature, timing, and extent of audit procedures performed, the auditor should record:

(a)   Who performed the audit work and the date such work was completed, and
(b)   Who reviewed the audit work and the date and extent of such review[3].

The auditor should complete the assembly of the final audit file on a timely basis after the date of the auditor's report.

After the assembly of the final audit file has been completed, the auditor should not delete or discard audit documentation before the end of its retention period.

When the auditor finds it necessary to modify existing audit documentation or add new audit documentation after the assembly of the final file has been completed, the auditor should, regardless of the nature of the modifications or additions, document:

(a)   When and for whom they were made, and (where applicable) reviewed
(b)   The specific reasons for making them, and
(c)   Their effect, if any, on the auditor's conclusions.

When exceptional circumstances arise after the date of the auditor's report that require the auditor to perform new or additional audit procedures, or that lead the auditor to reach new conclusions, the auditor should document:

(a) The circumstances encountered

(b) The new or additional audit procedures performed, audit evidence obtained, and conclusions reached, and

(c) When and by whom the resulting changes to audit documentation were made, and (where applicable) reviewed.

These standards guide the auditor to produce audit documentation that is of an acceptable standard. Understanding and applying the standards will protect the auditor from unwelcome and unnecessary litigation. ISA 230 (Revised) is more comprehensive than its predecessor and is likely to prove very useful.

Importance of working papers

Working papers are important because they:

- are necessary for audit quality control purposes

- provide assurance that the work delegated by the audit partner has been properly completed

- provide evidence that an effective audit has been carried out

- increase the economy, efficiency, and effectiveness of the audit

- contain sufficiently detailed and up-to-date facts which justify the reasonableness of the auditor's conclusions

- retain a record of matters of continuing significance to future audits.

Avoiding unnecessary papers

Before deciding to prepare a particular audit working paper, the auditor should be satisfied that it is:

- Necessary either because it will serve an essential or useful purpose in support of the auditor's report, or because it will provide information needed for tax or other client-related statutory/regulatory purposes

- Not practicable for the client staff to prepare the working paper, or for the auditor to make copies of papers that the client staff (including internal auditors) have prepared as part of their normal regular duties.

Content

Each audit working paper must be headed with the following information:

- The name of the client

- The period covered by the audit

- The subject matter

- The file reference

- The initials (signature) of the member of staff who prepared the working paper, and the date on which it was prepared

- In the case of audit papers prepared by client staff, the date the working papers were received, and the initials of the audit team member who carried out the audit work

- The initials of the member of staff who reviewed the working papers and the date on which the review was carried out

- Each audit paper should meet the characteristics of a good working paper, as detailed later in this article.

Papers prepared by client

Certain working papers required by the auditor may have already been prepared by client staff. The auditor should make arrangements, whenever possible, for copies of these to be made available to the audit team. If client staff prepare working papers which are to be retained by the auditor, the auditor should agree the form of the working papers with client staff at an early stage in the audit, and include this information in the audit timetable.

When arranging for working papers to be prepared, the auditor should take care to ensure that the working papers will give all the information required. All such working papers should normally be clearly identified as having been prepared by the client. The member of audit staff directly responsible for an audit area in which working papers prepared by client staff are included should sign those papers – this will show that they have been checked and that they can be reviewed by the manager and the partner, and by subsequent reviewers. The signature of the audit team member indicates that the working paper (prepared by client staff) has been 'audited'.

Some characteristics of a good working paper

On the basis of the discussion above, a good working paper should meet the requirements of ISA 230 by displaying the following characteristics:

- It should state a clear audit objective, usually in terms of an audit assertion (for example, 'to ensure the completeness of trade creditors').

- It should fully state the year/period end (eg 31 October 2006), so that the working paper is not confused with documentation belonging to a different year/period.

- It should state the full extent of the test (ie how many items were tested and how this number was determined). This will enable the preparer, and any subsequent reviewers, to determine the sufficiency of the audit evidence provided by the working paper.

- Where there is necessary reference to another working paper, the full reference of that other working paper must be given. A statement that details of testing can be found on 'another working paper' is insufficient.

- The working paper should clearly and objectively state the results of the test, without bias, and based on the facts documented.

- The conclusions reached should be consistent with the results of the test and should be able to withstand independent scrutiny.

- The working paper should be clearly referenced so that it can be filed appropriately and found easily when required at a later date.

- It should be signed by the person who prepares it so that queries can be directed to the appropriate person.

- It should be signed and dated by any person who reviews it, in order to meet the quality control requirements of the review.

The reviewer of audit working papers should ensure that every paper has these characteristics. If any relevant characteristic is judged absent, then this should result in an audit review point (ie a comment by the reviewer directing the original preparer to rectify the fault on the working paper).

Conclusion

Working papers provide evidence that an effective, efficient, and economic audit has been carried out. They should therefore be prepared with care and skill. They should be sufficiently detailed and complete so that an auditor with no previous experience of that audit can understand the working papers in terms of the work completed, the conclusions reached, and the reasoning behind these conclusions.

Notes

1   ISA 230 (Revised) became effective for audits of financial information for periods beginning on or after 15 June 2006. It resulted in conforming amendments to ISA 200, ISA 330, and ISQC 1. These conforming amendments are set out in the appendices to those standards.

2   Those shown in bold in the text of the ISA.

3   Paragraph 26 of ISA 220 establishes the requirement for the auditor to review the audit work performed through review of the documentation, which involves the auditor documenting the extent and timing of the reviews. Paragraph 25 of IAS 220 describes the nature of a review of work performed.

4   Each audit firm has its own file numbering and referencing system. Within each system, the best way of numbering working papers is to file them serially in each section and to cross-reference them. Where papers are intended to agree with or support items appearing in the financial statements, or in other working papers in the file, the auditor should normally prepare them so as to make such agreements obvious without the necessity of further investigation and reconciliation.

Planning your question practice

Planning your question practice

We have already stressed that question practice should be right at the centre of your revision. Whilst you will spend some time looking at your notes and Paper F8 Passcards, you should spend the majority of your revision time practising questions.

We recommend two ways in which you can practise questions.

- Use **BPP's question plan** to work systematically through the syllabus and attempt key and other questions on a section-by-section basis

- **Build your own exams** – attempt questions as a series of practice exams

These ways are suggestions and simply following them is no guarantee of success. You or your college may prefer an alternative but equally valid approach.

BPP's question plan

The BPP plan below requires you to devote a **minimum of 35 hours** to revision of Paper F8. Any time you can spend over and above this should only increase your chances of success.

Step 1 **Review your notes** and the chapter summaries in the Paper F8 **Passcards** for each section of the syllabus.

Step 2 **Answer the key questions** for that section. These questions have boxes round the question number in the table below and you should answer them in full. Even if you are short of time you must attempt these questions if you want to pass the exam. You should complete your answers without referring to our solutions.

Step 3 **Attempt the other questions** in that section. For some questions we have suggested that you prepare **answer plans** rather than full solutions. Planning an answer means that you should spend about 40% of the time allowance for the questions brainstorming the question and drawing up a list of points to be included in the answer.

Step 4 Attempt **Mock exams 1, 2 and 3** under strict exam conditions.

Syllabus section	2007 Passcards chapters	Questions in this Kit	Comments	Done ☑
Revision period 1				
Audit framework and regulation				
Assurance and audit limitations	1	1	Answer in full. It is very important to understand the assurance context in which the syllabus is set. This question is therefore good to work through at the beginning of your revision to ensure that you are aware of the quality of assurance given by an audit, and the limitations of an audit.	☐
Statutory audit	2	2	Answer in full. The regulatory context of auditing is extremely important and could be examined in a compulsory question. It is key that you can explain the basic purpose of an audit as it is the basis of the rest of the syllabus. This question also looks at the distinction between the interim and final audits. An answer plan is provided with this question.	☐
Regulatory environment	3	5	Answer in full. This question is a good one to practise to confirm your understanding of the regulatory environment that governs external audits. This topic could potentially come up in Question 2 of the paper.	☐
Corporate governance	3	6	Answer in full. This is an excellent scenario-based question on corporate governance and the requirements of the Combined Code. It tests both your knowledge of the Combined Code and your ability to apply that knowledge to a given scenario.	☐
		8	Plan an answer to this question.	☐
Revision period 2				
Professional ethics				
Independence and objectivity	4	9	Answer in full. This question covers the issue of objectivity and is therefore a good, broadly based question to attempt as part of your revision.	☐
Confidentiality	4	11	Answer in full. It is important to remember that whilst independence is a key ethical issue it is not the only one. This tests your basic knowledge of when the auditor can/cannot reveal information to third parties. Part (b) focuses on independence issues.	☐
Acceptance decisions	4	12	Answer in full. This is a scenario-based question looking at a wide range of issues affecting the decision to accept an appointment including legal, ethical and practical. Notice it also examines the purpose of the engagement letter. This demonstrates the importance of basic knowledge of the ISAs.	☐

Syllabus section	2007 Passcards chapters	Questions in this Kit	Comments	Done ☑
Auditors' rights and responsibilities	4	3	Answer in full. This question covers some important knowledge on auditors' responsibilities. Notice it also brings in other related issues, for example fraud. Testing of more than one topic in a question is possible.	☐
Revision period 3 *Internal audit*				
Internal audit – relationship with external audit	5	8	Answer in full. This question considers the role and objectives of internal audit and the types of assignments carried out.	☐
Internal audit objectives		14	Answer in full. It is important to have a good look through this question too, as internal audit is an important area in the syllabus. This question focuses more on the work of internal audit in a particular business.	☐
Internal audit assignments		15	Answer in full. This is a good question because it looks at the sort of work internal auditors would carry out within an organisation. It is scenario-based so you must be able to apply your knowledge to the circumstances in the question.	☐
Revision period 4 *Planning and risk assessment*				
Business risk	6/7	16	Answer in full. Run through this past exam question from the old syllabus to ensure that you can differentiate between audit risk and business risk. Although many of the issues will be common to both, business risk tends to involve a broader range of topics. Analysis is provided with this question.	☐
		22	Plan an answer to this question.	☐
Audit risk	6/7	18	Answer in full. Risk is a key topic in this syllabus and may be examined from the auditor's perspective or from the point of view of the business. Being able to identify risks will only come with practice, so this is a question on which to practise this important skill. Notice that in this case your identification of risk is based on an analysis of financial information. This makes it a demanding question but it is something which you need to be prepared to deal with.	☐
		20	Plan an answer to this question.	☐
Fraud	6/7	21	Answer in full. The development of recent ISAs has increased the emphasis on fraud and this could be reflected in the exam. If you do not have time to attempt this question in full at least try to produce an outline plan.	☐

Syllabus section	2007 Passcards chapters	Questions in this Kit	Comments	Done ☑
Revision period 5				
Audit evidence				
Evidence, sampling and documentation	8/11	23	Answer in full. This is an excellent revision question as it covers a number of different methods of obtaining evidence. It demonstrates the importance of being able to explain key audit principles and techniques.	☐
CAATs	8/11	25	Answer in full. This is a challenging question on CAATs. Part (a) is straightforward but parts (b) and (c) are more complex as they relate to the use of test data and audit software in a particular scenario.	☐
Using the work of others	8/11	55	Plan an answer to this question.	☐
Sampling	11	57	Answer in full. This is a good question to test your knowledge of sampling. It includes both knowledge-based and scenario-based requirements.	☐
Revision period 6				
Internal control				
Internal control	9	29	Answer in full. Internal controls is a key topic area and is very likely to come up. You need to be aware of the problems which result from poor controls and you need to be able to make recommendations that are useful and relevant to the organisation in question.	☐
Purchases system	10	33	Answer in full. Although this question covers purchases it also looks at controls over capital expenditure. Controls questions covering more than one business cycle are possible.	☐
Sales system	10	31	Answer in full. This question considers controls in specific aspects of the sales cycle. It also deals with procedures which auditors should perform if they wish to rely on internal controls. This makes it a very good all-round revision question.	☐
		32	Plan an answer to this question.	☐
Wages system	10	34	Plan an answer to this question.	☐
Revision period 7				
Audit of inventories				
Valuation and existence	13	43	Answer in full. This question looks at the issues of inventory counts and valuation and using an external valuer.	☐
		42	Answer in full. This question looks at inventory valuation but also asks you to draft a report to management.	☐

Syllabus section	2007 Passcards chapters	Questions in this Kit	Comments	Done ☑
Perpetual inventory system	13	41	Plan an answer to this question.	☐
Revision period 8 *Audit of other assets*				
Trade receivables' circularisation	12	44	Answer in full. This question is a good one as it tests both your knowledge of receivables circularisations and your ability to answer the 10 mark question in the time available.	☐
Bad and doubtful receivable balances	12	50	Plan an answer to this question.	☐
Bank	15	46	Answer in full. This question covers a bank reconciliation and controls over cash and bank, so is a good one to practise.	☐
Revision period 9 *Audit of non-current assets*				
Audit work	16	39	Answer in full. This question is split into two parts. The first asks you to consider the audit work to perform on sales and the second asks you to describe the audit work to do on a particular category of non-current assets.	☐
		42	Answer in full. This is a recent exam question that gives good coverage of non-current asset issues.	☐
Revision period 10 *Audit of payables*				
Liabilities	14	48	Answer in full. This is a good all-round question on liabilities audit and tests your application skills.	☐
Payroll	14	49	Answer in full. This question considers the audit of payroll balances	☐
Provisions	17	50	Answer in full. This question serves as a useful reminder that questions may require some accounting knowledge. Here IAS 37 *Provisions, contingent liabilities and contingent assets* is examined.	☐

Syllabus section	2007 Passcards chapters	Questions in this Kit	Comments	Done ☑
Revision period 11 *Review* Subsequent events	18	59	Answer in full. This is a good 10 mark knowledge-based question on subsequent events to do as it tests both your auditing and accounting knowledge.	☐
		60	Answer in full. This question is set in a scenario context and tests your knowledge and application skills.	☐
Revision period 12 *Reporting* Audit reports	19	62	Answer in full. This topic is likely to crop up in some form in every sitting. Practising this past exam question comparing and contrasting external audit reports and internal audit reports should stand you in good stead if you have to critique either in the real exam.	☐
		64	Plan an answer to this question.	☐
Going concern and audit reports	18/19	61	Answer in full. This question asks you to describe factors concerning going concern and also examines the impact on the audit report.	☐
		63	Answer in full. Going concern can be examined in a number of different contexts eg in a planning question. However, it is often combined with audit reports as it is here. You need to be able to identify going concern risk factors and describe the potential impact on the audit report.	☐
Audit and other reports	19	65	Answer in full. This recent past exam question looks at both audit reports and other assurance reports produced by auditors.	☐

BPP LEARNING MEDIA

Build your own exams

Having revised your notes and the BPP Passcards, you can attempt the questions in the Kit as a series of practice exams. You can organise the questions in the following way:

	Practice exams						
	1	2	3	4	5	6	7
1	37	40	41	42	43	57	29
2	1	3	8	14	55	62	4
3	6	7	9	10	11	12	13
4	20	26	32	33	27	35	38
5	58	60	61	63	65	53	47

- Whichever practice exams you use, you must attempt **Mock exams 1, 2 and 3** at the end of your revision.

Questions

AUDIT FRAMEWORK AND REGULATION

Questions 1 – 12 cover Audit framework and regulation, the subject of Part A of the BPP Study Text for F8.

1 Audit judgements   18 mins

ISA 200 *Objective and general principles governing an audit of financial statements,* deals with, amongst other matters, the responsibility for financial statements and the concept of reasonable assurance.

Paragraph 17 of the Statement states that:

'An auditor conducting an audit in accordance with ISAs obtains reasonable assurance that the financial statements taken as a whole are free from material misstatement whether due to fraud or error. Reasonable assurance is a concept relating to the accumulation of the audit evidence necessary for the auditor to conclude that there are no material misstatements in the financial statements taken as a whole. Reasonable assurance relates to the whole audit process.'

The effect on the audit is explained in paragraph 18:

'An auditor cannot obtain absolute assurance because there are inherent limitations in an audit that affect the auditor's ability to detect material misstatements.'

and paragraph 19:

'Also, the work undertaken by the auditor to form an audit opinion is permeated by judgement.'

Required

(a)   State the respective responsibilities for financial statements of the management of the entity and of its external auditors.   **(5 marks)**

(b)   Describe the inherent limitations facing auditors in undertaking their work.   **(5 marks)**

(Total = 10 marks)

2 Question with answer plan: External audit (AIR 12/04)

36 mins

The purpose of an external audit and its role are not well understood. You have been asked to write some material for inclusion in your firm's training materials dealing with these issues in the audit of large companies.

Required

(a)   Draft an explanation dealing with the purpose of an external audit and its role in the audit of large companies, for inclusion in your firm's training materials.   **(10 marks)**

(b)   The external audit process for the audit of large entities generally involves two or more recognisable stages. One stage involves understanding the business and risk assessment, determining the response to assessed risk, testing of controls and a limited amount of substantive procedures. This stage is sometimes known as the interim audit. Another stage involves further tests of controls and substantive procedures and audit finalisation procedures. This stage is sometimes known as the final audit.

Describe and explain the main audit procedures and processes that take place during the interim and final audit of a large entity.   **(10 marks)**

(Total = 20 marks)

3 Auditors' responsibilities (AIR 6/02) (amended)   18 mins

The responsibilities of external auditors are not always well understood, especially with regard to the detection and reporting of fraud. When external auditors provide non-audit services to their audit clients, it is essential that the auditors make a clear distinction between their audit and non-audit responsibilities.

Required

(a)   Explain the responsibilities of external auditors to directors and shareholders.   **(4 marks)**

(b)   Describe the limitations of the external audit in relation to the detection and reporting of fraud.   **(3 marks)**

(c)   Explain why it is essential for external auditors to be independent of their clients.   **(3 marks)**

(Total = 10 marks)

4 Audit regulation (AIR 12/01) (amended)   18 mins

Auditors and Auditing Standards are controlled and regulated in a number of different ways.

Required

(a)   Explain how International Standards on Auditing (ISAs) are developed by the International Auditing and Assurance Standards Board (IAASB), and explain the role and authority of ISAs.   **(4 marks)**

(b)   Explain the role of professional bodies in the regulation of auditors.   **(4 marks)**

(c)   Describe how ISAs and national auditing standards in individual countries influence each other.   **(2 marks)**

(Total = 10 marks)

5 International Standards on Auditing (AIR 6/06)   36 mins

International Standards on Auditing (ISAs) are produced by the International Audit and Assurance Standards Board (IAASB), which is a technical committee of the International Federation of Accountants (IFAC). In recent years, there has been a trend for more countries to implement the ISAs rather than produce their own auditing standards.

A school friend who you have not seen for a number of years is considering joining ACCA as a trainee accountant. However, she is concerned about the extent of regulations which auditors have to follow and does not understand why ISAs have to be used in your country.

Required

Write a letter to your friend explaining the regulatory framework which applies to auditors.

Your letter should cover the following points:

(a)   The due process of the IAASB involved in producing an ISA.   **(4 marks)**
(b)   The overall authority of ISAs and how they are applied in individual countries.   **(8 marks)**
(c)   The extent to which an auditor must follow ISAs.   **(4 marks)**
(d)   The extent to which ISAs apply to small entities.   **(4 marks)**

(Total = 20 marks)

6 Jumper (AIR 6/06)   36 mins

You are the audit manager of Tela & Co, a medium sized firm of accountants. Your firm has just been asked for assistance from Jumper & Co, a firm of accountants in an adjacent country. This country has just implemented the internationally recognised codes on corporate governance and Jumper & Co has a number of clients where the codes are not being followed. One example of this, from SGCC, a listed company, is shown below. As your country already has appropriate corporate governance codes in place, Jumper & Co have asked for your advice regarding the changes necessary in SGCC to achieve appropriate compliance with corporate governance codes.

Extract from financial statements regarding corporate governance

Mr Sheppard is the Chief Executive Officer and board chairman of SGCC. He appoints and maintains a board of five executive and two non-executive directors. While the board sets performance targets for the senior managers in the company, no formal targets or review of board policies is carried out. Board salaries are therefore set and paid by Mr Sheppard based on his assessment of all the board members, including himself, and not their actual performance.

Internal controls in the company are monitored by the senior accountant, although detailed review is assumed to be carried out by the external auditors; SGCC does not have an internal audit department.

Annual financial statements are produced, providing detailed information on past performance.

Required

Write a memo to Jumper & Co which:

(a)   Explains why SGCC does not meet international codes of corporate governance
(b)   Explains why not meeting the international codes may cause a problem for SGCC, and
(c)   Recommends any changes necessary to implement those codes in the company.

                                                                                          (20 marks)

7 ZX (AIR 6/05)   36 mins

You are a recently qualified Chartered Certified Accountant in charge of the internal audit department of ZX, a rapidly expanding company. Turnover has increased by about 20% p.a. for the last five years, to the current level of $50 million. Net profits are also high, with an acceptable return being provided for the four shareholders.

The internal audit department was established last year to assist the board of directors in their control of the company and to prepare for a possible listing on the stock

 exchange. The Managing Director is keen to follow the principles of good corporate governance with respect to internal audit. However, he is also aware that the other board members do not have complete knowledge of corporate governance or detailed knowledge of International Auditing Standards.

Required

Write a memo to the board of ZX that:

(a)   Explains how the internal audit department can assist the board of directors in fulfilling their obligations
       under the principles of good corporate governance.   **(10 marks)**

(b)   Explains the advantages and disadvantages to ZX of an audit committee.   **(10 marks)**

                                                                                  (Total = 20 marks)

8 Internal control evaluation

18 mins

There is a growing call internationally for public reporting about the control effectiveness of companies not just from a narrow statutory audit perspective but more from the wider perspective of corporate governance.

Required

(a)   Explain the key enquiries that an auditor would make in order to ensure that a company is managing effectively its corporate business risk.   **(7 marks)**

(b)   Explain what you understand by the term audit committee, and list the benefits of having one.   **(3 marks)**

(Total = 10 marks)

9 Objectivity (AIR 12/02)

36 mins

The objectivity of the external auditor may be threatened or appear to be threatened where:

(i)   There is undue dependence on any audit client or group of clients;

(ii)   The firm, its partners or staff have any financial interest in an audit client;

(iii)   There are family or other close personal or business relationships between the firm, its partners or staff and the audit client;

(iv)   The firm provides other services to audit clients.

Required

(a)   For each of the four examples given above, explain why the objectivity of the external auditor may be threatened, or appear to be threatened, and why the threat is important.   **(12 marks)**

(b)   Describe ACCA's requirements that reduce the threats to auditor objectivity for each of the four examples given above.   **(8 marks)**

Notes

In part (a) all parts carry equal marks.
In part (b) all parts carry equal marks.   **(Total = 20 marks)**

10 Ethical dilemma (AIR 6/02)

36 mins

(a)   You are a Chartered Certified Accountant and the newly appointed internal auditor of a company that is experiencing financial difficulties. As a condition for obtaining bank loans, the company has agreed to maintain specified liquidity ratios, asset to liability ratios, and gross profit margins. The draft financial statements for the period-end appear to show that the company has not succeeded in complying with some of these requirements. The profit figures are significantly affected by the calculation of bad debt and depreciation charges. There has been a suggestion to the effect that these could be changed, in order to meet the bank's conditions. There is a real danger that if the bank withdraws its funding, the company will become insolvent and will have to cease trading. The chief financial accountant has asked you to sign certain internal records that have been altered in order to show that the bank's conditions have been met.

Required

Explain the courses of action open to you in these circumstances.   **(10 marks)**

(b)   You are the external auditor of the company in financial difficulties described in (a) above. You have noted that the calculations of the bad debt allowance and depreciation provisions have been altered in the current year and that as a result, the bank's requirements have been met. You also note that certain accounting policy changes have been made in relation to accounting for leases and that as a result, the profit targets expected by certain investment analysts have now been met. If the changes had not been made, the targets would not have been met. You have asked to speak to the internal auditor but you have been told that he is on long-term sick leave. The chief financial accountant is away on holiday and will not be back until shortly before the audit is due to be completed.

Required

In relation to the facts above, explain the:

(i)   Implications for the audit of the financial statements;
(ii)   Potential effect, if any, on the auditor's report on the financial statements;
(iii) Implications for the continuing relationship between the audit firm and the client.   **(10 marks)**

(Total = 20 marks)

11 Confidentiality and independence (AIR 6/06)   36 mins

(a)   Explain the situations where an auditor may disclose confidential information about a client.   **(8 marks)**

(b)   You are an audit manager in McKay & Co, a firm of Chartered Certified Accountants. You are preparing the engagement letter for the audit of Ancients, a public limited liability company, for the year ending 30 June 2006.

Ancients has grown rapidly over the past few years, and is now one of your firm's most important clients. Ancients has been an audit client for eight years and McKay & Co has provided audit, taxation and management consultancy advice during this time. The client has been satisfied with the services provided, although the taxation fee for the period to 31 December 2005 remains unpaid.

Audit personnel available for this year's audit are most of the staff from last year, including Mr Grace, an audit partner and Mr Jones, an audit senior. Mr Grace has been the audit partner since Ancients became an audit client. You are aware that Allyson Grace, the daughter of Mr Grace, has recently been appointed the financial director at Ancients.

To celebrate her new appointment, Allyson has suggested taking all of the audit staff out to an expensive restaurant prior to the start of the audit work for this year.

Required

Identify and explain the risks to independence arising in carrying out your audit of Ancients for the year ending 30 June 2006, and suggest ways of mitigating each of the risks you identify.   **(12 marks)**

(Total = 20 marks)

12 Phones Anywhere   36 mins

You are the partner in charge of a four partner firm of certified accountants. Your firm has been invited to tender for the audit of Phones Anywhere for the year ended 31 December 20X6.

Phones Anywhere was established two years ago and it provides a mobile phone service for individuals and businesses. The system being established by the company comprises:

(a)   Small portable mobile phones which allow subscribers (users) to contact or be contacted by any other telephone.

(b)   The mobile phones can be used within range of a local relay station which receives calls from and sends calls to the mobile phones.

(c)   The local relay stations are linked to a central computer which connects the calls to other users. Frequently, this is through a competitor's telephone network.

(d) Currently, the local relay stations cover one large city with a population of about 1,000,000. Within the next year the system will cover all large cities in the country with a population of over 250,000. By the year 20Y0, the system will cover all motorways and cities with a population of over 100,000. Extending the coverage of the system will involve considerable capital expenditure on new relay stations and require additional borrowings.

(e) The cost of the relay stations and central computer are capitalised and are written off over six years.

(f) The mobile phones are manufactured by other companies and sold through retailers. Phone Anywhere does not sell the phones, but it pays $200 to the retailer for each phone sold and subscription signed by the customer to Phones Anywhere. This payment is capitalised in the financial statements of Phones Anywhere and written off over four years.

(g) Subscribers are invoiced monthly with a fixed line rental and a variable call charge. Other operators are charged for the time spent by their customers contacting Phones Anywhere's subscribers (customers). These charges are logged and calculated by the company's main computer.

(h) All the shares are owned by three wealthy individuals who are non-executive directors. They will receive a fixed salary. They do not plan to make any further investment in the company.

(i) Establishing the network of relay stations and subscribers will result in the company making losses for at least three years. Current borrowings are about 20% of shareholders' funds. Because of the substantial capital expenditure and trading losses, it is expected the company will be highly geared by the year 20X9.

(j) As the company will not be profitable, the non-executive directors have decided that executive directors should receive a basic salary and a bonus based on the number of subscribers to the system.

(k) The owners plan to float the company on a public exchange in the year 20Y0. The flotation will involve:

    (i)   Issuing new shares to the general public to provide funds for the company, and

    (ii)   The three non-executive directors selling some of their shares.

You are aware that Phones Anywhere has a number of very large competitors, each of which has a large number of users and comprehensive coverage (that is, over 90% of the population are within range of a relay station).

Required

In relation to the audit of Phones Anywhere:

(a) Consider the risks associated with the audit. **(8 marks)**

(b) Describe the ethical matters you should consider in deciding whether your audit firm should accept the audit. This should include considering whether your firm has the technical and logistical ability to carry out the audit. **(8 marks)**

(c) Come to a conclusion on whether you would advise your firm to accept or decline the audit, giving your principal reasons for coming to this decision. **(4 marks)**

(Total = 20 marks)

INTERNAL AUDIT

Questions 13 – 15 cover Internal audit, the subject of Part B of the BPP Study Text for F8.

13 Internal audit (AIR 6/03)

36 mins

Your firm is the newly appointed external auditor to a large company that sells, maintains and leases office equipment and furniture to its customers and you have been asked to co-operate with internal audit to keep total audit costs down. The company wants the external auditors to rely on some of the work already performed by internal audit.

The internal auditors provide the following services to the company:

(i)   A cyclical audit of the operation of internal controls in the company's major functions (operations, finance, customer support and information services);

(ii)   A review of the structure of internal controls in each major function every four years;

(iii)   An annual review of the effectiveness of measures put in place by management to minimise the major risks facing the company.

During the current year, the company has gone through a major internal restructuring in its information services function and the internal auditors have been closely involved in the preparation of plans for restructuring, and in the related post-implementation review.

Required

(a)   Explain the extent to which your firm will seek to rely on the work of the internal auditors in each of the areas noted above.   **(6 marks)**

(b)   Describe the information your firm will seek from the internal auditors in order for you to determine the extent of your reliance.   **(6 marks)**

(c)   Describe the circumstances in which it would *not* be possible to rely on the work of the internal auditors.
                                                                                                                (4 marks)

(d)   Explain why it will be necessary for your firm to perform its own work in certain audit areas in addition to relying on the work performed by internal audit.   **(4 marks)**

(Total = 20 marks)

14 Internal audit function (AIR Pilot paper) (amended)   18 mins

Required

(a)   Describe the role of internal audit in ensuring that organisations achieve their corporate objectives.**(5 marks)**

(b)   List the types of activity normally carried out by internal audit departments.   **(5 marks)**

(Total = 10 marks)

15 Value for money audit (AIR 12/06)   36 mins

(a)   Explain the purpose of the three 'Es' in relation to a value for money audit.   **(4 marks)**

(b)   You are an audit manager in the internal audit department of KLE Co. The internal audit department is auditing the company's procurement system in the company. Extracts from your system notes, which are correct and contain no errors, are provided below.

Details on ordering department:

–   Six members of staff – one buyer and five purchasing clerks.

–   Receives about 75 orders each day, many orders for duplicate items come from different departments in the organisation.

–   Initial evaluation of internal controls is high.

Procurement systems

Ordering department

All orders are raised on pre-numbered purchase requisitions and sent to the ordering department.

In the ordering department, each requisition is signed by the chief buyer. A purchasing clerk transfers the order information onto an order form and identifies the appropriate supplier for the goods.

Part one of the two part order form is sent to the supplier and part two to the accounts department. The requisition is thrown away.

Goods inwards department

All goods received are checked for damage. Damaged items are returned to the supplier and a damaged goods note completed.

For undamaged items a two-part pre-numbered Goods Received Note (GRN) is raised.

–   Part one is sent to the ordering department with the damaged goods notes.

–   Part two is filed in order of the reference number for the goods being ordered (obtained from the supplier's goods despatched documentation), in the goods inwards department.

Ordering department

GRNs are separated from damaged goods notes, which are filed. The GRN is forwarded to the accounts department.

Accounts department

GRNs matched with the order awaiting the receipt of the invoice.

Required

Using the system notes provided

(i)   Identify and explain the internal control weaknesses and provide a recommendation to overcome each weakness.   **(10 marks)**

(ii)   Identify and explain the additional weaknesses that should be raised by a value for money audit and provide a suitable recommendation to overcome each weakness.   **(6 marks)**

(Total = 20 marks)

PLANNING AND RISK ASSESSMENT

Questions 16 – 28 cover Planning and risk assessment, the subject of Part C of the BPP Study Text for F8.

16 Question with analysis: Twinkletoes (AIR 6/04)　　36 mins

Required

(a)　Explain how the classification of risks into categories such as 'high', 'medium' or 'low', helps entities manage their businesses.　　**(4 marks)**

You are the internal auditor of a large private company, Twinkletoes. Twinkletoes manufactures a high volume of reasonably priced shoes for elderly people. The company has a trade receivables ledger that is material to the financial statements containing four different categories of account. The categories of account, and the risks associated with them, are as follows:

(i)　Small retail shoe shops. These accounts represent nearly two thirds of the accounts on the ledger by number, and one third of the receivables by value. Some of these customers pay promptly, others are very slow;

(ii)　Large retail shoe shops (including a number of overseas accounts) that sell a wide range of shoes. Some of these accounts are large and overdue;

(iii)　Chains of discount shoe shops that buy their inventory centrally. These accounts are mostly well-established 'high street' chains. Again, some of these accounts are large and overdue; and

(iv)　Mail order companies who sell the company's shoes. There have been a number of large **new** accounts in this category, although there is no history of bad debts in this category.

Receivables listed under (ii) to (iv) are roughly evenly split by both value and number. All receivables are dealt with by the same managers and staff and the same internal controls are applied to each category of receivables. You do not consider that using the same managers and staff, and the same controls, is necessarily the best method of managing the receivables ledger.

Twinkletoes has suffered an increasing level of bad debts and slow payers in recent years, mostly as a result of small shoe shops becoming insolvent. The company has also lost several overseas accounts because of a requirement for them to pay in advance. Management wishes to expand the overseas market and has decided that overseas customers will in future be allowed credit terms.

Management has asked you to classify the risks associated with the receivables ledger in order to manage trade receivables as a whole more efficiently. You have been asked to classify accounts as high, medium or low risk.

Required

(b)　Classify the risks relating to the four categories of trade receivables as *high*, *medium* or *low* and explain your classification.　　**(8 marks)**

Note. More than one risk classification may be appropriate within each account category.

(c)　Describe the internal controls that you would recommend to Twinkletoes to manage the risks associated with the receivables ledger under the headings: *all customers*, *slow paying customers*, *larger accounts*, and *overseas customers*.　　**(8 marks)**

(Total = 20 marks)

16 Question with analysis: Twinkletoes (AIR 6/04)   36 mins

> It is as important to be able to identify where risk is **low** as well as instances where risk is high.

Required

(a)   Explain how the **classification** of risks into categories such as 'high', 'medium' or 'low', helps **entities** manage their businesses.

(4 marks)

> You are the internal auditor rather than the external auditor. Don't be put off by this. In some questions it may indicate that you need to think a bit more about operational issues. In this case as the question is dealing with risk related to accounts receivable the issues are essentially the same.

> Notice that you are looking at risk from the perspective of the **business** not the audit.

You are the **internal auditor** of a large private company, Twinkletoes. Twinkletoes manufactures a high volume of reasonably priced shoes for elderly people. The company has a trade receivables ledger that is material to the financial statements containing four different categories of account. The categories of account, and the risks associated with them, are as follows:

> There is a large number of relatively low value balances. How does this affect risk? If an individual account goes bad what will the overall effect be?

> Does the size of the retail organisation impact on risk?

(i)   **small** retail shoe shops. These accounts represent nearly **two thirds of the accounts** on the ledger by number, and **one third of the receivables by value**. Some of these customers pay **promptly**, others are very **slow**;

> Material to the balance overall?

> Reduced risk?

> Increased risk?

> Take care here not to jump to conclusions about the risk attached to overseas debts. Can you see any other relevant information? Don't always expect information to be conveniently grouped together.

> Think about the nature of the receivable. What is the likelihood that they will fail to pay?

(ii)   large retail shoe shops (including a number of **overseas accounts**) that sell a wide range of shoes. Some of these accounts are **large and overdue**;

> Materiality? Risk?

(iii)   chains of discount shoe shops that buy their inventory centrally. These accounts are mostly **well-established 'high street' chains**. Again, some of these accounts are **large and overdue**; and

(iv)   mail order companies who sell the company's shoes. There have been a number of large **new accounts** in this category, although there is **no history of bad debts** in this category.

> But ultimate will the amounts be recovered?

> This would normally increase risk as the company has no previous experience of this customer.

> What impact does this have on the fact that there are a large number of new accounts. Does it reduce our initial assessment of risk? Try to look at the relationship between different pieces of information.

ink about the
ative
ateriality of
ch category
relation to
tal
ceivables.

Receivables listed under (ii) to (iv) are **roughly evenly split** by both value and number. All receivables are dealt with by the same managers and staff and the same internal controls are applied to each category of receivables. You do not consider that using the same managers and staff, and the same controls, is necessarily the best method of managing the receivables ledger.

We are given more information about the small retail accounts which apparently increases risk but you must read it in the light of the earlier details provided.

Different type of risk? That is, affecting the business as a whole rather that just accounts receivable.

w risk?

Twinkletoes has suffered an increasing level of bad debts and slow payers in recent years, mostly as a result of small shoe shops becoming **insolvent**. The company has also **lost several overseas accounts** because of a requirement for them to **pay in advance**. Management wishes to expand the overseas market and has decided that overseas customers will in future be allowed credit terms.

is is where
e skill comes
. You need to
aluate the
ative merits
the
formation you
ve just read.
y to connect
fferent pieces
information
determine
nat the overall
ect will be.

Management has asked you to classify the risks associated with the receivables ledger in order to manage trade receivables as a whole more efficiently. You have been asked to classify accounts as high, medium or low risk.

Required

(b)   **Classify the risks** relating to the four categories of trade receivables as *high*, *medium* or *low* and **explain** your classification.   **(8 marks)**

Note. **More than one risk classification may be appropriate** within each account category.

Always pay attention to any extra notes or comments which the examiner includes in the question. Here the examiner is giving you an important clue. Try not to think about all the accounts in each category as being the same. For example the small retail shops which pay promptly will be low risk whilst those who pay slowly will be more risky.

a question
quiring judgement
ere is often more
an one acceptable
swer. The
planation is your
portunity to justify
ur conclusions.

A standard requirement but you must tailor your answer to the scenario.

Make sure that your suggestions of controls address the issues raised in the question ie
 recoverability. The examiner is not looking for a list of every control that could relate to the receivables ledger.

(c)   Describe the **internal controls** that you would recommend to Twinkletoes **to manage the risks** associated with the receivables ledger under the headings: *all customers*, *slow paying customers*, *larger accounts*, and *overseas customers*.   **(8 marks)**

(Total = 20 marks)

17 Rock (AIR 12/04)

36 mins

You are an audit senior responsible for understanding the entity and its environment and assessing the risk of material misstatements for the audit of Rock for the year ending 31 December 20X4. Rock is a company listed on a stock exchange. Rock is engaged in the wholesale import, manufacture and distribution of basic cosmetics and toiletries for sale to a wide range of stores, under a variety of different brand names. You have worked on the audit of this client for several years as an audit junior.

Required

(a) Describe the information you will seek, and procedures you will perform in order to understand the entity and its environment and assess risk for the audit of Rock for the year ending 31 December 20X4.

(10 marks)

(b) You are now nearing the completion of the audit of Rock for the year ending 31 December 20X4. Draft financial statements have been produced. You have been given the responsibility of performing a review of the audit files before they are passed to the audit manager and the audit partner for their review. You have been asked to concentrate on the proper completion of the audit working papers. Some of the audit working papers have been produced electronically but all of them have been printed out for you.

Describe the types of audit working papers you should expect to see in the audit files and the features of those working papers that show that they have been properly completed. **(10 marks)**

(Total = 20 marks)

18 Tempest (AIR 12/05)

36 mins

(a) International Standard on Auditing 300 (revised) '*Planning an audit of financial statements*', states that an auditor must plan the audit.

Explain why it is important to plan an audit. **(5 marks)**

(b) You are the audit manager in charge of the audit of Tempest, a limited liability company. The company's year end is 31 December, and Tempest has been a client for seven years. The company purchases and resells fittings for ships including anchors, compasses, rudders, sails etc. Clients vary in size from small businesses making yachts to large companies maintaining large luxury cruise ships. No manufacturing takes place in Tempest.

Information on the company's financial performance is available as follows:

	20X7 Forecast	20X7 Actual
	$'000	$'000
Revenue	45,928	40,825
Cost of sales	(37,998)	(31,874)
Gross profit	7,930	8,951
Administration costs	(4,994)	(4,758)
Distribution costs	(2,500)	(2,500)
Net profit	436	1,693

	20X7 Forecast	20X6 Actual
	$'000	$'000
Non-current assets (at net book value)	3,600	4,500
Current assets		
Inventory	200	1,278
Receivables	6,000	4,052
Cash and bank	500	1,590
Total assets	10,300	11,420
Capital and reserves		
Share capital	1,000	1,000
Accumulated profits	5,300	5,764
	6,300	6,764
Total shareholders' funds	1,000	6,764
Non-current liabilities	3,000	2,598
Current liabilities	10,300	11,420

Other information

The industry that Tempest trades in has seen moderate growth of 7% over the last year.

- Non-current assets mainly relate to company premises for storing inventory. Ten delivery vehicles are owned with a net book value of $300,000.

- One of the directors purchased a yacht during the year.

- Inventory is stored in ten different locations across the country, with your firm again having offices close to seven of those locations.

- A computerised inventory control system was introduced in August 20X7. Inventory balances are now obtainable directly from the computer system. The client does not intend to count inventory at the year-end but rely instead on the computerised inventory control system.

Required

Using the information provided above, prepare the audit strategy for Tempest for the year ending 31 December 20X7. **(15 marks)**

(Total = 20 marks)

19 Bridgford Products

36 mins

Your firm has been the auditor of Bridgford Products, a listed company, for a number of years. The engagement partner has asked you to describe the matters you would consider when planning the audit for the year ended 31 January 20X9.

During a recent visit to the company you obtained the following information.

(a) The management accounts for the 10 months to 30 November 20X8 show a revenue of $130 million and profit before tax of $4 million. Assume sales and profits accrue evenly throughout the year. In the year ended 31 January 20X8 Bridgford Products had sales of $110 million and profit before tax of $8 million.

(b) The company installed a new computerised inventory control system which has operated from 1 June 20X8. As the inventory control system records inventory movements and current inventory quantities, the company is proposing:

(i) To use the inventory quantities on the computer to value the inventory at the year-end
(ii) Not to carry out an inventory count at the year-end

(c) You are aware there have been reliability problems with the company's products, which have resulted in legal claims being brought against the company by customers, and customers refusing to pay for the products.

(d) The sales increase in the 10 months to 30 November 20X8 over the previous year has been achieved by attracting new customers and by offering extended credit. The new credit arrangements allow customers three months credit before their debt becomes overdue, rather than the one month credit period allowed previously. As a result of this change, trade receivables age has increased from 1.6 to 4.1 months.

(e) The financial director and purchasing manager were dismissed on 15 August. A replacement purchasing manager has been appointed but it is not expected that a new financial director will be appointed before the year end of 31 January 20X9. The chief accountant will be responsible for preparing the financial statements for audit.

Required

(a) Describe the reasons why it is important that auditors should plan their audit work. **(5 marks)**

(b) Describe the matters you will consider in planning the audit and the further action you will take concerning the information you obtained during your recent visit to the company. **(15 marks)**

(Total = 20 marks)

20 Question with student answer: Parker (AIR 6/05)   36 mins

(a) Explain the term 'audit risk'. **(4 marks)**

(b) You are the audit manager for Parker, a limited liability company which sells books, CDs, DVDs and similar items via two divisions: mail order and on-line ordering on the Internet. Parker is a new audit client. You are commencing the planning of the audit for the year ended 31 May 20X7. An initial meeting with the directors has provided the information below.

The company's turnover is in excess of $85 million with net profits of $4 million. All profits are currently earned in the mail order division, although the Internet division is expected to return a small net profit next year. Turnover is growing at the rate of 20% p.a. Net profit has remained almost the same for the last four years.

In the next year, the directors plan to expand the range of goods sold through the Internet division to include toys, garden furniture and fashion clothes. The directors believe that when one product has been sold on the Internet, then any other product can be as well.

The accounting system to record sales by the mail order division is relatively old. It relies on extensive manual input to transfer orders received in the post onto Parker's computer systems. Recently errors have been known to occur, in the input of orders, and in the invoicing of goods following dispatch. The directors maintain that the accounting system produces materially correct figures and they cannot waste time in identifying relatively minor errors. The company accountant, who is not qualified and was appointed because he is a personal friend of the directors, agrees with this view.

The directors estimate that their expansion plans will require a bank loan of approximately $30 million, partly to finance the enhanced web site but also to provide working capital to increase inventory levels. A meeting with the bank has been scheduled for three months after the year end. The directors expect an unmodified auditor's report to be signed prior to this time.

Required

(i) Identify and describe the matters that give rise to audit risks associated with Parker. **(10 marks)**

(ii) Explain the enquiries you will make, and the audit procedures you will perform to assist you in making a decision regarding the going concern status of Parker in reaching your audit opinion on the financial statements. **(6 marks)**

(Total = 20 marks)

21 Stone Holidays (AIR 12/04)   36 mins

Fraud and error present risks to an entity. Both internal and external auditors are required to deal with risks to the entity. However, the responsibilities of internal and external auditors in relation to the risk of fraud and error differ.

Required

(a) Explain how the internal audit function helps an entity deal with the risk of fraud and error. **(7 marks)**

(b) Explain the responsibilities of external auditors in respect of the risk of fraud and error in an audit of financial statements. **(7 marks)**

(c) Stone Holidays is an independent travel agency. It does not operate holidays itself. It takes commission on holidays sold to customers through its chain of high street shops. Staff are partly paid on a commission basis. Well-established tour operators run the holidays that Stone Holidays sells. The networked reservations system through which holidays are booked and the computerised accounting system are both well-established systems used by many independent travel agencies.

Payments by customers, including deposits, are accepted in cash and by debit and credit card. Stone Holidays is legally required to pay an amount of money (based on its total sales for the year) into a central fund maintained to compensate customers if the agency should cease operations.

Describe the nature of the risks to which Stone Holidays is subject arising from fraud and error. **(6 marks)**

(Total = 20 marks)

22 Grindsbrook Clothing Company (AIR 6/02)   36 mins

The Grindsbrook Clothing Company is a family-owned company that manufactures and sells high quality clothes by mail order. It has been in business for nearly ten years and has made a small profit during the last five years.

The company has a small, modern factory and employs some 150 staff including clerical staff who take orders over the telephone and prepare the accounting records. The accounting hardware and software are out of date and slow. Credit management and management of receivables and payables generally is poor.

The company does not yet have a presence on the Internet. The company's chief buyer, who is the managing director's son, buys high quality fabrics all over the world. He is an expert in fabrics but he pays too little attention to either the consistency of supply or the cost. As a result, budgeting is difficult and some lines of clothing are made and sold at very little profit, or even a loss.

The company out-sources the production of the company catalogue and does not spend a significant amount on other advertising because the managing director does not consider that it is necessary. He has consistently refused to employ a professional marketing manager. There are an increasing number of competitors in this profitable market and despite the fact that the market is growing overall, the company's market share is declining, although turnover is rising slowly.

The company is financed partly by the managing director and his wife (who are the only shareholders), and partly by short and long-term bank loans. The managing director's son does not have any investment in the business, because his father wishes to retain control of the company. The bank loans are small by comparison with the family's investment. The long-term bank loan is small by comparison with the short-term bank loan. The two daughters are not involved in the business. There are some disagreements among family members about how the business should be run.

The company's accounts have been prepared and audited by a series of firms of auditors. The managing director has refused to employ a qualified accountant. The company's budgets and statutory financial statements have been of poor quality and have often been produced late.

You are a very busy Chartered Certified Accountant working in practice on your own and the managing director's wife is your sister. You have considerable experience of providing advice to this type of business because you were once employed as internal auditor to a similar, but larger, clothing company. Your sister has decided that if the business is to prosper, outside professional help is needed.

The managing director's wife, your sister, considers that your previous experience as an internal auditor may be useful to the Grindsbrook Clothing Company. She has asked you to assess the risks facing the business and to make suggestions as to how these risks should be managed.

Required

(a)   List the factors you will take into account in deciding whether or not to accept the assignment from your sister.   **(6 marks)**

(b)   List the specific issues facing the business under appropriate headings such as external risks, financial risks, operational risks and compliance risks. Describe the actions that could be taken by the company to deal with each issue you identify.

        Note. You may use headings other then those suggested in the question.   **(14 marks)**

                                                                                                          (Total = 20 marks)

23 BearsWorld (AIR 6/05)   **36 mins**

You are the auditor of BearsWorld, a limited liability company which manufactures and sells small cuddly toys by mail order. The company is managed by Mr Kyto and two assistants. Mr Kyto authorises important transactions such as wages and large orders, one assistant maintains the payables ledger and orders inventory and pays suppliers, and the other assistant receives customer orders and despatches cuddly toys. Due to other business commitments Mr Kyto only visits the office once per week.

At any time, about 100 different types of cuddly toys are available for sale. All sales are made cash with order – there are no receivables. Customers pay using credit cards and occasionally by sending cash. Turnover is over $5·2 million.

You are planning the audit of BearsWorld and are considering using some of the procedures for gathering audit evidence recommended by ISA 500 as follows:

(i)   Analytical Procedures
(ii)   Inquiry
(iii)   Inspection
(iv)   Observation
(v)   Re-calculation

Required

(a)   For EACH of the above procedures:

        (i)   Explain its use in gathering audit evidence.   **(5 marks)**
        (ii)   Describe one example for the audit of BearsWorld.   **(5 marks)**

(b)   Discuss the suitability of each procedure for BearsWorld, explaining the limitations of each.   **(10 marks)**

                                                                                                          (Total = 20 marks)

24 CAATs

18 mins

CAATs are commonly used by auditors.

Required

(a)   State five audit benefits to be derived from using CAATs when carrying out testing of computer records.

(3 mins)

(b)   Describe and give an example of five typical functions of an audit software interrogation programme.

(3 mins)

(c)   Describe four problems associated with the use of audit interrogation programmes.   **(2 marks)**

(d)   Describe four examples by which computers and information technology can be used to enhance the administration procedures and control over an audit.   **(2 marks)**

(Total = 10 marks)

25 Porthos (AIR 12/05)

36 mins

(a)   Computer-Assisted Audit Techniques (CAATs) are used to assist an auditor in the collection of audit evidence from computerised systems.

Required

List and briefly explain four advantages of CAATs.   **(4 marks)**

(b)   Porthos, a limited liability company, is a reseller of sports equipment, specialising in racquet sports such as tennis, squash and badminton. The company purchases equipment from a variety of different suppliers and then resells this using the Internet as the only selling media. The company has over 150 different types of racquets available in inventory, each identified via a unique product code.

Customers place their orders directly on the Internet site. Most orders are for one or two racquets only. The ordering/sales software automatically verifies the order details, customer address and credit card information prior to orders being verified and goods being despatched. The integrity of the ordering system is checked regularly by ArcherWeb, an independent Internet service company.

You are the audit manager working for the external auditors of Porthos, and you have just starting planning the audit of the sales system of the company. You have decided to use test data to check the input of details into the sales system. This will involve entering dummy orders into the Porthos system from an online terminal.

Required

List the test data you will use in your audit of the financial statements of Porthos to confirm the completeness and accuracy of input into the sales system, clearly explaining the reason for each item of data.   **(6 marks)**

(c)   You are also considering using audit software as part of your substantive testing of the data files in the sales and inventory systems of Porthos Ltd.

(i)   List and briefly explain some of the difficulties of using audit software.   **(4 marks)**

(ii)   List the audit tests that you can program into your audit software for the sales and inventory system in Porthos, explaining the reason for each test.   **(6 marks)**

(Total = 20 marks)

26 Serenity (AIR 12/06)

36 mins

(a) ISA 315 *Understanding the entity and its environment and assessing the risks of material misstatement* states 'the auditor should perform . . . risk assessment procedures to obtain an understanding of the entity and its environment, including its internal control.'

Required

    (i)   Explain the purpose of risk assessment procedures.   **(3 marks)**

    (ii)   Outline the sources of audit evidence the auditor can use as part of risk assessment procedures.

        (3 marks)

(b) Mal & Co, an audit firm, has seven partners. The firm has a number of audit clients in different industrial sectors, with a wide range of fee income.

An audit partner of Mal & Co has just delegated to you the planning work for the audit of Serenity Co. This company provides a range of mobile communication facilities and this will be the second year your firm has provided audit services.

You have just met with the financial controller of Serenity prior to agreeing the engagement letter for this year. The controller has informed you that Serenity has continued to grow quickly, with financial accounting systems changing rapidly and appropriate control systems being difficult to maintain. Additional services in terms of review and implementation of control systems have been requested. An internal audit department has recently been established and the controller wants you to ensure that external audit work is limited by using this department.

You have also learnt that Serenity is to market a new type of mobile telephone, which is able to intercept messages from law enforcement agencies. The legal status of this telephone is unclear at present and development is not being publicised.

The granting of the licence to market the mobile telephone is dependent on the financial stability of Serenity. The financial controller has indicated that Mal & Co may be asked to provide a report to the mobile telephone licensing authority regarding Serenity's cash flow forecast for the year ending December 2007 to support the licence application.

Required

As part of your risk assessment procedures for the audit of Serenity Co for the year ending 31 December 2006, identify and describe the issues to be considered when providing services to this client.

        (10 marks)

(c) When reporting on a cash flow forecast, explain the term 'negative assurance' and why this is used.

        (4 marks)

        (Total = 20 marks)

27 Tam (AIR 12/06)

36 mins

(a)   (i)   In the context of ISA 530 *Audit Sampling and Other Means of Testing*, explain and provide examples of the terms 'sampling risk' and 'non-sampling' risk.   **(4 marks)**

    (ii)   Briefly explain how sampling and non-sampling risk can be controlled by the audit firm.   **(2 marks)**

(b) Tam Co, is owned and managed by two brothers with equal shareholdings. The company specialises in the sale of expensive motor vehicles. Annual revenue is in the region of $70,000,000 and the company requires an audit under local legislation. About 500 cars are sold each year, with an average value of $140,000, although the range of values is from $130,000 to $160,000. Invoices are completed manually with one director signing all invoices to confirm the sales value is correct. All accounting and financial statement preparation is carried out by the directors. A recent expansion of the company's showroom was financed by a bank loan, repayable over the next five years.

The audit manager is starting to plan the audit of Tam Co. The audit senior and audit junior assigned to the audit are helping the manager as a training exercise.

Comments are being made about how to select a sample of sales invoices for testing. Audit procedures are needed to ensure that the managing director has signed them and then to trace details into the sales day book and sales ledger.

'We should check all invoices' suggests the audit manager.

'How about selecting a sample using statistical sampling techniques' adds the audit senior.

'Why waste time obtaining a sample?' asks the audit junior. He adds 'taking a random sample of invoices by reviewing the invoice file and manually choosing a few important invoices will be much quicker.'

Required

Briefly explain each of the sample selection methods suggested by the audit manager, audit senior and audit junior, and discuss whether or not they are appropriate for obtaining a representative sample of sales invoices. **(9 marks)**

(c) Define 'materiality' and explain why the auditors of Tam Co must form an opinion on whether the financial statements are free from material misstatement. **(5 marks)**

(Total = 20 marks)

28 Question with answer plan: Ajio (AIR 12/03)   36 mins

Ajio is a charity whose constitution requires that it raises funds for educational projects. These projects seek to educate children and support teachers in certain countries. Charities in the country from which Ajio operates have recently become subject to new audit and accounting regulations. Charity income consists of cash collections at fund raising events, telephone appeals, and bequests (money left to the charity by deceased persons). The charity is small and the trustees do not consider that the charity can afford to employ a qualified accountant. The charity employs a part-time bookkeeper and relies on volunteers for fund raising. Your firm has been appointed as accountants and auditors to this charity because of the new regulations. Accounts have been prepared (but not audited) in the past by a volunteer who is a recently retired Chartered Certified Accountant.

Required:

(a) Describe the risks associated with the audit of Ajio under the headings inherent risk, control risk and detection risk and explain the implications of these risks for overall audit risk. **(10 marks)**

(b) List and explain the audit tests to be performed on income and expenditure from fund raising events. **(10 marks)**

Note. In part (a) you may deal with inherent risk and control risk together. You are not required to deal with the detail of accounting for charities in either part of the question.

(Total = 20 marks)

INTERNAL CONTROL

Questions 29 – 35 cover Internal control, the subject of Part D of the BPP Study Text for F8.

29 Cliff (AIR 12/04) (amended)

54 mins

Day-to-day internal controls are important for all businesses to maximise the efficient use of resources and profitability.

Your firm has recently been appointed as auditor to Cliff, a private company that runs a chain of small supermarkets selling fresh and frozen food, and canned and dry food. Cliff has very few controls over inventory because the company trusts local managers to make good decisions regarding the purchase, sales and control of inventory, all of which is done locally. Pricing is generally performed on a cost-plus basis.

Each supermarket has a stand-alone computer system on which monthly accounts are prepared. These accounts are mailed to head office every quarter. There is no integrated inventory control, sales or purchasing system and no regular system for inventory counting. Management accounts are produced twice a year.

Trade at the supermarkets has increased in recent years and the number of supermarkets has increased. However, the quality of staff that has been recruited has fallen. Senior management at Cliff are now prepared to invest in more up-to-date systems.

Required

(a)   Describe the problems that you might expect to find at Cliff resulting from poor internal controls.**(10 marks)**

(b)   Make four recommendations to the senior management of Cliff for the improvement of internal controls, and explain the advantages and disadvantages of each recommendation.   **(12 marks)**

(c)   Explain the impact that the internal control environment at Cliff is likely to have on your audit approach.

(5 marks)

(d)   Briefly discuss the benefits of a report to management at the interim stage of an audit.   **(3 marks)**

(Total = 30 marks)

30 Internal control (AIR Pilot paper)

36 mins

There are many reasons for maintaining internal control. These include the need to ensure that:

(i)   Transactions are properly authorised
(ii)   Transactions are promptly and accurately recorded
(iii)   Access to assets and records is properly authorised
(iv)   Recorded assets represent actual assets.

In the absence of internal control, errors, omissions and misappropriation of assets are likely and external and internal auditors pay attention to both the design and operation of internal control.

Receivables is an area in which most organisations expect internal controls to be operating effectively.

Required

(a)   In the context of receivables, list and describe the types of error, omission and misappropriation of assets that can occur in practice where internal controls are weak or non-existent.   **(4 marks)**

(b)   Explain why even good internal control will not necessarily prevent or detect errors, omissions and the misappropriation of assets in a receivables system, and explain why effective internal control is important to auditors.   **(4 marks)**

(c)   List the main internal control activities that you would expect to be in operation in the receivables system at a small manufacturing company with a computerised accounting system.   **(9 marks)**

(d)   Explain why external auditors seek to rely on the proper operation of internal control wherever possible.
   (3 marks)

   (Total = 20 marks)

31 Risk assessment and internal control (AIR 12/02)   36 mins

(a)   There are a number of key procedures which auditors should perform if they wish to rely on internal controls and reduce the level of substantive testing they perform. These include:

(i)   Documentation of accounting systems and internal control;
(ii)   Walk-through tests;
(iii)   Audit sampling;
(iv)   Testing internal controls;
(v)   Dealing with deviations from the application of control activities.

Required

Briefly explain each of the procedures listed above.   **(10 marks)**

Note. (i) – (v) above carry equal marks.

(b)   Flowers Anytime sells flowers wholesale. Customers telephone the company and their orders are taken by clerks who take details of the flowers to be delivered, the address to which they are to be delivered, and account details of the customer. The clerks input these details into the company's computer system (whilst the order is being taken) which is integrated with the company's inventory control system. The company's standard credit terms are payment one month from the order (all orders are despatched within 48 hours) and most customers pay by bank transfer. An accounts receivable ledger is maintained and statements are sent to customers once a month. Credit limits are set by the credit controller according to a standard formula and are automatically applied by the computer system, as are the prices of flowers.

Required

Describe and explain the purpose of the internal controls you might expect to see in the sales system at Flowers Anytime over the:

(i)   Receipt, processing and recording of orders   **(6 marks)**
(ii)   Collection of cash   **(4 marks)**

   (Total = 20 marks)

32 Atlantis Standard Goods (AIR 6/06)   36 mins

(a)   State the control objectives for the ordering, despatch and invoicing of goods.   **(5 marks)**

(b)   Atlantis Standard Goods (ASG) Co has a year end of 30 June 2006. ASG is a retailer of kitchen appliances such as washing machines, fridges and microwaves. All sales are made via the company's Internet site with dispatch and delivery of goods to the customer's house made using ASG's vehicles. Appliances are purchased from many different manufacturers.

The process of making a sale is as follows:

(1)   Potential customers visit ASG's website and select the kitchen appliance that they require. The website ordering system accesses the inventory specification file to obtain details of products ASG sells.

(2)   When the customer chooses an appliance, order information including price, item and quantity required are stored in the orders pending file.

(3)   Online authorisation of credit card details is obtained from the customer's credit card company automatically by ASG's computer systems.

(4)   Following authorisation, the sales amount is transferred to the computerised sales day book. At the end of each day the total from this ledger is transferred to the general ledger.

(5)   Reimbursement of the sales amount is obtained from each credit card company monthly, less the appropriate commission charged by the credit card company.

(6)   Following authorisation of the credit card, order details are transferred to a goods awaiting despatch file and allocated a unique order reference code. Order details are automatically transferred to the dispatch department's computer system.

(7)   In the despatch department, goods are obtained from the physical inventory, placed on ASG vehicles and the computerised inventory system updated. Order information is downloaded on a hand held computer with a writable screen.

(8)   On delivery, the customer signs for the goods on the hand held computer. On return to ASG's warehouse, images of the customer signature are uploaded to the orders file which is then flagged as 'order complete'.

This year's audit planning documentation states that a substantive approach will be taken on the audit.

Required

Tabulate the audit tests you should carry out on the sales and despatch system, explaining the reason for each test.

(15 marks)

(Total = 20 marks)

33 Cosmo (AIR 12/01)

36 mins

(a)   Internal control is designed, amongst other things, to prevent error and misappropriation.

Required

Describe the errors and misappropriations that may occur if purchases and capital expenditure are not properly controlled.

(5 marks)

(b)   Cosmo is a high-quality, private motor manufacturing company. It has recently joined a consortium for the purchase of parts. Cosmo's purchases and capital expenditure systems are not integrated.

Purchases and capital expenditure

There are complex internal rules relating to what constitutes a purchase, and what constitutes capital expenditure and the budgets for both are tightly controlled. Problems associated with the internal rules result in a significant number of manual adjustments to the management accounts which take up an excessive amount of management time.

The system for authorising capital expenditure is not well controlled which results in some capital items being acquired without proper consideration, at the monthly meetings of the capital expenditure committee.

Purchase orders

Purchase orders are generated automatically by the computerised inventory system when inventories levels fall below a given level in the context of scheduled production. This system does not work well because the system uses outdated purchasing and production patterns and many manual adjustments are required. The orders are reviewed by the production controller and her junior managers and changes are made informally by junior clerical staff in the production controller's department.

Some of the purchases are input into the buying consortium system which shows the optimum supplier for any combination of cost, delivery time and specification. This system has only been in operation for a few months. The system takes up a substantial amount of disk space on the company's computers and is suspected of causing problems in other systems. It is difficult to use and so far, only two of the production controller's junior managers are able to use it. As a result, the parts ordered through the system are sometimes of the incorrect specification or are delivered late. The remaining purchases are ordered directly from manufacturers, as before, through a reasonably well-controlled buying department.

Required

Set out, in a form suitable for inclusion in a report to management, the weaknesses, potential consequences and your recommendations relating to the purchases and capital expenditure systems of Cosmo.

(15 marks)

(Total = 20 marks)

34 Dinko (AIR 12/03)   36 mins

A proper understanding of internal controls is essential to auditors in order that they understand the business and are able to effectively plan and execute tests of controls and an appropriate level of substantive procedures.

You are the auditor of a small manufacturing company, Dinko, that pays its staff in cash and by bank transfer and maintains its payroll on a small stand-alone computer.

Required

(a) For the payroll department at Dinko, describe the:

     (i)   internal control *objectives* that should be in place;   **(4 marks)**

     (ii)   internal control *environment* and internal control *activities* that should be in place to achieve the internal control objectives.   **(6 marks)**

(b) For the payroll charges and payroll balances (including cash) in the financial statements of Dinko:

     (i)   describe the external auditor *audit objectives*;   **(4 marks)**

     (ii)   list *the tests of controls* and *substantive procedures* that will be applied in order to achieve the audit objectives identified in (b) (i) above.   **(6 marks)**

(Total = 20 marks)

35 Burton Housing   36 mins

Your firm is the auditor of Burton Housing, which is a small charity and housing association. Its principal asset is a large freehold building which contains a restaurant, accommodation for 50 young people, and recreational facilities.

The charity is controlled by a management committee which comprises the voluntary chairman and treasurer, and other voluntary members elected annually. However, day-to-day management is by a chief executive who manages the full-time staff who perform accounting, cleaning, maintenance, housing management and other functions.

You are auditing the company's financial statements for the year ended 31 October 20X5. Draft accounts have been prepared by the treasurer from accounting records kept on a microcomputer by the bookkeeper. The partner in charge of the audit has asked you to consider the audit work you would perform on income from rents, and the income and expenditure account of the restaurant.

For income from rents:

(a) The housing manager allocates rooms to individuals, and this information is sent to the bookkeeper.

(b)   Each week the bookkeeper posts the rents to each resident's account on the sales ledger. All rooms are let at the same rent.

(c)   Rents are received from residents by reception staff who are independent of the housing manager and bookkeeper. Reception staff give the rents to the bookkeeper.

(d)   The bookkeeper posts cash received for rents to the sales ledger, enters them in the cash book and pays them into the bank.

(e)   The housing manager reports voids (that is, rooms unlet) to the management committee.

The restaurant comprises the manager and four staff, who prepare and sell food to residents and other individuals.

Cash takings from the restaurant are recorded on a till and each day's takings are given to the bookkeeper who records and pays them into the bank. Details of cash takings are recorded on the till roll.

The system for purchasing food comprises the following:

(a)   The restaurant manager orders the food by sending an order to the supplier.

(b)   Food received is checked by the restaurant manager.

(c)   The restaurant manager authorises purchase invoices, confirming the food has been received.

(d)   The bookkeeper posts the purchase invoices to the payables ledger.

(e)   The bookkeeper makes out the cheques to pay the suppliers, which the chief executive signs. The cheques are posted to the payables ledger and cash book.

The bookkeeper is responsible for paying the wages of staff in the restaurant. The restaurant manager notifies the bookkeeper of any absences of staff.

You should assume that the income and expenditure account of the restaurant includes only:

(a)   Income from customers who purchase food

(b)   Expenditure on purchasing food and wages of restaurant staff

Required

Consider the control activities which should be in operation and the audit procedures you will carry out to verify:

(a)   For rents received:

     (i)   Recording of rental income on the sales ledger
     (ii)   Receipt and recording of rents received from residents
     (iii)   Posting of adjustments, credit notes and write off of bad debts on the sales ledger   **(11 marks)**

(b)   The income and expenditure account of the restaurant.   **(9 marks)**

(Total = 20 marks)

AUDIT EVIDENCE

Questions 36 – 57 cover Audit evidence, the subject of Part E of the BPP Study Text for F8.

36 Materiality considerations (AIR 6/02) (amended)   18 mins

The concept of materiality is fundamental to the work of auditors. Matters that are immaterial are not reported in financial statements.

Required

(i)	Explain the concept of materiality;	**(4 marks)**
(ii)	Describe how materiality affects the audit work performed by auditors;	**(4 marks)**
(iii)	Give an example of *qualitative* materiality.	**(2 marks)**

(Total = 10 marks)

37 Question with analysis: Springfield Nurseries (AIR Pilot paper) (amended)   54 mins

Your firm is the auditor of Springfield Nurseries, a company operating three large garden centres which sell plants, shrubs and trees, garden furniture and gardening equipment (such as lawnmowers and sprinklers) to the general public. You are involved in the audit of the company's non-current assets. The main categories of non-current assets are as follows:

(i)   Land and buildings (all of which are owned outright by the company, none of which are leased)
(ii)   Computers (on which an integrated inventory control and sales system is operated)
(iii) A number of large and small motor vehicles, mostly used for the delivery of inventory to customers
(iv)   Equipment for packaging and pricing products.

The depreciation rates used are as follows:

(i)	Buildings	5% each year on cost
(ii)	Computers and motor vehicles	20% each year on the reducing balance basis
(iii)	Equipment	15% each year on cost

You are concerned that these depreciation rates may be inappropriate.

Required

(a)   List and explain the main financial statements assertions tested for in the audit of non-current assets.

(5 marks)

(b)   Explain the main risks associated with the assertions relating to non-current assets.   **(4 marks)**

(c)   List the sources of evidence available to you in verifying the ownership and cost of:

(i)   The land and buildings
(ii)   The computers and motor vehicles.   **(10 marks)**

(d)   List the audit procedures you would perform to check the appropriateness of the depreciation rates on each of the three categories of non-current asset.   **(6 marks)**

(e)   Describe the action you would take if you disagreed with any of the depreciation rates used and explain the potential effect of the disagreement on your audit report.   **(5 marks)**

(Total = 30 marks)

37 Question with analysis: Springfield Nurseries (AIR Pilot paper)

54 mins

Your firm is the auditor of Springfield Nurseries, a company operating **three large garden centres which sell plants**, **shrubs and trees, garden furniture and gardening equipment** (such as lawnmowers and sprinklers) to the general public. You are involved in the audit of the company's non-current assets. The main categories of non-current assets are as follows:

Think about scena

So make sur you don't mention leas assets in you answer.

(i)   Land and buildings (all of which are owned outright by the company, **none of which are leased**)

(ii)   Computers (on which an integrated inventory control and sales system is operated)

(iii)   A number of large and small motor vehicles, mostly used for the delivery of inventory to customers

(iv)   Equipment for packaging and pricing products.

The depreciation rates used are as follows:

Note different methods

(i)   Buildings   5% each year on **cost**

(ii)   Computers and motor vehicles   20% each year on the **reducing balance basis**

(iii)   Equipment   15% each year on **cost**

You are concerned that these depreciation rates may be **inappropriate**.

Make sure you comment on this in your answer.

Required

Note the question requirement for each part and the mark allocations.

(a)   **Listen and explain** the main financial statement assertions tested for in the audit of non-current assets.

(5 marks)

(b)   **Explain** the main risks associated with the assertions relating to non-current assets.   **(4 marks)**

(c)   **List** the sources of evidence available to you in verifying the ownership and cost of:

(i)   The land and buildings

(ii)   The computers and motor vehicles.   **(10 marks)**

(d)   **List** the audit procedures you would perform to check the appropriateness of the depreciation rates on each of the three categories of non-current asset.   **(6 marks)**

(e)   **Describe** the action you would take if you disagreed with any of the depreciation rates used and **explain** the potential effect of the disagreement on your audit report.

(5 marks)

(Total = 30 marks)

38 Wear Wraith (AIR 6/06)

36 mins

Wear Wraith (WW) Co's main activity is the extraction and supply of building materials including sand, gravel, cement and similar aggregates. The company's year end is 31 May and your firm has audited WW for a number of years. The main asset on the balance sheet relates to non current assets. A junior member of staff has attempted to prepare the non-current asset note for the financial statements. The note has not been reviewed by the senior accountant and so may contain errors.

	Land and buildings $	Plant and machinery $	Motor vehicles $	Railway trucks $	Total $
COST					
1 June 20X5	100,000	875,000	1,500,000	–	2,475,000
Additions	10,000	125,000	525,000	995,000	1,655,000
Disposals	–	(100,000)	(325,000)	–	(425,000)
31 May 20X6	110,000	900,000	1,700,000	995,000	3,705,000
Depreciation					
1 June 20X5	60,000	550,000	750,000	–	1,360,000
Charge	2,200	180,000	425,000	199,000	806,200
Disposals	–	(120,000)	(325,000)	–	(445,000)
31 May 20X6	62,200	610,000	850,000	199,000	1,721,200
Net Book Value					
31 May 20X6	47,800	290,000	850,000	796,000	1,983,800
Net Book Value					
31 May 20X5	40,000	325,000	750,000	–	1,115,000

– Land and buildings relate to company offices and land for those offices.

– Plant and machinery includes extraction equipment such as diggers and dumper trucks used to extract sand and gravel etc.

– Motor vehicles include large trucks to transport the sand, gravel etc.

– Railway trucks relate to containers used to transport sand and gravel over long distances on the railway network.

Depreciation rates stated in the financial statements are all based on cost and calculated using the straight line basis.

The rates are:

Land and buildings	2%
Plant and machinery	20%
Motor vehicles	33%
Railway trucks	20%

Disposals in the motor vehicles category relates to vehicles which were five years old.

Required

(a) List the audit work you should perform on railway trucks. **(10 marks)**

(b) You have just completed your analytical procedures of the non-current assets note.

 Required

 (i) Excluding railway trucks, identify and explain any issues with the non-current asset note to raise with management.

 (ii) Explain how each issue could be resolved. **(10 marks)**

Note. You do not need to re-cast the schedule.

(Total = 20 marks)

39 Tracey Transporters (AIR 6/05)   36 mins

You are the external auditor of Tracey Transporters, a public limited company (TT). The company's year end is 31 March. You have been the auditor since the company was formed 24 years ago to take advantage of the increase in goods being transported by road. Many companies needed to transport their products but did not always have sufficient vehicles to move them. TT therefore purchased ten vehicles and hired these to haulage companies for amounts of time ranging from three days to six months.

The business has grown in size and profitability and now has over 550 vehicles on hire to many different companies. At any one time, between five and 20 vehicles are located at the company premises where they are being repaired; the rest could be anywhere on the extensive road network of the country it operates in. Full details of all vehicles are maintained in a non-current asset register.

Bookings for hire of vehicles are received either over the telephone or via e-mail in TT's offices. A booking clerk checks the customer's credit status on the receivables ledger and then the availability of vehicles using the Vehicle Management System (VMS) software on TT's computer network. E-mails are filed electronically by customer name in the e-mail programme used by TT. If the customer's credit rating is acceptable and a vehicle is available, the booking is entered into the VMS and confirmed to the customer using the telephone or e-mail. Booking information is then transferred within the network from the VMS to the receivables ledger programme, where a sales invoice is raised. Standard rental amounts are allocated to each booking depending on the amount of time the vehicle is being hired for. Hard copy invoices are sent in the post for telephone orders or via e-mail for e-mail orders.

The main class of asset on TT's balance sheet is the vehicles. The net book value of the vehicles is $6 million out of total shareholders' funds of $15 million as at 31 March 20X5.

Required

(a)   List and explain the reason for the audit tests you should perform to check the completeness and accuracy of the sales figure in TT's financial statements.   **(10 marks)**

(b)   List and describe the audit work you should perform on the balance sheet figure for vehicles in TT's financial statements for the year ended 31 March 20X5.   **(10 marks)**

(Total = 20 marks)

40 Snu (AIR 6/03) (amended)   54 mins

Some organisations conduct inventory counts once a year and external auditors attend those counts. Other organisations have perpetual systems (continuous inventory counting) and do not conduct a year-end count.

Snu is a family-owned company which retails beds, mattresses and other bedroom furniture items. The company's year-end is 31 December 20X3. The only full inventory count takes place at the year-end. The company maintains up-to-date computerised inventory records.

Where the company delivers goods to customers, a deposit is taken from the customer and customers are invoiced for the balance after the delivery. Some goods that are in stock at the year-end have already been paid for in full – customers who collect goods themselves pay by cash or credit card.

Staff at the company's warehouse and shop will conduct the year-end count. The shop and warehouse are open seven days a week except for two important public holidays during the year, one of which is 1 January. The company is very busy in the week prior to the inventory count but the shops will close at 15.00 hours on 31 December and staff will work until 17.00 hours to prepare the inventory for counting. The company has a high turnover of staff. The following inventory counting instructions have been provided to staff at Snu.

(i)   The inventory count will take place on 1 January 20X4 commencing at 09.00 hours. No movement of inventory will take place on that day.

BPP
LEARNING MEDIA

(ii) The count will be supervised by Mr Sneg, the inventory controller. All staff will be provided with pre-printed, pre-numbered inventory counting sheets that are produced by the computerised system. Mr Sneg will ensure that all sheets are issued, and that all are collected at the end of the count.

(iii) Counters will work on their own, because there are insufficient staff for them to work in pairs, but they will be supervised by Mr Sneg and Mrs Zapad, an experienced shop manager who will make checks on the work performed by counters. Staff will count inventory with which they are most familiar in order to ensure that the count is completed as quickly and efficiently as possible.

(iv) Any inventory that is known to be old, slow-moving or already sold will be highlighted on the sheets. Staff are required to highlight any inventory that appears to be soiled or damaged.

(v) All inventory items counted will have a piece of paper attached to them that will show that they have been counted.

(vi) All inventory that has been delivered to customers but that has not yet been paid for in full will be added back to the inventory quantities by Mr Sneg.

Required

(a) Explain why year-end inventory counting is important to the auditors of organisations that do not have perpetual inventory systems. **(5 marks)**

(b) Describe audit procedures you would perform in order to rely on a perpetual inventory system in a large, dispersed organisation. **(6 marks)**

(c) Briefly describe the principal risks associated with the financial statements assertions relating to inventory. **(4 marks)**

(d) Describe the weaknesses in Snu's inventory counting instructions and explain why these weaknesses are difficult to overcome. **(15 marks)**

(Total = 30 marks)

41 Textile Wholesalers   54 mins

Your firm is the auditor of Textile Wholesaler, a limited liability company, which buys textile products (eg clothing) from manufacturers and sells them to retailers. You attended the inventory count at the company's year-end of Thursday 31 October 20X6. The company does not maintain book inventory records, and previous years' audits have revealed problems with purchases cut-off.

Your audit procedures on purchases cut-off, which started from the goods received note (GRN), have revealed the following results:

	Date of GRN	GRN Number	Supplier's Invoice No	Invoice value $	On purchase ledger before year end	In purchase accruals at year end
1	28.10.X6	1324	6254	4,642	Yes	No
2	29.10.X6	1327	1372	5,164	Yes	Yes
3	30.10.X6	1331	9515	7,893	No	Yes
4	31.10.X6	1335	4763	9,624	No	No
5	1.11.X6	1340	5624	8,243	Yes	No
6	4.11.X6	1345	9695	6,389	No	Yes
7	5.11.X6	1350	2865	7,124	No	No

Assume that goods received before the year-end are in inventories at the year-end, and goods received after the year-end are not in inventories at the year-end.

A purchase accrual is included in payables at the year-end for goods received before the year-end when the purchase invoice has not been posted to the trade payables ledger before the year-end.

Required

(a)   At the inventory count:

    (i)   Describe the procedures the company's staff should carry out to ensure that inventories are counted accurately and cut-off details are recorded

    (ii)   Describe the procedures you could carry out and the matters you would record in your working papers.   **(12 marks)**

(b)   Briefly explain why cut-off is an important issue in the audit of inventory.   **(4 marks)**

(c)   From the results of your purchases cut-off test, described in the question:

    (i)   Identify the cut-off errors and produce a schedule of the adjustments which should be made to the reported profit, purchases and payables in the financial statements to correct the errors   **(5 marks)**

    (ii)   Comment on the results of your test, and state what further action you would take.   **(4 marks)**

(d)   Where a company uses a perpetual inventory counting system, describe the audit work that auditors would carry out to satisfy themselves that inventory was fairly stated.   **(5 marks)**

(Total = 30 marks)

42 Chingford Potteries (AIR Pilot paper) (amended)   54 mins

Your firm is the external auditor of Chingford Potteries, and you recently attended the year-end inventory count at the company's warehouse. The company manufactures high quality tableware (plates, cups and saucers etc.) and it maintains an integrated computerised system that shows the inventory held at any given point in time. At the year-end inventory count, the various categories of inventories (but not the quantities) are printed off the system and the quantities of inventories actually counted are inserted manually by the counters, for later comparison with the computerised quantity. This system has proved successful in recent years but unfortunately, your notes show a number of weaknesses in the current year-end count.

The count instructions were received by both you and the counters the day before the count was due to take place. Many areas in which the count took place were untidy and inventory was sometimes difficult to find, because it was not in the allocated area. The same categories of inventories were sometimes found in several different areas and some inventory was incorrectly labelled. The count was conducted in a hurry in order to close the warehouse before a public holiday and there were insufficient counters to conduct the count properly in the time available. The issue was receipt of inventory sheets (on which the quantities were recorded by counters) was not properly controlled. It was difficult to reconcile the inventory quantities recorded at the count to the computerised records and some significant differences remain outstanding.

Required

(a)   Explain why inventory valuation and the year-end inventory count are important to the audit of financial statements and describe the alternatives to a year-end count as a basis for the year-end valuation. **(6 marks)**

(b)   Draft for the inclusion in a report to the management on Chingford Potteries:

    (i)   The weaknesses you found

    (ii)   The potential consequences

    (iii) Your recommendations for remedying the weaknesses in the current year count, and your recommendations for future years.   **(9 marks)**

(c)   Describe the basis for valuing inventories as required by IAS 2 *Inventories* and list the types of inventories which may be worth less than cost at Chingford Potteries.   **(8 marks)**

(d)   Describe the work that you would perform to establish which inventories are worth less than cost at Chingford Potteries.   **(7 marks)**

Note. In part (c), you are not required to deal with construction contracts.

(Total = 30 marks)

43 Rocks Forever (AIR 12/05) (amended)　　54 mins

You are the audit manager in the firm of DeCe & Co, an audit firm with ten national offices.

One of your clients, Rocks Forever, purchases diamond jewellery from three manufacturers. The jewellery is then sold from Rocks Forever's four shops. This is the only client your firm has in the diamond industry.

You are planning to attend the physical inventory count for Rocks Forever. Inventory is the largest account on the balance sheet with each of the four shops holding material amounts. Due to the high value of the inventory, all shops will be visited and test counts performed.

With the permission of the directors of Rocks Forever, you have employed UJ, a firm of specialist diamond valuers who will also be in attendance. UJ will verify that the jewellery is, in fact, made from diamonds and that the jewellery is saleable with respect to current trends in fashion. UJ will also suggest, on a sample basis, the value of specific items of jewellery.

Counting will be carried out by shop staff in teams of two using pre-numbered count sheets.

Required

(a) Describe the main risks associated with the financial statement assertions relating to inventory.　(3 marks)

(b) Briefly describe the main risks associated with inventory in a company such as Rocks Forever.　(4 marks)

(c) List and explain the reason for the audit procedures used in obtaining evidence in relation to the inventory count of inventory held in the shops.　(12 marks)

(d) Explain the factors you should consider when placing reliance on the work of UJ.　(6 marks)

(e) Describe the audit procedures you should perform to ensure that jewellery inventory is valued correctly.

(5 marks)

(Total = 30 marks)

44 Receivables circularisations (AIR 12/01) (amended)　18 mins

ISA 505 *External confirmations* deals with a number of different types of external confirmation. External confirmation is a useful method of obtaining audit evidence in relation to accounts receivable.

Required

(a) In relation to external confirmation of accounts receivable:

(i) Explain the difference between a positive and a negative confirmation
(ii) Explain the two different types of positive confirmation and the advantages and disadvantages of each
(iii) List the reconciling items highlighted by external confirmation of accounts receivable　(7 marks)

(b) Describe the principal risks associated with assertions relating to receivables.　(3 marks)

(Total = 10 marks)

45 Coogee　　36 mins

Coogee is a medium sized, privately owned and incorporated engineering company with an annual revenue of $23 million. Most of its sales are on credit. At its financial year end 31 December 20X8 its accounts receivable ledger contained 2,000 accounts with balances ranging from $50 to $10,000 and totalling $2,300,000. As a staff member of Coogee's external auditors you have been assigned to the audit of the allowance for bad and doubtful debts which has been set as $120,000. Your initial enquiries established that $80,000 relates to the allowance against specific bad and doubtful debts and $40,000 is a general allowance determined as a percentage of overdue debts with an increasing percentage being applied against the longest overdue accounts.

Required

(a) Explain the approaches adopted by auditors in obtaining sufficient appropriate audit evidence regarding accounting estimates. **(3 marks)**

(b) Describe the procedures you would apply in verifying the general allowance for bad and doubtful debts. **(9 marks)**

(c) Describe the procedures you would apply in verifying the specific allowance for bad and doubtful debts. **(8 marks)**

(Total = 20 marks)

46 Duckworth Computers   36 mins

The firm of Chartered Certified Accountants you are employed by is the external auditor of Duckworth Computers, a privately owned incorporated business.

Accounting records are maintained on a computer using proprietary software.

You have worked on the audit for three years and this year you are in charge of the audit. Your assistant is a newly recruited business graduate who has done an accounting course but has no practical experience.

Because of the small size of the company there is limited opportunity for segregation of duties. You decide, as in previous years, that the appropriate audit strategy is to obtain evidence primarily through the performance of substantive procedures. You also plan to perform the audit around the computer as the proprietary software is known to be reliable and details of all transactions and balances can be readily printed out.

On arriving at the company's premises in December 20X9 to perform the final audit on the 31 October 20X9 financial statements, you obtain a copy of the year end bank reconciliation prepared by the bookkeeper and checked by the managing director. This is reproduced below.

Duckworth Computers
Bank Reconciliation 31 October 20X9

	$	$
Balance per bank statement 31 October 20X9		18,375.91
Deposits outstanding		
30 October	1,887.00	
31 October	1,973.00	3,860.00
		22,235.91
Outstanding cheques		
2696	25.00	
2724	289.40	
2725	569.00	
2728	724.25	
2729	1,900.00	
2730	398.00	
2731	53.50	
2732	1,776.00	
2733	255.65	5,990.80
		16,245.11
Cheque returned 'not sufficient funds' 29 October		348.00
Bank charges October		90.00
Balance per books 31 October 20X9		$16,683.11

You have already obtained the bank confirmation and lists of cash (and cheque) receipts and payments printed out from the computer. These lists have been added and the totals agreed with ledger postings. You decide the first task to set for your assistant is the verification of the bank reconciliation.

BPP)))
LEARNING MEDIA

Required

(a)   (i)   List the audit procedures to be followed by your assistant in verifying the bank reconciliation in sufficient details for an inexperienced staff member to follow.   **(6 marks)**

        (ii)   Explain the purpose of each procedure in terms of audit objectives.   **(5 marks)**

(b)   Discuss the reliability of bank statements as audit evidence. What steps can be taken if it is considered desirable to increase their reliability?   **(3 marks)**

(c)   (i)   Distinguish between 'auditing around the computer' and 'auditing through the computer   **(3 marks)**

        (ii)   Explain the circumstances when it would be inappropriate for the auditor to rely on auditing around the computer.   **(3 marks)**

(Total = 20 marks)

47 Cash audit (AIR 6/02)   36 mins

(a)   Internal control is designed, amongst other things, to prevent error and misappropriation.

Required

Describe the errors and misappropriations that may occur if the following are not properly controlled:

(i)   Receipts paid into bank accounts;   **(2 marks)**
(ii)   Payments made out of bank accounts;   **(3 marks)**
(iii)   Interest and charges debited and credited to bank accounts.   **(2 marks)**

(b)   A book selling company has a head office and 25 shops, each of which holds cash (banknotes, coins and credit card vouchers) at the balance sheet date. There are no receivables. Accounting records are held at shops. Shops make returns to head office and head office holds its own accounting records. Your firm has been the external auditor to the company for many years and has offices near to the location of some but not all of the shops.

Required

List the audit objectives for the audit of cash and state how you would gain the audit evidence in relation to those objectives at the year end.   **(8 marks)**

(c)   The external auditors of companies often write to companies' bankers asking for details of bank balances and other matters at the year end.

Required

Explain why auditors write to companies' bankers and list the matters you would expect banks to confirm.   **(5 marks)**

(Total = 20 marks)

48 Liabilities (AIR 12/02)   36 mins

(a)   Company A has a number of long and short-term payables, accruals and provisions in its balance sheet.

Required

Describe the audit procedures you would apply to each of the three items listed below, including those relating to disclosure.

(i)   A 10-year bank loan with a variable interest rate and an overdraft (a bank account with a debit balance on the bank statement), both from the same bank.   **(5 marks)**

(ii)   Expense accruals   **(4 marks)**

(iii)   Trade payables and purchase accruals   **(6 marks)**

(b)   Company B has a provision in its balance sheet for claims made by customers for product defects under 1 year company warranties.

Required

Describe the matters you would consider and the audit evidence you would require for the provision.

(5 marks)

(Total = 20 marks)

49 Question with helping hand: Boulder (AIR 12/04)   36 mins

ISA 500 *Audit evidence* states that management implicitly or explicitly makes assertions relating to the various elements of financial statements including related disclosures. Auditors may use three categories of assertions to form a basis for risk assessments and the design and performance of further audit procedures. The three categories suggested by ISA 500 relate to (i) classes of transactions, (ii) account balances, and (iii) presentation and disclosure. One assertion applicable to all three categories is completeness: that all transactions, events, assets, liabilities, equity interests and disclosures that should be included, are included in the financial statements.

Required

(a)   List and describe six financial statement assertions, other than completeness, used by auditors in the audit of financial statements.   **(6 marks)**

(b)   Boulder is a small company that manufactures hosiery products. It employs approximately 150 staff, all of whom are paid by bank transfer.

Temporary factory staff are hired through an agency and are paid on piece rates (i.e. for the number of items that they produce or process) on a weekly basis. Supervisors at Boulder authorise documentation indicating the number of items produced or processed by agency staff. The agency is paid by bank transfer and it, not Boulder, is responsible for the deduction of tax and social insurance.

Permanent factory staff are paid on a weekly basis on the basis of hours worked as evidenced by clock cards. Administration and sales staff are paid a monthly salary. The two directors of the company are also paid a monthly salary.

Sales staff are paid a quarterly bonus calculated on the basis of sales. Directors are paid an annual bonus based on profits.

You will be performing the audit of the financial statements for the year ending 31 December 2004 and you will be responsible for the figures in the financial statements relating to payroll.

Required

Describe the substantive audit procedures you will perform on:

(i)   the payroll balances in the balance sheet of Boulder;   **(10 marks)**
(ii)   the payroll transactions in the income statement of Boulder.   **(4 marks)**

(Total = 20 marks)

Helping Hand. Part (a) of this question is a straight test of knowledge. ISA 500 is a key standard so you must make sure you know its main principles.

Part (b) is quite challenging. This is not because the audit of payroll is very difficult but rather because the high mark allocation indicates that the examiner wants a very detailed answer covering a wide range of different procedures, especially on payroll balances in part (i).

To start generating ideas, think first about what these balances will be, using the detail in the question:

*   A liability for unpaid wages and salaries
*   Statutory liabilities for tax and social insurance
*   Accrued bonus for sales staff
*   Accrued bonus for directors

Once you do this it gets easier to see how to find enough procedures. A useful memory jogger is to run through the types of audit procedure:

- Analytical procedures
- Inquiry
- Inspection
- Observation
- Confirmation
- Recalculation
- Reperformance

This should help you generate enough ideas, which leaves the final challenge of expressing them in such a way that the marker will give you a full mark for each point. You need to write out each point in detail to show that you understand exactly what the procedure would involve, rather than just listing out a few bits of jargon as bullet points.

For example, if you write "*perform analytical procedures*" you will get no marks. If you describe a particular analytical procedure, you will get full credit.

50 Newthorpe
36 mins

You are auditing the financial statements of Newthorpe Engineering Co, a listed company, for the year ended 30 April 20X7.

(a) In March 20X7 the Board decided to close one of the company's factories on 30 April 20X7. The plant and equipment and inventories will be sold. The employees will either be transferred to another factory or made redundant.

At the time of your audit in June 20X7, you are aware that:

(i) Some of the plant and equipment has been sold
(ii) Most of the inventories have been sold
(iii) All the employees have either been made redundant or transferred to another factory

The company has provided you with a schedule of the closure costs, the realisable values of the assets in (i) and (ii) above and the redundancy cost.

Details of the plant and machinery are maintained in a non-current asset register.

A full inventory count was carried out at 30 April 20X7. Audit tests have confirmed that the inventory counts are accurate and there are no purchases or sales cut-off errors.

You are aware the redundancy payments are based on the number of years service of the employee and their annual salary (or wage). Most employees were given redundancy of one week's pay for each year's service. A few employees have a service contract with the company and were paid the amount stated in their service contract which will be more than the redundancy pay offered to other employees. Employees who are transferred to another factory were not paid any redundancy.

As part of the audit of the closure cost, you have been asked to carry out the audit work described below.

Required

For the factory being closed, describe the audit procedures you will carry out to verify the company's estimates of:

(i) The net realisable value of plant and equipment, and inventories **(7 marks)**
(ii) The redundancy cost **(4 marks)**

Notes

(1) In auditing inventories you are required only to verify that the price per unit is correctly determined.

(2) For the redundancy cost, you should ignore any national statutory rules for determining redundancy procedures and minimum redundancy pay.

(b) In February 20X7 the directors of Newthorpe Engineering suspended the managing director. At a disciplinary hearing held by the company on 17 March 20X7 the managing director was dismissed for gross misconduct, and it was decided the managing director's salary should stop from that date and no redundancy or compensation payments should be made.

The managing director has claimed unfair dismissal and is taking legal action against the company to obtain compensation for loss of his employment. The managing director says he has a service contract with the company which would entitle him to two years' salary at the date of dismissal.

The financial statements for the year ended 30 April 20X7 record the resignation of the director. However, they do not mention his dismissal and no provision for any damages has been included in the financial statements.

Required

(i) State how contingent losses should be disclosed in financial statements according to IAS 37 *Provisions, contingent liabilities and contingent assets*. **(3 marks)**

(ii) Describe the audit procedures you will carry out to determine whether the company will have to pay damages to the director for unfair dismissal, and the amount of damages and costs which should be included in the financial statements. **(6 marks)**

Note. Assume the amounts you are auditing are material. **(Total = 20 marks)**

51 Crighton-Ward (AIR 6/05) 36 mins

(a) Explain the purpose of a management representation letter. **(5 marks)**

(b) You are the manager in charge of the audit of Crighton-Ward, a public limited liability company which manufactures specialist cars and other motor vehicles for use in films. Audited turnover is $140 million with profit before tax of $7·5 million.

All audit work up to, but not including, the obtaining of management representations has been completed. A review of the audit file has disclosed the following outstanding points:

Lion's Roar

The company is facing a potential legal claim from the Lion's Roar company in respect of a defective vehicle that was supplied for one of their films. Lion's Roar maintains that the vehicle was not built strongly enough while the directors of Crighton-Ward argue that the specification was not sufficiently detailed. Dropping a vehicle 50 metres into a river and expecting it to continue to remain in working condition would be unusual, but this is what Lion's Roar expected. Solicitors are unable to determine liability at the present time. A claim for $4 million being the cost of a replacement vehicle and lost production time has been received by Crighton-Ward from Lion's Roar. The director's opinion is that the claim is not justified.

Depreciation

Depreciation of specialist production equipment has been included in the financial statements at the amount of 10% pa based on reducing balance. However the treatment is consistent with prior accounting periods (which received an unmodified auditor's report) and other companies in the same industry and sales of old equipment show negligible profit or loss on sale. The audit senior, who is new to the audit, feels that depreciation is being undercharged in the financial statements.

Required

For each of the above matters:

(i)   Discuss whether or not a paragraph is required in the representation letter; and

(ii) *If appropriate*, draft the paragraph for inclusion in the representation letter.   **(10 marks)**

(c)   A suggested format for the letter of representation has been sent by the auditors to the directors of Crighton-Ward. The directors have stated that they will not sign the letter of representation this year on the grounds that they believe the additional evidence that it provides is not required by the auditor.

Required

Discuss the actions the auditor may take as a result of the decision made by the directors not to sign the letter of representation.   **(5 marks)**

(Total = 20 marks)

52 Jayne (AIR 12/06)   36 mins

(a)   ISA 505, *External confirmations*, states that 'the auditor should determine whether the use of external confirmations is necessary to obtain sufficient appropriate audit evidence at the assertion level'.

Required

(i)   List four examples of external confirmations.   **(2 marks)**

(ii) For each of the examples in (i) above explain:

One audit assertion that the external confirmation supports, and
One audit assertion that the external confirmation does NOT support.   **(8 marks)**

(b)   Jayne Co has a significant number of cash transactions and recent non-current asset purchases have been financed by a bank loan. This loan is repayable in equal annual instalments for the next five years.

Required

(i)   Explain the procedures to obtain a bank report for audit purposes from Jayne Co's bank and the substantive procedures that should be carried out on that report.   **(5 marks)**

(ii) List the further substantive procedures that should be carried out on the bank balances in Jayne Co's financial statements.   **(5 marks)**

(Total = 20 marks)

53 FireFly Tennis Club (AIR 12/02)   36 mins

The FireFly Tennis Club owns 12 tennis courts. The club uses 'all weather' tarmac tennis courts, which have floodlights for night-time use. The club's year end is 30 September.

Members pay an annual fee to use the courts and participate in club championships. The club had 430 members as at 1 October 2005.

Income is derived from two main sources:

1.   Membership fees. Each member pays a fee of $200 per annum. Fees for the new financial year are payable within one month of the club year end. Approximately 10% of members do not renew their membership. New members joining during the year pay 50% of the total fees that would have been payable had they been members for a full year. During 2006, 50 new members joined the club. No members pay their fees before they are due.

2.   Court hire fees: Non-members pay $5 per hour to hire a court. Non-members have to sign a list in the club house showing courts hired. Money is placed in a cash box in the club house for collection by the club secretary. All fees (membership and court hire) are paid in cash. They are collected by the club secretary and banked on a regular basis. The paying-in slip shows the analysis between fees and court hire income. The secretary provides the treasurer with a list of bankings showing member's names (for membership fees) and the amount banked. Details of all bankings are entered into the cash book by the treasurer.

Main items of expenditure are:

1.   Court maintenance including repainting lines on a regular basis.

2.   Power costs for floodlights.

3.   Tennis balls for club championships. Each match in the championship uses 12 tennis balls.

The treasurer pays for all expenditure using the club's debit card. Receipts are obtained for all expenses and these are maintained in date order in an expenses file. The treasurer also prepares the annual financial statements.

Under the rules of the club, the annual accounts must be audited by an independent auditor. The date is now 13 December 2006 and the treasurer has just prepared the financial statements for audit.

Required

(a)   Describe the audit work that should be performed to determine the completeness of income for the FireFly Tennis Club.   **(10 marks)**

(b)   Describe the audit procedures that should be performed to check the completeness and accuracy of expenditure for the FireFly Tennis Club.   **(5 marks)**

(c)   Discuss why internal control testing has limited value when auditing not-for-profit entities such as the FireFly Tennis Club.   **(5 marks)**

(Total = 20 marks)

54 Walsh (AIR 12/06)   **36 mins**

Walsh Co sells motor vehicle fuel, accessories and spares to retail customers. The company owns 25 shops.

The company has recently implemented a new computerised wages system. Employees work a standard eight hour day. Hours are recorded using a magnetic card system; when each employee arrives for work, they hold their card close to the card reader; the reader recognises the magnetic information on the card identifying the employee as being 'at work'. When the employee leaves work at the end of the day the process is reversed showing that the employee has left work.

Hours worked are calculated each week by the computer system using the magnetic card information. Overtime is calculated as any excess over the standard hours worked. Any overtime over 10% of standard hours is sent on a computer generated report by e-mail to the financial accountant. If necessary, the accountant overrides overtime payments if the hours worked are incorrect.

Statutory deductions and net pay are also computer calculated with payments being made directly into the employee's bank account. The only other manual check is the financial accountant authorising the net pay from Walsh's bank account, having reviewed the list of wages to be paid.

Required

(a)   Using examples from Walsh Co, explain the benefits of using Computer-Assisted Audit Techniques to help the auditor to obtain sufficient appropriate audit evidence to be able to draw reasonable conclusions on which to base the audit opinion.   **(8 marks)**

(b)   List six examples of audit tests on Walsh Co's wages system using audit software.   **(6 marks)**

(c) Explain how using test data should help in the audit of Walsh Co's wages system, noting any problems with this audit technique. **(6 marks)**

(Total = 20 marks)

55 Audit confirmations (AIR 12/02) (amended) **18 mins**

Auditors obtain several different confirmations from various sources during the course of their audit.

Required

Describe the audit evidence provided by each of the confirmations listed below, the practical difficulties in obtaining them and the alternative audit evidence available when they are not provided:

(a) Management representations **(3 marks)**
(b) Direct confirmation of receivables **(4 marks)**
(c) Confirmation of inventory held by third parties **(3 marks)**

(Total = 10 marks)

56 ZPM (AIR 6/06) **36 mins**

ISA 610 *Considering the Work of Internal Auditing* states that 'when the external auditor intends to use specific work of internal auditing, the external auditor should evaluate and perform audit procedures on that work to confirm its adequacy for the external auditor's purposes.'

Required

(a) In relation to ISA 610, explain the factors the external auditor will consider when evaluating the work of the internal auditor. **(5 marks)**

(b) ZPM is a listed limited liability company with a year end of 30 June. ZPM's main activity is selling home improvement or 'Do-It-Yourself' (DIY) products to the public. Products sold range from nails, paint and tools to doors and showers; some stores also sell garden tools and furniture. Products are purchased from approximately 200 different suppliers. ZPM has 103 stores in eight different countries.

ZPM has a well-staffed internal audit department, who report on a regular basis to the audit committee. Areas where the internal and external auditors may carry out work include:

(1) Attending the year end inventory count in 30 stores annually. All stores are visited on a rotational basis.

(2) Checking the internal controls over the procurement systems (eg ensuring a liability is only recorded when the inventory has been received).

(3) Reviewing the operations of the marketing department.

Required

For each of the above three areas, discuss

(i) The objectives of the internal auditor; **(5 marks)**

(ii) The objectives of the external auditor; and **(5 marks)**

(iii) Whether the external auditor will rely on the internal auditor, and if reliance is required, the extent of that reliance. **(5 marks)**

(Total = 20 marks)

57 Strathfield

54 mins

The recorded value of Strathfield's accounts receivable as at 31 October 20X9, was $2,350,000.

Out of the 5,350 accounts receivable, Sarah Jones selected 120 accounts for confirmation as part of the external audit of the company.

In selecting accounts for confirmation Sarah picked the 10 largest accounts totalling $205,000 and 110 other accounts selected haphazardly. Her working paper states that she rejected any accounts that were less than $100 as not being worth confirming and accounts with government bodies since she knew they never bother replying to confirmation requests.

Each of the 10 largest accounts was satisfactorily confirmed. Sarah analysed the responses to confirmation of the other 110 accounts as follows:

Result of confirmation	Number of accounts	Recorded amount $	Amount confirmed $
Satisfactorily confirmed	75	245,000	245,000
Confirmation returned marked 'gone away – address unknown'	4	950	0
Cut-off differences due to cash or goods in transit	8	6,800	5,750
Invoicing errors	4	2,800	2,200
Invoices posted to the wrong customer's account	2	1,300	980
Disputed as to price or quantity or quality of goods	3	2,800	1,300
Not confirmed - verified by alternative procedures	14	5,800	5,800
Totals	110	265,450	261,030

Sarah is about to draw up her working paper in which she reaches a conclusion as to whether the results of the confirmation of accounts receivable enables her to conclude that the recorded balance is not materially misstated. She is aware that ISA 530 *Audit sampling and other means of testing* requires her to:

(1) Consider the qualitative aspects of errors and whether any of these relate to a sub-population and not to accounts receivable as a whole

(2) Project the error results of the sample to the population from which the sample was selected.

Required

(a) Briefly explain the principal risks associated with the financial statement assertions for trade receivables.

(3 marks)

(b) Discuss Sarah's method of selecting items to be confirmed. Your answer should:

    (i) Identify any aspects of her approach that might be considered inconsistent with sampling

    (ii) Suggest alternative means of selecting a sample ensuring that the more material balances stand the greatest chance of selection

    (iii) Compare and contrast the haphazard method of selection with random selection and systematic selection.

(10 marks)

(c) Consider qualitative aspects of each of the five categories of error or other reported differences analysed by Sarah. Suggest which of them should be included in arriving at an estimate of population error. **(7 marks)**

(d) Calculate the projected error in accounts receivable based on the results of the sample test consistent with the qualitative considerations in your answer to (b). **(5 marks)**

(e) Discuss the extent to which Sarah could use computer-assisted audit techniques in her work. **(5 marks)**

(Total = 30 marks)

REVIEW

Questions 58 – 60 cover Review, the subject of Part F of the BPP Study Text for F8.

58 LALD (AIR 12/05)

36 mins

You are the auditor of LALD Ltd. The main activity of the company is the construction of buildings ranging in size from individual houses to large offices and blocks of flats.

Under the laws of the country LALD operates in, LALD must add sales tax to all buildings sold and they pay this tax to the government at the end of each month.

The largest non-current asset on LALD's balance sheet is the plant and machinery used in the construction of buildings. Due to the variety of different assets used, four different sub-classes of plant and machinery are recognised, each with its own rate of depreciation.

You are now reaching the end of the audit work for the year ended 30 September 20X5. There are two specific matters where additional audit work is required:

(i)   The sales tax for the month of August was not paid to the government. This appears to have been an accidental error and the amount involved is not material to the financial statements.

(ii)   The complicated method of calculating depreciation for plant and machinery appears to have resulted in depreciation being calculated incorrectly, with the result that depreciation may have been under-provided in the financial statements.

Required

(a)   Explain the additional audit procedures you should take regarding the accidental underpayment of sales tax.

(7 marks)

(b)   Explain the additional audit procedures you should take regarding the possible underprovision of depreciation.

(7 marks)

(c)   You have determined that the under-provision is material to the financial statements and therefore need to qualify the audit report. The directors have informed you that they do not intend to take any action regarding the underprovision of depreciation. They also disagree with your action and have threatened to remove your company as the auditors of LALD unless you agree not to qualify your report.

Required

Explain the procedures that the directors must follow in order to remove your company as the auditors of LALD.

(6 marks)

(Total = 20 marks)

59 Question with helping hand: Sheraton

18 mins

You are the auditor of Sheraton Co, a limited liability company, the year-end of which is 30 November. You are currently planning the 20X1 audit and want to incorporate procedures which will ensure that, in finalising its financial statements, the company has complied with IAS 10 *Events after the balance sheet date.*

Required

(a)   List the procedures that you would incorporate into the audit plan.   **(6 marks)**

(b)   Briefly describe the types of events, as defined in the standard, and their accounting treatment.   **(4 marks)**

(Total = 10 marks)

Helping hand. In part (a), first look at the requirement ('list') and the mark allocation (six marks). You need to make enough points to score as many of the marks available as possible. Think about events after the balance sheet date and what audit procedures you would need to perform in order to test this period adequately. Make sure the procedures you suggest are specific and well-explained – vague points wont score marks.

In part (b), you need to be brief and to the point. Split your answer into 'adjusting events' and 'non-adjusting events'. Your explanations for each will need to be succinct and accurate, given that each is worth two marks only. If you can, suggest an example of each type of event to illustrate your explanation.

60 OilRakers (AIR 12/05)   36 mins

(a)   International Standard on Auditing 560 *Subsequent events* explains the audit work required in connection with subsequent events.

Required

List the audit procedures that can be used prior to the auditors' report being signed to identify events that may require adjustment or disclosure in the financial statements.   **(5 marks)**

(b)   You are the auditor of OilRakers, a limited liability company which extracts, refines and sells oil and petroleum related products.

The audit of OilRakers for the year ended 30 June 20X5 had the following events:

Date	Event
15 August 20X5	Bankruptcy of major customer representing 11% of the trade receivables on the balance sheet.
21 September 20X5	Financial statements approved by directors.
22 September 20X5	Audit work completed and auditors' report signed.
1 November 20X5	Accidental release of toxic chemicals into the sea from the company's oil refinery resulting in severe damage to the environment. Management had amended and made adequate disclosure of the event in the financial statements.
23 November 20X5	Financial statements issued to members of OilRakers.
30 November 20X5	A fire at one of the company's oil wells completely destroys the well. Drilling a new well will take ten months with a consequent loss in oil production during this time.

Required

For each of the following three dates:

–   15 August 20X5;
–   1 November 20X5; and
–   30 November 20X5.

(i)   State whether the events occurring on those dates are adjusting or non-adjusting according to IAS 10 *Events after the balance sheet date*, giving reasons for your decision.   **(6 marks)**

(ii)   Explain the auditor's responsibility and the audit procedures that should be carried out.

                                                                                                    (9 marks)

Note: Marks are allocated evenly across the three dates.   **(Total = 20 marks)**

Questions 61 – 65 cover Reporting, the subject of Part G of the BPP Study Text for F8.

61 Mowbray Computers   36 mins

You are carrying out the audit of Mowbray Computers, a limited liability company, for the year ended 30 April 20X4. The company assembles microcomputers from components purchased from the Far East and sells them to retailers, and to individuals and businesses by mail order. In the current year, there has been a recession and strong competition which has resulted in a fall in sales and the gross profit margin. This had led to a trading loss and the company experiencing going concern problems.

Required

(a)   Describe the factors which indicate that a company may not be a going concern. Your list should include all factors, and not just those which apply to Mowbray Computers.   **(12 marks)**

(b)   Consider the form of audit report you would use on Mowbray Computers' financial statements, if you conclude that the company is experiencing serious going concern problems, in the following two situations:

   (i)   You conclude that the financial statements give sufficient disclosure of the going concern problems.

   (ii)   There is no disclosure of the going concern problems in the financial statements and you believe there is a serious risk that the company will fail in the foreseeable future.   **(8 marks)**

   In each case you should say how the audit report will differ from an unqualified audit report (that is, as in ISA 700 *The independent auditor's report on a complete set of general purpose financial statements*).

(Total = 20 marks)

62 Audit Reports (AIR 6/03) (amended)   18 mins

Reports produced by internal auditors are different from audit reports produced by external auditors performing audits under International Standards on Auditing. The reports are produced for different purposes, and are directed at different users. They differ substantially in both form and content.

Internal audit reports often comprise the following:

(i)   A cover page;
(ii)   Executive summary;
(iii) The main report contents;
(iv)   Appendices.

Required

(a)   List and briefly describe the general categories of information that you would expect to find in an internal audit report under each of the four headings above.   **(4 marks)**

(b)   List the main contents of most external audit reports.   **(2 marks)**

Note. You are not required to reproduce a full external audit report.

(c)   Explain why the contents of external audit reports prepared under International Standards on Auditing and internal audit reports are different.   **(4 marks)**

(Total = 10 marks)

63 Question with helping hand: Corsco (AIR 12/03)   36 mins

(a)   Describe external auditor's responsibilities and the work that the auditor should perform in relation to the going concern status of companies.   **(5 marks)**

(b)   Describe the possible audit reports that can be issued where the going concern status of a company is called into question; your answer should describe the circumstances in which they can be issued.   **(5 marks)**

Corsco is a large telecommunications company that is listed on a stock exchange. It is highly geared because, like many such companies, it borrowed a large sum to pay for a licence to operate a mobile phone network with technology that has not proved popular. The company's share price has dropped by 50% during the last three years and there have been several changes of senior management during that period. There has been considerable speculation in the press over the last six months about whether the company can survive without being taken over by a rival. There have been three approaches made to the company by other companies regarding a possible takeover but all have failed, mainly because the bidders pulled out of the deal as a result of the drop in share prices generally.

The company has net assets, but has found it necessary to severely curtail its capital investment program. Some commentators consider this to be fundamental to the future growth of the business, others consider that the existing business is fundamentally sound. It has also been necessary for the company to restructure its finances. Detailed disclosures of all of these matters have always been made in the financial statements. No reference has been made to the going concern status of the company in previous auditor's reports on financial statements and the deterioration in circumstances in the current year is no worse than it has been in previous years.

Required

(c)   On the basis of the information provided above, describe the audit report that you consider is likely to be issued in the case of Corsco, giving reasons.   **(4 marks)**

(d)   Explain the difficulties that would be faced by Corsco and its auditors if Corsco's audit report made reference to going concern issues.   **(6 marks)**

(Total = 20 marks)

Helping Hand

(a)   Part (a) of this question considers the external auditor's responsibilities and the audit work that should be performed in relation to going concern.

(b)   The auditor's responsibilities are set down in ISA 570 so if you are familiar with this you should be able to produce a good answer. If you are not sure what the ISA says don't give up but try to think logically. Remember it is ultimately the management's responsibility to assess whether the business is viable so what role can the auditor play? How can we be sure that what management have concluded is reasonable? Also remember that with going concern issues disclosure is normally a key consideration.

(c)   For audit work try to think about what you are attempting to prove. You are trying to confirm that the business will continue for the foreseeable future and that the conclusion formed by management is the right one. Audit work will therefore concentrate on obtaining evidence concerning factors that might cast doubt on the future of the company and also on the process by which management have evaluated the situation. Also remember that going concern may be affected by the outcome of factors which already exist (eg the outcome of litigation) and factors which might arise in future. Your audit work should address both of these aspects.

(d)   Part (b) considers the possible audit reports which might be issued where going concern is called into question. The key here is to give the full range of possibilities in your answer. Remember the audit report would be affected in the following circumstances:

•   Where going concern assumption is appropriate but a material uncertainty exists which is adequately disclosed.

- As above but where disclosure is not adequate.

- Where the auditor disagrees with the preparation of accounts on a going concern basis.

- Where there is a limitation on scope.

- If the management are unwilling to extend its assessment where the period considered is less than twelve months from the balance sheet date.

(e) In part (c) you are asked to describe the appropriate audit report in the case of Corsco. This is potentially the trickiest part of the question as you are being asked to apply your knowledge to the scenario. Try to avoid basing the opinion on one or two pieces of information but try instead to understand the relative importance of all statements made. Just because some factors are presented which may cause concern does not automatically mean the audit opinion will be qualified.

(f) In part (d) you are asked to consider the difficulties that would be faced by Corsco and the auditors if the audit report referred to going concern issues. Here you need to think practically. From the company's point of view if suppliers, lenders and customers think there is a potential problem what action are they likely to take? From the auditors' perspective what will happen to client relations? Also note that historically no reference has been made to this issue by the auditor. What are the implications of this?

64 Theta

18 mins

In November 20X3, the head office of Theta was damaged by a fire. Many of the company's accounting records were destroyed before the audit for the year ended 31 January 20X4 took place. The company's financial accountant has prepared financial statements for the year ended 31 January 20X4 on the basis of estimates and the information he has been able to salvage. You have completed the audit of these financial statements.

Required

(a) Explain how your audit report would be affected by the fire at the head office of Theta. **(4 marks)**

(b) Explain the reasons for your audit opinion. **(3 marks)**

(c) Explain and distinguish between the following forms of qualified audit opinion:

(i) Disagreement

(ii) Disclaimer

(iii) Adverse opinion **(3 marks)**

(Total = 10 marks)

65 Hood Enterprises (AIR 6/05)

36 mins

You are the audit manager of Hood Enterprises a limited liability company. The company's annual turnover is over $10 million.

Required

(a) Compare the responsibilities of the directors and auditors regarding the published financial statements of Hood Enterprises. **(6 marks)**

(b) An extract from the draft audit report produced by an audit junior is given below:

Basis of Opinion

'We conducted our audit in accordance with Auditing Standards. An audit includes examination, on a test basis, of evidence relevant to the amounts and disclosures in the financial statements. It also includes an assessment of all the estimates and judgements made by the directors in the preparation of the financial statements, and of whether the accounting policies are appropriate to the company's circumstances, consistently applied and adequately disclosed.

'We planned and performed our audit so as to obtain as much information and explanation as possible given the time available for the audit. We confirm that the financial statements are free from material misstatement, whether caused by fraud or other irregularity or error. The directors however are wholly responsible for the accuracy of the financial statements and no liability for errors can be accepted by the auditor. In forming our opinion we also evaluated the overall adequacy of the presentation of information in the company's annual report.'

Required

Identify and explain the errors in the above extract.

Note. You are not required to redraft the report. **(10 marks)**

(c)   The directors of Hood Enterprises have prepared a cash flow forecast for submission to the bank. They have asked you as the auditor to provide a negative assurance report on this forecast.

Required

Briefly explain the difference between positive and negative assurance, outlining the advantages to the directors of providing negative assurance on their cash flow forecast. **(4 marks)**

(Total = 20 marks)

Answers

1 Audit judgements

> **Text reference.** Chapter 1
>
> **Top tips.** Part (a) to this question should have been reasonably straightforward, book learning. Part (b) is more complicated. It is important that you are able to understand the types of judgements accountants make when providing assurance services, and also be able to link that to the level of assurance the accountant is able to give.
>
> **Easy marks.** These are available in part (a). It is important that you are comfortable with the responsibilities of management and those of the external auditors.

(a) **Responsibilities of directors**

- To keep sufficient accounting records to show the position of the company at any given time

- To select suitable accounting policies and apply them consistently within the financial statements

- To make reasonable judgements and estimates regarding figures appearing in the financial statements

- To state whether applicable accounting standards have been followed and give details of any departures

- To prepare the financial statements on a going concern basis unless it is unreasonable to do so

- To prevent and detect fraud and error

- To prepare true and fair accounts

- To implement a suitable system of controls

Responsibilities of auditors

- To form an independent opinion on the financial statements
- To report their opinion to the members

(b) **Inherent limitations facing auditors undertaking their work**

Auditing is not objective, **judgements** often have to be made, and these judgements are subject to human error.

Auditors do not check every balance in the statements, they test on a **sample** basis. This means that there will never be a 100% correct solution, just persuasive evidence.

There are inherent **limitations in any internal control and accounting system**, so even if the auditor has tested controls and found them to be reliable, errors may still have been made which the auditor is unlikely to pick up during the course of his testing.

There is a **possibility of dishonesty** from client staff or their **collusion in fraud**. If the auditor is not told the truth then he is likely to draw incorrect conclusions.

There is always a **time lag between reporting period and audit** itself. This can be substantial, say four to five months. This lack of immediacy can give rise to errors.

There **are limitations to a standardised audit report**. The standardised audit report may make it **difficult to express the opinion accurately**, or it may give rise to **misunderstanding by its readers**.

2 Question with answer plan: External audit

Text references. Chapters 1 and 7

Top tips.

Read the requirements carefully.

Part (a) asks for an explanation of the purpose and role of the audit in the context of a large company.

For 10 marks it is clearly not going to be enough to give a basic definition so you need to think about how to expand on the definition.

This requirement does not give you any help in structuring your answer so before you start to write decide on two or three headings to use and plan how you will arrange the points you want to make under these headings.

Part (b) is more clearly sub-divided. The requirement asks about the interim and final audit and the body of the question lists out the main procedures at each of these stages. You should be able to use this as a plan for your answer.

Notice that it is not **enough** to list procedures; the requirement asks you to "**explain**". Re-read the points you have made to check that each is **explained**.

Easy marks. In part (a) there are few easy marks, but you should be able to explain in general terms the purpose and role of an audit.

In part (b) the easy marks were to be found by looking at each stage of the audit flagged in the question and explaining one or two basic procedures for each.

Examiner's comments.

In part (a), most candidates made important statements regarding the purpose of the audit in terms of providing an opinion on the financial statements. However, following this, most answers tended to spend an excessive amount of time explaining issues of auditor independence and liability rather than focusing on other purposes of an audit.

Common errors included focusing the answers on too few points and not considering the effect of the audit on third parties.

Part (b) was answered well where candidates provided an overview of the procedures and processes, mentioning six to eight different points in their answers. The main area where comment was not expected in answers was on the initial process of client acceptance, as the implication was that the client had been accepted and the interim audit was commencing. A common error was spending too much time on one area, especially the determination of audit risk and explanation of the risk model.

Marking scheme

		Marks
(a)	Training material: purpose of external audit and its role Up to 2 marks per point to a maximum of	10
(b)	Main audit procedures and processes: interim and final audit Up to 1 mark per point to a maximum of	$\underline{10}$ $\underline{\underline{20}}$

Answer plan

Part (a)

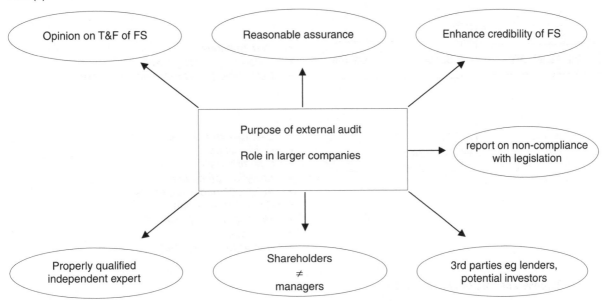

Part (b)

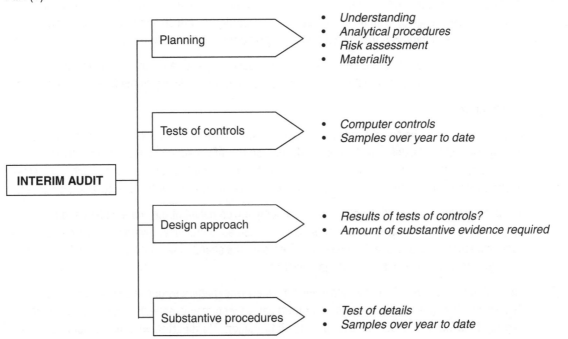

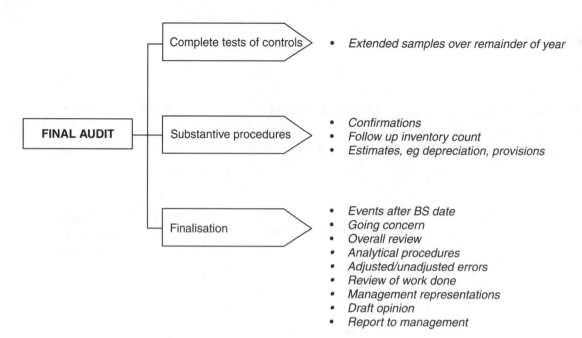

(a) **Purpose and role of external audit**

Basic definition

(1) ISAs describe the objective of an audit as being "the expression of an opinion whether the financial statements are prepared, in all material respects, in accordance with an applicable accounting framework. The opinion is normally worded as …*give a true and fair view* or *present fairly*.

(2) The nature of the audit is to give reasonable (but not absolute) assurance that the financial statements are free from material error. This should add to the credibility of the financial statements.

Regulatory framework

(1) In a large company, the owners of the business, the shareholders, are unlikely to be involved in the management of the business and therefore depend on the information provided to them by the directors to let them assess the performance of the business and to make decisions such as whether to stay invested in that business or how to cast their votes in respect of the directors' appointment.

(2) The directors have a duty of stewardship of the company on behalf of the shareholders and the preparation of annual financial statements is part of their accountability towards the shareholders. An audit opinion without any qualification should reassure the shareholders that the information is free from any significant misstatement or manipulation.

(3) The role of the auditor is that of an independent expert who gathers evidence and issues an opinion that will indicate, to shareholders and other third parties who may use the financial statements, the degree of reliance that should be placed on the information. Third parties who may benefit from the assurance given in the auditor's report could include lenders, potential investors or potential suppliers.

(4) Under the legal framework, and the rules of recognised professional bodies such as the ACCA, there are strict requirements as to who may carry out audits to ensure that only properly qualified people can perform this service. The ACCA also issues ethical rules to ensure that the auditor is genuinely independent. This regulatory framework should maintain the credibility of the role of the audit.

(b) (i) **Main audit procedures and practices during the interim audit**

(1) The auditor will obtain a thorough knowledge of the business by discussion with client management and reading relevant trade publications.

(2) Preliminary analytical procedures will be performed on interim accounts in order to identify any major changes in the business or unexpected trends.

(3) The client's accounting systems will be documented, or documentation prepared in prior year audits will be updated.

(4) An assessment will be made of **inherent risk** and **control risk**.

(5) An appropriate **materiality** level will be estimated.

(6) The information obtained during the planning stage will be **documented** along with an outline of the audit strategy to be followed.

(7) If control risk has been assessed as low in particular areas, then **controls testing** will need to be performed on the controls to confirm the initial assessment of the risk. These tests of controls will be started at the interim audit although they will generally need to be performed on a sample of items extending right over the accounting period so may need to be completed at the final audit.

(8) The **detailed audit approach** should be prepared. Programmes of audit procedures, both tests of controls and substantive procedures, will be designed to show the work that needs to be done and to enable subsequent review of audit completion.

(9) If substantive procedures are to be performed that involve checking a sample of transactions selected to cover the whole accounting period, it is likely that some of these procedures will also be started at the interim audit, but these will again be completed at the final audit.

(ii) **Main audit procedures and practices during the final audit**

(1) The tests that were started at the interim visit, both tests of controls and substantive procedures should be completed.

(2) Year-end balances may be verified through confirmations obtained from third parties such as:

- Receivables
- Payables
- Banks

(3) If the client has carried out a year-end inventory count, detailed procedures will be carried out to check the accuracy of the compilation of the year-end inventory listing and also to follow up any evidence gathered by the auditor when attending the inventory count.

(4) Detailed calculations will need to be obtained of any estimates the client has made at the year-end such as allowances for receivables, depreciation and provisions. Procedures will need to be performed to:

- Assess the reasonableness of the methods used to make the estimates
- Check the calculations; or
- Make an independent estimate.

(5) Analytical procedures will be performed on the draft accounts to consider whether the view given by the financial statements is in line with the auditor's understanding of the business.

(6) The auditor must review the directors' assessment of whether the business is a going concern. The auditor must consider whether the assumptions made by the directors are reasonable and whether it is appropriate to prepare the accounts on the going concern basis.

(7) A review of events after the balance sheet date must be performed in order to assess whether any appropriate adjustments or disclosures as required by IAS 10 have been dealt with correctly.

3 Auditors' responsibilities

Text references. Chapters 4 and 7

Top tips. This is a straightforward question looking at the topical issue of the role and responsibilities of the external auditor. However, you do need to plan your answer carefully and decide which points you are going to make in each section to avoid repetition. Note that the emphasis is on **explanation**. Don't fall into the trap of repeating rote learned knowledge. The examiner is looking for your **understanding** of this.

Easy marks. All the marks in this question are very achievable. This question is based on basic knowledge which is an essential starting point for success in this exam.

Examiner's comments. Candidates demonstrated a sound knowledge of most of the issues with the exception of the limitations of the external audit. In part (c) many simply repeated the independence rules rather than explaining the importance of independence.

Marking scheme

		Marks
(a)	Responsibilities of external auditors to directors and shareholders Up to 1 mark per point to maximum of	4
(b)	Limitations of the external audit – fraud Up to 1 mark per point to maximum of	3
(c)	External auditor independence Up to 1 mark per point to maximum of	$\underline{3}$ $\overline{10}$

(a) **Responsibilities**

    (i) *To shareholders*

        The auditor is required, normally by law, to **express an opinion** as to the truth and fairness of the financial statements (or that they present fairly). In doing this the auditor is acting on behalf of the shareholders and protecting their interests.

    (ii) *To directors*

        The auditor **does not have any specific legal responsibility** to the directors, although in practice it is important that they work together. Auditing standards do set out some responsibilities. For example, if the auditor detected fraud he would have a responsibility to inform management. Similarly as a result of work performed on internal control, management would expect to receive a letter of weakness.

(b) **Limitations**

Limitations of the audit arise due to the **expectations of the public** for the audit to fulfil a role which is outside the scope set down by national legislation or auditing standards.

Examples include the fact that an unqualified audit report does not indicate a 'complete bill of health'. It does not certify the accounts as being 100% correct, but reasonable within the benchmarks of materiality.

It is also believed that the auditor is responsible for detecting all fraud. In fact the primary responsibility for this lies with the directors and whilst the auditor will plan his work to have a **reasonable expectation of detecting material fraud** this is not his primary objective.

Confusion can also arise from the work performed on internal control. A letter of weakness is produced for management but is not intended to be a comprehensive list of all potential issues. It will simply highlight those which have come to light in the course of the audit.

(c) **Importance of independence**

Independence is important as it is the basis of the role of the auditor. The directors are required to account for the **stewardship** of the assets placed under their control. They do this by preparing the financial statements which are presented to the shareholders. The auditor's opinion enhances the **credibility** of the financial statements by providing assurance from an unbiased source.

If the auditor has an interest in the company, for example a financial or personal interest, he can no longer be seen as objective and impartial.

4 Audit regulation

Text reference. Chapter 3

Top tips. The issue of regulation of auditors is important and it is certainly a topical issue. If you are well prepared, you should be able to attempt a question like this well and gain good marks. It does not involve application of your knowledge and really just requires you to explain what you have learnt. All three parts of the question should be reasonably straightforward.

Easy marks. All the marks in this question are reasonably achievable providing you plan your answer before you start.

Examiner's comments. This question was not a popular question, although candidates who did attempt it made a good effort. Many candidates appreciated the broad role of professional bodies in the regulation of auditors and did not stick rigidly to professional ethics in part (b), which is encouraging, and a high number of candidates appreciated the relationship between national and international auditing standards. The understanding of the overall regulatory regime is essential to an understanding of the role of external audit and it is an area that may be tested in the compulsory section of the paper in future.

Marking scheme		Marks
(a)	Development, role and authority of ISAs 1 mark per valid point to maximum of	4
(b)	The role of the ACCA in the regulation of auditors 1 mark per point to maximum of	4
(c)	How ISAs and national standards influence each other ½ mark per point to a maximum of	$\frac{2}{10}$

(a) **Development, role and authority of ISAs**

ISAs

ISAs are International Standards on Auditing that set out basic procedures and guidance that auditors should adhere to in the audit of financial statements. The auditing standards are in bold type. Narrative in grey type in ISAs is guidance on how to apply the standards.

Authority

ISAs apply to material items in all financial statements which are audited so as to express an opinion in the true and fair terms. They are developed with due regard for national standards.

Development

ISAs are set by IAASB, the International Auditing and Assurance Standards Board: it is a committee of IFAC, the International Federation of Accountants. IAASB is made up of representatives of the profession who are members of IFAC.

ISAs are developed in consultation with interested parties within the profession and outside of it. They are also developed with due regard for national standards on auditing.

(b) **Role of professional bodies in the regulation of auditors**

One of the key professional bodies is the ACCA.

The role of the ACCA varies from country to country depending on the legal requirements for the regulation of auditors in those countries.

In some countries governments regulate auditors directly, in others, the profession is self regulating or a mixture of the two. In Europe, there is a tradition of government being directly involved in the regulation of auditors.

However, in the UK, regulation of the profession is devolved to Recognised Supervisory Bodies (RSB) and ACCA is one such RSB.

Training and entry requirements

The ACCA imposes certain requirements which must be fulfilled before a person can become a member of ACCA, and student members have to qualify by passing exams and fulfilling training requirements. There is also a commitment to Continuing Professional Development (CPD).

Ethics

The ACCA issues an ethical code which all students and members must comply with.

Investigation and discipline

The ACCA monitors its members' work and conduct and may impose punitive measures such as fines or exclusion from membership.

(c) **ISAs and National Standards**

There is increasing global interest in harmonising auditing standards because in the increasingly global marketplace it is important that sets of figures, and the assurance given on them, are comparable.

The requirement for listed EC companies to report group accounts in IASs from 2005 added to this requirement. It makes little sense to report according to the same standards but then be audited to differing ones.

In recent years, countries with a mature accounting profession have increasingly sought to harmonise their standards with ISAs.

This is not always possible, or may be a drawn out process due to the fact that some matters in national standards are required as a result of law. Nevertheless, many countries have accepted ISAs in their entirety, or with some local variations.

Many countries where standard-setting is mature make significant contributions to the development of ISAs by providing members to IFAC who sit on the committees and help to develop standards.

5 International Standards on Auditing

Text reference. Chapter 3

Top tips. Make sure you answer each requirement in turn, putting your answer in the required letter format, and using sub-headings based on the requirements to give your answer more structure.

Easy marks. As suggested above, easy marks are available if your knowledge in this area of the syllabus is sound.

Examiner's comments. This question was based on a short scenario, but otherwise was essentially factual, requiring knowledge of the ISA setting process.

Most candidates provided a letter to their friend, obtaining some presentation marks. Part (a) was almost always well answered, with many candidates obtaining full marks. Part (b) caused some confusion, although the key points regarding how different jurisdictions apply ISAs were normally made. In part (c), most candidates correctly stated that auditors should follow ISAs. In part (d), again, most candidates correctly noted that ISAs apply to any size of entity.

Weaknesses included explaining what happens when a company does not follow an ISA, rather than when an audit or does not follow an ISA, stating that small companies did not need an audit, without then going on to show that the principles of ISAs actually applied to any size of entity and in the UK, explaining the process of SAS setting rather than ISA setting.

Marking scheme

			Marks
One mark for each valid point			
(a)	Due process to produce an ISA		
	Subcommittee – areas for ISAs	1	
	Exposure draft (ED) via IAASB and issued	1	
	Comments on ED	1	
	Amendment of ED and issue of ISA	1	
	Other relevant points (each)	1	
	Maximum marks		4
(b)	Authority of ISAs		
	Apply to audit of FS	1	
	May apply to other statements	1	
	Basic principles in bold type	1	
	Explanatory text in normal type	1	
	Must read all ISA to understand application	1	
	ISA not override requirements of national countries	1	
	Where relevant country use ISA and not issue own guidance	1	
	National requirements differ – use national	1	
	Adopt changes so that the ISA can be used	1	
	Other relevant points (each)	1	
	Maximum marks		**8**
(c)	Extent to which auditor follows ISAs		
	Should follow wherever possible	1	
	Do not follow where audit more efficient	1	
	Must justify departure	1	
	Other relevant points (each)	1	
	Maximum marks		**4**

(d)   ISAs apply to small entities
      Applicable to any entity   1
      Appropriate ISAs to be followed   1
      Letter format/why writing   1
      Other relevant points (each)   1

                                          Maximum marks   <u>4</u>
                                                                           <u>20</u>

---

                                                                1 Any Road
                                                                Any Town
                                                                NT1 1ZZ

Dear Carmen,

Thanks for your letter, it was really nice to hear from you.

I'm going to set out in my letter the queries you raised regarding the regulatory framework which applies to auditors.

(a)   The due process of the IAASB involved in producing an ISA

      ISAs are produced by the International Audit and Assurance Standards Board, IAASB, which is a technical standing committee of the International Federation of Accountants, IFAC.

      Initially an exposure draft is produced for consideration by the IAASB. If this is approved, it is circulated to the member bodies of the IFAC (such as ACCA) and any other interested parties. It is also published on the IAASB's website. These bodies make comments on the exposure draft which is then amended as necessary. The exposure draft is then re-issued as an ISA or an International Auditing Practice Statement, IAPS. This process can take as long as two years.

(b)   The overall authority of ISAs and how they are applied in individual countries

      ISAs must be applied in the audits of historical financial information.

      ISAs contain basic principles and essential procedures (bold type) together with related guidance in the form of explanatory and other material. The whole text must be considered in order to understand and apply the basic principles and essential procedures.

      ISAs do not override the requirements for the audit of entities in individual countries. To the extent that ISAs conform with local regulations in regard to a particular subject, the audit in that country in accordance with local regulations will automatically comply with the ISA on that subject. Where local regulations differ from or conflict with ISAs, member bodies should comply with the obligations of members in the IFAC constitution, ie encourage changes in local regulations to comply with ISAs.

(c)   The extent to which an auditor must follow ISAs

      There may be exceptional circumstances under which the auditor may judge it necessary to depart from an ISA in order to achieve the objective of an audit more effectively. In this case, the auditor must be prepared to justify the departure. This situation is likely to be the exception rather than the rule.

(d)   The extent to which ISAs apply to small entities

      ISAs apply to the audit of financial information of any entity, regardless of its size. However, small entities possess distinct characteristics, such as a lack of segregation of duties, which mean that auditors must adapt their audit approach when auditing the financial statements of a small company. This is likely to include a substantive-based audit approach and more reliance on management representations, for example.

      The IAASB has published IAPS 1005, The special considerations in the audit of small entities. This was issued in March 1999 and discusses how various ISAs apply to the audit of small enterprises.

I hope this helps. Please let me know if I can be of any more assistance to you. Hope to hear from you soon.

Yours sincerely,

Amy Chan

6 Jumper

Text reference. Chapter 3

Top tips. Make sure you answer this question using a memo format as stated in the requirement (presentation marks are available). The best way to approach this question is to take each issue in turn from the scenario and deal with it separately. Your answer should include sub-headings for each issue as this will give it more structure. A detailed knowledge of the Combined Code is not required so don't panic. Use the clues in the scenario, for example, the company does not have an internal audit department, Mr Sheppard is both the Chief Executive and the Chairman of the company.

Easy marks. There aren't many easy marks as such in this question but use the question scenario to structure your answer and apply your knowledge of corporate governance.

Examiner's comments. The overall standard for this answer was quite good, with many international stream candidates obtaining very high marks. However, common errors included providing a history of corporate governance regulations (normally with a UK focus), not explaining the points made, providing detailed lists on the work of an audit committee, not providing the memo format required by the question and thus not gaining the mark for presentation.

Marking scheme

	Marks
1 mark for identifying the corporate governance problem, 1 for explaining why this is a problem and 1 for recommending a solution	
CEO and chairman	3
Composition of board	3
Director appointment	3
Review of board appointment	3
Board pay	3
Internal control	3
Internal audit	3
Financial statements	3
Audit committee	
Other relevant points (each – but limit to 1.5 marks if not	
mentioned in the scenario)	1.5
Memo format/why writing	2
Total	20

Memorandum

To: Jumper & Co
From: A Manager, Tela & Co
Date: Today
Subject: SGCC and Corporate Governance

SGCC does not appear to be following corporate governance codes for a number of reasons which are outlined below. Recommendations of changes to address these weaknesses are also suggested.

Chief Executive and Chairman Roles

Mr Sheppard is both the Chief Executive Officer and the board chairman of the company. Corporate governance codes indicate that there should be a clear division of responsibilities between running the board of directors and running the company's business, i.e. no single individual should have unfettered powers of decision.

In order to address this, the company should appoint a separate chairman who meets the independence criteria set out in the codes. This would ensure that Mr Sheppard does not have too much power within the company.

Board Composition

The board consists of five executive and two non-executive directors. To follow good corporate governance practice, the board should consist of a balance of executive and non-executive (preferably independent) directors such that no one individual or group of individuals can dominate the board's decision-making. Half the board (excluding the chairman) should preferably be independent non-executive directors (unless the company is small). In the case of SGCC, there are only two non-executive directors out of seven and it is not clear how independent they are.

The company should appoint more independent non-executive directors to the board to achieve a balance of half non-executive directors and half executive directors.

Board Appointments

Mr Sheppard makes appointments to the board himself. Good corporate governance suggests that any appointments to the board should be done through a nomination committee, the majority of the members of which should be independent non-executive directors and which should be chaired by the chairman or an independent non-executive director. This ensures transparency of appointment of board members.

The company should establish a nomination committee consisting of mainly non-executive directors. Formal job descriptions should also be published to make the appointment process as transparent as possible.

Monitoring of Targets

At present there are no formal targets or reviews of board policies carried out. The board should undertake a formal and rigorous review of its own performance, its committees and of individual directors annually. This should also be stated in the annual report. The performance evaluation of the chairman should be undertaken by the non-executive directors.

SGCC should address this by ensuring that performance targets are set for each director and that their performance is reviewed annually. Non-executive directors should review the performance of the Chairman.

Remuneration of Board Members

Currently Mr Sheppard decides the level of remuneration for himself and the board members without considering performance. A significant proportion of executive directors' remuneration should be structured so that rewards are linked to performance. For non-executive directors, remuneration should reflect the time commitment and responsibilities of the role.

A remuneration committee should be set up for determining the level of remuneration for directors and no director should be involved in deciding his own remuneration. This committee should consist of at least three non-executive directors to set the remuneration for executive directors and the chairman. The remuneration of non-executive directors should be determined by the board itself (or the shareholders if required by the articles of association of the company).

Review of Internal Controls

The internal controls of the company are monitored by the senior accountant and a detailed review assumed to be undertaken by the external auditors. It is not sufficient to rely on this to test the overall effectiveness of controls within the company.

The board should conduct a review of the company's internal controls at least annually and report to shareholders that this has been undertaken. This could be facilitated by establishing an internal audit department.

Audit Committee

It is not clear whether there is an audit committee. Good corporate governance would require an audit committee, comprising at least three members who are independent non-executive directors, which can monitor the external auditors.

The board should set up an audit committee to allow them to maintain an appropriate relationship with the external auditors.

Internal Audit Department

SGCC does not have an internal audit department. Listed companies, such as SGCC, should review the need for an internal audit department at least annually.

Given the lack of formal controls at SGCC, an internal audit department should be established as soon as possible. It should report its findings to the audit committee.

Financial Statements

The company produces annual financial statements with detailed information on past performance. However, the board of directors should also produce information in the annual report setting out their view of how the company will perform in the future for the benefit of shareholders and potential investors.

Kind regards,

A Manager

7 ZX

Text references. Chapters 3 and 5

Top tips. Firstly note the requirement for a memo format – make sure you do this as marks are available for presentation. Structure your answer by using sub-headings for each of the two requirements. For both the requirements you are asked to 'explain' so make sure that you don't simply produce a list of points. You need to explain each point in order to score the marks available.

Easy marks. There were no very obvious easy marks in this question but at the time it was set, the examiner had recently written an article about the regulatory framework and corporate governance. If you had read that article it would have provided a basic framework that would let you identify some of the key principles of corporate governance that would have got you started in planning an answer.

Examiner's comments. The standard of answers to part (a) was unsatisfactory. The majority of answers took a page or two of the answer book to explain the background to corporate governance. This approach showed one of the classic mistakes in writing exam answers – not reading the question. The question was actually about the role of internal audit in corporate governance, not about the history of corporate governance. Reasons for weaker answers included:

- Not providing a memo format (one mark was available for this)
- Stating areas where internal audit could assist with corporate governance but not how that would be provided. For example, stating that internal audit could assist with fraud, but not stating that their presence could act as a deterrent.
- Explaining the duties of directors – not internal audit

Answers to part (b) were of a higher standard than those for part (a) mainly because candidates started writing straightaway about the advantages and disadvantages of an audit committee. Some weaker answers tended to explain the composition of the audit committee, rather than moving straight into the advantages and disadvantages.

Marking scheme

		Marks
(a)	Board reports	2
	Internal control	2
	Application of ISAs	2
	Communication with external auditors	2
	Communication to the board	2
	Risk management	2
	Communication with external auditors	2
	Prevent/detect fraud	2
	Allow other relevant points	2
	Maximum marks	**10**
(b)	One mark for explaining the area and one mark for applying to the situation in ZX	
	Advantages	
	Public confidence	2
	Financial reporting	2
	Communication	2
	Friend of the board	2
	Disadvantages	
	Lack of understanding of function	2
	Role of non-executive directors	2
	Cost	2
	Allow other relevant points	2
	Maximum marks	**10**
Total		**20**

From:	Chief Internal Auditor
To:	Board of ZX Ltd
Subject:	Role of Internal Audit and Audit Committee
Date:	Today

(a)   Areas where the internal audit department can assist the directors with the implementation of good corporate governance include:

(i)   **Internal controls**

The directors are responsible for assessing the risks faced by the company, implementing appropriate controls and monitoring the effectiveness of those controls.

The internal audit department could assist the board in a number of ways:

- They could review the directors' risk assessment and report on its adequacy

- In certain areas (perhaps in respect of the accounting system) they could actually carry out the risk assessment

- They could review and report on the adequacy of the controls that are to be implemented

- They could carry out annual audits of the effectiveness of controls (performing tests of the controls), identifying weaknesses and making recommendations for improvements

It would be inappropriate for them to be involved at every stage, ie assessing risks, designing controls and reviewing their effectiveness as this would mean that they are checking their own work. This would undermine the credibility of their reports.

In some sense the existence of an internal audit serves as a control procedure in its own right. An example would be that the existence of an internal audit department is likely to act as a deterrent against fraud, and so helps the directors meet their responsibilities to implement appropriate controls to prevent and detect fraud.

(ii) **Financial statements**

Good corporate governance requires the directors to prepare financial statements that give a balanced and understandable view. As the internal audit department has experience in accounting and auditing and is led by a qualified Chartered Certified Accountant it can assist the directors in applying accounting standards and meeting the expectations of readers of the accounts (particularly as these expectations will greatly increase if ZX proceeds with the possible listing).

(iii) **Board reports**

A principle of good corporate governance is that the board should be properly briefed. The internal audit department can review the reports that are presented to the board to ensure that they are properly prepared and presented in a way that can be easily understood.

(iv) **Communication with external auditors**

Although it is mainly the audit committee (if one has been established) that will act as a channel of communication between the external auditors and the board, it will often be the case that the external and internal auditors will work together on some areas. This could be the case if the external auditor found it appropriate to rely on internal audit reports on some areas (for example, on periodic inventory counting procedures) or where the external auditor wants to extend computer assisted testing over the whole year under the supervision of the internal auditors. This could add value to information available to the board where areas have been considered by both groups of auditors.

(v) **Knowledge of corporate governance and auditing standards**

As qualified professionals the internal audit department will have up to date knowledge of corporate governance requirements and of developments in auditing standards. They will be able to help the board keep up to date with what is expected of them under the codes of corporate governance and with what will be expected of them from the external auditors.

(b) **Advantages and disadvantages of an audit committee**

(i) **Advantages**

Proposed listing

If ZX is listed it will in all probability have to follow tighter requirements such as the Combined Code on corporate governance in the UK. The establishment of an audit committee is considered good practice under this code. If ZX did not establish one it would have to disclose the non-compliance with the code in that respect and this might affect shareholder confidence in respect of the accounting and auditing functions within the company.

'Critical friend' of the board

An effective audit committee will be made up of individuals with relevant knowledge and experience, who are independent of the day-to-day running of the company. This will give the shareholders confidence that there is some independent oversight of the board which should help ensure that the company is being run in the best interests of the shareholders. They should also be able to advise the executive directors on areas such as corporate governance where their own knowledge may be incomplete.

Communication

The existence of an audit committee gives an effective channel of communication for the external auditors. It means there is a quasi-independent body with whom the external auditor can discuss contentious audit issues such as disagreements over accounting treatments rather than going directly to the board who have made the decisions on those matters.

This may increase stakeholders' confidence in the financial statements and the audit process.

Financial reporting

The non-executive directors are expected to have a good knowledge of financial reporting. In the case of ZX this should prove a useful source of advice to the board. Also, externally, it should increase confidence in the financial reporting processes and reports of ZX.

Appointment of external auditors

The audit committee, rather than the board, would recommend which auditors should be appointed. They would also review annually any circumstances, such as provision of other services, which might threaten the perceived independence of the external auditor. This should again increase the confidence that readers of the financial statements have in the objectivity of the opinion given by the external auditors and hence the credibility of the financial statements,

(ii) **Disadvantages**

Cost

Although the non-executive directors will not require full time salaries, the level of fees that will be required to attract suitably experienced individuals may be significant but must be weighed against the benefits which will be derived especially in view of the planned listing.

Knowledge and experience

The board may question whether individuals from outside ZX will have adequate experience of the business to make a useful contribution to the board. As explained above, it is their very independence that adds value to their role as well as their particular experience in respect of financial accounting and corporate governance issues.

Responsibilities

The current board may be concerned that the establishment of an audit committee of non-executive directors may diminish their powers in running the company. It could be seen as another tier of management. They should be assured that the audit committee would act in support of the board, not as an alternative to it.

8 Internal control evaluation

Text reference. Chapter 3

Top tips. You may read this and think that it is a really tough question. It is tricky, but using your common sense should earn you marks.

You may find it easier in part (a) to think about the ways in which a company might manage business risk. Having established this you can then develop the enquiries that the auditor would make.

Easy marks. These are available in part (b). The issue of corporate governance is an important one and you should have a basic understanding.

(a) **Corporate business risk**

The questions the auditor should ask include:

(i) Does the company address the **issues**?

The auditors should ensure that the company is aware of the issues raised by the Turnbull guidance and that they have taken steps to follow the guidance. Indicators of such steps might include having one director put in charge of complying with the Turnbull guidance, and information issued to staff about what this will involve.

(ii) Do the directors identify **significant risks**?

It is possible that 'risks' are defined narrowly by the directors, in other words that they have tried to set out what issues the company might face, and that other significant risks may slip through the net.

Again, reading the documentation that has been prepared for staff may indicate whether this is the case. It might also emerge in the course of discussions with the director designated to control compliance.

(iii) Does the board **evaluate and manage** significant risks?

The board must be able to do this stage effectively, or the entire process is pointless. The auditors should assess the director's action plan in the event of significant risks being identified, and perhaps review minutes of past meetings when the directors have had to respond to a risk.

(iv) Does the board **consider the probability** of the risk arising?

(v) Does the board **consider the potential operational and financial impact** in the event of the risk arising?

(vi) Have the board **implemented controls** which would maintain the business risk between certain specified tolerance limits? (Have the directors set specified tolerance limits?)

(vii) Does the board **regularly review its processes** for identifying and dealing with risks arising?

(viii) Does the board include **meaningful reports** about the systems to identify and manage risks in the annual report so that shareholders can understand their actions?

(b) **Audit committees**

An audit committee reviews financial information and liaises between the auditors and the company. It normally consists of the non-executive directors of the company, though there is no reason why other senior personnel should not be involved.

Benefits include:

- Improvement to the quality of financial reporting

- Increased discipline and control which will reduce the opportunity for fraud

- Enabling non-executive directors to play a positive role

- Providing a forum for the finance director to raise concerns

- Providing a channel of communication for the external auditor

- Strengthening the position of internal audit functions by providing a greater degree of independence from management

- Increasing public confidence in the credibility and objectivity of financial statements

9 Objectivity

Text reference. Chapter 4

Top tips. This is a relatively straightforward question dealing with ethical issues. You should be familiar with the basic principles involved as well as having a detailed knowledge of the ACCA's own ethical guidance. Although not a difficult question, you should take care to structure your answer carefully and only include the relevant points. The examiner does not want to read everything you know about the ethical guidance but instead is looking for an ability to apply your knowledge to the question.

Easy marks. All the marks in this question should be reasonably achievable as in spite of the high level of application it is a topic with which you should be familiar.

Examiner's comments. Although there were some good answers many candidates lost marks for the following reasons:

* Not appreciating that in some instances it is possible to retain a client where objectivity is threatened, provided that safeguards are met.

* Lack of planning leading to repetitive answers.

* Regurgitating knowledge without application.

Marking scheme

		Marks
External auditor objectivity		
(a)	**Why external auditor objectivity may be, or appear to be, threatened** Up to 1 mark per point to a maximum of Subject to a maximum of 3 for each of the four categories	12
(b)	**Requirements** Up to 1 mark per point to a maximum of subject to a maximum of 2 for each of the four categories	8
		20

(a) **Objectivity**

    (i) *Undue dependence*

        An auditor is likely to become dependant on an individual client or a group of connected clients where they provide a **significant proportion of the firm's fees**. These may be audit fees or fees for other services.

        Objectivity may be impaired as the auditor's judgement may be affected by his need to keep the client. For example the auditor may be more reluctant to question accounting policies and accounting treatments adopted for fear of losing the income.

        In extreme situations it may be that the auditor fails to issue a modified audit report due to pressure applied by the client not to do so. This action would constitute negligence and the firm could be sued as a result. In some instances the professional indemnity insurance may not cover the size of the claim.

(ii) *Financial interest*

A firm, its partners or staff may have a **financial interest** in a client in a number of ways. This could arise through the ownership of shares or by making loans to the client. (Overdue fees of a large amount could constitute a loan.)

The role of the auditor is to provide the shareholders with an **independent opinion** of the position and performance of the company. If the auditor is also a shareholder himself, or has some other financial interest, that opinion can no longer be seen as objective. It may be difficult for the auditor to make professional decisions rather than those based on personal interest.

For example, the auditor may be inclined to allow accounting policies and treatments which inflate performance on the basis that this would have a positive effect on the share price. As above, in extreme circumstances the auditor may be reluctant to issue a modified audit report as this may have a detrimental impact on the price.

(iii) *Family or other close personal or business relationships*

Where there are family or other close relationships between the client and the auditor, objectivity is impaired as the auditor's decisions may be affected by his wish to support the family member or friend or to enhance his own business interests.

Obviously the extent of the problem depends on the nature of the relationship and the seniority of those involved. The audit partner being married to the finance director would be more of a risk than the audit junior being related to one of the sales staff.

Again the key issue is the **effect this may have on the financial statements and the audit report**. The auditor may feel pressured to allow the company to present results in a better light than the facts would suggest. An auditor may also be reluctant to issue a modified audit report if this will damage a personal relationship or another business interest exposing the firm to possible claims of negligence.

(iv) *Other services*

Most audit firms provide their clients with other services. These include, for example, tax and IT advice, and for smaller companies can also include accountancy services.

In many cases the fees generated from these exceed the income generated from the provision of the basic audit. Whilst this is obviously beneficial to the firm this does cause a problem with objectivity. Where other services make up a significant part of the firm's income the auditor's judgement may be impaired. As with undue dependence, the auditor may fear that if he tries to enforce decisions which are unpopular with the management the firm may lose the audit and therefore the income from the other services as well. The situation would be particularly sensitive where the auditor wishes to issue a modified audit report.

The other risk to objectivity is that of **self review**. The auditor may find himself in the situation where he is expressing an opinion on information which has been prepared by the firm in the first place, or has been produced by a system set up under its guidance. If errors or mistakes are identified the auditor may be tempted to overlook these rather than have to admit that these problems have arisen.

(b) **ACCA requirements**

(i) *Undue dependence*

- Where the recurring work paid by one client or group of connected clients exceeds 15% of the gross practice income additional safeguards should be put in place (eg rotation of engagement partner). In the case of listed and other public interest companies this would apply where fees exceeded 10% of the gross practice income. (New practices may not be able to satisfy such criteria and extra care will be necessary in such circumstances.)

- A review of the risk to independence should be instituted for all large fees ie where gross fee income exceeds 10% of gross practice income (5% for listed and other public interest companies). All firms are required to have professional indemnity insurance to cover them against claims of negligence.

(ii) *Financial interest*

- No partner in a firm or any member of staff working on a particular audit should hold shares in a client business. Where the shares are acquired involuntarily (by marriage or inheritance) then they should be disposed of at the earliest opportunity. Where the articles of the client company require the auditor to be a shareholder, then the auditor should hold only the minimum number of shares. Any voting rights should not be exercised.

- Beneficial holdings in unit trusts, modest personal savings in a client building society or other similar institution are not precluded.

- No loans or guarantees should be undertaken between a client and the auditor.

(iii) *Family or other close relationships*

- An officer or employee of the company (or the partner or employee of such a person) is prohibited from being appointed as auditor.

- An auditor may also be ineligible if closely connected with an officer or senior staff member of the client company. The following are normally regarded as being closely connected:

  - Spouses or cohabitees

  - Minor children including stepchildren

  - A company in which a 20% interest or more is held

  - Any relative to whom regular financial assistance is given

  - An individual who has been an officer or employee of a company within the two years prior to the commencement of the first day of the period reported on should not take part in the audit.

(iv) *Other services*

- For listed companies and other public interest companies a practice should not participate in the preparation of the company's accounts and accounting records except in relation to assistance of a routine clerical nature or in emergency situations.

- Where a practice is involved in the preparation of accounting records care must be taken not to make management decisions or to perform management functions. The auditor should ensure that the client accepts responsibility for the records as its own and that appropriate audit tests are performed even where it has processed or maintained the records.

- The auditor may advertise for and interview prospective key financial and administrative staff including the provision of a short list with recommendations. However the final decision must be that of the client.

- A firm should not audit a client's financial statements which include the product of a specialist valuation carried out by it or an associated practice or organisation.

10 Ethical dilemma

Text reference. Chapter 4

Top tips. This question looked at the issue of an ethical dilemma faced by an internal auditor. The key here is to use a little common sense and to ensure that the comments which you make are as specific to the scenario as possible. Part (b) is a more typical type of question but you do need to think carefully about the impact which the situation has on the audit report.

Easy marks. Part (a) is the more straightforward section.

Examiner's comments. On the whole part (a) was well answered with most candidates being aware of the fact that a member of the ACCA should not falsify documents even if instructed to do so by his employer. A number of candidates said that they would inform the bank of the situation, therefore breaching confidentiality. This course of action would normally only be taken regarding issues of national security or public interest. Part (b) was not well answered with many candidates showing a lack of understanding of the effect of the issue on the auditors' report.

Marking scheme

		Marks
(a)	Request to alter accounts Up to 2 marks per point up to a maximum of	10
(b)	Implications for the audit, the auditor's report and the relationship between the firm and the client Up to 2 marks per point up to a maximum of	10
		20

(a) **Course of action**

(i) *Legitimate changes*

The action taken will depend on the **nature of the changes** made to the documents. Bad debt and depreciation charges are balances which are subject to a great deal of judgement. They are not absolutes and are often revised from one period to the next. Provided that any changes made to these are in order to present information more fairly, rather than to achieve specific results, the internal auditor would be able to accept these as **legitimate**. For example information about the recoverability of certain debts may have been received or perhaps the usage of certain assets may have been revised. Whilst these types of change do not constitute changes in policy and therefore do not need to be disclosed in the financial statements it would be important to bring them to the attention of the bank.

Before the internal auditor could sign off the documentation he would review the records to ensure that they do in fact show that the bank's targets have been met.

(ii) *Falsification of records*

It would be **unethical** for a member of the ACCA to falsify the internal control records and it would be in contravention of the ACCA's *Code of Ethics and Conduct*. Depending on the nature of the alterations they could constitute fraud which is a criminal offence.

As the internal auditor is being asked to do this by his employer it is obviously a difficult situation. Steps which he might take would include discussing the matter with the Board of Directors and the Audit Committee to ensure that they are aware of the legal implications. Concerns should also be made in writing.

The internal auditor may also wish to **seek legal advice** in order to protect himself and could also contact the ACCA for clarification of the ethical implications.

The internal auditor should not bring the issue to the attention of the bank as this would be a **breach of confidentiality**. Reporting to third parties is normally confined to matters of public interest and national security, neither of which seems to be relevant here.

Ultimately if the internal auditor is not satisfied with the response of the directors he needs to consider his position and whether he should **resign**.

(b)   **Implications**

(i)   *Audit of financial statements*

The fact that changes are being made, apparently to satisfy criteria set down by the bank **increases audit risk**. The auditor will need to be sensitive to the possibility of the existence of other areas where changes may have been made with the same objective in mind. Risk is also increased by the absence of two key members of staff, a situation in itself which appears highly unusual.
The external auditor needs to assess the materiality of the changes made to bad debts, depreciation and in respect of the leases. The criteria set down by the bank may be more sensitive than audit materiality, therefore whilst an issue for the bank it may not be as significant from the audit point of view.

The external auditor will need to establish **the reasons for the changes** in the treatment of bad debts, depreciation and leases to determine whether they can be justified. As the change in the treatment of leases constitutes a change in accounting policy the auditor needs to ensure that this is based on a truer and fairer view and that the impact has been **adequately disclosed**.

(ii)   *Auditors' report*

Depending on the results of the audit work the auditors' report may be affected as follows:

Qualified on the grounds of disagreement – if the auditor does not agree with the changes made to bad debts, depreciation and leases including the level of disclosure provided (assuming they are material).

Modified (but unqualified) – if the auditor believes there is doubt about the ability of the company to continue as a going concern this would be drawn to the attention of the readers. If the situation was not properly disclosed this could result in a qualified audit report.

(iii)   *Continuing relationship*

If the external auditor is satisfied that changes made to treatments and accounting policies are legitimate there are no implications for the ongoing relationship.

If the external auditor has concerns over the integrity and honesty of the client in the way it has presented financial information the auditor should consider whether he wishes to continue with the relationship at all.

11 Confidentiality and independence

Text reference. Chapter 4

Top tips. This is a fairly straightforward question dealing with client confidentiality and the ethical issues around independence. In part (b), use the scenario to identify the risks to independence and take each issue in turn, using a separate sub-heading for each. There are plenty of clues in the scenario to help you, for example, the company has been an audit client of the firm for eight years, the finance director is the daughter of the audit partner. As well as identifying the risks to independence, make sure you suggest how to mitigate those risks – this is specifically asked for in the question requirement.

Easy marks. These are available in part (a). You should be familiar with the guidelines to auditors concerning client confidentiality and the situations where an auditor may disclose information as set out in the ACCA's *Code of ethics and conduct*.

Examiner's comments. Part (a) required candidates to explain situations where an auditor could disclose confidential information concerning a client. While this was a factual question, it did focus on an important ethical area with which candidates should be familiar. Most candidates obtained a pass standard in this section, with a minority obtaining full marks. However weaker candidates did not provide enough detail for some of the comments made or suggested that disclosure would be made to any government department for virtually any reason.

Part (b) was based on a scenario and asked candidates to identify and explain the risks to independence identified in the scenario. Many candidates provided a clear format to their answer, identifying individual points with a heading and clearly explaining the issues involved. The only major common error was that some candidates correctly identified and explained the independence risk, but then did not explain how that risk could be mitigated. However, many candidates used a three-column format (for the risk, why it was an independence issue, and how to mitigate the risk) which limited the extent to which this error occurred.

Marking scheme

		Marks
(a)	General rules	
	Statement don't normally disclose without good reason	1
	Simply stating rules	1
	Client consent	
	Public duty to disclose	1
	Legal or professional duty to disclose	1
	ACCA Code of ethics – obligatory disclosure	
	Implied agreement not to disclose	1
	Exemptions	1
	Disclose to proper authority	1
	Court demands disclosure	1
	ACCA Code of ethics – voluntary disclosure (0.5 area 0.5 example)	
	Protect member's interest	1
	Public duty	1
	Also allow other ethics where appropriate, eg person not considered fit and proper to carry out work	1
	Allow 1 bonus mark where specific information about a candidate's jurisdiction is given	<u>1</u>
	Maximum marks	**8**

		Marks
(b)	1 for identifying and explaining area	
	1 for explaining why an ethical issue	
	1 for the resolution of the problem	
	Gives potential for 3 marks per section	
	Areas for discussion per the scenario	
	Audit partner – time in office	3
	Unpaid taxation fees	3
	Fee income	3
	Allyson Grace	3
	Meal	3
	Maximum marks	**12**
	Total	**20**

(a) **Situations where an auditor may disclose confidential information about a client**

Auditors have a professional duty of confidentiality and this is an implied term of the agreement made between the auditor and the client. However there may be a legal right or duty to disclose confidential information or it may be in the public interest to disclose details of clients' affairs to third parties. Also the client may have given the auditor consent to disclose confidential information. These are general principles only and there is more specific guidance which is discussed below.

Obligatory Disclosure

If the auditor knows or suspects that his client has committed money-laundering, treason, drug-trafficking or terrorist offences then he is obliged to disclose all the information he has to a competent authority.

Under ISA 250 *Consideration of laws and regulations in an audit of financial statements* auditors must also consider whether non-compliance with laws and regulations may affect the accounts. They might have to include in the audit report a statement that non compliance with laws and regulations has led to significant uncertainties, or that non compliance has meant that there is a disagreement over the way specific items have been treated in the accounts.

Voluntary Disclosure

Voluntary disclosure includes where the auditor considers that disclosure is reasonably necessary to protect his interests, for example to allow him to sue for outstanding fees or to defend an action for negligence.

Other examples of voluntary disclosure include when disclosure is compelled by law such as when the auditor has to give evidence in court. There may be a public duty to disclose such as if an offence has been committed which is contrary to the public interest. Disclosure may be required to non-governmental bodies which have statutory powers to compel disclosure.

(b) **Risks to independence**

Audit Partner

Mr Grace has been the audit partner on the audit of Ancients for the last eight years. His independence and objectivity are likely to be impaired as a result of this close relationship with a key client and its senior management.

This threat could be addressed by appointing another audit partner to the audit of Ancients and rotating partners at suitable intervals thereafter.

Tax Fees Outstanding

There are taxation fees outstanding from Ancients for work that was done six months previously. In effect, McKay & Co are providing an interest-free loan to Ancients. This can threaten independence and objectivity of the audit firm as it may not want to qualify the accounts in case the outstanding fees are not paid.

This can be addressed by discussing the issue with the directors of Ancients and finding out why the fees have not been paid. If the fee is still not paid the firm should consider delaying the start of the audit work or even the possibility of resigning.

Fee Dependence

Ancients is one of McKay & Co's most important clients and the firm provides other services to this client as well as audit, including taxation services. Also the company is growing rapidly. Generally objectivity and independence are considered to be threatened if the fees for audit and recurring work exceed 10% of the firm's total fees for a listed client such as Ancients.

This threat could be mitigated by reviewing the total of the audit and recurring fee income from Ancients as a % of McKay & Co's total fee income on a regular basis and possibly limiting the provision of the other services if Ancients is providing 5-10% of the total fee income of the firm.

Relationship to Financial Director of Ancients plc

Allyson Grace, the daughter of Mr Grace, has recently been appointed the Financial Director of Ancients. The independence of Mr Grace could be threatened because of their close family relationship. The code of ethics does not define 'close family relationships' but lists factors that should be considered, such as the position the immediate family member holds with the client and the role of the professional on the assurance team. As Financial Director, Allyson has direct influence over the financial statements and as engagement partner, Mr Grace has ultimate responsibility for the audit opinion, so there is a clear threat to objectivity and independence.

This threat to independence could be mitigated by the appointment of another audit partner to this client.

Meal

The fact that Allyson Grace wants to take the audit team out for an expensive meal before the audit commences could be considered a threat to independence as it might influence the audit team's decisions once they start the audit of the financial statements. The ethics rules state that gifts or hospitality from the client should not be accepted if the benefit is significant.

This threat could be mitigated by declining the invitation.

12 Phones Anywhere

Text references. Chapters 4 and 7

Top tips. To score marks on this question, you need to explain your reasons clearly. In (a) your answer will be clearer if you group the risks under major headings, such as going concern. Your answer to (b) should focus on the most important risks indicated by the information given, but you should not neglect the general ethical considerations. Your answer to (c) should be backed with reasons whatever your conclusion; but it is difficult to see how the firm could possibly have accepted this appointment.

A potential problem with this question is the overlap between the answers to the different parts. If this occurs you should discuss the relevant issue in detail where most appropriate (eg going concern in part (a)), and make brief reference to it elsewhere (as a significant factor in part (c)).

Easy marks. These are available in part (b). It is important to be familiar with the ethical guidance regarding the acceptance of an audit assignment. Where possible try to make points that relate to the scenario. This will add to your score.

(a)   There are a number of significant risks that will influence the audit work, and there are also various professional issues connected with the audit.

Inherent risks

(i)   **Indications that the company may not continue as a going concern**

(1)   The company's **commercial prospects** appear doubtful. The company's current limited coverage might well make it unappealing to subscribers, as it does not cover a large number of towns or motorways, unlike its competitors.

(2)   The company is **recently established,** and subscribers may prefer longer-established companies with better known names.

(3)   The company's **present financial situation** is not good. Gearing is increasing and the company is making significant trading losses. We are not told whether the company's competitors are making profits, or whether they are likely to adopt aggressive strategies which result in them making losses, but losses that they are better able to bear than Phones Anywhere can.

(4)   **Significant investment** will be required over the next few years. It will be needed for **new relay stations,** and to incorporate **technical advances** that will inevitably occur in the industry. Significant **advertising** and **marketing expenditure** will also be required to improve the company's profile in the market.

(ii)   **Risks associated with the directors**

(1)   The **role** of the **non-executive director owners** appears to be uncertain. The information given does not make clear how actively they are involved in the company, and whether they are fulfilling their responsibilities as directors.

(2)   The arrangements for **remuneration** of the **executive directors** give the directors an incentive to maximise subscribers, which is not the same as maximising profits, since the directors may attract subscribers by offering excessive discounts.

(3)   We need also to consider what we know about the **reputation** of the directors, particularly the finance director.

(iii)   **Computer risks**

The company appears to be very **reliant** on a **single computer**, which both connects subscribers and calculates bills. The company's operations would be very seriously, perhaps fatally, affected if the computer crashed and there were **no emergency back-up arrangements.** We also do not know what would be involved in updating the computer and whether the computer has sufficient capacity to cope with an expanded network of relay stations.

(iv)   **Accounting policies**

Some of the company's **accounting policies** appear to be **questionable.** Six years is likely to be too long an amortisation period for the computer equipment. The amortisation period for the discount to retailers may also be too long if subscribers are likely to change the operator they use within four years or buy a different model of phone.

Professional risks

There are a number of indications that the risk of a negligence claim may be higher than normal on this client.

(i)   The **going concern problems** discussed above may lead to the company failing and our being sued for negligence if our audit reports have failed to give sufficient warning.

(ii)   Given the need for new funds, the company may be vulnerable to a **take-over bid,** or new shareholders may purchase a significant number of shares. The risk of material error may be high because of the **questionable accounting policies**, and my firm may be vulnerable to an action from the new shareholders.

In addition we should consider the likely **profits.** These may be low because of the audit work required in the light of the risks discussed above and the work required if the company is floated on the Stock Exchange.

(b) **Principal ethical concerns**

(i) The audit fee may form **too large** a **percentage** of my firm's annual income. The ACCA guidelines recommend that the recurring work paid by one client should not exceed **15%** of the gross practice income. In the case of **listed** and **other public interest companies**, the figure should be 10% of the gross practice income. Even if the fee does not currently exceed these limits, it is likely to do so in the near future if the company expands or becomes listed. Even if the fees do not exceed the limits, they are likely to be significant enough for the firm to exercise quality control procedures such as hot review by a second partner.

(ii) Our firm must have the resources to perform the work properly, as well as any relevant **knowledge** or **skills.** For this client, we shall need **specialist computer auditing** knowledge to be able to understand how the client's system records calls and deals with bills. We also need to have someone with knowledge of the **accounting policies** that are used in this industry, to decide whether the accounting policies on discounts and capitalisation of the computer equipment is reasonable.

(iii) **Other ethical matters**

    (1) No partner or member of the audit team should have a **close personal relationship** with the directors of the company.

    (2) No partner or employee of the audit firm should **own shares** in the company. If the shareholding is unavoidable (because say a staff member cannot dispose of their shares), the person concerned should not vote on the appointment of auditors.

    (3) No partner or employee who has a **beneficial interest** in a trust holding shares in the company should be employed on the audit.

    (4) Ideally no partners or staff who are **trustees** of a **trust** holding shares in the client should be involved on the audit. The problems are greater if the trust holds more than **10%** of the **company's issued share capital** or the **total assets** comprised in the trust. If the company becomes a public company, our firm can no longer act for it if the 10% limit is breached.

(iv) Certain formalities will be required as part of the appointment process.

    (1) Our firm should request permission from the client to **contact** the **current auditors.** If permission is refused we should decline nomination. If permission is granted, we should ask the current auditors to tell us in writing all the information they have that they think will enable us to decide whether to accept appointment as auditors. If the existing auditors supply important information, we must then consider whether we can accept nomination.

    (2) If we consider the client to be of sufficiently high risk, we may carry out **further investigations** on the individuals involved, check the client's credit rating and obtain further references.

    (3) If we are appointed as auditors, we should agree an **engagement letter** with the client.

(c) I believe that my firm should not accept nomination as the auditors of Phones Anywhere for the following reasons:

(i) It is likely that the **fees** from the assignment are in **excess** of the ACCA's limits or will exceed them in the next two to three years.

(ii) My firm probably does not have the **experience** and **knowledge** to audit this type of client.

(iii) It is very difficult to gauge **how much work** will be involved in the audit, particularly if the going concern problems prove to be serious.

(iv) The risk of a **negligence claim** arising from the audit appears to be much higher than average.

(v) The **fees** from the client may not justify the risks involved. If the company does go into liquidation, there is a risk that some of the fees will never be paid. We are unlikely also to be the auditors for very long; if the company is floated on a public exchange, a larger firm will most likely be appointed.

13 Internal audit

Text reference. Chapter 5

Top tips. This question covers the relatively straightforward topic of internal audit and the extent to which it can be relied on by the external auditor. The main problem is that the requirements cover the same aspects albeit from different angles. In this situation it is important to plan your answer to avoid repeating the same points. Also remember the importance of using the scenario. Three specific internal audit services are described. Think about their relevance to the external auditor. They may not all be equally useful.

Easy marks. These are available in part (a) and part (c). Notice that you can use your knowledge of the ISA 610 criteria for assessing the internal audit function as a framework for your answer (organisational status, scope, technical competence, due professional care).

Examiner's comments. This was a very straightforward question for which many candidates were well prepared. More marks would have been scored if candidates had dealt separately with the three internal audit functions described. A large number of candidates incorrectly assumed that the same independence requirements applied to both internal and external auditors.

Marking scheme

		Marks
(a)	Reliance on work of internal auditors Up to 2 marks per point to a maximum of	6
(b)	Information required Up to 2 marks per point to a maximum of	6
(c)	Circumstances in which it would not be possible to rely on the work of internal audit Up to 2 marks per point to a maximum of	4
(d)	External auditor work Up to 1.5 marks per point to a maximum of	4 20

(a) **Extent of reliance on internal audit**

In general terms the extent to which the external auditor relies on the work performed by the internal auditor depends on:

- Their **organisational status**
- The **scope** of the work they perform
- Their **technical competence**
- Whether the work is performed with **due professional care**

This applies to the three situations noted as follows:

Cyclical audit of internal controls

The extent of reliance will depend on whether the work is **properly planned, supervised, reviewed and documented**. It will also depend on the **scope** of the work performed. Work on controls relating to finance and information services will be of more relevance to the external auditor as they are likely to have a greater impact on the financial statements than operations or customer support.

The external auditors will wish to rely on the work done by the internal auditors regarding the information services' restructure. The amount of independent work which will need to be performed will depend on the results of the post-implementation review as this will provide evidence as to the success of the restructuring.

Structure review every four years

This information will be useful to the external auditor in his assessment of the overall **control environment**. The extent of reliance will depend largely on when the last review was performed. A review performed this year will be of more relevance than one carried out four years ago.

Review of risk management

ISA 315 requires the external auditor to obtain an understanding of the business risks faced by the company in order to assess their potential implications for the financial statements. The internal auditor's review of the **effectiveness of risk management** measures would be invaluable in obtaining this understanding. The extent to which this could be relied upon however would be affected by any constraints placed on the internal auditor in his ability to perform this work and express his conclusions. The external auditor would also need to consider whether management have acted on the recommendations and the way in which these actions have been evidenced.

(b) **Information required**

- Records detailing the qualifications and experience of internal audit staff.

- Procedure manuals setting out the organisation's quality control standards for internal audit and evidence that this is monitored and reviewed.

- For the cyclical audit of the operation of internal controls working papers showing:
    - That the work is adequately planned, executed and reviewed
    - The results of tests of controls particularly in respect of finance and information systems

- For the restructuring of the information services function:

    - Documentation showing the way in which the restructure was planned and the basis on which decisions were made

    - The results of the post-implementation review

    - Any documents relating to this function prior to the change (as part of the year would have been based on the old system)

- For the review of the structure of internal controls:

    - The most recent report produced to determine how up to date the information is.

- For the annual review of risk management measures working papers showing:

    - Planning of this work
    - Results of key tests performed (controls, substantive)
    - Key conclusions
    - Management responses

(c) **It may not be possible to rely on the work of internal audit in the following situations:**

- If severe restrictions are placed on internal audit by management such that they cannot act independently.

- If the scope of the work is such that it covers aspects of the business which are of little relevance to the external auditor.

- If internal audit does not have access to senior management and/or no action is taken as a result of internal audit recommendations.

- If the team members lack the technical competence to perform the work. This might include the lack of an appropriate qualification, lack of experience and training.

- If internal audit work is not conducted with due professional care ie it is not properly planned, reviewed and documented.

(d) **It will be necessary for the external auditor to perform his own work in the following circumstances:**

- Where balances are **material** to the financial statements. This is because the external auditor cannot delegate responsibility for the audit opinion. The external auditor needs sufficient appropriate evidence on which to form his opinion and auditor generated evidence is the most reliable.

- In areas of **increased risk**. This will include areas where complex accounting treatments are involved or where judgement is required. In this instance inventory is likely to be a risk area, as well as being material. Leasing transactions may also be complex and will therefore require independent appraisal by the external auditor.

- Where the **objectives of the internal audit work differ** from those of the external auditor. The roles of the internal and external auditor are very different. In some instances whilst the internal auditor may have done some work on a particular area the approach taken may not be adequate for the purposes of expressing an opinion on truth and fairness. This is particularly the case where the internal audit department concentrates on operational aspects rather than matters which affect the financial statements.

14 Internal audit function

Text reference. Chapter 5

Top tips. It is very important in these short 10 mark question to stick to the time allocation. Don't be tempted to run over because you know lots about this topic. The key is to answer the requirements in the time you have available, and then move on to the next question.

Easy marks. These are in part (b) of the question. You should be aware of the different activities that internal audit will be involved in. You are required to produce a list so bullet points will be sufficient.

(a) **Role of internal audit**

Internal audit is an appraisal and monitoring function. It is established by directors for the **review of accounting and control systems**. It exists to provide assurance to the directors that systems are sufficient to achieve their aims and that they are operating effectively.

The role of internal audit is however, constantly expanding, particularly in the light of the importance placed on good corporate governance.

Government committees set up to investigate the issue of corporate governance have stated how an internal audit function can help directors achieve good corporate governance in their traditional role, and by assessing the **risk management** of the company.

(b) **Types of internal audit activities**

Internal auditors have routine functions, and can be involved in special projects as well.

Routine

- Reviews of systems (internal control, management, operational, accounting)
- Monitoring of systems against targets and making recommendations
- Value for money, best value, information technology or financial audits
- Operations audits (such as procurement, treasury or human resources)

- Monitoring or risk management

Special projects

Special investigations rely on situations arising within the business, but could encompass issues such as fraud detection.

15 Value for money audit

Text references. Chapters 5 and 10

Top tips. This is a question on weaknesses in the purchases system of a company, but from an internal audit point of view. Don't be put off by this – stay focussed and use the information in the scenario to generate your answer in part (b). A good way to set out your answer to part (b) (i) is by using a columnar format – this ensures that you link weaknesses to recommendations and gives more structure to your answer. Part (a) should be very straightforward for four marks. Part (c) is trickier because you need to think of other weaknesses that would be generated by a value for money audit so you need to apply your knowledge to this particular company.

Easy marks. In part (a), easy marks are available for explaining the purpose of the three Es in relation to a value for money audit.

ACCA examiner's answer. The examiner's answer to this question is included at the back of this Kit.

Marking scheme

		Marks
(a)	One mark per point	
	Explanation of	
	Value for money	1
	Economy	1
	Efficiency	1
	Effectiveness	1
	Maximum marks	**4**
(b)	Weaknesses two marks each. One for identifying the weakness and one for recommendation to overcome that weakness	
(i)	Transfer info – purchase requisition to order form	2
	Purchase requisition destroyed	2
	Order form no copy in ordering department	2
	No copy order form in goods inwards department	2
	GRNs filed in part number order	2
	Other relevant points (each)	2
	Maximum marks	**10**
(ii)	Chief buyer authorising all orders	2
	Individual items ordered	2
	Routing of GRN	2
	GRNs filed in part number order	2
	Lack of appropriate computer system	2
	Other relevant points (each)	2
	Maximum marks	**6**
	Total	**20**

(a)   The three 'Es' relate to economy, efficiency and effectiveness in value for money audits.

Economy relates to the attainment of the appropriate quantity and quality of physical, human and financial resources (inputs) at the lowest cost.

Efficiency is the relationship between goods or services produced (outputs) and the resources used to produce them. An efficient process would produce the maximum output for any given set of resource inputs, or would have minimum inputs for any given quantity and quality of product or service provided.

Effectiveness is concerned with how well an activity is achieving its policy objectives or other intended effects.

(b)   (i)

Internal control weakness	Recommendation
A clerk transfers information from the order requisition to an order form. This could result in errors in orders being made after the buyer has authorised the requisition.	The order form should be signed off as authorised to confirm that the details on the requisition match those on the order form.
The order requisition is thrown away once the chief buyer has authorised it. Any subsequent queries on orders cannot be checked back to the original requisition.	The order requisition form should be retained with the order form in case of query or dispute regarding items ordered.
No copy of the order form is retained by the ordering department. This means that goods could be ordered twice in error or deliberately. It also means that queries on deliveries cannot be chased up.	A three-part pre-numbered order form should be used and one copy should be retained by the ordering department with the requisition form.
The Goods Inward Department does not retain a copy of the Damaged Goods note. If the note is lost on the way to the ordering department, or there is a query, the Goods Inward Department has no record of goods returned.	Four copies of the Damaged Goods note should be retained. One copy could be retained by the Goods Inward Department, one sent to the ordering department, one to the department who requested the goods, so they are aware that there will be a delay and one to the supplier.
The Ordering Department does not keep a record of goods received, so is unable to check which orders are closed or to chase up suppliers.	The Ordering Department should match orders to GRNs and mark orders as closed once all goods have been received.
The Goods Inwards Department files GRNs in order of the supplier's goods reference. This could make it difficult to find a GRN at a later date if the department is not aware of the supplier's reference.	GRNs should be filed in date order, or by PO number.

(b)   (ii)

Additional weaknesses	Recommendations
There is no delegated level of authority for authorising order requisitions – the chief buyer has to authorise all requisitions.	A delegated level of authority should be introduced for the authorisation of order requisitions.
The ordering department receives many orders in the day and some of these are for duplicate items. Any volume discounts for ordering bulk items would therefore not be obtained.	Orders should be reviewed on a daily or weekly basis so that orders for the same item from different departments can be aggregated to take account of volume discounts.

Additional weaknesses	Recommendations
The structure of the department could be improved; there is just one buyer and five purchasing clerks. This could cause problems when the buyer is on holiday, sick or leaves permanently. It may indicate inefficiency.	The department's staffing structure should be reviewed with a view to training one of the purchasing clerks to fill the buyer's role in instances of holiday or sickness.
There is insufficient communication to the department that created the purchase requisition of how the order is progressing. They do not know that their order has been made and would not find out if the goods are delivered but have to be returned due to damages.	A tracking system should be developed for orders so that the department that made the requisition can check when their goods have been ordered, the expected delivery date and then find out about any problems with the delivery.

16 Question with analysis: Twinkletoes

Text references. Chapters 6, 7 and 9

Top tips. This question looks at the familiar topic of risk but rather than being asked to identify risks you are asked to consider risk classification. The key here is not to panic but to try to think through the issues. Notice for example that you are the internal not the external auditor. This means that you need to think about risk from management's perspective. This is particularly important in part (a) and (b). Also notice that the examiner tries to give you a clue in part (b) in the note. The examiner is trying to get you to think about the fact that not all the receivables within the same category will be as risky as others. Even in a generally high risk category those balances that have no history of non-payment will be less risky. What makes this category risky or not? What is the impact of this category on receivables overall? Are all the balances within a category the same or do some have characteristics which either increase or decrease the risk? These are the types of question which you should be asking.

Easy marks. These are available in part (c) of the question where you are asked to recommend internal controls. You should be familiar with the basic examples eg credit checks, credit limits etc but make sure that you try to adapt these according to the nature of the balance. For example major accounts are likely to be managed in a different way to smaller accounts.

Examiner's comments. Most candidates demonstrated appropriate knowledge although a minority focused on the audit of receivables.

In part (a) errors included discussing audit risk and the risk model. This was not required as the question was focusing on risks within the business. No marks were awarded for these points.

In part (b) common errors included not explaining the choice of risk category and inappropriate classification. This was particularly apparent in relation to overseas receivables. In spite of the fact that they were paying in advance many candidates still classified them as high risk purely based on the fact that they were overseas.

In part (c) most candidates appreciated the need to split their answer into sections. However in spite of this, there was a lack of discrimination between the controls which would be applied to each of the different categories with the same controls being repeated several times over. Higher marks were scored where candidates thought about the nature of the different debts, suggested appropriate controls and described why these controls were necessary.

Common errors in part (c) included confusing control risk with internal controls and therefore documenting audit tests and listing controls over the whole of the sales system rather than confining their answer to the receivables ledger.

		Marks
(a)	Risk classification Up to 1 mark per point to a maximum of	4
(b)	Classification of risks for receivables Up to 2 marks per point for each category to a maximum of	8
(c)	Internal controls Up to 1 mark per point to a maximum of	8 20

(a) Risk classification

- Risk classification helps management run the business because it is part of the overall process of identifying and assessing risks. Risk can exist on an individual department level or on a strategic level and will potentially affect all aspects of the business. As such it is an essential part of business management.

- Risk must be managed by the company. The company will aim to identify risk, determine a policy and implement a strategy. The classification of risk will be a key factor in deciding the best policy and how to implement the strategy.

- Risk classification enables effective use of resources. Resources can be directed towards dealing with high and medium risk problems so that the benefits are maximised.

- Risk classification assists management in adopting the right response to risk. For example a low risk might be accepted. A high or medium risk should be reduced (eg by instituting a system of internal control as protection) or transferred (eg by taking out insurance).

(b) Risks relating to trade receivables

(i) *Small retail shops*

This group of balances collectively is significant as it represents one third of the total value of receivables. Risk is also affected by the increase in the insolvency rate of small shoe shops. However accounts that are overdue are medium risk (as opposed to high risk) as individual balances will not have a material impact on receivables overall as the amounts involved are comparatively small. Balances which are not overdue are low risk.

(ii) *Large retail shoe shops*

The overseas accounts are low risk as they pay for goods in advance although the fact that this business is being lost may represent a different type of risk to the business in future. Large overdue accounts are likely to be assessed as high to medium risk depending on the proportion which are overdue. This category in total accounts for approximately 22% of receivables. If the majority of these were overdue the risk would be high. If, as is more likely, fewer of these are overdue the risk is medium. The accounts which are not overdue are low risk.

(iii) *Chains of discount shoe shops*

The large overdue accounts will be medium/low risk. The risk is reduced from high/medium to medium/low in spite of the size of the accounts due to the fact that the shops are well established high street chains. Whilst they may take a little 'unofficial' credit it is unlikely that they will be unable to pay.

(iv) *Mail order companies*

Existing accounts will be low risk as there has been no history of bad debts in this category. The new accounts will be assessed as medium risk. New accounts would normally be assessed as high risk particularly where there are a large number of them as there are in this case. However as this category has not experienced any problems in the past the overall risk can be reduced to medium.

(c) **Internal controls**

All customers

- Credit checks and references should be obtained for all new customers before credit is given.

- Where new customers place large orders before a credit history has been established payment should be in advance or on delivery.

- Credit limits should be set for all customers. These should be regularly reviewed to ensure that sales are not being made to customers who have already exceeded their credit limit.

- Standard credit terms should be applied eg 30 days for local customers and 45 days for overseas customers. Any extension to these standard terms should be authorised in advance.

Slow paying customers

- Credit controllers should be specifically assigned the task of chasing these debts on a regular basis.

- Where customers consistently fail to pay and balances are significantly overdue no further credit sales should be made to the account in question.

Larger accounts

- These should be allocated an account manager who would not only be responsible for securing the sale but also for ensuring that payment is received on a reasonable basis.

Overseas customers

- Controls will be required as the company is due to offer overseas customers credit terms. (Currently they pay up front.)

- Payment terms should reflect the practical difficulties of transferring funds eg terms could be extended.

- Controls should be in place to minimise the exposure of Twinkletoes to exchange rate differences eg payment in the local currency of Twinkletoes.

17 Rock

Text references. Chapters 6 and 7

Top tips.

On reading the requirements you should have spotted that both parts of this question were essentially asking you to demonstrate your knowledge of audit planning and documentation.

There is very little in the way of a scenario but you should make an effort to refer in some way to the details given rather than just reproducing a list of general points.

The wording of requirement (a) should be broken down to identify the different points you were being asked to make, ie

- Information
- Procedures
- Planning
- Risk assessment
- Determination of audit approach

Once you have done this it becomes much easier to see where you will find enough separate points to make in your answer.

Again in part (b) you should split out the requirements. To produce a good answer you would need to cover both the types of working papers and the features of working papers as described in the requirement.

Easy marks. In both parts (a) and (b) there were some easy marks available for listing out relevant points. In (a) it would have been easy to list standard pieces of information and procedures and in (b) to list types of working papers. In order to build on this you would need to make part (a) relevant to the details in the question and in (b) to explain the *features* of the working papers.

Examiner's comments.

Typical answers to part (a) provided six to eight points regarding planning procedures with the better answers linking these where possible to the information provided in the scenario. Common errors included:

- Providing detailed explanation of the audit risk model

- Explaining issues relevant to client acceptance. This was inappropriate because audit planning takes place after acceptance of the audit. Also the scenario clearly stated that the auditor had been involved in the audit for a number of years.

Pass standard answers to part (b) took on one of two formats. Firstly, describing about six or seven different working papers with details on how they would be completed. The second category of answer was a detailed list of working papers followed by a separate list of completion notes.

Common errors included:

- Explaining the purpose of the permanent file and current file rather than the different working papers that are found in these files.

- Listing all of the income statement and balance sheet areas and stating that working papers were available on those areas.

Marking scheme

		Marks
(a)	Information and procedures: understanding the entity and its environment and risk assessment for Rock Up to 1 mark per point to a maximum of	10
(b)	Types and features of audit working papers Up to 1 mark per point to a maximum of	10 20

(a) **Information and procedures at the planning stage in the audit of Rock**

  (i) The information that must be gathered at the planning stage will include:

   - Any problem areas identified in last year's audit file

   - The latest interim accounts of Rock

   - A current organisation chart

   - Details of key customers and suppliers

   - Relevant internal audit reports

   - Changes in regulations or accounting standards that may have an effect on the financial statements of Rock

- Information from external sources such as banks, analysts, rating agencies or from trade journals

- Performance measures prepared by management

(ii) Procedures to be carried out at the planning stage will include:

- A meeting with the management of Rock to discuss

    - Significant events during the year
    - Changes in systems
    - Any proposed changes in accounting policies
    - Their views on the current situation of the company

- A review of systems documentation held on file from prior years to identify whether it will need to be updated for any changes that have occurred.

- Inspection of business plans and strategies

(iii) In the light of the information gathered the auditor will perform preliminary analytical procedures to help identify any unexpected trends or changes that may indicate increased risk of error. Unusual movements in key figures (such as inventory and non-current assets for this manufacturing and distribution company) will need careful investigation during the audit as these would have a material effect on the profit of this business. Other specific risks may be attached to the recognition and valuation of brands.

(iv) The level of risk assessed may well vary between different areas of the financial statements and based on these assessments the auditor will determine the approach to be used in each area. The combination of tests of controls, substantive procedures, either tests of detail or analytical procedures, will vary according to the level of risk assessed and the auditor's judgement as to the most effective means of gathering sufficient evidence in each area.

(v) The initial assessment of risks along with the estimates of materiality and tolerable error will be used in establishing sample sizes.

(vi) The information gathered, the key results of the initial analytical procedures, along with the risk assessment and outline audit approach, should be documented so that the members of the audit team can commence their work properly briefed as to the key issues and the rationale for the procedures they are being asked to carry out.

(b) **Types of audit working papers**

(i) There are two main types of working papers, those that are carried forward from one audit to the next, on the **permanent file,** and those that relate purely to the current period's audit, kept in the **current file.**

The permanent file will normally contain:

- Prior year audited financial statements
- Systems documentation
- Engagement letter
- Memorandum and Articles of Association
- Key legal documents, such as leases
- Loan agreements
- Regulatory documentation in respect of the Stock Exchange listing

The current file will contain:

- Planning documentation

- Current year audited financial statements referenced to a trial balance

- Lead schedules linking the amounts in the financial statements to the detailed working paper documenting the related procedures

- Working papers showing the procedures performed, the results obtained and conclusions drawn
- Papers showing the calculation of sample sizes
- Schedules of unadjusted differences
- Schedules of review queries
- Completion checklists
- Disclosure checklists
- Draft report to management
- Management representation letter

(ii) *Features of working papers*

The features that will show that the working papers have been properly completed are:

- All working papers should be dated and signed to show who has completed the work and when, and also signed and dated as evidence of review.
- Audit plans should be cross referenced to the working papers where the procedures have been carried out to enable the reviewer to see immediately if any procedures are still outstanding.
- All points on lists of review queries should have been signed off to show that the matters raised have been resolved.
- There should be clear cross referencing between:
    - The audited financial statements
    - The trial balance
    - The audit plan
    - The lead schedules, and
    - The detailed working papers

    so that the reviewer can follow either from the financial statements to the work done or *vice versa*.

- The list of unadjusted differences should be cross referenced to detailed working papers

18 Tempest

Text references. Chapters 6 and 7

Top tips. When a case study question includes both narrative and numerical information, you must take time to read all of the information several times to identify all the points that you can develop in your answer. While you should not get too bogged down in number crunching, a little bit of basic ratio analysis here, eg profit margins and days sales in receivables will give you some more practical points to raise in your audit strategy.

If you need to do detailed calculations, such as the ones for materiality in this answer, it is a good idea to put them into an appendix.

Easy marks. The only genuinely easy marks here were in part (a) where sound knowledge of ISA 300 could give you full marks.

Examiner's comments. Part (a) was answered well although there was a tendency for some students to provide answers that were far too detailed for the marks available. In part (b), where a risk was identified, not all students succeeded in explaining why the risk was important. Some answers to part (b) did not take into account the scenario, ie the type of company and its business.

Marking scheme

		Marks
(a)	**ISA 300 – Planning**	1
	Audit work performed in an effective manner	1
	General approach and strategy for audit	1
	Attention to critical areas	1
	Amount of work	1
	Discussion with audit committee	1
	Basis to produce audit program	1
	Other relevant points	1
	Maximum marks	5
(b)	**List of tests at 1 mark per relevant point**	
	Audit strategy	
	Type of audit	1
	ISAs to be used	1
	Overview of Tempest	1
	Key dates for audit	1
	Overview of approach	
	Industry details	1
	Fall in GP%	1
	Materiality	
	How determine	1
	Risk areas (state with reason for risk)	
	COS	1
	Inventory	1
	Trade receivables	1
	Non-current assets	1
	Long term liabilities	1
	Audit approach	
	Compliance testing	1
	New inventory system – transfer of balances	1
	New inventory system – test end of year balances	1
	New inventory system – test during year	1
	Other risk areas	
	Information on going concern	1
	Related party transactions	1
	Inventory count assistance	1
	Any other general points 0.5 mark	
	Maximum marks	15

(a)   Audit planning is important for the following reasons:

- It ensures that appropriate attention is devoted to important areas of the audit. For example, materiality will be assessed at the planning stage and this will mean that when the detailed audit plan is drawn up, more procedures will be directed towards the most significant figures in the financial statements.

- Planning should mean that potential problems are identified and resolved on a timely basis. This could be in the sense of identifying financial statement risks at an early stage, so allowing plenty of time to gather sufficient relevant evidence. It could also relate to identifying practical problems relating to the gathering of evidence and resolving those through actions such as involving other experts being built into the detailed audit plan.

- Planning helps ensure that the audit is organised and managed in an effective and efficient manner. This could relate to, for example, ascertaining from the client when particular pieces of information will be available so that the timings of the audit are organised so as to minimise waste of staff time and costs.

- Planning assists in the proper assignment of work to engagement team members. Once the main risk areas have been identified at the planning stage, the engagement partner can then make sure that staff with suitable experience and knowledge are allocated to the engagement team.

- Planning facilitates direction, supervision and review of the work done by team members. Once procedures have been designed and allocated to members of the team, it is easier for the manager and partner to decide when work should be completed and ready for review. It will also make it easier for them to assess during the audit whether work is going according to the original plan and budget.

(b) **Audit Strategy**

Client: Tempest Ltd
Year-end: 31 December 20X7
Prepared by: A. Manager

Scope of audit

Tempest is subject to a normal statutory audit. It cannot take advantage of any reporting or audit exemptions.

The financial statements are prepared under IFRS.

The audit will be carried out under International Standards on Auditing.

Tempest trades in fittings for ships and stores its inventory at ten different locations. As in previous years, we have carried out year-end procedures at the three locations with the most significant inventory balances plus three others on a rotational basis, using staff from our most conveniently located offices. This year, due to the change in accounting systems we will carry out year-end procedures at all of the locations.

> **Tutorial note.** In a genuine audit strategy, the specific locations and relevant offices would be detailed but there is not enough information in the question to allow this.

Timings

> **Tutorial note.** Again in a genuine audit strategy, the specific dates would be listed out here but there is not enough information in the question to allow this.

- Interim audit
- Final audit
- Audit staff planning/briefing meetings
- Meeting with directors (or audit committee, if one exists)
- Approval of financial statements by the board
- Issue of audit report

Materiality

Preliminary calculations of materiality based on the forecast financial statements are set out in Appendix 1. The materiality levels will need to be reassessed when the actual financial statements for the year ended 31 December 20X7 are available.

Materiality for income statement items should be set in the region of $40,000 (being at the upper end of the range based on profit before tax).

Materiality for balance sheet items should be set in the region of $75,000, based on total assets.

Materiality levels are generally lower than those for the prior year, which will increase sample sizes for procedures; this is appropriate in light of the indications that there may an increased risk of error this year.

Higher risk areas

(1) **Inventory**

The forecast year end inventory figure is significantly lower than in the prior year. Coupled with the mid-year change in the accounting system for inventory there is a risk of material error in inventory quantities or valuation.

(2) **Sales**

Sales are forecast to have increased by 12% over the prior year. Compared to the average year on year growth of only 7% for the industry in general there is a risk that sales may be overstated.

(3) **Profit**

Gross profit margin has fallen to 17.3% (20X6 21.9%) and net profit margin has fallen to 0.9% (20X6 4.1%). This could indicate errors in cut off or allocation or that the company has been cutting prices in order to win market share and has let profitability suffer. Although there is no specific indication of immediate going concern difficulties, this strategy may not be sustainable in the longer term.

(4) **Receivables**

Days' sales in receivables are forecast to have increased to 47 days (36 days in 20X6). This may indicate problems with the recoverability of the receivables and a risk that impairments in value of the receivables' balances are not recognised.

(5) **Non-current assets**

There is a decrease in this balance of $900,000. This is far in excess of what could be explained by depreciation of assets that comprise mainly properties. It may be that there have been disposals in the year. This raises the possibility of incorrect accounting or inadequate disclosures.

Also in relation to the non-current assets, if the inventory balance has genuinely decreased to approximately 15% of its previous level, some of the storage locations may be redundant. It could be that the reduction relates to impairment write-downs and it could be the case that further write-downs are needed.

(6) **Related party transactions**

Given the information that one of the directors purchased a yacht during the year it may be that he has purchased fittings from Tempest Ltd. There is a risk that any related party transactions have not been fully disclosed.

Audit approach

> **Tutorial note.** Again it is impossible to be very precise here given the limited information in the question.

Where possible evidence should be obtained from tests of control so that detailed substantive procedures can be reduced.

Special emphasis will be needed in respect of inventory accounting. Procedures will include:

- Obtaining an understanding of how the transfer of balances to the new system was carried out. Direct testing of balances from the old to new systems may be needed as well as reviewing evidence of control procedures carried out by the client at the point of changeover.

- A sample of sales and purchase transactions should be traced through the new system to check whether additions to and deletions from inventory are being made correctly.

- Test counts of inventory at the various locations should be performed at the year-end and agreed to the inventory records as at that date.

Testing of items in the income statement will need to include:

- Consideration of the revenue recognition policies being used
- Cut-off testing on sales and costs of sales
- Comparison of expense classifications from year to year

The review of events after the balance sheet date should focus on:

- Any substantial adjustments to the inventory figure
- Evidence of recoverability of receivable balances
- Any information suggesting further reductions in profitability of the business
- Management accounts and cash flow projections for the post year end period

19 Bridgford Products

Text references. Chapters 6, 7 and 9

Top tips. You need to read part (b) of this question carefully as the examiner wants you to focus on the problems highlighted in the question; a general essay on planning procedures is not required. If you were unsure, you should have realised when planning your answer that there was sufficient information given for you only to have time to discuss the points mentioned.

Easy marks. These are available in part (a). You must be able to explain the basic importance of planning an audit.

(a) Auditors should plan their work for the following reasons.

(i) The **objectives** of the audit are **set**. For a company this is producing an audit report in accordance with legislation and ISA 700, but there may be other regulatory requirements involved, for example if the client is a financial services company.

(ii) Attention is **devoted** towards the **key audit areas**. These will be areas which are **large** in **materiality** terms, where there is significant risk of material misstatement, or which have had **significant problems** in previous years.

(iii) **Staff** are **briefed**. The audit strategy should provide enough detail about the client to enable staff to carry out the detailed work effectively. Budgets should ensure that appropriate time is spent on each audit area.

(iv) The **efficiency** of the **audit process** should be **enhanced**. Good planning should ensure that the **right staff** are **selected**, that **information technology** is used **appropriately,** and that maximum use is made of schedules prepared by the client and of the work of **internal audit**.

(v) The **timing** of the audit is **appropriate**. Staff will need to be available to carry out an inventory count and circularisation of receivables at the year-end. If use is to be made of work done by the client or internal audit, then this work will need to have been completed in time for the final audit. The timing should also allow sufficient time for the audit to be completed so that the financial statements can be signed on the date desired by the client.

(vi) **Review** is **facilitated**. Setting out an audit plan and budgets at the planning stage means that the reviewer has measures against which the work can be examined at the end of the assignment.

(b) (i) **Management accounts revenue and profit**

Assuming the level of sales is maintained until January, revenue for the year will be $156 million, which is a 42% increase on last year. However on the same assumptions profit will be $4.8 million, a decrease of 40%. The auditors will need to determine the reasons for the differences, in particular:

(1) **Erosion** of the **gross profit margin** because of decreased selling prices or problems with purchases (discussed below).

(2) **Increased bad debt allowance** or **contingency provision** (discussed below).

(ii) *Computerised inventory control system*

(1) The **reliability** of the new computerised inventory system will have to be **tested**. The auditors will have to check whether the system is in accordance with the **needs** of the **client**, the **staff** properly **trained, proper documentation provided** and **inventory quantities transferred correctly**. The auditors, using **computer-assisted audit techniques,** will need to check that the system adequately identifies and ages inventory.

(2) The auditors will also need to assess the **reliability** of the **inventory count procedures**. This will mean ascertaining **how often inventory** is **counted** and the procedures for **correcting differences** found between actual counted inventory and inventory recorded on the computer. The auditors would need to arrange to **attend** one or more of the **inventory counts** to check whether the laid-down procedures are being followed. They should check the **reasons** for the **differences** found on other inventory counts, because if the differences are large, this will indicate the computer records and/or inventory count procedures are inadequate.

(3) Ideally the work on the computer system and perpetual inventories procedures should be carried out before the year-end, in case problems with the system warrant the auditors asking for a **full inventory count** to be done at the year-end.

(iii) *Reliability problems*

(1) The auditors would need to check that **appropriate allowance** had been made against the balances outstanding on these customers' accounts by reviewing correspondence and any payments made since the year-end.

(2) There may be **claims** over and above the amounts owed. The auditors would need to check the likelihood of the claims being successful by examining correspondence with the customers and the company's lawyers, and discussions with the directors and lawyers. The company may also be in difficulties with the trading standards authorities.

(3) The problems with reliability may mean that some **existing inventories** has to be **written down.** The auditors will need to check what the company has done about the reliability problems, and the allowance that need to be made against year-end inventories to reduce it to net realisable value, and for credit notes.

(4) The problems over reliability may lead to **further bad debts** and **claims** of which the client and auditors are not yet aware. The auditors should also consider whether the legal consequences and bad publicity might impact so seriously as to call into question the company's ability to continue as a **going concern.**

(iv) *Sales increase*

(1) The concern here is that the new customers to whom credit has been granted are **poor credit risks.** The client does not have the assurance of previous settlement records that it has with existing customers. The more attractive terms may attract new customers who are having difficulty paying their current suppliers within the agreed credit period.

(2)   The volume of new customers may mean that **credit granting** and **credit control procedures** have been **less strict** than in previous years. This may be evidenced by the increase in the age of receivables from 1.6 to 4.1 (and the increase in actual period over allowed period from 0.6 to 1.1 months).

(3)   The increased age may mean that the client and auditors have **difficulty** in **identifying doubtful debts** until some months after the debt arises.

(4)   The failure to receive cash may mean that the client is suffering **cash flow problems.** The auditors will need to check that the increases in settlement times have been incorporated into cash flow forecasts.

(v)   *Management changes*

(1)   The auditors need to **ascertain** the **reasons** for the dismissal. They need to confirm whether the dismissal was for **fraud**. If it was, the auditors will need to assess whether the company has identified the true **extent** of the fraud, what the **monetary loss** was and whether **other staff** were involved. Extensive substantive work will be needed on the areas affected.

(2)   The financial director and purchases manager may be pursuing a claim for **unfair dismissal**; if so, disclosure or a provision may be required.

(3)   The absence of the finance director may mean that certain **controls**, for example that all significant transactions have to be approved, have **lapsed**. The auditors would also need to assess the **qualifications** and **reliability** of the chief accountant, because these factors will impact upon whether the accounts will be prepared in time, and the likelihood of problems with them. The auditors may have to allow for spending significant time on checking the adequacy of accounting records. They may also have to spend more time overall on the audit than in previous years, as the client may be less able to assist because of its staff problems.

(4)   The effect of the **absence** of the **purchasing manager** needs to be considered. Again controls may have lapsed, and this may have increased the risks of **other frauds** in the areas of inventory or purchases. Also there may be problems of **over-valuation of inventory**, caused by purchase of the wrong inventory or purchase of inventory at excessive prices. The auditors would also need to assess whether the **new** purchasing **manager** appears to be **operating effectively.**

20 Question with student answer: Parker

Text references. Chapters 6 and 7

Top tips. Read the scenario carefully. Think carefully about the context. Going concern involves auditing future projections, not past transactions.

Easy marks. Part (a) is fairly straightforward and the mark allocation gives a clue as to the level of detail required – a basic definition of *"audit risk"* cannot be worth four marks on its own. You need to add an explanation of the three component parts of audit risk.

In part (b)(i) a careful reading of the scenario should give you some ideas about issues to mention in your answer. It is not enough simply to restate phrases from the question; you need to clarify *why* you think they will give rise to risks.

You should have learned about the main procedures an auditor would follow to review the directors' assessment of the going concern status of a company. This would give a good foundation to your answer to part (b) (ii) but you should try to make it detailed and relevant to the question.

Student answer. Two student answers for this question are included. The first is an example of a good pass standard answer, whilst the second is a clear fail.

In the first student answer, part (a) is answered very well, beginning with an excellent overall definition of audit risk. It then goes on to the components of audit risk, however the answer should have included a definition of detection risk. In the second student answer, the student clearly has no idea what audit risk is and would probably have scored no marks for this part of the question.

In part (b) (i), the first student answer clearly identifies the matters – using them as sub-headings for the answer – and then going on to explain them in detail. The second student answer is far too brief to score enough marks to pass this part of the question.

In part (b) (ii), although the first student answer correctly identifies enquiries to make, the answer would have been better structured by splitting it into audit procedures and enquiries. In the second answer, the student wastes time by writing about going concern factors and then making suggestions of procedures that would have been done at planning or audit fieldwork stages.

Examiner's comments. Part (a) was answered very well.

In part (b) most candidates showed appropriate application of knowledge to the scenario, identifying the risks and explaining the effect of those risks. Some candidates split the answer into three sections of *inherent, control* and *detection* risks but marks were awarded for relevant points whether or not this split was made. A minority of candidates simply identified the risk areas but did not explain the relevance of the point being made.

Part (b) (ii) allowed candidates to show their knowledge of going concern reviews but the focus of answers should be on Parker so issues such as possible lack of forecasts, (lack of director control) could be mentioned. Some answers emphasised the audit of the balance sheet but not the audit work going forward into the future; these answers were not adequate.

Marking scheme

			Marks
(a)	**One mark each explaining the following. Allow 0.5 where explanation incomplete**		
	Audit risk		1
	Inherent risk		1
	Control risk		1
	Detection risk		<u>1</u>
	Maximum marks		<u>4</u>

(b)   (i)   **1 mark per point**

        Overtrading (expanding rapidly turnover, new product lines, cash reserves, credits/liquidation)

        Internet trading (different products, naïve directors, new systems, higher returns, inventory obsolescence)

        Control environment (overall weak, extent of errors not known, directors attitude, lack of skill Fin accountant, material error FS)

        Bank loan (additional finance, audit disclaimer, liquidation)

        First year of audit (audit report expectations, unreliable accounting systems, time needed – resist director pressure)

        Maximum marks   <u>10</u>

(ii)	**Key points 1 for each point**	**Marks**
	Financial position of company – budgets etc	2
	Bank letter	1
	Bank correspondence	1
	Enquiries with directors	2
	Management accounts	1
	Letter of representation	1
	Final decision going concern	1
	Board minutes – review after year enc	1
	Other good relevant points	1
	Maximum marks	**6**
	Total	**20**

Student answer

> This is an excellent pass standard answer.

1 (a) Audit risk is the risk that the auditor will give the wrong audit opinion ie issue an unqualified audit report when a qualified audit report should have been issued and vice versa.

Good introduction to audit risk.

The audit risk of a company should always aim to be low. Audit risk is determined by a number of factors given by the below formula.

Nice, short paragraphs and spacing used.

$$\text{Audit risk} = \text{inherent risk} \times \text{control risk} \times \text{detection risk}$$

The inherent risk of a company is the risk due to the nature of the business. These include the integrity of the directors and if the business is cash based.

Should also have mentioned detention risk here.

Control risk is the risk that internal controls will not prevent or detect errors and frauds within the business.

If both inherent risk and control risk, then in order for the audit risk to be low, detection risk must also be low. That is, the risk that an error or fraud wont be identified through the audit procedures of the auditor.

(b) Parker is a new client

Notice that matters are used as sub-headings with explanation below.

Because Parker is a new client, the auditor has no accumulated knowledge or experience of the audit client. This means that they know very little about their internal controls, the way the business is run, the integrity of the managers and directors and no basis to make their opinion on.

All of these factors will increase the audit risk of the client. As with any new audit client, additional work is required to be done in the first year of audit to limit audit risk.

Tight reporting deadline

A tight reporting deadline (less than 3 months after the year end) will also increase audit risk in two ways.

The first being the lack of post balance sheet information. Past balance sheet information is important as its occurrence or non-occurrence of events can confirm items in the financial statements.

Another way is that it may not give the audit company enough time to carry out appropriate procedures in order to be confident in their audit evidence.

Occurrence of errors

The occurrence of errors recently, and the reliance on manual input of orders indicates a lack of internal controls within the system.

Given this, control risk would be high and therefore increasing audit risk.

The fact that the individual errors are minor, does not mean that the overall error is not material.

Good
presentation
throughout.

Employment of the company accountant

There are several issues regarding the company accountant that increase the audit risk of the client.

He is not qualified which may mean that he does not have appropriate knowledge and experience of preparation of financial statements. He may not be aware of accounting regulations and how to deal with certain matters. This may mean that the accounts have not been prepared properly.

A second area for concern is that he is a personal friend of the director. This reduces his independence and objectivity. This will increase the chance that he would overlook any untoward dealings occurring through the business to remain friends with the director.

This point could
have been
expanded
further.

Internet based business

Internet based businesses are inherently risky due to their nature. This alone will increase the audit risk.

(i)   Going concern appears to be a significant area in the case of Parker Limited, particularly since post year end information is only available for a maximum of 3 months.

It is stated that turnover is growing at a rate of 20% per annum. Previous increases in turnover should be examined to see if this is the case. It should also be examined as to whether this is sustainable ie if growing at this rate in the past has the company managed to cope.

Given that a bank loan of £30m is needed, it suggests that the company is suffering from cash flow problems which are a strong indication that the company may not be able to continue as a going concern.

An enquiry should be made as to when this loan will be received. Estimated interest cover could be calculated to see whether the loan could be sustained.

is part of the question
uld have been better
swered by splitting the
swer into 'Enquiries'
d 'Audit procedures'.

An enquiry should be made into the future plans for expansion, although it does not appear that there are any. If expansion is not properly planned then the business may end up not having enough funds to continue trading.

Student answer

> This answer is a clear fail.

1   (a)   *Audit risk*

> This is not the correct explanation of audit risk and would have scored zero or very low marks.

(i)   Audit risks are areas that could compromise the audit procedures and results.

Vulnerable areas such as heavy reliance on one person to process all the paperwork.

Understanding the lack of knowledge and understanding of the business could pose a large audit risk.

Planning a successful audit is a planned audit with a sound structure.

Responsibilities placing reliance on a person who has little or no knowledge of the company would pose an audit risk.

A risk to a combined audit may come about if the client has influence or a relationship with the auditor or their team, however it is recommended that no more than 15% of a audit firms business is supported by anyone client.

(b)   (i)   *Accounting system*

> Although the points made here are valid, they are not sufficient to pass this part of the question.

In order to place reliance on the accounting system it needs to be reliable and accurate.

The evidence proves this not to be the case as errors have been found. Efficient with the volume of transactions to be handled it would be more appropriate to phase out the manual element and try to bring in computerisation.

The fact that the company accountant has been appointed through a personal relationship causes concern on the independent workings within their role. Training could be implemented to rectify the lack of appropriate qualifications.

(ii)   Value and diversity the amount of product to be treated would cause a risk to the business. Mis-appropriation of stock would be extremely easy as the business appears not to have an adequate stock procedures in place.

> These points are not relevant to the question asked.

(iii)   Turnover given the growth of 20% per annum the question of net profit remaining static would cause concern as there appears to be inefficiencies and waste occurring.

(iv)   Expansion plans the rapid growth of Parker Ltd and the level of increase in net profit together with bank borrowings indicates over trading by the company. When the evidence proves otherwise then an unqualified audit might not be available.

(v)   The directors are bringing pressure on the auditors by saying they expect an unqualified audit report which might cause concern on the fairness of the audit, and whether the commission should be taken on.

(b)   (ii)   *Accounts*

> These are procedures done at planning and fieldwork stages!

Procedures: Systems would be examined to ascertain the accuracy of recording information. Test samples of records to include purchases and sales invoicing procedures.

Bank reconciliation procedures would be examined for their accuracy.

Payment procedures and examining split role functions to incorporate more than one person in the paying or banking procedures.

Stock control reviewing the validity of stock control and the actual storage and physical viewing of the stock. Whether on site or by the suppliers stock control ??.

This is relevant but again, insufficient to pass this part of the question.

Financial

Reviewing loan facilities and security held by the bank. Looking at rates analysis such as R.O.C.E. current ratios and stock ratios.

Reviewing turnover and why there has been an increase in net profit.

BPP answer

(a) The term "audit risk" literally means the risk that the auditor will give an incorrect opinion. The concern for the auditor is that he/she may issue an unmodified opinion in circumstances where there are material misstatements in the financial statements.

It can be analysed into three separate components:

(i) **Inherent risk**

This arises from factors specific to the business or its operating environment and which make errors more likely to occur. It could result from complex transactions, such as leases, or from pressures on management to achieve particular targets.

(ii) **Control risk**

This is the risk that the audit client's internal control does not prevent errors occurring or detect them after the event so that they may be corrected. This could be due to failures in the control environment, such as management allowing a culture of carelessness towards control procedures to develop or to failures of specific control procedures, for example, a lack of proper reconciliation of payables ledger balances to supplier statements could allow misstatements in trade payables to go undetected.

(iii) **Detection risk**

This is the risk that the auditor's substantive procedures do not detect material errors that exist. One component of this is sampling risk. Many audit procedures are performed using samples so introducing the possibility that whilst the sample may have been free from errors, there could be material misstatements elsewhere in the population.

There are a variety of other reasons why the auditor may fail to detect errors. These include lack of experience and time pressure.

(b) (i)

Matters		Audit risks associated with Parker Ltd
(1)	The company sells books, CDs, DVDs and similar items	These goods are subject to fashions and trends, and this is a very competitive business where undercutting of sales prices is common. As a result, inventory values could be overstated if some lines cannot be sold or have to be sold at substantially discounted prices.
(2)	Parker is a new audit client	This increases the detection risk for the auditor, as the firm has no previous experience of the company. This makes it harder to establish which areas of Parker's accounting systems are most susceptible to errors and also means that less reliance can be placed on analytical procedures.

Matters	Audit risks associated with Parker Ltd
(3) Online ordering over the internet	This may increase the control risk as the ordering and sales system is reliant on the security and procedures of not only Parker itself but also its counter parties and service provider etc.
(4) Expanding the range of goods	The proposed new products are also subject to fashions and trends so may increase the risk of incorrect inventory valuation. It may also be the case that the directors are moving into areas of business where they have less experience so the problems may be increased by poor buying decisions. If the expansion is unsuccessful, the company's going concern status may be threatened.
(5) Mail order accounting system	The high level of manual input appears to introduce many errors into the records. This could lead to errors in sales and receivables in the financial statements. The related invoicing errors may destroy customer goodwill and in the longer term may add to the threats to the company's going concern status.
(6) Directors' attitude to internal control	The directors appear to disregard the importance of internal control, meaning that no efforts are being made to detect and correct the errors mentioned above.
(7) Unqualified company accountant	The accountant seems to have been appointed solely because he is a friend of the directors rather than for his skill and experience. Also, as he is not a member of a reputable professional body, he is under no ethical obligations if he does have any doubts about the integrity of management.
(8) Requirement for high level of borrowing	There must be doubts over whether a business which is suffering so much pressure on its margins and is moving into new areas of activity is going to be able to generate sufficient profit to repay its loans. This will also raise the question of whether the company can continue as a going concern.
(9) Meeting with bank after the year end	The directors will want to present a healthy set of financial statements to the bank manager so there will be a risk that figures may have been manipulated. There will be an increased risk of error throughout the financial statements, particularly in areas that are at all subjective.
(10) Directors expect an unqualified audit report to be signed before the meeting with the bank	This increases detection risk as the auditor is under time pressure and also will lack evidence of events after the balance sheet date. If the new loan is essential to the company's going concern status it may be difficult for the auditor to reach an opinion before the completion of the loan negotiations.

(b)   (ii)   **Enquiries**

    (i)   Enquire about management's views on the prospects for profitability of the planned new lines of business.

    (ii)   Enquire into any planned cost cutting to improve the company's profit margins.

    (iii)   Enquire into whether there have been any problems with the operation of the online ordering system.

Procedures

    (i)   Obtain management's forecasts and projections and:

        –   Assess reasonableness of assumptions (for example, compare projected margins with those achieved by similar businesses)

        –   Review projections to verify that they have been based on these assumptions

        –   Review projections to check that all the information is consistent. For example, as the directors are planning to increase the inventory levels, check that allowance has been made for related increases in inventory holding costs.

        –   Calculate ratios, eg receivables days, to check reasonableness

    (ii)   Review loan agreements for terms and conditions of existing borrowings and consider whether it appears likely that interest and capital payments can be met.

    (iii)   Review minutes of board and committee meetings to assess management's views of the proposed new lines of business.

    (iv)   Review correspondence with bank for any indications of the current relationship between Parker and its bankers and the likelihood of the bank providing more finance

    (v)   These reviews should all be continued in the period after the balance sheet date right up to the date of the auditor's report.

    (vi)   Obtain written representations from management acknowledging their responsibility for:

        –   Assessing the going concern status of the company
        –   Making reasonable assumptions in preparing forecasts and projections
        –   Deciding on the appropriate basis of preparation of the financial statements

21 Stone Holidays

Text references. Chapters 5 and 7

Top tips. Read all parts of the requirements carefully. Requirements (a) and (b) are essentially rote-learning points while (c) involves application of your knowledge to a scenario.

Try to identify the relevant technical areas being tested in (a) and (b). It is important here to spot that in (a) the focus is on internal auditors and in (b) on external auditors. In (a) you should be thinking about internal audit and corporate governance, while in (b) you need to demonstrate a good knowledge of ISA 240.

Notice that the mark allocation is the same for (a) and (b). When planning your answer you should jot down the two headings and make very brief notes about the points you are going to make under the two requirements. This should help you answer in appropriate depth in each, avoid repetition and distinguish properly between the two types of audit.

Your answers should be presented as a "list of sentences". That way you will give enough detail to meet the requirement to "explain" and also be able to see how many separate points you have made.

In (c) you need to read the requirement first then read through the scenario several times to identify the points that should trigger ideas about potential frauds and errors. Highlight those as you go through but also jot down briefly what the possible error or fraud involves as there is a danger that you could lose marks by merely stating facts from the question without adding any description of the nature of the risks.

Easy marks. Parts (a) and (b) largely involve straight recall of knowledge. Providing that you could remember some basic points here *and* expressed those in *sentences* it should be reasonably easy to find enough points to make in these two sections to get close to the total of 10 marks needed to pass the question as a whole.

Examiner's comments. In part (a) most candidates mentioned that internal auditors were a management control, and mentioned the role of internal audit in good corporate governance. Common errors included explaining the controls needed to prevent fraud and error such as segregation of duties and authorisation controls and implying that internal auditors established, checked, amended and reported on internal controls systems without identifying the self-review threat from the audit of controls established by internal audit.

In part (b) most candidates identified the reporting duty of external auditors and the issue of reporting only on material fraud and error. The main weakness was the amount of detail provided on audit testing itself while the question attempted to focus attention on the responsibilities, not the tests that would be done to carry out those responsibilities. Common errors included a significant minority of candidates stating that the auditor was responsible for detecting all fraud and error and suggesting that the auditor would not report immaterial fraud at all and that confidentiality precluded any external reporting.

In part (c) good answers identified specific areas of risk such as commissions payable and payments to the central fund. However, a significant number focused on general risks facing the organisation, not risks of fraud and error as was required by the question.

Marking scheme

		Marks
(a)	Internal audit function: risk of fraud and error Up to 1 mark per point to a maximum of	7
(b)	External auditors: fraud and error in an audit of financial statements Up to 1 mark per point to a maximum of	7
(c)	Nature of risks arising from fraud and error: Stone Holidays Up to 1 mark per point to a maximum of	6 — 20

Internal audit and the risk of fraud and error

(a) (i)   The management of an entity have the primary responsibility of preventing and detecting fraud and error. An internal audit function may assist them in this responsibility. This is encouraged under the Combined Code on Corporate Governance. The role of the internal audit function in respect of fraud and error will be decided by the entity's management but is likely to include some of the following:

- **Risk assessment** – the internal audit function may carry out risk assessments identifying the main risks of fraud and error or may review that process if it is carried out by management.

- **Control recommendations** – internal audit reports may recommend controls to address the risks of fraud and error identified by management.

- **Control procedures** – the internal audit function may be involved in carrying out certain control functions such as counting cash or inventories and comparing to book records. It may be management's objective to detect even low value frauds and misappropriations.

- **Monitoring controls** - the internal audit function may perform procedures to monitor whether the control procedures implemented by management are operating effectively. This could involve inspecting documents for evidence of appropriate authorisation or using test data to check the operation of computerised controls.

(ii) It would not be appropriate for the internal audit function to be involved in all of these areas in a particular entity, as they would effectively be checking their own work thus undermining their credibility.

(iii) The existence of an internal audit function within an entity is likely to act as a deterrent against fraud and error.

External audit and the risk of fraud and error

(b) (i) The ultimate responsibility of external auditors is to give an opinion on the **truth and fairness** of the financial statements. This means that the auditors give **reasonable assurance** that the financial statements are free from **material misstatement.** ISA 240 sets out the principles of how the external auditor should deal with the risk of fraud and error within the overall audit approach.

(ii) **Professional scepticism** – the auditor should maintain an attitude of professional scepticism during the audit, maintaining a questioning attitude and being alert to circumstances that may suggest that there is a risk of fraud or error.

(iii) **Discussion** – the members of the audit team should discuss the possibility of the entity's financial statements containing material misstatements resulting from fraud or error.

(iv) **Risk assessment** – when obtaining an understanding of the entity, the external auditor should consider any indications of frauds that may lead to material errors. This would involve both enquiries of management and analytical procedures.

(v) **Design of audit procedures** – this should address the assessed risk of fraud and error. This would involve increasing sample sizes where the risk is assessed as high and ISA 240 also recommends that the auditor should introduce an element of unpredictability into the nature and timing of audit procedures.

(vi) **Management representations** – the external auditor should obtain written representations from management

- Acknowledging their responsibility for internal control to prevent and detect fraud; and

- Confirming that they have disclosed to the auditor their own assessment of the risk of fraud and any knowledge of fraud or suspected fraud in the entity.

(vii) **Limitations** – It is not reasonable to expect external auditors to identify all instances of material misstatements especially where fraud is involved even when the audit is properly planned and performed in accordance with the ISAs. Where a fraud has been perpetrated, particularly if it is at management level, it is likely to be carefully concealed and collusion may be involved.

(viii) **Materiality in the opinion given to the shareholders** – As the external auditor's reporting responsibilities only relate to **material** misstatements, he/she cannot be expected to detect frauds and errors where the resulting misstatement is immaterial.

(ix) **Reporting** – Where the external auditor detects or suspects that a fraud has occurred, this should be reported to the appropriate level of management. In certain circumstances, for example in matters subject to legislation such as money laundering, the auditor may have to report to external bodies.

(c)   **Risks arising from fraud**

   (i)   Staff are paid on a **commission basis**. This may result in deliberate overstatement of sales figures as individuals try to inflate their own income.

   (ii)   The use of the networked reservations system introduces the risk that information may be lost or corrupted in transmission.

   (iii)   Errors may occur in the computerised accounting system if the controls within that system are not operating effectively. It may also be the case that certain employees have discovered how to circumvent the controls and are able to amend records perhaps to hide misappropriations of assets.

   (iv)   Some payments are received in **cash.** This introduces the risk that cash may be misappropriated and the records falsified to conceal this.

   (v)   The amount that the entity is required to pay in to the central compensation fund is based on the sales figure for the year. There may be management bias towards understating sales to reduce the amounts payable or delaying revenue recognition thus deferring the due date of the payment.

   (vi)   Customers may attempt to defraud Stone holidays by using stolen credit or debit cards.

22 Grindsbrook Clothing Company

Text references. Chapters 4, 6 and 7

Top tips. You may have read this question and been put off by part (b). We'll get to the ins and outs of part (b) soon, but, especially as this is a compulsory question, do not let it put you off from answering part (a) well. Part (a) is an extremely straightforward question and you should be able to score highly on it. You should approach this question by dealing with part (a) first, ensuring that you do not run over the allotted time on it, of course, and then worry about part (b).

Part (b) lists a series of risks that may be off-putting as they are not the types of risk (audit risk, inherent risk etc) that you are comfortable with. However, the question clearly states that you may use other headings, so if those terms put you off, ignore them, and use your common sense instead. As a trainee accountant, you should have sufficient business awareness to spot the sorts of issues which this business is faced with that will cause it problems. Brainstorm, prioritise, spot links between factors, construct an answer plan and then answer the question. Remember, the question is (i) to list the problems and (ii) to describe actions the company could take to remedy them. You are likely to find it helpful to adopt a two-column strategy in your answer to this question, but you don't have to.

Easy marks. Part (a) represents the easier marks in this question.

Examiner's comments. Many candidates lost marks by failing to appreciate that this question related to the internal not external auditor and therefore failing to deal with commercial issues. In part (b) it was important to show the ability to analyse the information provided.

Marking scheme

		Marks
(a)	Factors to be taken into account in deciding whether to accept the assignment Up to 1.5 marks per point to a maximum	6
(b)	Risks and actions to deal with them Up to 2 marks per point to a max of	14 20

(a)   **Factors in acceptance decision**

Ability factors

I have considerable experience in a comparable position and am therefore well-qualified to take on this role.

Ethical factors

Internal auditors are required to have '**personal objectivity**' to enable them to perform their duties properly.

While I would be **independent** of the organisation to the extent that I would not be employed by it, the fact that I am **closely connected** to the owners (the managing director's wife/major shareholder being my sister) suggests that personal objectivity might be an issue if I were to accept this engagement.

The fact that there are already **family disputes** over the way that the business is run adds to the fact that I would not be able to ensure my personal objectivity in the role as internal auditor. It is unclear whether my sister has an **executive position** at the company. If she does not, I might find that I am expected to become her voice in the management of the company.

My sister appears to consider **objectivity** an **important value** in an internal auditor, as she thinks **outside professional help** is needed. As a family member, I am **not able to provide the objectivity** she appears to want.

Practical issues

The other factors that will affect my decision are that I am already **very busy** with my existing clients, and I am a **sole practitioner**, so it will be impossible to share the responsibilities in relation to Grindsbrook Clothing Company (GCC) with another person.

It is also interesting to note that GCC does not appear to value consistency in its dealings with **professional advisers** and the external auditors have been changed several times. This indicates to me that GCC might not be a good client to have on my client list. I should also add that GCC have a record of **poor credit management** and of seeking to avoid additional costs, whatever the associated benefit. This would also affect my decision in relation to taking on their work. As the managers of the company are family, trying to collect **overdue** and **disputed fees** could become embarrassing.

(b)   **Risks facing the business**

External risks	Action
The key external risk facing the company is that there are a number of **new competitors** entering the market. As there are **no significant barriers to entry** in the market, this trend is likely to continue until the market is **saturated**.	
A saturated market is a very competitive one, and with an aversion to spending on marketing and no Internet presence (discussed below), GCC might find that it is **pushed out of the market** if it refuses to fight for its market share.	However, as GCC is an established company, if it **acts** in response to the new competition, it should be able to successfully fight and retain/extend market share. This '**fight back**' should include investing in an **Internet** presence, renovating the **catalogue** and possibly employing a marketing manager.

Operational risks	Action
GCC appears to suffer from a host of operational problems:	
It has **out of date systems**, which are likely to make processing slow, increase possibilities of errors or of controls being overridden and also are at risk from viruses. The company also has **no Internet presence**. While the family might believe in the catalogue system and the personal touch, other companies in the sector are likely to have Internet facilities and so not doing so makes GCC **uncompetitive**.	GCC should consider **investing in new software** to improve its processing of customer orders. It might be possible to combine such a system upgrade with the **introduction of an Internet presence** and **integrated email order processing** to make it as easy as possible for customers to make orders and to ensure that customers can receive their orders in the smallest possible amount of time.
The mail order **catalogue** which the company uses to market its collection appears to have had **little investment** and the company may have **very little control over the quality/content** of the publication as the production of it is outsourced. This is the prime source of company publicity, and GCC must ensure that it is of a high quality to encourage custom.	While it may still be appropriate to outsource the catalogue, the directors must ensure that they have **substantial input** into the catalogue and ensure that it is **updated** so that it does not become 'samey' and tired. If they were to employ a **marketing manager**, control of the catalogue and liasing with the service organisation could be delegated to them.
The company appears to have **poor controls**, for example, over **purchasing**, and over **credit management** and **receivables collection**. Good quality controls are important to prevent **error, fraud and slow operations**. Suppliers may withdraw credit if bills are not paid. Such inefficiencies will be **passed on to customers** who may choose to take future business elsewhere.	The directors should **review** their **internal control** and **amend** it where necessary, or alternatively **enforce** it, where it has simply become lax. They should ensure that the systems are **communicated to staff** and **implemented**.
The directors also appear to have **disputes over company strategy** and such issues. This will ensure that the company runs inefficiently and runs the risk of being pressed out of the market.	It is vital that the **directors develop an agreed and coherent strategy** to running the company. If the directors and management cannot agree how to run the company, the son, who does not appear to have a shareholding, should consider whether it might be better to consider alternative employment options, as it is likely that the company will fail.

Financial risks	Action
The company appears to have **significant financing potential which it has not taken up**, and which could be used to finance improvements in the company's systems and investment in staff and new fixed assets, such as the computer systems.	The company should **assess its current financing** and consider seeking new finance from additional family members. If control is an issue, the managing director should first assess why, when the future plan is for the family to retain control over the business but secondly, consider further bank finance. As the bank borrowing is currently low, the bank is likely to lend more, particularly if security could be given, perhaps over the factory.

Compliance risks	Action
As the company deals with **consumers** it is subject to the laws relating to **quality** of products. The company is likely to meet **statutory requirements** in this area already, but should be aware of future developments, and also be careful in choosing suppliers and ensuring that quality is consistent.	The purchasing manager should institute further **controls** in his department, such as checking quality on goods inwards, to ensure that deliveries from suppliers are of a **consistently high standard** so that this **quality is passed on** to customers.

23 BearsWorld

Text reference. Chapter 11

Top tips. Part (a) should be reasonably straightforward for 10 marks. Each procedure is worth two marks, one for explaining it and one for an example. This should give you an idea of how much to write for each one. Part (b) is trickier but again you can split the question up as you are asked to consider each procedure in turn. Use the clues in the scenario to help you with your answer.

Easy marks. Part (a) contained the easiest marks. ISA 500 *Audit evidence* is a key standard so you should be able to explain the main techniques of gathering audit evidence. As long as you took care to avoid the traps, eg talking about procedures relating to receivables when the question states there are none, it should have been reasonably easy to think of relevant examples for most of them.

Examiner's comments. Part (a) required an explanation of five different types of evidence and then applied this knowledge to a scenario where controls were weak – by implication the auditor would be looking for substantive evidence and this should be shown in the examples provided.

Answers were generally of a high standard. The main weaknesses were:

- Provision of examples without actually explaining what the collection method was. For example forgetting to mention that inspection actually meant looking at assets or documents to check existence or other assertions

- Some confusion between observation and inspection

- Some confusion relating to the use of analytical procedures

Answers to part (b) varied. Weaker answers tended to repeat information from part (a) or provide inappropriate examples. A significant minority did not attempt part (b), possibly due to time pressure at the end of the exam.

Marking scheme

Marks

Types of evidence

(a) (i) Types of audit evidence
Award one mark for each well explained point. Allow 0.5 for simply stating the appropriate area.
Analytical procedures 1
Enquiry 1
Inspection 1
Observation 1
Computation 1

Marks

(ii) Examples of evidence
Award one mark for each well explained point. Allow 0.5 for simply mentioning the appropriate test

	Marks
Analytical procedures	1
Enquiry	1
Inspection	1
Observation	1
Computation	1
Maximum marks	**10**

Suitability of methods of gathering evidence

(b) Part (a) required candidates to state tests that could be carried out in BearsWorld. (b) takes this forward to actually considering whether each type of testing would be used in BearsWorld. Candidates should be able to identify that some methods of gathering evidence such as enquiry are of more use than others. Note – also allow procedures as if used in BearsWorld by director – question could be read this way.

Types of audit evidence

Award one mark for explaining whether each technique is suitable for BearsWorld and one mark for explaining limitations in that technique to a maximum of   **10**

Total   **20**

(a) **Analytical procedures**

(i) Analytical procedures mean the study of trends and ratios in financial and non-financial information. It is used within audit planning to identify risk areas and also as a means of gathering substantive evidence, for example by calculating an estimate of a particular figure based on knowledge of the business and comparing this to the actual figure.

(ii) A comparison of gross profit percentages month by month for BearsWorld could be performed and any unusual fluctuations investigated as these could indicate errors such as omission of sales, loss of inventory or other errors.

Enquiry

(i) Enquiry means requesting information. This could be from individuals within the company, either orally or in written representations, or in formal written requests to third parties.

(ii) In BearsWorld a relevant example would be to send a standard confirmation letter to the company's bank (could be illustrated with an example of enquiry to client staff).

Inspection

(i) Inspection means looking at documentation, books and records or assets. This could be done to confirm existence of an asset, to verify values or to provide evidence that a control has taken place.

(ii) The inventory of cuddly toys at the year-end could be inspected as part of the evidence relating to its value. The inspection would give evidence as to whether the inventory was in good saleable condition (could be illustrated with an example of inspection of documentation).

Observation

(i) Observation means watching a procedure being carried out. It is usually used as a means of gathering evidence about the internal controls in a company.

(ii) In BearsWorld it night be appropriate to observe the procedures that are carried out when the post is opened to assess whether controls exist to prevent the misappropriation of cash.

Recalculation

(i) Recalculation means the reperformance of an arithmetical process within the accounting system. This could involve re-checking a manual calculation or using a computer-assisted audit technique to reperform casts within the accounting records.

(ii) Depreciation is likely to be a significant expense within a manufacturing company such as BearsWorld. The auditor should recalculate this expense.

(b) The usefulness of **analytical procedures** depends on a number of factors including the reliability of the underlying information. It seems that, as a small business, BearsWorld has little segregation of duties and formal controls. This casts doubt on the reliability of the information and hence the conclusions that might be drawn from the analytical procedures.

Enquiry evidence from third parties will be essential in the audit of BearsWorld. As well as the bank confirmation it may be necessary to send confirmation letters to creditors to obtain third party evidence of the liabilities at the year-end.

Enquiry evidence from sources within BearsWorld will be obtained mainly from Mr Kyto and its reliability will be very dependent on how the auditors assess his integrity.

Inspection of documents will be a major part of the evidence gathered in the audit of BearsWorld. Supplier invoices will be inspected to verify values and to confirm that purchases and expenses are genuinely business items. There may be limits to the reliance that can be put on this as in a poor control environment it may be difficult to confirm whether documentation is complete.

Observation may be the only way to gather evidence about controls such as any that may exist over the opening of post. This type of evidence is limited in its usefulness for two reasons:

– It only provides evidence that the control operated at the point in time that the auditor carried out the test

– Client staff are likely to perform their duties exactly according to the company's procedures manual when they are aware that the external auditor is observing them whereas this may not be the case on any other day of the year

To place reliance on controls and reduce substantive testing the auditor needs evidence that controls operated effectively over the whole of the accounting period so the observation would be of limited usefulness.

Observation of controls in operation over the year-end inventory count might be more useful as this is a one-off, rather than daily, procedure. If the auditor could see that the inventory count was being carried out in a well-controlled way then it may be possible to reduce substantive testing on the inventory sheets.

24 CAATs

Text reference. Chapter 11

Top tips. Notice that this question specifies the number of points to be made in each section. Always follow this kind of instruction. Our answer provides more than the required number of points to provide a comprehensive answer for revision purposes.

(a) **Benefits of using Computer-Assisted Audit Techniques (CAATs)**

(i) Computer programs often perform tasks for which there is **no visible record**. CAATs can be used to check the **correct operation** of **these tasks and controls.**

(ii) **Testing 'round the computer'** by comparing input and output may **not** be **possible** if there are significant gaps in the trail of processing linking input and output. Use of CAATs may be the only way that the auditors can gain sufficient assurance about the processing of transactions.

(iii) Testing '**round the computer'** by detailed comparison of input and output may be a very **time-consuming** way of testing the correctness of processing if a large number of items have been processed. CAATs may give the required assurance as a result of processing only a handful of items.

(iv) Testing 'round the computer may mean that clients have to be asked for **print-outs** that they would otherwise not need to make or retain.

(v) For certain procedures, use of CAATs guarantees a correct answer, whereas the same tasks would be **prone to error** if carried out **manually.** Examples include carrying out complex calculations and checking that all items have been processed.

(b) **Functions of an audit software interrogation program**

(i) **Analytical procedures.** Programs can **identify trends in data**, and also **highlight exceptions** and **potential areas of concern**.

(ii) **Identification of items that fulfil certain criteria.** Programs can pick out items according to criteria set by the auditors, for example debtor balances that are larger than a specified amount.

(iii) **Confirming completeness of processing.** Programs can check to see whether all items in a sequence of invoices have been processed.

(iv) **Checking calculations**. Programs can check that the ageing of receivables has been carried out correctly.

(v) **Random sampling**. A program can select a sample of balances or transactions for testing.

(vi) **Stratification**. A program can stratify a population by amounts, so that auditors can concentrate testing on larger balances or transactions.

(vii) **Testing for unauthorised relationships**. Programs can achieve this by comparison of different data, for example employee and supplier addresses.

(c) **Problems with using interrogation programs**

(i) Audit staff may need a very **detailed knowledge** of systems analysis, operating systems and the programming language being used.

(ii) The **costs** and **time** involved in setting up the procedures may be significant.

(iii) The **interrogation software available** may not be compatible with the client's computer system.

(iv) The interrogation programmes may be **time-consuming** to operate.

(v) The client may not **allow access** to its computers at times that are convenient to the auditors.

(vi) The client may lack **full knowledge** of its computer system, and may not be able to comment on the **auditors' findings.**

(d) **Use of computers in audit administration**

(i) **Word processing software** can be used to record **audit plans** and **working papers**.

(ii) Relevant packages can be used to record the **accounting systems** in whatever way is deemed clearest. This record can **easily be updated** in subsequent years.

(iii) Automated packages can **reduce recording time** by automatically cross-referencing and balancing.

(iv) **Decision support systems**, such as automated questionnaires which follow different logic paths depending on the answers given, can be used to **focus audit attention** on key areas.

(v) Software can be used to analyse the results of **sampling procedures**.

(vi)   Software can be used for **reference** purposes.

(vii)   Computerised working papers can be **emailed** to the office for review, thus **improving** the **timeliness** of review, and perhaps **reducing** the **travelling** that senior staff need to undertake.

(viii)   **Management software** can be used for **control** purposes, to check actual time and cost against budgeted time and cost.

25 Porthos

Text reference. Chapter 11

Top tips. The important thing here is to read the question and apply your knowledge to the requirements. Key words to notice were *"advantages"* in part (a), *"difficulties"* in part (c) (i) and *"explaining the reasons"* in both parts (b) and (c)(ii).

The other thing to remember here is that you can get a long way with common sense. You may not have much audit experience but the chances are that you have ordered goods (not necessarily tennis racquets!) over the Internet. In part (b) you should think about what you'd expect to happen when you do that. Once you have thought about it in this way it should be much easier to think what sort of test data the auditor could use to test the system.

Take care not to confuse test data and audit software, a common mistake which could lead to a score of zero in either (a) or (c) (ii).

Easy marks. This was a fairly tough question but basic, rote-learned knowledge of CAATs would help you get started on parts (a) and (c).

Examiner's comments. The standard of answers to this question varied considerably. Part (a) was answered very well. In part (b), areas of weakness included confusing test data and audit software and relating answers to the scenario.

Part (c)(i) was answered well but part (c)(ii) was not, with weaknesses including repeating examples of test data or explaining systems testing but without using audit software. In summary, this is an area to revisit in a future examination.

Marking scheme

		Marks
(a)	**Advantages of CAATS – 1 mark each**	
	Test program controls	1
	Test more items quickly	1
	Test actual records	1
	Cost effective after initial setup	1
	Supplement traditional testing	1
	Other relevant points	1
	Maximum marks	4
(b)	**Examples of test data 0.5 for test and 0.5 for explanation**	
	Negative quantities	1
	High quantities	1
	Lack of payment details	1
	Invalid inventory code	1
	Invalid credit card details	1
	Invalid address	1
	Other relevant points	1
	Maximum marks	6

			Marks
(c)	(i)	**Difficulties of using audit software – 1 mark each**	
		Setup costs	1
		Not available for bespoke systems	1
		Too much output/program errors	1
		Dangers of live testing	1
		Other relevant points	1
		Maximum marks	4
	(ii)	**Tests using audit software – 1 mark each**	
		Cast SDB	1
		Inventory ageing	1
		Sample inventory year end	1
		Sales invoices sample	1
		Completeness of recording – numeric sequence check	1
		Invoices paid for – should be no receivables	1
		Large credit notes	1
		Other relevant points	1
		Maximum marks	6

(a)   **Advantages of Computer-Assisted Audit Techniques (CAATs)**

Time savings

Potentially time-consuming procedures such as checking casts of ledgers can be carried out much more quickly using CAATs.

Reduction in risk

Larger samples can be tested, giving greater confidence that material errors have not been missed

Testing programmed controls

Without CAATs many controls within computerised systems cannot be tested, as they may not produce any documentary evidence. This gives greater flexibility of approach.

Cost effective

Many CAATs have low set-up costs, such as where information is downloaded from the client's system onto the auditor's copy of the same system. Even where CAATs have had to be written specially for a particular audit, the on-going costs will be minimal as they can be reused until the client changes its systems.

(b)

Test data	Reason
Order for unusually high quantities, eg 20 racquets	This would identify whether any reject controls requiring special authorisation for large orders are effective. This control would also prompt the customer to recheck the quantity if they had accidentally keyed in the wrong quantity.
Orders with fields left blank	This would give evidence as to whether orders could be accepted that prove impossible to deliver because, for example, the name of the town has been omitted from the delivery address.
Orders with invalid credit card details	This will identify whether the controls over the ordering system will protect the company from losses arising from credit card frauds.

Test data	Reason
Orders with details of customers on retailers' 'blacklists' or of cards that have been reported as stolen	This will identify whether the company has effective procedures to ensure that their system is regularly updated for security. This should reduce the risk of bad debts.
Order with invalid inventory code	This will show whether the system will alert the customer to the code error and prompt them to check it. This should ensure that the correct goods are dispatched.
Order with complete and valid details	This order should be accepted by the system so will allow the auditor to inspect the order confirmation to determine whether the order details are transferred accurately into the dispatch system.

(c)   (i)   **Difficulties of using audit software**

- The costs of designing tests using audit software can be substantial as a great deal of planning time will be needed in order to gain an in-depth understanding of the client's systems so that appropriate software can be produced.

- The audit costs in general may increase because experienced and specially trained staff will be required to design the software, perform the testing and review the results of the testing.

- If errors are made in the design of the audit software, audit time, and hence costs, can be wasted in investigating anomalies that have arisen because of flaws in how the software was put together rather than by errors in the client's processing.

- If audit software has been designed to carry out procedures during live running of the client's system, there is a risk that this disrupts the client's systems. If the procedures are to be run when the system is not live, extra costs will be incurred by carrying out procedures to verify that the version of the system being tested is identical to that used by the client in live situations.

(ii)   **Audit tests using audit software**

Test	Reason
Test casts and extensions of inventory listing	To verify the accuracy of the calculation of the final inventory figure.
Reperformance of the ageing of inventory in the inventory listing	To ensure that the ageing is accurate before using an aged listing to identify items that might be obsolete and hence need to be written down.
Selecting a sample of inventory lines to count at the year-end inventory count	This will be a quicker and more objective method of selecting a sample rather than doing this manually.
Performing a sequence check on the sales invoice numbers issued over the year.	This will give assurance in respect of the completeness of recording of sales.
Select a sample of credit notes, perhaps including all those over a certain value	This will be an effective means of selecting a sample so that the auditor can trace supporting documentation to check that credit notes have only been issued for valid reasons eg returns of racquets, and with appropriate authorisation.
Cast the sales day books for the year	This will give evidence that the sale figure has been calculated accurately.
Match dates of sales invoices/date posted to ledgers with date on related despatch data	This will give evidence that sales cut-off has been performed accurately.

26 Serenity

Text references. Chapters 6 and 19

Top tips. Part (a) of this question should be straightforward as you are asked to explain the purpose of risk assessment procedures and outline sources of audit evidence that can be used for this part of the audit. In part (b), you have to identify issues to be considered during the planning stage of an audit. There are lots of clues in the question scenario so the best way to approach this part of the question is to go through the scenario line-by-line, jotting down issues as you go. This will give more structure to your answer, as will the use of sub-headings for each issue you identify.

Easy marks. These are available for basic technical knowledge in part (a) for six marks on risk assessment procedures and sources of evidence and part (c) for four marks on explaining what negative assurance means.

ACCA examiner's answer. The examiner's answer to this question is included at the back of this Kit.

Marking scheme

			Marks
(a)	One mark per point		
	(i)	Purpose of risk assessment – understand client	1
		Material misstatements	1
		Knowledge of classes of transactions	1
		Association risk	1
	(ii)	Evidence from enquiry (with example)	1
		Analytical review (with example)	1
		Observation (with example)	1
		Maximum marks	6
(b)	One mark per point		
	Skills necessary?		1
	Self-review threat		1
	Acceptance non-audit work		1
	Fee income		1
	Internal audit – fee pressure		1
	Client growth		1
	Association threat		1
	Advocacy threat		1
	Report on cash flow		1
	Possible going concern		1
	Other relevant points (each)		1
	Maximum marks		10
(c)	Key points one for each point = knowledge outside scenario		
	Accuracy of cash flow not confirmed		1
	'Reasonable' – not T&F		1
	Nothing to indicate cash flow is incorrect		1
	Forecast relates to future – uncertainty		1
	Conditions may not turn out as expected		1
	Other relevant points (each)		1
	Maximum marks		4
Total			20

(a)　(i)　Risk assessment procedures are performed at the planning stage of an audit to obtain an understanding of the entity being audited and to identify any areas of concern which could result in material misstatements in the financial statements. They allow the auditor to assess the nature, timing and extent of audit procedures to be performed.

　　(ii)　Sources of audit evidence that can be used as part of risk assessment procedures.

- Enquiries of management
- Prior year financial statements
- Current year management accounts and budgets
- Analytical procedures
- Observation and inspection

(b)　*Poor internal controls and rapid growth*

The accounting systems of Serenity Co are changing rapidly and the control systems are difficult to maintain as the company continues to grow. This indicates that the internal controls are likely to be poor so control risk and the risk of material misstatements in the accounts will be high. Therefore a fully substantive audit is likely and Mal & Co must ensure it has enough time and resources to obtain sufficient audit evidence to support the figures in the financial statements.

Reliance on internal audit department

Serenity Co has only recently established its internal audit department so Mal & Co needs to be very careful in deciding whether it can place reliance on the work performed by internal audit and ultimately in a reduced external audit fee, as desired by the financial controller. Additional time and work would be required to assess internal audit so an immediate reduction in the fee is very unlikely.

Additional services required

Serenity Co requires additional services of review and implementation of control systems but Mal & Co must consider whether it has sufficiently skilled resources to carry out this additional work as it is a small firm with a number of clients in different sectors.

Fee income

The additional work required by Serenity Co will result in increased fee income to Mal & Co. The audit firm must ensure that its fee income from this one client does not breach the guidelines set by the ACCA's Code of Ethics. These state that the fee income from an unlisted client should not exceed 15% of the firm's total fees.

Self-review threat

The additional work required on the review and implementation of control systems at Serenity Co could result in the risk of self-review. Mal & Co must ensure it implements appropriate safeguards to mitigate this risk, such as separate teams to carry out the review work and the external audit. This may be difficult in a small audit firm. It would also be essential to ensure that the client makes all the management decisions in relation to the systems.

Legal status of new mobile

The legal status of the new mobile product is not known – it may be illegal. Any adverse publicity generated as a result will impact on Mal & Co as the auditors of the company. The audit firm needs to consider carefully whether it wants to be associated with Serenity Co. The fact that the company is planning to make a product of dubious legality raises questions about the integrity of the directors, and the audit team should be cautious in relying on any management representations.

Reliance on cash flow statement for licence

The granting of the licence to market the mobile is dependent on the financial stability of the company. Mal & Co may be asked to provide a report on the company's cash flow statement for the following financial year. This needs to be considered carefully – Mal & Co must ensure it has sufficient experienced resources for this work and determine what kind of assurance is required.

Going concern assumption

The company is growing rapidly and is relying on the granting of a licence for the new mobile, whose legal status is not known. These factors may indicate a possible going concern risk which should be monitored carefully.

(c)   'Negative assurance' refers to when an auditor gives an assurance that nothing has come to his attention which indicates that the financial statements have not been prepared according to the identified financial reporting framework, i.e. he gives his assurance in the absence of any evidence to the contrary.

Negative assurance is given on review assignments such as the review of a company's cash flow statement. Such a statement relates to the future so is based upon assumptions that cannot be confirmed as accurate. The auditor cannot therefore confirm positively that the statement is materially true and fair.

27 Tam

Text references. Chapters 6, 7 and 11

Top tips. This is a question on audit sampling and includes both knowledge-based and scenario-based aspects. In parts (a) and (c), don't just simply produce one line definitions for the terms in the question – you need to explain them fully in order to score well. In part (b), break the question down into three parts for each of the comments made by each of the audit team – this means you need to aim to write sufficiently to score three marks for each comment. Breaking the question down like this into smaller parts makes it more manageable and less daunting.

Easy marks. These are available in parts (a) and (c) of the question, provided you are comfortable with audit sampling and the concept of materiality.

ACCA examiner's answer. The examiner's answer to this question is included at the back of this Kit.

Marking scheme

			Marks
(a)	One mark per point		
	(i)	Sampling risk	
		Explanation	1
		Example	1
		Non-sampling risk	
		Explanation	1
		Example	1
	(ii)	Sampling risk	
		Controlled by	1
		Non-sampling risk	
		Controlled by	1
		Allow other relevant points	1
		Maximum marks	**6**
(b)	One mark per point		
	Audit manager comments		
	Explanation of sampling method		1
	Small population		1
	Transactions material		1
	Audit senior points		
	Explanation of sampling method		1
	Population homogenous – therefore use statistical sampling		1
	Time to produce sample		1
	Audit junior points		
	Explanation of sampling method		1

	Marks
Sample selection not random	1
Can't draw valid statistical conclusion	1
Allow other relevant points	1
Maximum marks	9

(c) One mark per point

Definition	
Materiality – omission or misstatement	1
Materiality – size of the item	1
Important because:	
Financial statements incorrect	1
Directors/owners know of errors; auditor reporting to	1
Third parties rely on financial statements	1
Other relevant points	1
Maximum marks	5
Total	**20**

(a) (i) 'Sampling risk' is the risk that the auditor's conclusion, based on a sample, may be different from the conclusion reached if the entire population were subject to the same audit procedure. There are two types of sampling risk. In the first type, the auditor concludes in a test of controls, that controls are more efficient than they actually are, or in a test of details, that a material error does not exist when it actually does. In the second type, the auditor concludes in a test of controls, that controls are less efficient than they actually are, or in a test of details, that a material error exists when it actually does not.

'Non-sampling risk' arises from factors that cause the auditor to reach an incorrect conclusion for any reason not related to the size of the sample. For example, the auditor may rely on audit evidence that is persuasive rather than conclusive, the auditor may use inappropriate audit procedures, or the auditor misinterprets audit evidence and fails to recognise an error.

(ii) Sampling risk can be controlled by the audit firm by increasing sample size for both tests of control and tests of detail.

Non-sampling risk can be controlled by the audit firm by proper engagement planning supervision and review.

(b) The audit manager wants to check all the invoices in the year. This would involve checking around 500 invoices. This would be impractical in terms of time and cost for the directors of Tam Co. Although 500 is not a huge population, it is unlikely that the firm would test 100% in practice.

The audit senior wants to select a sample using statistical sampling techniques. This would involve calculating a sample size appropriate to the auditor's assessment of factors such as risk, required confidence level, tolerable error and expected error. Such a sample can still produce valid conclusions and in this case, the population consists of items showing similar characteristics. Where statistical sampling is used all the items in the population must have an equal chance of being selected, so the sample should be picked using a method such as random number tables or a systematic basis. Provided that the sales invoices are sequentially numbered, this should be easy to apply in the example.

The audit junior's suggestion is to use a 'random' method of selecting samples manually and choosing a few important ones. This approach would not be appropriate because the auditor is not choosing the sample randomly as there would be bias involved and implies that 'haphazard' selection would be used. Valid conclusions would not be able to be drawn because statistical sampling had not been used to select the sample.

(c) Information is material if its omission or misstatement could influence the economic decisions of users taken on the basis of the financial statements. Materiality depends on the size of the item or error judged in the particular circumstances of its omission or misstatement. Materiality also has qualitative, as well as quantitative, aspects which must be considered.

Materiality is often calculated as a percentage of different items in the financial statements, such as revenue, profit before tax or net assets. In the case of Tam Co, materiality is likely to be based on 0.5 – 1% of revenue, ie $350-700k.

The auditors of Tam Co must form an opinion on whether the financial statements are free from material misstatement because there is a requirement for an audit under local legislation for this company. Other users of the accounts may also be relying on the outcome of the audit, such as the bank since the company has recently taken out a five year bank loan to finance an expansion. The bank would be very interested in the accounts of Tam Co as a basis for assessing whether the company will be able to repay the loan. Users of the financial statements expect to receive reasonable assurance that the information is 'true and fair'. This implies that there are no material errors or omissions.

28 Question with answer plan: Ajio

Text references. Chapters 6 and 7

Top tips. The key to part (a) of the question is to ensure that you explain the risk rather than simply identifying the risk factor. For example you may decide that the fact that the organisation is a charity as opposed to a company is a risk in itself but to score well you need to expand and explain why eg volunteers lack expertise. Also notice that you are asked to consider the implications for overall audit risk. Here you need to think about the relationship between the different components of risk.

In part (b) you do need to think sensibly about the practicalities of the fund raising events. How is the cash collected? What happens to it when it is returned to Ajio? How is the income recorded? Once you have thought about the sequence of events it will be much easier to devise audit tests for each stage.

Easy marks. In part (a) although you should ideally explain the risks make sure that you at least identify the risk factors. Remember these can normally be taken from the scenario itself. In part (b) audit tests relating to expenditure should be relatively straightforward. In this case the fact that the entity is a charity does not make a significant difference.

Examiner's comments. Generally the answers were good however many candidates did not read the information carefully and answered the question as if Ajio was a company. In part (b) candidates were asked for audit tests relating to fund raising events. Many candidates gave answers based on the charity as a whole. Some answers did not take into account the fact that the charity was a small one. These went into great detail about segregation of duties and other control procedures which would not have been appropriate in these circumstances.

Marking scheme

		Marks
(a)	Risks and implication for audit risk	
	Up to 2 marks per point to a maximum of	10
(b)	Audit tests – fund raising events	
	Up to 2 marks per point to a maximum of	10
		20

Answer plan

(a) **Risks**

Inherent and control risks

- Complexity and extent of regulations-risk of failure to comply
- Completeness of income-risk of misstatement of income

- Uncertainty of future income-risk to projects/going concern
- Skills and qualifications of trustees-control risk
- Use of volunteers-control risk
- Quality of paid staff-risk of errors
- Lack of formal procedures-poor control environment

Detection risk

- Recent appointment
- Reduced reliance on analytical procedures

Implications

- Inherent risk/control risk = high/medium
- Detection risk needs to be low-increase sample sizes, target risk areas

(b) **Audit tests**

Income

- Attend fund raiser and observe procedures
- Count cash and agree to returns
- Match returns to paying in slips
- Trace entries
- Bank recs
- Analytical procedures
- Representations

Expenditure

- Check nature of cost
- Trace to supporting invoices
- Analytical procedures
- Authorisation

(a) **Risks**

Inherent and control risks (risk of material misstatement)

The complexity and extent of regulations

There is a risk that the charity will **fail to comply** with new and existing regulations. It may also be involved in activities which are not compatible with its charitable status. This is particularly the case where small charities like Ajio are involved as they may not be run by individuals with the required expertise. The fact that the accounts are prepared by a recently retired accountant should reduce the auditor's assessment of this risk however.

Completeness of income

There is a risk that **income may be misstated**. This risk is increased by the high levels of cash donations made as these are not supported by any documentary evidence. Cash may be misappropriated or errors could be made in counting and recording. Completeness of income from bequests would also be difficult to confirm as there is no predictable pattern in terms of their receipt. This risk is likely to be increased by the fact the Ajio is unlikely to have sophisticated controls in place.

Uncertainty of future income

Due to the **unpredictable nature of income** there is a risk that the charity will undertake projects which it subsequently finds it is unable to finance. This factor will also make it more difficult for the auditor to assess whether the charity is viable on an ongoing basis.

Skills and qualifications of trustees

Control risk is increased if the trustees do not have the skills required to manage the affairs of the charity. It will also be affected by the extent to which they are involved and the amount of time which they are able to devote to its affairs.

Use of volunteers

Control risk is increased by the use of volunteers. The charity is dependent upon their integrity and commitment. Shortcomings may arise from a lack of training and from their attitude in that they may resent formal procedures. Bogus volunteers may commit fraud.

Quality of paid staff

Lack of resources may result in staff being employed who are not sufficiently qualified. In the case of Ajio a part-time bookkeeper has been employed instead of a full time accountant. If this individual is under constant time pressure the **risk of errors** in the accounts is increased.

Lack of formal procedures

There is a risk that the charity may be run in an informal manner which will result in a **poor control environment**. This problem is likely to be accentuated by a lack of segregation of duties due to the small number of staff involved.

Detection risk

Recent appointment

Detection risk is increased by the fact that the firm has only recently been appointed. The audit team will not be able to rely on their experience of this audit from previous years. In addition the regulations are new. There is a risk that the auditors will fail to perform specific procedures required by the regulations due to a lack of familiarity with them. Adequate planning will reduce this risk.

Reduced reliance on analytical procedures

Due to the unpredictable nature of income it may be more difficult to rely on the results of analytical procedures to assess the **completeness of income**. This increases detection risk as analytical procedures are one of the key tests in this area. The results of alternative procedures will reduce this risk.

Implications for overall audit risk

The aim of the auditor is to reduce overall audit risk (the risk of issuing an inappropriate opinion) to a reasonable level. Audit risk is a function of the risk of material misstatement (inherent risk and control risk) and detection risk. As inherent risk and control risk in Ajio appear to be high/medium **detection risk will need to be low**. This will be achieved by increasing audit work eg increasing sample sizes. Risk areas will also be targeted, in this case income and cash being key balances.

(b) **Audit tests**

Income:

- Attend a fund raising event and observe procedures to confirm that they are in accordance with the guidance set down by the charity eg use of sealed collection boxes.

- Count cash at the end of the day and agree to returns submitted by volunteers.

- Match returns submitted with amounts on the bank paying-in slips.

- Trace entry of cash received to cash book and bank statements.

- Review the preparation of monthly bank reconciliations.

- Compare amounts received by cash collections with previous years balances and forecasts. Discuss major fluctuations with trustees.

- Obtain representations from the trustees regarding the completeness of income.

Expenditure:

- Obtain a breakdown of expenditure relating to fund raising events and check that the nature of the cost is reasonable.

- For a sample of expenses trace the cost to a supporting invoice or other documentation.

- Compare the overall level of expenditure with previous years and with budgets. Discuss any major fluctuations with management.

- For a sample of major expenses confirm that the expenditure has been authorised by the trustees.

29 Cliff

Text reference. Chapter 10

Top tips. When you read the requirements you should spot that this is a very practical question based on a scenario. You need to identify the tasks you are being given in the requirements then read the scenario carefully, several times, to find practical points to make.

For part (a), highlight relevant points in the scenario and make a brief note in the margin to remind you of what the related "problem" is.

For each point you should write one or two sentences only. To score well on this sort of requirement, you need to make enough (here the "target" is 8) separate points rather than elaborate at great length on any one point.

In (b) you should spot that the requirement effectively gives you an answer plan. You need to make FOUR recommendations, along with advantages and disadvantages of each. This makes it easy to guess how the 12 marks are being allocated.

Spend some time thinking up recommendations – if you think of more than four, select the four you have most to say about and use only those.

Keep yourself on track and help the marker by using subheadings of **'Recommendation'**, **'Advantages'** and **'Disadvantages'** for each of your points.

Easy marks. Some people may well feel that there are no "easy marks" in a question of this type! There are certainly no marks available here for simply repeating facts that you have memorised from your studies. The best advice on tackling this sort of scenario is to use your common sense and imagination and make some practical points about the business being discussed. The easiest way to improve your mark would be to re-read your answer and check if all your points are obviously addressing a supermarket – if not, it's worth using a couple of minutes to sharpen up the commonsense detail.

Examiner's comments. Many candidates correctly used the information provided in the scenario to include relevant comments in their answers. Good answers to part (a) contained about five or six problems with some explanation to show their relevance to the scenario. Poorer answers to part (a) tended to be repetitive or to cover insufficient relevant points.

Common errors included:

- Stating a potential problem but not showing exactly why it was a problem. For example, making the point *"management accounts produced twice a year"* was a repeat of part of the scenario. Additional explanation was needed to show why this is a problem.

- Spending time on less relevant areas. For example, explaining detailed problems with the receivables' ledger which was not mentioned in the scenario.

Part (b) was normally very well answered with candidates providing four recommendation/advantages/ disadvantages sections in their answers.

Common errors included:

- Including less relevant recommendations in the answer.

- Not explaining the points being made. Some answers were in bullet point format with limited explanation.

Marking scheme

		Marks
(a)	Problems expected at Cliff: poor internal control Up to 1-1½ marks per point to a maximum of	10
(b)	Four recommendations, explanation of advantages and disadvantages: improvements to internal control Up to 3 marks per issue to a maximum of	12
(c)	Impact on audit approach 1 mark per point to a maximum of	5
(d)	Interim report to management 1 mark per point to a maximum of	3 30

(a) **Problems at Cliff resulting from poor internal control**

(i) The local decision-making in respect of purchasing may lead to Cliff missing out on discounts that would be available if goods were bought in greater quantities.

(ii) As the nature of the inventory is foodstuff, and as such, perishable, the lack of control over inventory could mean that Cliff has to write off significant amounts of unsaleable food that is past its sell by date.

(iii) If no controls exist to identify when fresh food is past its sell by date the business could be at risk of prosecution under Food Safety legislation.

(iv) If the local managers are not making good decisions regarding purchasing there could be stock outs of certain lines of goods, losing potential sales and perhaps losing future business if customers decide to shop at other, better-stocked supermarkets.

(v) There is a lack of centralised control over the accounting system. Errors arising on the stand-alone computers in each supermarket may go undetected and senior management will not have good quality information for decision-making.

(vi) Misappropriations of inventory may go undetected, as there is no regular system of inventory counting. Supermarket products are at high risk of being stolen either by staff or others.

(vii) The fact that management accounts are only produced twice a year reduces their usefulness. Pilfering or other fraudulent activity could be going on for several months before there is any chance of it being identified through review of management accounts.

(viii) All of the above problems are likely to be exacerbated by the declining quality of staff employed by Cliff.

(b) **Recommendations to the senior management of Cliff**

(i) **Recommendation 1**

A new computerised accounting system should be implemented, integrating the sales, purchases and inventory accounting systems.

Advantages

This would give the head office management up to date information about inventory levels so that purchase orders can be placed in time to avoid stock outs. More information about sales patterns would assist in better purchasing planning in the medium to longer term.

Disadvantages

The cost of implementing this system would be substantial. Also, there would be further costs of training the staff who will operate the system. It is also likely that there will be "teething problems" when the system is first used. Information may be flawed and the problems that the new system is supposed to solve may in fact be made worse temporarily.

(ii)   **Recommendation 2**

Management accounts should be produced monthly and reviewed by senior management. Ideally these accounts should be prepared for each individual supermarket and also analysed by different product lines.

Advantages

This should allow senior management to identify any poorly performing supermarkets promptly allowing action to be taken to rectify problems. Unprofitable product lines could also be identified and dropped from the supermarkets' range.

Disadvantages

If these accounts are used as part of a more centralised decision-making process it could be that decisions are made that are not in the best interest of a particular supermarket as demand for various types of food is likely to vary between different geographical areas of the country.

(iii)   **Recommendation 3**

Sales pricing decisions should be taken centrally.

Advantages

This should help the business maximise its profits by charging appropriate prices for products. Management could also implement policies of discounting on certain lines designated as "loss-leaders" which may have the effect of attracting new customers into the supermarkets.

Disadvantages

Again the centralised decisions may not be optimal for each individual supermarket. In addition, this would imply a significant change in the culture of the business and established supermarket managers, used to having a great deal of autonomy, may become de-motivated or leave.

(iv)   **Recommendation 4**

There should be regular inventory counts at the supermarkets.

Advantages

For efficiency in inventory management and ordering in the food business it is essential to have reliable inventory records. The inventory counts, if properly followed up with amendments being made to book inventory figures, will ensure the quality of the inventory records. This should also act as a deterrent against any staff pilferage of goods.

Disadvantages

Significant staff time will be needed to plan and carry out these inventory counts. This will result in extra costs to the business. It may also cause some disruption to the business if supermarkets have to be closed while the inventory counting is done.

(c)   **Internal control environment at Cliff**

The internal control systems at Cliff appear to be very poor. This is demonstrated by the lack of adequate monitoring (management accounts are produced only twice a year), lack of procedures to count inventory regularly, lack of integration of systems and poor quality staff.

This will result in the auditors being unable to place reliance on the controls in place because control risk will be high. Tests of controls would not be undertaken and the audit will most likely have to take a fully **substantive-based approach**, using both analytical procedures and tests of detail on all the key account areas (inventory, sales, purchases and cash).

The impact of this is that the audit will be **less efficient** than it would be if controls could be relied upon and therefore it is more likely to be **more expensive** to the client as it will require more time to be spent on audit work. A detailed report to management will also have to be prepared, setting out the weaknesses in the various systems and recommendations to mitigate those weaknesses.

(d)   **Report to management**

The report to management can be a very useful tool for the management of an entity, even though it is just a by-product of the external audit. It sets out weaknesses in the control system, the implications of those weaknesses and recommended controls to overcome them.

At the interim stage of the audit, the report to management can be issued to highlight any such weaknesses that have come to the attention of the auditors during this visit and allows management time to start implementing the recommendations.

It is also preferable to report weaknesses identified at this stage of the audit on a timely basis, rather than waiting for the end of the audit process, as the issues will be fresh in the minds of the auditors and client. It also shows the auditor's continuing interest in the future of the company and demonstrates the added value of the external audit, which can sometimes be perceived negatively by organisations and their staff.

In summary, sending the letter out on a timely basis gives a favourable impression to the client and could encourage an early and positive response to the recommendations being made.

30 Internal control

Text references. Chapters 9 and 10

Top tips. Remember that the receivables system is part of the **sales** system. It is important that you get to grips with the issue in parts (a), (b) and (d). Application (part c) is more straightforward if you have a good grip of the theory behind specific internal controls. Given the one mark per valid point system, you need to list at least nine controls in part (c). Make sure you focus on genuine and valid controls and don't just write an over-long list hoping to pick up marks. You should ensure that you spend time on each of the parts so that you pick up the marks for obvious points in each.

Easy marks. Overall this is a reasonably straightforward question so whilst there are no easy marks as such all the marks are reasonably achievable. You should feel particularly confident with part (c) and as this is worth nine marks a good answer here will put you well on the way to passing the question overall.

(a) **Errors, omissions and misappropriations which may arise**

Where internal control is weak or non-existent, the following errors, omissions and misappropriations may arise:

- **Invoices** may be **processed twice**, resulting in the accounting system recording a bigger asset than actually exists.

- **Invoices** may be **processed** for which **no goods have been sent out**, resulting in the accounting system recording two assets (receivables and inventory) instead of one.

- Alternatively, **goods** may be **sent out** to customers and then **no invoice** sent out in respect of those goods. This will result in inventory being given away to customers.

- If the system does not contain delivery notes matched to invoices, it will be easier for people to **misappropriate inventory**.

- **Lack of segregation of duties** will increase the risk of **receipts** being **misappropriated** in a fraud such as 'teeming and lading'.

(b) **Inherent limitations of internal control**

Good controls will not necessarily prevent and detect errors, omissions and misappropriation of assets in a receivables system because of the inherent limitations of any system. These are:

- The fact that the control system cannot always account for **human error**

- The fact that employees may **collude in a fraud** such as teeming and lading: mismatching receipts with receivables and skimming cash away for private use.

Importance of internal control to auditors

There is always an element of risk on audit assignments. Audit risk is the risk that the auditor will give an incorrect opinion on the financial statements.

Audit risk is broken down into three elements. One of the elements is control risk, the risk that a material misstatement could occur in an assertion which will not be prevented, detected or corrected by internal control. If the accounting systems are good and the chances of it allowing error or fraud are small, then the overall risk of misstatement will be reduced.

Of course, control risk can never be as low as zero, because of the inherent limitations in any accounting system, as noted above.

(c) **Main internal control activities to be found in a receivables system**

Ordering

- New customers should be given a credit check before the company deals with them
- Customers should be allocated credit limits which are reasonable and observed
- Sales orders should be checked to the ledger to ensure that they are within credit limits
- Sales orders should be authorised for processing

Goods

- Goods should be agreed to the sales order, prior to despatch
- Multiple copies of all documents should be maintained to ensure that a record is retained

Invoicing

- Invoice should be agreed to dispatch note prior to dispatch
- Invoice should be checked to ensure that adds and extensions are correct
- Invoice should be batched to ensure that all items are included in processing

Ledgers

- Invoices should be posted to the ledgers on a frequent and regular basis
- The receivables ledger should be posted to the general ledger on a regular basis
- The receivables ledger should be reconciled to the control account on a regular basis

Receipts

- Receivables should be extended clear credit terms which are enforced
- Receivables should be sent regular statements of the balance due
- Post should be opened by two people and listings of cash receipts made
- Cash receipts should be banked promptly and frequently
- Cash receipts should be posted to the ledgers frequently
- Cash receipts should be posted to the ledger by a different person to the initial recorder

(d) **Reason auditors seek to rely on proper operation of internal control**

In many cases, auditors seek to rely on the proper operation of internal control because if controls are operating satisfactorily, they can reduce substantive testing. This will make the audit more efficient.

Making the audit more efficient will also probably have the effect of making it cheaper, which will benefit the client.

However, it is not always the case that auditors will seek to rely on internal control. In the audit of smaller entities, it is often more cost effective to undertake substantive testing than to undertake detailed controls testing.

31 Risk assessment and internal control

Text references. Chapters 9, 10 and 11

Top tips. This question tests your knowledge in two different ways. Part (a) requires an explanation of five key procedures which are fundamental to the audit process. You should have a sound understanding of these. Part (b) is more demanding as it examines internal controls in the context of a scenario. The key here is to ensure you consider the elements of the cycle mentioned in the question (ie receipts, processing and recording of orders and collection of cash) and that you both **describe** and **explain the purpose** of the controls you would expect to see.

Easy marks. Part (a) represents 10 relatively straightforward marks as you should be able to explain the five procedures listed.

Examiner's comments. Overall part (a) of the question was reasonably well answered. Those who lost marks did so because their answers were too general. Some candidates also seemed confused about the difference between the various types of test. In part (b) candidates lost marks for failing to address all aspects of the requirement. For example, (b) (i) asked for controls regarding the receipt, processing **and** recording of orders. Other problems included the out-dated approach taken to segregation of duties with many candidates failing to take account of modern computerised systems.

		Marks
(a)	Key procedures Up to 1 mark per point up to a maximum of subject to maximum of 2 for each of the five categories	10
(b)	Internal controls	
	(i) Receipt, processing and recording Up to 1 mark per point to a maximum of	6
	(ii) Collection of cash Up to 1 mark per point to a maximum of	$\frac{4}{20}$

(a) **Explanation of procedures**

(i) *Documentation of accounting systems and internal control*

Auditors are required to obtain an understanding of the business they are to audit. As part of that process they record the accounting and internal control systems to enable them to plan the audit and develop an effective audit approach. This allows the auditor to determine the adequacy of the system for producing the financial statements and to perform an initial risk assessment.

There are a number of different techniques which may be used to record the system. These include **narrative notes, flowcharts and questionnaires**. The extent of the work will depend on the **nature of the organisation and the practical circumstances**. For example in a smaller company where a substantive rather than controls based approach is to be taken, a detailed record of internal control would not be necessary. For a new client with a large and complex system a much more detailed review would be required.

(ii) *Walk-through tests*

Walk through tests are performed by the auditors to confirm that their **recording and understanding of the system is correct**. They are often performed as the recording of the system takes place or in conjunction with the tests of controls.

The process involves the tracing of a sample of transactions from the start of the operating cycle to the end and *vice versa*. For example a sales transaction could be traced from the initial order through to the entry in the nominal ledger accounts.

(iii) *Audit sampling*

Audit sampling involves the **application of audit procedures to a selection of transactions** within a population (ie rather than applying the procedures to 100%). The auditor then obtains and evaluates the evidence in order to form a conclusion about the population as a whole.

Sampling is normally adopted for practical reasons as in most cases it would be too time consuming to audit the whole population. A number of different techniques can be used in order to select the sample including random, systematic or haphazard selection. When designing the size and the structure of the audit sample the auditor will need to consider **sampling risk** – the risk that the sample is not representative of the population as a whole, meaning that results cannot be extrapolated.

(iv) *Testing internal controls*

Tests of controls are used to **confirm the auditor's assessment of the operation of the control system**. They are tests to obtain audit evidence which confirm that controls have been carried out correctly and consistently.

For example a control activity over the payment of supplier invoices could be that all invoices are authorised by the purchases manager's signature. The auditor would test this control by looking for evidence of this on a sample of paid purchase invoices. As this is a test of controls rather than a substantive procedure the size of the balance on the invoice is irrelevant and any exceptions potentially show a failure in the system.

The results of this work will then determine **the extent to which further substantive procedures are required**. If controls have proved to be effective less additional work is required. If controls are not in place or are not effective more additional evidence will be required.

(v) *Deviations*

If deviations from the application of control activities are found the auditor will need to determine whether this is an isolated incident or evidence of a more comprehensive breakdown in procedures. This will normally be confirmed by extending the sample size and testing more transactions.

If the problem is an isolated incident no further formal action is required (although the auditor may wish to mention it to management informally).

If the breakdown is more comprehensive the auditor needs to consider the impact this will have on this particular aspect of the audit and the **audit approach as a whole**. If a compensating control cannot be identified and tested satisfactorily, a substantive approach will need to be adopted. In addition, the auditor will need to reassess audit risk.

(b) **Internal control activities**

(i) *Receipts, processing and recording of orders*

All orders should be recorded on **pre-printed sequentially numbered documentation**. This could be a four part document, one copy being the order, one copy being the despatch note, one copy being sent to the customer as evidence of the order and the last copy retained by the accounts receivable clerk.

To ensure completeness of orders a **sequence check** should be performed on the documents either manually or by computer. Any missing documents should be traced.

As the clerk inputs the order the system should automatically check whether the customer remains within its **credit limit**. Any orders which exceed the credit limit should be rejected.

In exceptional circumstances where credit limits are to be exceeded this should be authorised by the department manager. Orders should also be rejected if the customer has a significantly overdue balance.

As the order is being input the system should check whether the item required is **in stock**. This is possible as the ordering and inventories systems are integrated. If items are unavailable the order should be rejected. This will enable the clerk to inform the customer which will enhance customer service.

Periodically an **independent review should be performed of the standing data on the system**. A sample of credit limits should be checked to ensure that they have been calculated in accordance with the standard formula. Any breaches should be investigated. Similarly the price of flowers should be matched against an up to date price list.

Sales invoices should be posted automatically to the sales daybook and accounts receivable ledger. An accounts receivable control account reconciliation should be performed on a monthly basis and any discrepancies should be investigated and dealt with.

Customer statements should be generated by the system automatically. Any queries raised by the customer on receipt of these should be investigated promptly. Any resulting credit notes should be authorised.

(ii) *Collection of cash*

Details of all **bank transfers** received should be input into the cash book/bank control account and the accounts receivable ledger and accounts receivable control account.

Entries in the accounts receivable ledger should be **matched** against specific invoices. Any unallocated cash should be investigated via an exception report.

On a monthly basis a **bank reconciliation** should be performed. Together with the accounts receivable control account reconciliation and the following up of queries on customer statements this will help to ensure that the cash is correctly recorded and allocated.

On a monthly basis an **aged rec**eivables listing should be generated. The company should have procedures in place for the chasing of debts which the credit controller would follow ranging from a telephone reminder to the threat of legal action.

32 Atlantis Standard Goods

Text reference. Chapter 10

Top tips. Part (a) of this question should be straightforward as you should be very familiar with the sales cycle and the control objectives over sales. In part (b), note that the requirement is asking you to tabulate the audit tests and explain why you are carrying them out. A structured approach would take each point in turn from the scenario. Think about the assertions you are testing against and make sure that your audit tests are specific to the company and not vague. The reason for the test should explain clearly why you are doing it, for example, 'To verify that order details are accurately recorded on the website'.

Easy marks. These are available in part (a). It is important that you are familiar with the control objectives for both sales and purchases.

Examiner's comments. In part (a), many candidates obtained full marks by providing five clear objectives, however, many candidates spent far too much time writing about systems which scored few marks and wasted time. Common errors included writing too much for the five marks available and poor explanation of objectives.

In part (b) the scenario was built around an internet trading company (such as Amazon). The issue being addressed was that the control objectives within a computerised system would be the same as in a manual system, although the methods of implementation and testing would be different. The standard of answers here was very variable. The main weaknesses were writing in general terms about sales systems or providing tests that were not relevant to the scenario. Given that this type of question is focused on basic audit work, candidates are strongly advised to revise how systems are tested.

Marking scheme

			Marks
(a)	One mark for each valid control objective		
	Supply of goods – good credit card rating	1	
	Orders correctly recorded	1	
	Orders despatched to correct customer	1	
	Despatches correctly recorded	1	
	Despatches relate to orders	1	
	Invoices relate to goods supplied	1	
	Other similar correct points (each)	1	
	Maximum marks		**5**
(b)	Key points 1 for each test and 0.5 for explanation of why the test is required		
	Input of order details	1.5	
	Orders pending to despatch file	1.5	
	Completeness of receivables – credit card company	1.5	
	Orders pending to receivables file – sales complete	1.5	
	Review orders pending – old items	1.5	
	Cast receivables ledger – completeness	1.5	
	Goods awaiting despatch file to despatch department	1.5	
	Despatch department – agree back to orders awaiting despatch	1.5	
	Update of inventory records	1.5	
	Customer signature for receipt of goods	1.5	
	Incomplete information despatch department computer	1.5	
	Items not flagged 'order complete' despatch department computer	1.5	
	Other good relevant points (each)	1.5	
	Maximum marks		**15**
	Total		**20**

(a) Control objectives for the ordering, despatch and invoicing of goods:

- To ensure that orders are correctly recorded
- To ensure that orders are fulfilled correctly
- To ensure that goods are supplied to authorised customers only
- To ensure that all goods sold are invoiced correctly
- To ensure that goods are sent to the correct customer
- To ensure that all goods despatched are recorded
- To ensure that all invoices raised relate to goods and services supplied by the business

(b) Audit tests on the sales and despatch system:

Audit tests	Reason for test
For a sample of days, cast the sales day book and agree the total to the nominal ledger accounts for that day.	To check the numerical accuracy and to ensure that the amount updated to the ledger is complete and accurately posted.
Access the website and input order details for selected goods. Then trace these details to the orders pending file.	To ensure that order details are accurately recorded on the website.

Audit tests	Reason for test
Take a sample of orders from the orders pending file and perform the following:	To ensure that the details of the order on the website have been completely and accurately transferred to the orders awaiting despatch file.
Review the goods awaiting despatch file for old items and inquire why these are still on file.	To ensure that reasons for orders not being processed are being obtained. Overdue items could indicate delays in obtaining credit and authorisation.
Take a sample of orders from the goods awaiting despatch file and agree the details to the information on the despatch department computer.	To ensure that orders are transferred to the despatch department correctly.
Take a sample of items on the despatch department computer: • Agree to inventory records for correct updating • Confirm that the customer signature is on file agreeing receipt of the goods	To ensure that the inventory system records the item and that inventory records are accurate. To confirm that evidence of receipt of goods is present to confirm that goods ordered have been delivered.
Take a sample of goods from the computer in the despatch department and check for evidence of delivery. Where no evidence is available, investigate further.	To ensure that goods have been received and that processes for following up non-delivery/receipt are operating.
Take a sample of items from the despatch department computer that are not flagged 'order complete' and investigate further.	To confirm that the despatch of goods process is operating correctly and that incomplete items are investigated fully.

33 Cosmo

Text reference. Chapter 10

Top tips. Read through the examiner's comments about the real answers to this question (below). Notice that again, a point is raised that candidates should answer the question set. Always read the requirement carefully once or twice to make sure that you are not suffering from a case of wishful thinking. It sometimes helps if you read a requirement before reading through a scenario attached to a question – although you have to beware answering the question without reference to the scenario. You should be capable of identifying control problems and setting them out in a 'weaknesses, consequences, recommendations' format. You might find that using a columnar format is useful in such questions. The answer below has not used that format, but has been set out more as it is likely such a letter would be in practice. It would have been acceptable to use the columnar presentation in your answer, however.

Easy marks. These are available in part (a) of the question. In addition in part (b), having identified the weakness, the consequence and recommendation should follow, so you should feel confident of scoring a substantial number of the 15 marks available.

Marking scheme

		Marks
(a)	Error and misappropriations 1 mark per point to maximum of	5
(b)	Report to management 3 marks per point to maximum of	15
	Note: To obtain full marks in this section, the weakness, consequences and recommendations must be identified.	$\overline{\underline{20}}$

(a) **Errors and misappropriations – purchases system**

- Goods could be bought which are not genuinely for the company
- Goods/materials could be bought at inappropriately high prices
- Goods which have not been ordered could be accepted/paid for
- Genuine liabilities might be unrecognised, resulting in loss of supply
- Liabilities which are not genuine might be created as part of a fraud

(b) **Report to management – Cosmo**

Complex purchasing system

Weakness

The purchasing system is complex. This can be seen in the distinction between capital and revenue purchases and also the use of two systems to purchase goods running in parallel.

Consequence

The complexity of the system wastes management time and at worst, could in itself result in errors being made in classification or purchase which could result in business interruption or dissatisfied suppliers.

Recommendation

The purchases system should be revisited and simplified. This could be done by the internal audit department. Alternatively, we would be happy to be engaged separately to provide advice on the simplification of your system.

Consortium system

Weakness

The new system of purchasing is not used comprehensively for all purchases.

Consequences

This is likely to lead to confusion and could lead to the company making necessary purchases twice or not at all.

Recommendation

Steps should be taken to integrate the entire purchasing function with the consortium system to avoid confusion.

Weakness

The consortium system can only be operated by two of the production controller's junior staff.

Consequences

This has two significant consequences:

- There are insufficient people trained to operate the major purchasing system and the company may find that they could be unable to operate their systems if those capable are absent.

- The people who can use the system are employed in the production department, meaning that there is a lack of segregation of duties in the purchasing function, which could lead to error and/or purchasing fraud.

Recommendation

The purchasing department staff should be trained to use the new Consortium system and they should be the only people who use the system, so that they operate as an authorisation function to purchases.

Circumvention

Weakness

The automatic re-ordering system and the capital expenditure system both operate inefficiently and staff members are required to circumvent the system in order to be able to get on with their jobs.

Consequence

Staff may become accustomed to habitually overriding the systems, which will cause systems to be inefficient and fail to achieve company objectives.

Recommendation

The system should be improved and staff reminded that circumvention of the system is not acceptable. This is likely to have to be an initiative led by senior staff, who may have permitted/encouraged circumvention of systems in the past.

Information Technology Systems

Weakness

The new purchasing system appears to take up a significant amount of disk space and cause problems to other programmes.

Consequence

This may result in a significant 'jam' in the company's overall system, or even cause errors in related systems.

Recommendation

Technical advisers should be engaged to review the system and discover whether there is an error with the new system, or whether the capacity of the company's infrastructure is sufficient. It may be that the company's IT policy needs to be reviewed. Again, we could provide such a service for the company, if required.

34 Dinko

Text reference. Chapter 10

Top tips. In this question you need to take a structured approach. Notice that in this case the requirements actually take you through the logical thought process which you need to follow, so for example part (a) asks you to identify control objectives before asking you to explain the practical measures which can be taken to achieve these (ie control environment and control activities). Make sure you can distinguish between a control objective and a control activity. Remember an objective will normally commence with the phrase 'to ensure that....'. A control activity will be a procedure built into the information system by management eg authorisation of overtime by a supervisor.

Easy marks. These are available in part (b)(i) as audit objectives can be based on the financial statement assertions found in ISA 500 ie completeness, accuracy etc.

Examiner's comments. Many candidates struggled to make a distinction between internal control objectives, the internal control environment and internal control procedures. Answers generally consisted of long lists of 'check this' and 'check that' for which little credit was given. In part (b) many candidates simply repeated information from their answers to part (a).

(a)   **Payroll department**

(i)   Internal control objectives

To ensure that:

- Genuine staff are only paid for work performed

- Gross pay has been calculated correctly

- Deductions from gross pay are calculated and recorded accurately

- The correct employees are paid what they are entitled to

- Wages and salaries paid are accurately recorded in the bank and cash records

- The right amounts due in respect of tax and social insurance are paid to the relevant authority on a timely basis

(ii) Internal control environment and control activities

Internal control environment

The control environment includes the governance and management functions and the attitudes, awareness and actions of management and those charged with governance in terms of the importance of internal control within the business. More specifically it would include the following:

- The way in which management **communicate** to staff the need for integrity and enforce it.

- The consideration which management gives to ensure that the payroll staff have the **requisite skills** and **knowledge** through proper recruitment and training.

- Management's **philosophy** and **operating style** including the way in which the importance of internal control in the processing of payroll is translated into positive action, for example providing sufficient resources to address security risks regarding access to the computer.

- The way that **authority** and **responsibility** is assigned. For example the chief accountant might act in a supervisory role whilst the payroll clerk is responsible for the detailed calculations and processing.

Internal control activities

- Responsibility for the preparation of the payroll should be delegated to a responsible, adequately trained member of staff.

- For hourly paid employees the payroll should be prepared on the basis of timesheets/clockcards authorised by a factory supervisor.

- Standing data used by the computerised payroll system should be checked on a regular basis eg gross pay to personnel records.

- Any changes should be authorised by the chief accountant eg change in pay rates, overtime, joiners and leavers.

- For a sample of employees calculations for gross pay, net pay and deductions should be reperformed by the chief accountant.

- The payroll software should include computerised controls eg hierarchical password access and range checks. Exception reports should be produced and investigated.

- The managing director should review the payroll by comparing the total monthly cost with the budget and previous months actual figures.

- The bank transfer list and wage cheque should be authorised by the managing director.

- Cash should be kept securely in the company safe until it is distributed.

- There should be segregation of duties between the member of staff responsible for processing the payroll and the individual handling the cash.

- The chief accountant should maintain and reconcile a wages and salaries control account.

(b)

Audit objectives	Tests of controls/substantive procedures
Occurrence and cut-off: All payroll transactions and events that have been recorded have occurred and relate to the correct accounting period.	Cut-off tests should be performed. Hours worked immediately before and after the year end should be traced from the payroll records and agreed to an authorised time sheet specifying the period to which the work related.
Completeness: All payroll transactions which should have been included have been accounted for. There are no unrecorded payroll liabilities (or assets).	Review of exception reports eg highlighting staff for which no information regarding hours worked has been input. For a sample of starters and leavers agree the dates for which payment has commenced/terminated per the payroll with personnel records. For a sample of employees agree hours worked per the payroll with hours recorded on the time sheets. Obtain evidence of a review for reasonableness being performed by the financial controller eg authorisation signature.
Accuracy and valuation: Amounts relating to the payroll transactions and the resulting assets and liabilities have been correctly recorded.	For a sample of employees agree standing data to source documentation eg pay rates to personnel records. For a sample of payments reperform the payroll calculations. Check that deductions from gross pay have been calculated correctly.
Existence: Liabilities for payments to staff and to tax authorities in respect of deductions made exist. The asset of cash used to pay payroll exists.	For a sample of employees chosen from the payroll check the existence of personnel records (to confirm that the individual exists and therefore that liabilities in respect of them exist). Check for the existence of physical security of cash by observing the payment process for cash wages. Perform a cash count of any amounts of cash in hand eg where cash wages have not been claimed. The reasons why this cash has not been claimed should be established. Check for evidence that bank reconciliations are performed on a monthly basis which take into account bank transfers in respect of wages.
Classification and understandability: The financial information is appropriately presented and described, and disclosures are clearly expressed.	Agree the accounting treatment and disclosure of income statement charges and balance sheet assets and liabilities to local legislation and accounting standards.

35 Burton Housing

> **Text references.** Chapters 10 and 17
>
> **Top tips.** Don't forget what you are auditing here - it is useless to suggest controls or audit tests which are suitable for a large manufacturing organisation. Questions on organisations other than commercial companies are often based on their income and expenditure.
>
> **Easy marks.** This question is made more difficult by the fact that it is based on a small charity rather than a company. The requirements themselves however are familiar. Provided you are prepared to think about the nature of the organisation and tailor your comments you should be able to pick up good marks.

(a) (i) **Rental income**

Internal control over the system for recording rents are weak because there are no real checks on the work of the bookkeeper who could therefore easily commit a fraud or make undiscovered errors.

The main control problems here are as follows.

(1) **Lack of segregation of duties** between recording invoices, recording cash, receiving cash and banking cash.

(2) **Authorisation of bad debt write offs** should rest with the chief executive not the housing manager.

(3) An **independent check** is required to compare amounts received to expected rent based on occupancy levels.

My audit procedures will be greater in the areas of weakness of internal controls and I will perform the following procedures:

(1) **Compare rental income to previous levels and to budget**. Analytical review can be used to check occupancy, the level of empty flat/weeks and the level of bad debts. The theoretical rental income is 30 × weekly rent (ie on full occupancy).

$$\therefore \text{Occupancy (\%)} = \frac{\text{Actual rental income}}{\text{Theoretical rental income}} \% \text{, so:}$$

Empty flat rate (%) = 100 − Occupancy (%)

The level of occupancy can be checked to the housing manager's reports and compared to prior years. Investigate discrepancies between calculated occupancy and reported occupancy.

(2) Select a sample of weeks from the year and **check** the **posting** of all **invoices** for rent for all flats to the sales ledger. Where there is no invoice I will check to the occupancy report that the flat was empty. This will check that the invoices have been posted to the correct sales ledger account.

(ii) **Control over receipt and recording of rent**

Control activities which should be in operation here include the following.

(1) **Reception** staff should **issue receipts** for rent, reconciling cash to copy receipts before handing over the money to the bookkeeper. **Differences** between cash and receipts should be **investigated** and a note kept of the cash handed over.

(2) A **check** should be made by a senior (independent) official, eg the chief executive, between the **cash received** by the reception staff and the **cash** banked and **posted** to the sales ledger.

(3) **Complaints** from residents about rent payments should be **investigated** by an independent member of the management committee, particularly where residents claim to have paid rent,

but it has not been received. (The use of rent books for residents might avoid the loss of individual receipts.)

Main audit checks to be carried out

(1) Select a sample of days from during the year and **check** from the **reception staff's receipts** and record of cash to the **banked cash** and the postings to the sales ledger. Check that the money is banked promptly.

(2) **Check** that **disputes** about rent are **investigated** independently and a written report made to the management committee.

(3) **Investigate** any **problems** found. Any weaknesses in the system should be reported to the management committee.

(iii) **Postings of credit notes/bad debts/adjustments**

There should not be too many adjustments of this type, but they should be reviewed as any fraud could be 'lost' in such adjustments.

I will select a sample of all these items (probably based on size) and carry out the following procedures.

(1) **Agree to supporting documentation** (explaining why rents returned, or steps to recover rent before writing it off).

(2) **Check authorisation** has been given by the chief executive (for all these items).

(3) **Adjustments** to correct errors will be **checked** to the original entry and the calculations redone.

(4) Where a **credit note** has been issued, I will **check** that the **resident was originally charged** for that period and that amount.

(5) For **bad debts**, I will check that the **debt was old** and that the **resident had left**; also check that the Association tried to chase the debtor and collect the money.

At the year end, any credit balances which exist may indicate overpayment by residents. I will also **look** for any **old balances** which may need to be written off. These bad debts should be checked by the chief executive to ensure that they are not a result of misappropriation by staff.

(b) **Income and expenditure of restaurant**

(i) Select a sample of days during the year. For each day obtain the till roll and **compare** the **amount of money** taken in sales with the **amount banked**. (The till rolls should be retained for each year at least until the audit is over.) Small discrepancies can be ignored, but substantial differences must be investigated in full.

(ii) Use the above sample to check that any **credits given** by the till (ie after the total button has been pressed) have been **authorised** by the restaurant manager.

(iii) **Observe the cashier(s) at work**, as unobtrusively as possible, in order to ascertain whether they are using the till correctly and whether they have few opportunities to misappropriate cash (ie by not recording sales). Relevant controls will include frequent and regular supervision by the restaurant manager, use of video cameras etc (these should also help to prevent shoplifting of chocolate bars and other small objects).

(iv) **Calculate an average actual gross profit** for the restaurant by comparing selling price to the cost of ingredients for a range of meals/snacks. Amounts used can be assessed by sampling meals and the restaurant manager's calculations of amounts to be purchased can be assessed. I will compare the average gross profit I have assessed to the gross profit in the draft accounts. Any difference will represent **wastage** and should be reasonable compared to previous years (and perhaps the level of wastage seen at other restaurants etc audited by the firm).

(v)   The **gross profit** in the draft accounts should be **compared to the previous year's accounts** and any differences investigated.

(vi)   The **ratio of wages to sales** should be **calculated and compared** to previous periods. Any discrepancies or differences should be investigated. The weekly/monthly wages bill should be reviewed and any significant variations investigated (including variations in tax paid). Any variations caused by staff leaving/joining should be checked to the relevant tax forms.

(vii)   Select a sample of purchase invoices as listed in the purchase ledger and **trace the authorised purchase invoice** (ie the food was received) and **the purchase order**. I will check that all purchases are appropriate to the sales made in the restaurant. To overcome the weakness in control where the restaurant manager orders the food and authorises the invoice, the chief executive should authorise the invoice instead.

(viii) The **closing inventories** of food should be **checked**. Most inventory should not be very old and its age and value should be comparable with previous years (frequency of delivery will indicate the inventory age).

(ix)   **Discover** whether there are any **fictitious staff** being paid by **meeting** each member of staff. The **documentation for leavers and joiners** can be **checked** and that no payments were made to them after leaving or before joining. **Rates of pay** should be **agreed to personnel files** or management committee minutes. **Overtime** should be **authorised** by the restaurant manager (on the timesheet) and by the chief executive (on payment). Employees should sign for their pay packets and I might attempt to witness this in operation.

(x)   **Consider** whether, overall, the **figures** in the restaurant accounts are **reasonable**, based on the above audit work. If any **large costs** have been found I will **vouch** these to **authorised documentation**. In particular, I will look carefully for possible understatement of sales or overstatement of costs (both of which might indicate a fraud).

Criticisms of the system should be reported to the chief executive and the management committee. Any material unexplained differences might cause me to qualify my report ('material' amounts may not be very large in this situation).

36 Materiality considerations

Text reference. Chapter 6

Top tips. You should be familiar with materiality and should be able to explain and illustrate it well.

Easy marks. These should be available throughout this question although note the examiner's comment below. It is essential that you are able to explain a basic auditing concept like materiality.

Examiner's comments. The answers to this question were disappointing with few able to describe the concepts well. Many struggled to come up with an example of qualitative materiality and also thought it acceptable to do no work in immaterial areas.

Marking scheme		Marks

Materiality

(i)	Concept Up to 2 marks per point to a maximum of	4
(ii)	Audit work Up to 2 marks to a maximum of	4
(iii)	Qualitative example Up to 2 marks	$\frac{2}{10}$

Materiality

(i) *Concept*

Information is material if its omission or misstatement **could influence the economic decisions of users** taken on the basis of the financial statements. It is therefore a relative measure which can have **qualitative** as well as **quantitative** aspects. In other words something can be material due to its size or due to its nature. Material omissions/misstatements affect the true and fair view (fair presentation) and therefore the auditor's opinion.

(ii) *Impact on audit work*

Materiality is assessed together with risk so that **audit work can be targeted towards the significant and high risk areas**. This ensures that the audit is effective and efficient. It assists the auditor in deciding which items to examine and whether to use sampling and analytical procedures.

It assists the auditor evaluating the impact of errors. This may result in the auditor extending audit procedures or requesting management to adjust the financial statements.

(iii) *Qualitative example*

An example of qualitative misstatements would be the inadequate or improper description of an accounting policy when it is likely that the user would be misled by the description.

37 Question with analysis: Springfield Nurseries

Text reference. Chapter 16

Top tips. You shouldn't find this question on the audit of non-current assets too tricky. Part (c) is probably the most difficult part. This question is typical of the sort of question you should expect on any balance sheet area on your exam paper. You need to be able to explain issues and identify audit tests to gain sufficient evidence about them. You might also have to comment on the implications of a situation for your audit conclusion and report.

Easy marks. Parts (a) and (b) are the more straightforward parts of the question. For part (a) a sensible approach would be to consider the relevant assertions first and then consider the associated risks.

For part (b) ensure that you deal with ownership and cost separately. You should also consider the reliability of the evidence you suggest.

(a)   **Financial statement assertions for non-current assets**

Completeness

The amounts stated in the balance sheet for non-current assets must represent all non-current assets used in the operations of the entity. Significant omissions could have a material effect on the financial statements. Where an entity has lots of small capital items, recording and tracking these can be an issue so good controls are important.

Existence

Recorded assets must represent productive assets that are in use at the balance sheet date. Where assets have been disposed, they must not be included in the balance sheet. Items that are susceptible to misappropriation can also present issues.

Valuation

Non-current assets must be stated at cost or valuation less accumulated depreciation. Whether an entity has a policy or not of revaluing certain categories of its non-current assets can have a material effect on its financial statements. The depreciation policy in place must be suitable as this can also have a significant bearing on asset values on buildings and larges items of plant and equipment.

Rights and obligations

This is a key assertion for non-current assets because the entity must own or have rights to all the recorded non-current assets at the balance sheet date. For example, where an asset is leased by the entity, it may not have substantially all the risks and rewards associated with ownership and therefore should not recognise the asset on its balance sheet.

Classification and understandability

Non-current assets must be disclosed correctly in the financial statements. This applies to cost or valuation, depreciation policies and assets held under finance leases.

(b)   **Risks associated with non-current assets**

(i)   *Existence*

There is a risk that the assets held in the books and reported in the financial statements are not represented by the assets actually in use in the garden centres. Alternatively, items may have been wrongly capitalised, when in actual fact they should have been charged to the income statement in the year in which they occurred.

(ii)   *Rights*

There is a risk that assets are not actually owned by the company, but are hired or leased.

(iii)   *Valuation*

There is a risk that assets are overstated. Depreciation may not have been charged correctly, to represent the use that has been gained from the asset.

(c)   **Evidence available**

Asset	Ownership	Cost
Land and Buildings	Title deeds. These may be held at the bank or the client's solicitors. It may be possible to obtain confirmation of ownership from the central land registry office. The insurance policy should be checked to see whom the cover is in favour of.	The cost of the land and building can be traced to original invoices. The company may also have retained the original completion documents from the solicitor on the purchase of the land.
Computers	The software licence will reveal who owns the software on the computer. There may also be a contract with a computer company.	The cost can be obtained from the original invoice.
Motor Vehicles	Ownership can be verified by obtaining the registration documents for the motor vehicles.	Again, invoices will reveal the cost. If the original invoice is not available, the list price might be available from a publication such as Glasses Guide.

(d)   **Procedures re depreciation**

The purpose of depreciation is to write off the cost of the asset over the period of its useful economic life.

(i)   *Buildings*

The buildings are being depreciated over 20 years.

To check the appropriateness of the depreciation rate of 5%, the auditor should:

- Consider the physical condition of the building and whether the remaining useful life assumption is reasonable

- Review the minutes of board meetings to ensure there are no relocation plans

- Consider the budgets and ensure that they account for the appropriate amount of depreciation. If they do not, they may give an indication of management's future plans.

(ii)   *Computers and Motor vehicles*

The computers are depreciated at 20% reducing balance. This reflects the fact that the computers will wear out more of their value in the earlier years.

The reducing balance basis seems reasonable, given that computers and their software are updated frequently and therefore do wear faster early on in life.

The auditor should consider whether the assets are still in use.

He should review the board minutes to ascertain whether there are any plans to upgrade the system. He should also discuss the replacement policy with the directors.

The auditor should estimate the average age of the motor vehicles according to their registration plates and consider whether the life is reasonable in light of average age and recent purchases.

He should ask management what the replacement policy of the assets is.

(iii) *Equipment*

The motor vehicles are depreciated at 15% per year, or over 6-7 years.

The auditor should consider whether this is reasonable for all the categories of equipment, or whether there are some assets for which the technology advances more quickly than others.

He should consider the replacement policy.

(e) **Disagreement**

(i) *Action*

The auditor should discuss the reason why he disagrees with the depreciation policy with management. They may agree to amend the accounts.

He should then consider the materiality of the item in question. If it is depreciation it will impact on the balance sheet and the income statement.

It is unlikely to be material to the balance sheet. The net book value of assets other than buildings is likely to be small in relation to other assets such as inventory, and the impact of a change in rate not material. However, depreciation could be material to the income statement, particularly if the result was marginal and amendment would change the result from a profit to a loss.

(ii) *Impact on the audit report*

If the disagreement is material, it will impact on the audit report. However, despite its materiality, a disagreement about depreciation rates is unlikely to be fundamental to the basis of the accounts, so it would result in an 'except for…' qualification.

38 Wear Wraith

Text reference. Chapter 16

Top tips. This is a fairly straightforward question on non-current assets. In part (a), think about the objectives when testing non-current assets, i.e. ownership, existence, valuation, completeness. You are asked to 'list' the audit work so make sure you are specific and succinct in your answers. In part (b), the best approach is to take each category of non-current assets in turn and deal with each separately. Note that the requirement specifically tells you to ignore the railway trucks. The motor vehicles are a bit more complicated than the land and buildings and plant and machinery categories but you should, from the scenario, spot that the disposals in the year relate to vehicles that were five years old whereas the policy is to depreciate these over three years.

Easy marks. In part (b), easy marks are available for considering the land and buildings and plant and machinery categories first. You should remember from your financial reporting studies that land is normally not depreciated. From the plant and machinery figures, you should be able to identify fairly quickly from a quick scan of the figures that the depreciation on the disposals exceeds their cost value.

Examiner's comments. In part (a), many candidates obtained a good pass by stating six or seven clear audit tests on non-current assets. The tests were clearly related to the scenario. Some candidates, however, simply stated every possible test on non-current assets with no regard at all for the scenario. Spending a little time planning and thinking about the scenario is advisable prior to writing the answer. Overall, the standard was disappointing, with the average standard being a very marginal pass.

In part (b), candidates were required to identify any issues concerning the note that should be raised with management. The implication was that such issues would be unusual, not basic issues such as obtaining evidence of existence of the assets. It was therefore disappointing to see some candidates simply repeating all the audit tests again, having already done this in part (a). Weaknesses included a lack of knowledge of the information provided in a non-current asset note and suggesting that the note had arithmetical errors when the question explicitly stated that this was not the case.

The overall standard for this question was disappointing. The content of many answers showed that candidates are not always familiar with the use of scenarios in auditing questions. Question practice on how to apply scenario information to specific question requirements is needed.

Marking scheme

			Marks
(a)	One mark for each valid test		
	Board minutes	1	
	Non-current asset ledger	1	
	Non current asset note	1	
	Inspect trucks	1	
	Purchase invoices	1	
	Depreciation policy OK?	1	
	Depreciation disclosure amount	1	
	Depreciation accurate calculation	1	
	Treatment of any sales tax	1	
	Confirm NBV using specialist or trade journal	1	
	Other relevant points (each)	1	
	Maximum marks		**10**
(b)	Key points up to 2 marks for explaining the problem and 1 mark for stating the solution		
	Land and buildings – depreciation of land	3	
	Plant and machinery – depreciation eliminated > cost	3	
	Motor vehicles – depreciation calculated not = disclosure note	3	
	Motor vehicles – may be depreciating too quickly	3	
	Maximum marks		**10**
Total			**20**

(a) **Audit work to perform on railway trucks**

- Reconcile the draft note figures for railway trucks to the non-current asset register and general ledger to ensure that the amount stated in the accounts is accurate.

- Cast the non-current assets note and check that it agrees to the amount disclosed in the balance sheet.

- Vouch a sample of additions in the year to supporting third party documentation such as invoices from suppliers to ensure that the amounts stated are correct and to confirm ownership.

- Review board minutes authorising purchase of the trucks in the year to confirm authorisation.

- Recalculate the depreciation charge for the year based on the total cost of the trucks and the stated depreciation policy and check that this has been charged in the income statement and stated correctly in the non-current assets note.

- Vouch the existence of a sample of railway trucks in the accounting records to the physical asset.

- Verify completeness of railway trucks by taking a sample of trucks by physical inspection and checking that they have been recorded in the accounting records and the non-current asset register.

- Check that the depreciation policy for railway trucks is appropriate by reference to industry standards and the accounts of other similar companies to Wear Wraith.

- Check the treatment of sales tax for a sample of assets to ensure it is correct, e.g. capitalised where it is non-recoverable.

(b) **Non-current asset issues to discuss with management**

Land and Buildings

The depreciation rate of 2% has been correctly applied however the charge for the year has been based on the total balance i.e. land and buildings. Per IAS 16, land is not generally depreciated as it is considered to have an unlimited life. Therefore the building element of the total should be separated out in order to calculate the charge for the year on the buildings element only.

Plant and Machinery

The depreciation charge for additions and existing plant and machinery has been correctly calculated by applying 20% to the year-end balances (i.e. charging a full year's depreciation in the year of acquisition for new additions). Disposals costing $100,000 occurred in the year but the depreciation eliminated on these is $120,000, which is greater than the total cost, has been adjusted for which is incorrect. This must be discussed with management and any identified errors should be adjusted for accordingly.

Motor Vehicles

The depreciation charge on the motor vehicles sold has correctly been adjusted for at $325,000 as they were fully depreciated assets at the time of disposal. However, the motor vehicles were 5 years old, whereas the policy for motor vehicles is to depreciate them over 3 years. This indicates that management should review the useful economic life of motor vehicles in order to assess whether the current policy is still appropriate.

The charge for the year appears to have been incorrectly calculated, as it seems to have been charged over 4 years rather than over 3 years. The charge for the year of $425,000 is less than it should be according to the rate per the depreciation policy for motor vehicles. Therefore either the policy has changed or the calculation has been performed incorrectly. This issue should be discussed with management to ascertain the reason and the appropriate amendment made, i.e. either to the policy note or to the charge for the year. This would not constitute a change in accounting policy (as it is a change in an accounting estimate, per IAS 18) so there would be no need to amend prior year figures.

39 Tracey Transporters

Text references. Chapters 12 and 16

Top tips. In part (a), a good way of setting your answer out and giving it more structure would be to use a tabular format, ie 'Audit test' in one column and 'Reason for test' in the other column. Make sure that you do explain the reasons why you are carrying out each test – this is specifically requested in the question requirement. In part (b), think about the audit assertions first and make sure your audit work adequately covers them in your answer.

Easy marks. The marks in this question should be achievable fairly easily. Use the information in the scenario and give your answers as much structure as possible.

Examiner's comments. Answers to part (a) varied considerably. Well-prepared candidates provided excellent lists of tests, with appropriate explanations, which were relevant to the scenario. However the majority of candidates had difficulty explaining the tests.

Specific reasons for weak answers included:

- Including tests on the non-current assets register. Given that this was a sales audit, it was not clear why these tests were included here, and again in part (b)

- Providing comments such as 'check casting' without specifying which documents are to be cast, or why

- Explaining the audit of receivables without linking this to the objectives of completeness and accuracy of sales

- Explaining the systems and controls that should be in place rather than auditing the system. This did not meet the requirement of explaining audit tests.

The overall standard of answers to part (b) was much higher than for part (a). The majority of candidates managed to provide a sufficiently broad list of tests. Specific reasons for weaker answers included:

- Not fully explaining the points, e.g. saying, 'Obtain company records for ownership' but not actually stating which records needed to be obtained.

- Stating unclear or incorrect audit procedures, e.g. 'obtain non-current asset register, take sample of vehicles and see vehicle to check completeness of the register'. This is actually checking the accuracy of the register. Checking for completeness would normally involve seeing an asset then checking that it was included.

- A small minority of candidates mentioned tests on other areas of the balance sheet. It was not clear whether the need to audit non-current assets had been identified. More focused answers are needed to obtain a pass standard.

Many candidates would benefit from taking a minute to jot down the assertions and then ensure that their answer covered all of them.

Marking scheme

		Marks
(a)	Sales testing	
	Audit tests on completeness and accuracy of sales income	
	Watch for tests being combined – be generous where two tests are given in the same point	
	Normally award 1 mark per point to a maximum of	
(b)	Non-current asset testing	10
	List of tests at 1 mark per relevant test to a maximum of	10
	Total	**20**

(a)

Audit test	Reason
Enquire about and observe the procedures used when bookings are received over the telephone.	The biggest risk of incomplete recording of orders relates to those received by telephone. Evidence is needed that checking and supervision occurs at this point.
With the client's permission, enter a sample of test data into the VMS booking system and review the details logged on the system.	This will confirm that there are no flaws in the system causing omission or error at the input stage.
For a sample of e-mail orders, agree details to the VMS booking system.	This will identify errors arising when the e-mail details are input to the VMS system.
For a sample of booking records within the VMS system, agree the details to the corresponding invoice produced by the receivables ledger programme.	This will identify whether information is transferred completely and accurately between the two modules of the system.
For a sample of invoices, agree the hire prices charged to the master file record of approved prices.	This will identify whether the full approved prices are being charged to customers.
For a sample of credit notes issued in the year, agree to supporting documentation and check for evidence of authorisation by the appropriate level of management.	This will check that credit notes are only issued and sales entries reversed when there is a valid reason.

Audit test	Reason
Cast the list of invoices issued in one month (or other appropriate period) and agree the total to the entry made to the nominal ledger.	This will identify whether the journals posted to the nominal ledger are complete and accurate.
Cast the sales account in the nominal ledger and agree the total to the sales figure in the draft profit and loss account.	This will identify whether any arithmetical errors have arisen in the accounting system and whether any errors have arisen in the transfer of information from the accounting system to the financial statements.
Perform analytical procedures, comparing the following ratios to prior years (or month by month if the information is available): – Turnover per vehicle – Gross profit margin Obtain explanations and corroborate evidence for any unexpected variations.	If material amounts have been omitted from sales it would be likely to have a significant effect on these ratios.
Review the results of audit procedures on receivables, such as the results of any direct confirmation of balances, and consider whether any errors identified also have an effect on the sales figure.	The double entry effect of errors needs to be considered and if, say, a confirmation reply from a customer reveals that an amount has been incorrectly posted to the receivables account, this will have a corresponding effect on sales.

(b) **Audit work on vehicles**

(i) Obtain a schedule reconciling the movement on the vehicles cost account and vehicles depreciation account over the year and agree:

- Opening balances to prior year audit files
- Closing balances to non-current asset register and nominal ledger

(ii) Cast the columns for costs, depreciation and net book value in the non-current asset register.

(iii) Select a sample of additions in the year from the non-current asset register and:

- Agree to the purchase invoice to confirm ownership *(rights and obligations assertion)* and that the correct amount has been capitalised, excluding any revenue items such as petrol or road tax *(valuation and allocation assertion)*.

- From the date on the purchase invoice confirm that the purchase has been recorded in the correct accounting period *(occurrence assertion)*.

- Physically inspect the vehicle to confirm existence (or alternatively, if the vehicle is out on hire at the time inspect the hire documentation, insurance policy and vehicle registration document) *(existence assertion)*.

(iv) From the company's insurance policy, agree a sample of vehicles currently owned (and hence insured by TT) to the non-current asset register *(completeness assertion)*.

(v) Review the repairs and maintenance expense account and agree any unusually large amounts to invoices to check that no purchases of a capital nature have been misclassified *(completeness assertion)*.

(vi) Obtain a list of disposals in the year and:

- Check that the vehicle has been removed from the non-current assets register
- Agree sales proceeds to the cash book

(vii) Perform a proof in total of the depreciation charge for the year, applying the depreciation rate as disclosed in the financial statements to the opening balance *(valuation assertion)*.

(viii) For a sample of individual vehicles from the non-current asset register, reperform the depreciation calculation *(valuation assertion)*.

(ix) Review the depreciation policy for reasonableness *(valuation assertion)* by:

- Checking for consistency with prior years

- Comparing it with that used by other companies in the industry

- Considering whether significant gains or losses have arisen on disposals during the year

- Comparing the useful life applied in the depreciation calculation to the age of the lorries that were sold during the year

(x) Review the notes to the accounts to check that:

- The depreciation policy has been disclosed, and

- The movements on the vehicles cost and deprecation have been appropriately disclosed in the non-current assets note *(disclosure assertion)*.

(Note. The audit testing assertions are included in the answer as candidates are likely to structure their answer around these headings but there are no specific marks for mentioning them.)

40 Snu

Text reference. Chapter 13

Top tips. This is a relatively straightforward question dealing with inventory count procedures. The main trap to avoid however is confusing the year-end count with the perpetual inventory system in part (a). Remember the perpetual inventory system involves maintaining book inventory records with continuous inventory counting to ensure that the records are accurate and up to date. Also note the need to read the question carefully and to reflect the information in the answer. For example, part (b) asks for the audit procedures which would be performed, not the continuous inventory count procedures themselves. In part (c) notice that you are not being asked to describe **how** to overcome the weaknesses but to describe **why** the weaknesses are difficult to overcome.

Easy marks. There are plenty of easy marks in this question. Parts (a) and part (b) are essentially knowledge based requirements so you should be looking to pick up good marks here. In part (a) think about why the auditor attends the year end inventory count. What is important about this balance (materiality?), what evidence is obtained (existence, value?).

Part (b) mentions a large, dispersed organisation. You need to think about the effect of this on the audit procedures (use of other offices, other firms, role of internal audit?).

Examiner's comments.

Part (a) of the question was generally well answered.

In part (b) many described the continuous inventory counting procedures rather than the audit procedures.

Part (c) was well answered but too many candidates offered solutions to the weaknesses rather than explaining why they were difficult to overcome.

		Marks
(a)	Importance of inventory counting Up to 2 marks per point to a maximum of	5
(b)	Perpetual inventory system Up to 1 mark per point to a maximum of	6
(c)	Risks associated with inventory Up to 1 mark per point to a maximum of	4
(d)	Weakness in counting instructions – why they are difficult to overcome Up to 2 marks per point to a maximum of	$\underline{15}$ $\underline{\underline{30}}$

(a) **Importance of year-end inventory counts**

(i) Auditors are required to obtain **sufficient appropriate** evidence to support the inventory figure stated in the accounts. This is particularly relevant where inventories are material to the financial statements. Where perpetual inventory systems are not maintained the year-end count is the most reliable means by which the auditor can obtain the following audit evidence:

- **Quantity and existence** of inventory

- An indication of the **value** of inventory and the means by which management identify slow and obsolete items

- **Cut-off** details

- The overall **control environment** in which the inventory system operates

- Evidence of **fraud or misappropriation**

(b) **Audit procedures**

The following procedures would be performed in order to rely on a perpetual inventory system:

- **Check management procedures** to ensure that all inventory lines are counted at least once a year.

- Confirm that **adequate inventory records** are maintained and that they are kept up-to-date. Tests would include a comparison of sales and purchase transactions with inventory movements. Inventory records would also be checked for correct casting and classification of inventory.

- For a sample of counts at a number of locations the inventory count **instructions should be reviewed**.

- **Attend and observe** the counts at a sample of locations. (As the organisation is dispersed this may involve the use of staff from other offices.) Those visited should be chosen on the basis of the materiality of the inventory balance and whether the site is identified as high risk eg where controls have been weak historically. The remainder could then be visited on a rotational basis.

- Assess the extent to which the results of **internal audit work** can be relied on. As the organisation is large it is likely to have an internal audit function. Results of test counts performed by internal audit may reduce the extent of external audit test counts.

- Check that procedures are in place to **correct book inventories** for discrepancies identified at the inventory counts. Changes should be **authorised** and made accurately and on a timely basis.

(c) **Principal risks associated with the financial statement assertions for inventory**

One of the risks associated with inventory is its appropriate valuation. Inventory should be valued at the lower of cost and net realisable value per IAS 2 *Inventories*. Inventory can be a material figure in the financial statements of many entities, particularly manufacturing companies, and therefore appropriate valuation of inventory is very important, particularly for obsolete and slow-moving items. The valuation can also be a matter of judgement and this increases the risk associated with inventory.

Inventory in the balance sheet must **exist** - this is another key assertion. Inventory can be subject to theft and misappropriation, and is often held at more than one location, and so controls to safeguard it are very important.

Cut-off is another key issue for inventory. All purchases, transfers and sales of inventory must be recorded in the correct accounting period as again inventory can be a material figure for many companies. Incorrect cut-off can result in misstatements in the financial statements at the year-end and this can be of particular concern where inventory is material. Auditors therefore need to consider whether the management of the entity being audited have implemented adequate cut-off procedures to ensure that movements into and out of inventory are properly identified and reflected in the accounting records and ultimately in the financial statements.

(d)

Weakness	Explanation
Timing of the inventory count The count is due to take place on New Year's Day. This is unlikely to be popular with staff. Resentment and a desire to get the job done as quickly as possible may mean that the counts are not done thoroughly. There is also little time given to preparation before the count, a problem exacerbated by the fact that both the shops and warehouse are very busy in the period leading up to the count.	As the company operates seven days a week it would be difficult to find an alternative date for the inventory count. In addition it is at this time of year to coincide with the company's December year end. It would be expensive and difficult to find alternative staff to perform the task and it is unlikely that the business will change its year end simply because the inventory count is inconvenient. It may be possible to perform the count a week before or a week after the year end and roll forward/back the inventory calculation. This would involve closing the business for an extra day and would also involve a degree of reliance on inventory records.
There is a **lack of segregation of duties**. Mr Sneg is the inventory controller as well as being the count supervisor and count checker. This means that he is responsible for the physical assets as well as maintaining the book records. It would be possible therefore for Mr Sneg to cover up theft of inventory or mistakes made by himself. This situation affects the control environment of the overall performance of the inventory count.	In some respects this situation could be resolved if an alternative senior member of staff were made the inventory supervisor. However in family businesses it is common for a small number of loyal and trusted staff to bear the majority of the responsibility. There is likely to be strong resistance from Mr Sneg himself who would feel that his good character was being questioned. Other senior members of staff are also likely to be reluctant to take on a role for which they may feel they have little experience and understanding.
Counters will work on their **own**. Normally counts should be performed by pairs of counters as this reduces the risk of error.	Where there is a limited number of staff it may be difficult to work in pairs and get the count completed in the available time scale. Due to the timing of the count it will not be easy to get staff from other areas of the business to volunteer to take part.

Weakness	Explanation
This is of particular concern in this case as the company has a high turnover of staff. Counters are likely to be inexperienced and may not be motivated to do a good job.	Where staff turnover is high it is difficult to resolve the problem of inexperience in the short term. Management could consider the factors which contribute to staff leaving eg poor pay to determine whether these can be addressed in the medium term. However warehouse work is often unskilled and therefore an element of staff turnover is inevitable.
The treatment of inventory delivered to customers that has not yet been paid for is **incorrect.** The inventory should not be added back and the unpaid balances should be included as receivables.	There is no reason why this matter cannot be dealt with. The treatment of inventory not paid for should be corrected.

41 Textile Wholesalers

Text reference. Chapter 13

Top tips. This question deals with the year-end inventory count and cut-off procedures. This is a popular exam topic. When considering the inventory count procedures try to think through the practical steps involved. This will help you to generate ideas and will provide a sensible structure for your answer. Cut-off is an important area of your studies. Management should ensure they have proper cut-off procedures to cover all stages of the movement of inventories (ie receipt of goods, internal transfers and final sales).

Easy marks. These are available in part (a). Notice how (ii) follows on from (i). Once you have identified the procedures that the company's staff should be carrying out you can then use these points as a basis for the audit procedures. For example if the company procedure is to have full inventory count instructions the audit procedure would be to review these.

(a)   (i)   The procedures that the company's staff should carry out to ensure that inventories is counted accurately and cut-off details are recorded are as follows.

      (1)   Staff carrying out the inventory count should be issued with **full instructions** and so know how to proceed.

      (2)   Staff **counting inventories** should be **independent** of warehouse staff. They should count in **pairs**.

      (3)   A **senior member of staff** should **supervise the count**, carry out test counts and check at the end all inventories have been counted.

      (4)   All **inventory movements** should **stop** whilst the inventory counting is in progress.

      (5)   **Pre-numbered inventory sheets** should be used to record the counts and should be completed in ink signed by the counter. All sheets should be accounted for at the end of the inventory counting.

      (6)   The number of the **last Goods Received Note** and **Goods Dispatched Note** to be issued before the inventory counting should be recorded.

      (7)   Staff should **note the condition of inventories** where it is old or in poor condition.

      (8)   Staff should be designated **clearly defined areas** for counting to avoid double counting or inventory being missed. It may be possible to mark items in some way once they have been counted.

(ii)   As auditor I would carry out the following checks.

    (1)   **Review** the company's **inventory counting instructions** to ensure they were comprehensive and complete.

    (2)   **Observe** the client's **staff** during the count to ensure they were complying with issued instructions.

    (3)   **Carry out some test counts** and note the results in my working papers. My test counts will be in both directions (from the inventory sheets to the inventories, thus checking the inventories exists, and *vice versa* to ensure inventories has been completely recorded).

    (4)   **Note any items** considered to be **old** or in **poor condition**.

    (5)   **Note** the **sequence** of inventory sheets issued.

    (6)   **Note down the last Goods Received Note and Goods Despatched Note** numbers, also details of last returns to suppliers and from customers.

    (7)   **Take copies of inventory sheets** and check during final audit to ensure client's staff have not subsequently changed them.

(b)   **Importance of cut-off in the audit of inventory**

Cut-off is a key issue in the audit of inventory. All purchases, transfers and sales of inventory must be recorded in the correct accounting period as inventory can be a material figure for many companies, particularly manufacturing ones.

The points of purchase and receipt of goods and services are particularly important in order to ensure that cut-off has been correctly applied. The transfer of completed work-in-progress to finished goods is also important as is the sale and despatch of such goods.

Incorrect cut-off can result in misstatements in the financial statements at the year-end and this can be of particular concern where inventory is material. Auditors therefore need to consider whether the management of the entity being audited have implemented adequate cut-off procedures to ensure that movements into and out of inventory are properly identified and reflected in the accounting records and ultimately in the financial statements.

(c)   Errors have been made in cut-off for items 2, 4, 5 and 6

(i)

GRN No	Goods received in June 20X6	Adjustment $
2	Invoice included in the purchase ledger and in accruals	5,164
4	Invoice not included in the purchase ledger and in accruals	(9,624)
	Goods received in July 20X6	
5	Receipt included in purchase ledger	8,243
6	Receipt included in accruals	6,389
	Increase in profit	10,172

Both purchases and payables will be decreased by this amount.

(ii)   The incidence of error in this test is very high - four out of the seven items tested had been incorrectly treated. I would therefore **extend my test** to cover a larger number of GRNs over a longer period, both before and after the year end.

I would also ensure purchases that were treated as accruals had been **accrued correctly**.

I would check the treatment of goods on **invoices posted** early on the **following year** and check that invoices relating to following year deliveries had not been posted for this year.

I would also consider the results of the audit reconciliation of suppliers' statements to purchase ledger balances. This may highlight items which have been posted incorrectly (eg pre year-end invoices for goods received pre-year-end but not posted).

(d)   **Perpetual inventory counting systems**

Perpetual inventory counting systems are where an entity uses a system of inventory counting throughout the year and are commonly used by larger organisations.

Where such a system is in place, the auditors used carry out the following work:

- Talk to management to establish whether all inventory lines are counted at least once a year.

- Inspect inventory records to confirm that adequate inventory records are kept up-to-date.

- Review procedures and instructions for inventory counting and test counts to ensure they are as rigorous as those for a year-end inventory count.

- Observe inventory counts being carried out during the year to ensure they are carried out properly and that instructions are followed.

- Where differences are found between inventory records and physical inventory, review procedures for investigating them to ensure all discrepancies are followed-up and resolved and that corrections are authorised by a manager not taking part in the count.

- Review the year's inventory counts to confirm the extent of counting, the treatment of differences and the overall accuracy of records, and to decide whether a full year-end count will be necessary.

- Perform cut-off testing and analytical review to gain further comfort over the accuracy of the year-end figure for inventory in the financial statements.

42 Chingford Potteries

Text reference. Chapter 13

Top tips. This tests all the important areas of inventory, the inventory count and valuation. You should be well prepared in these areas though. In part (b) to gain good marks you have to note implications and recommendations as well as weaknesses.

Easy marks. This is a straightforward question so you should be able to score well here. All the marks are very achievable.

(a)   **Importance of the inventory count and inventory valuation**

Inventory count

The inventory count provides the primary evidence for the existence of inventories. Inventories is very often material to the financial statements. It affects both the balance sheet and the income statement (the trading account includes closing inventories). In a manufacturing company, such as Chingford Potteries, inventories is highly likely to be material.

Valuation

Valuation is a key assertion with regard to inventories because **inventory valuation can be complex**, particularly if the company has work in progress.

Alternatives to an inventory count

While an inventory count is commonly the primary evidence for the existence of inventory, there are alternatives to a year end inventory count. These are:

- A **perpetual inventory system**, where inventories is checked on a regular basis to ensure that book and physical inventories correspond

- A **roll-back or forward** of inventory from an inventory count at a time other than the year end. This involves counting the inventories at a time other than the year end and then performing a reconciliation to what inventories would have been at the year end, using goods delivered and received records.

(b) **Items for inclusion in Report to Management**

(i) **Planning**

Weakness

The inventory count was poorly planned.

Consequence

Inventories could have been omitted from the count or items counted twice due to confusion over the location of inventory. Items which were obsolete or damaged may have been included in the count due to them not being properly identified or segregated.

Recommendation

In future, the inventory count should be planned more carefully, inventories should be organised so that like inventories is placed together in the factory and warehouse and obsolete inventories should be clearly identified.

Staff should be properly briefed so that they know what they have to do to ensure that the count is completed smoothly and correctly.

For the purposes of this year's audit, the count may have to be planned again and repeated, with a roll-back reconciliation subsequently taking place.

(ii) **Inventory counting sheets**

Weakness

The inventory count sheets were not properly controlled. Employees were not required to sign for them and records were not kept of who was working from which sheet.

Consequence

Sheets may be lost or not counted from. This could result in inventories being counted and not recorded in the final inventory count, or not counted at all. This means that inventories will be understated in the financial statements.

Recommendation

In future years, inventory sheets should be signed in and out by the person who is in charge of them, and that person should keep a record of which employee has which sheet.

As noted above, for the purposes of this year's audit, this problem might also require the inventory count to be repeated.

(c) **Basis of valuing inventory**

According to IAS 2, inventories should be valued at the **lower of cost and net realisable value**. Net realisable value means the price that will be obtained for the inventories.

There are a number of categories of inventories which may have a net realisable value that is lower than cost at Chingford Potteries, because it is obsolete. These categories are:

- **Broken crockery.** It is reasonable to assume that given the fragile nature of Chingford's inventories, some of the inventories may have suffered damage.

- **Seconds.** It is common in this industry that items which do not meet required standards are produced. These are often referred to as seconds. There is a market for such inventories, but it may be at a price less than cost.

- **Out-of-line inventory.** Chingford may also produce seasonal items, for example, Christmas crockery, or may be contracted to large retailers for specific periods with certain designs. Such inventories will not be worth the original selling price if it is out of season.

(d) **Work to establish inventories where NRV is lower than cost**

In order to establish if NRV is lower than cost, the following procedures should be undertaken:

- The current catalogues should be reviewed to check inventory and prices, and particularly, any sale catalogues should be scrutinised.

- Enquire into the quality control processes and identify if there is a typical percentage of inventory which is categorised as seconds. It may be possible to apply a percentage to the total of inventory as a seconds provision.

- Ask management, particularly those in charge of inventories whether any inventories is particularly slow moving.

- Review the inventory movement records to identify any particularly slow moving inventories.

- Compare the inventory sheets to the prior year to see if any inventories has not moved in the year.

- Review the inventory count notes to see if any damaged or obsolete inventories was noted by audit staff at the inventory count.

43 Rocks Forever

Text reference. Chapter 13

Top tips. Part (a) asks you to list and explain the reasons for the audit procedures used in obtaining evidence at an inventory count. Here a sensible structure would be to produce your answer in two columns but remember to answer fully and not to use a note form style. Think through the various aspects of the auditor's work. The role of the auditor is to assess the overall performance of the count to determine its reliability, not just to perform test counts. Also remember the importance of collecting information regarding cut-off. For 10 marks you are looking for about 10 points with 0.5 marks for the procedure and 0.5 for the explanation.

Part (b) asks for factors to consider when placing reliance on the work of the expert. For five marks you need about five points so you will need to generate a few ideas. If you are not familiar with ISA 620 don't panic. You should be able to produce a reasonable answer with a bit of common sense.

For part (c) the key is your accounting knowledge. Inventory should be valued at the lower of cost and net realisable value. Approach this part by thinking about the ways in which the cost of stock can be confirmed. Then think about the way in which net realisable value can be established.

Easy marks. Overall this is a reasonably straightforward question looking at an aspect of the audit with which you should be familiar. All the marks are reasonably achievable, which is good news although you do need to apply your knowledge to the scenario. Part (b) is probably the most straightforward as you can use your knowledge of ISA 620 *Using the work of an expert* to structure your answer.

Examiner's comments. Part (a) was not answered well. The standard of answers indicated that students were unclear about procedures for inventory counting. Two common errors were providing detailed work on inventory valuation and explaining how to audit the control systems over the receipt and despatch of goods. Marks were lost for not providing a reason for the procedure.

Part (b) was answered satisfactorily on the whole, although some answers were too brief to obtain the five marks available.

Part (c) was not answered well at all, with students focusing on assertions other than valuation or on the inventory count.

Marking scheme

		Marks
(a)	Risks associated with inventory Upto 1 mark per point to a maximum of	3
(b)	Risks associated with inventory in Rocks Forever Upto 1 mark per point to a maximum of	4
(c)	One mark each for explaining each procedure. 0.5 for the audit procedure and 0.5 for explaining the relevance of the procedure. **Maximum marks**	__12__
(d)	Key points 1 for each point	
	Confirm need for expert – auditor not have appropriate skill	1
	Scope of work – relevant experience	1
	Scope of work – professional body	1
	No conflict with client	1
	Obtained appropriate evidence – appears reasonable	1
	Other good relevant points	_1_
	Maximum marks	6
(e)	Key points 1 for each point	1
	Statement of accounting standard	1
	Determination of cost	1
	Determination of NRV	1
	Professional values report – NRV evidence	1
	Other obsolete inventory	1
	Other good relevant points	1
	Maximum marks	_5_
		30

(a)   **Principal risks associated with the financial statement assertions for inventory**

One of the risks associated with inventory is its appropriate valuation. Inventory should be valued at the lower of cost and net realisable value per IAS 2 *Inventories*. Inventory can be a material figure in the financial statements of many entities, particularly manufacturing companies, and therefore appropriate valuation of inventory is very important, particularly for obsolete and slow-moving items. The valuation can also be a matter of judgement and this increases the risk associated with inventory.

Inventory in the balance sheet must **exist** at the balance sheet date - this is another key assertion. Inventory can be subject to theft and misappropriation, and is often held at more than one location, and so controls to safeguard it are very important.

Cut-off is another key issue for inventory. All purchases, transfers and sales of inventory must be recorded in the correct accounting period as again inventory can be a material figure for many companies.

(b)   **Risks associated with inventory in Rocks Forever**

Rocks Forever is a company specialising in the sale of diamond jewellery. Inventory is therefore a material figure in the accounts of Rocks Forever.

Specific risks associated with inventory in Rocks Forever include existence – the nature of the inventory means that it is highly susceptible to theft and loss as it is a very attractive and valuable commodity.

Valuation is another key risk. The amount in the financial statements is material and the valuation of the jewellery is subjective as it is reliant on the judgement of expert valuers. The inventory should be valued at the lower of cost and net realisable value in accordance with accounting standards. However, given the nature of the inventory and the fact that sales are subject to changing trends and fashions, this is a key risk area.

(c) **Inventory count: procedures and reasons**

Audit procedures	Reason
Check that the client staff are following the inventory count instructions. This would include the following:	If proper procedures are not followed the auditor will not be able to rely on the count as relevant reliable audit evidence.
• Confirming that prenumbered count sheets are being used and that there are controls over the issue of count sheets.	Prenumbering of count sheets means that a completeness check can be performed and any missing sheets can be chased.
• Checking that counters are working in pairs of two.	This helps to prevent fraud and error.
• Confirming that inventory is marked once it has been counted.	Marking of inventory helps to prevent double counting of items.
• Confirming procedures to ensure that inventory is not moved during the count.	If inventory is moved eg sold during the count the counters may become confused as to which inventory has been counted and which has not. Movements of inventory would also make it more difficult to establish whether proper cut-off procedures have been followed.
• Confirming that inventory held for third parties is separately identified.	Customer jewellery held eg for repair should not be included in the inventory figure.
• Confirming that the counters are aware of the need to note down any items which they identify as damaged.	Damaged items may need to be written down to their recoverable amount. This will affect the overall value of inventory.
Gain an overall impression of the levels and values of inventory held.	This will assist the auditor in the follow up procedures to judge whether the figure for inventory in the financial statements is reasonable.
For a sample of inventory lines perform test counts and match results to those recorded by the client staff.	This provides evidence to confirm that the inventory exists and that the counting has been performed accurately and completely.
Check that all inventory sheets issued have been accounted for at the end of the count.	This provides evidence that a complete record of the results of the inventory count has been obtained. If missing count sheets were undetected inventory would be understated.
Take copies of the count sheets at the end of the inventory count and retain on file.	This prevents management from being able to adjust the figures subsequently. It also enables the auditor, in his follow up procedures to trace inventory counted to the final inventory calculation.
Obtain cut off details ie record details of the last sales invoice issued before the count and the last goods in record before the count.	This information will allow the auditor to determine whether cut off is correct. Items sold before the count should be included as sales and not recorded in inventory. Items received from suppliers before the count should be recorded as liabilities and in inventory. Sales and purchases after the inventory count should not be accounted for in this year's financial statements.

Audit procedures	Reason
Discuss with the valuer the results of his findings (eg that the diamonds are genuine and any obsolete/damaged goods which have been identified).	This evidence will support the subsequent valuation of inventory.
Conclude whether the inventory count has been properly carried out.	This will help the auditor to determine whether the procedure is sufficiently reliable as a basis for determining the existence of inventory.

(d) **Factors to consider**

- The need for an expert

  The auditor should consider the risk of material misstatement and whether there is the required expertise within the audit firm. In this case as inventory is material and this is the only client in the diamond industry which the firm has it would seem appropriate to use an expert. This need is increased by the specialised nature of the client's business.

- The competence of the expert

  The expert should be a member of a relevant professional body. The auditor should also consider the individual's experience and reputation in his field.

- The objectivity of the expert

  The opinion of UJ could be clouded if for example, if they were related in some manner to Rocks Forever. This could be a personal relationship or one of financial dependence.

- The scope of the expert's work

  If the auditor is to rely on this evidence it must be relevant to the audit of inventory. In this case UJ is considering issues which will impact on the valuation of inventory. This is of great importance to the auditor and is therefore relevant.

- Evaluation of the work performed

  The auditor will need to assess the quality of the work performed by the expert. The auditor will consider the following:

  - Source data used
  - Assumptions and methods used and their consistency with previous years
  - The results of UJ's work in the light of DeCe's overall knowledge of the business.

  In spite of the fact that the auditor's expertise is limited in this field DeCe may test the data used by UJ. For example comparative price information may be available from other shops or industry sources.

(e) **Inventory valuation: audit procedures**

The key principle is that inventory should be valued at the lower of cost and net realisable value.

Cost

For a sample of items agree the cost price to the original purchase invoice. Care should be taken to ensure that the invoice relates specifically to the item in question.

Net realisable value

Review the report produced by UJ for any indication that items are fake. (This is unlikely to be the case but should be confirmed.)

For a sample of items sold after the year end check that the sales price exceeds cost. Where this is not the case the item should be written down to its net realisable value.

Check that items valued by the valuer have been included in the inventory total at this valuation. If there are discrepancies the inventory balance should be revised to include UJ's valuation.

Obtain a schedule of the ageing of inventory. For items identified as slow moving discuss with management the need to make an allowance.

44 Receivables circularisations

Text reference. Chapter 12

Top tips. Parts (a) and (b) of this question are simple book learning. You should have found these sections of the question straightforward. If you did not, revise this area using the suggested solution and go back to Chapter 12 of your Study Text.

Easy marks. These should have been available in part (a) as this is primarily knowledge based, however note the examiner's comment below. The importance of being able to explain key audit procedures cannot be underestimated.

Examiner's comments. Part (a) was not well answered. Not enough candidates were aware of the two types of positive circularisation and instead wrote about the advantages and disadvantages of positive and negative circularisations. A worrying number of candidates also appeared to think that the type of circularisation involved telephoning the client's customer. In part (b) the principal risks were required. Many included all risks and did not seem to appreciate that overstatement is the principal risk.

Marking scheme

			Marks
(a)	External confirmation		
	(i)	Positive and negative confirmations 1 mark per point to maximum of	2
	(ii)	Positive confirmations 1 mark per point to maximum of	3
	(iii)	Reconciling items 0.5 marks per point to maximum of	2
(b)	Financial statement assertions – receivables 1 mark per point to a maximum		3
			10

(a) **Receivables circularisations**

(i) *Positive and negative circularisation*

Positive circularisation is where the auditor requests a response to their circularisation, whatever that response might be.

Negative circularisation is where an auditor requests that the person circularised only replies if they disagree with the balance stated on the circularisation letter. This method of circularisation is used less then the positive method, and only where controls are strong.

(ii) *Types of positive circularisation*

There are two types of positive circularisation:

(1) **Amount stated**. The auditor states the amount on the client's ledger and asks the debtor to agree or disagree with the balance. He is asked to give reasons if he disagrees. The disadvantage of this method is that the customer may simply agree without checking, or because the amount is understated. An advantage is that the customer providing explanation for disagreement might bring relevant matters to the auditors' attention, such as faulty inventory which may be more widespread, or pricing problems etc.

(2) **Amount requested**. Under this method, the auditor asks the customer to confirm the amount owed. A customer may be less likely to respond to such a request, as it involves more effort. It also does not enable the customer to provide a reconciliation between his ledger and the client's.

(iii) *Reconciling items*

These may include:

- Items in transit (inventory/invoices)
- Payments in transit
- Disputed invoices
- Credit notes requiring issue
- Debit notes
- Simple errors (on either part)
- Contras

(b) **Assertions**

Assets generally are at risk of overstatement of **valuation** by the client. This may be achieved by providing insufficiently for bad debts, by delaying the issue of credit notes, or by not netting credit notes off year-end receivables.

It is also important to ascertain that debts **exist** and that they represent **genuine rights** of the company to be paid. This can generally be discovered by payment of those debts to the company.

45 Coogee

Text reference. Chapter 12

Top tips. To answer this question you need a good knowledge of ISA 540 *Audit of accounting estimates*. Try to establish which assertions you are trying to test, as this will help you to focus testing in the right area. In part (c), for example, you will need to verify the completeness of the allowance, amongst other things.

Easy marks. To score well in this type of question you need to identify the key issues. In this case you are dealing with balances which are estimates made by management. The focus of your audit work will therefore be to establish how management estimated the figure, and then to determine how reasonable this is.

(a) **Approaches to gaining audit evidence re estimates**

- Review and perform procedures on the process used by management to arrive at the estimate
- Use an independent estimate for comparison
- Review subsequent events which confirm the estimate made

(b) **General allowance: procedures**

Two approaches can be taken.

(i) *Review and perform procedures on the process*

    (1)   Obtain details of the general allowance and the aged receivables analysis which supports it.

    (2)   Review the results of sales transactions tests to ensure that the system for ageing receivables works effectively.

    (3)   Find out from management the method of calculation of the allowance.

    (4)   Check whether it is the same method as in previous years and if not whether the amendment is reasonable. Consider management's explanation for the method and ensure that the method has been correctly applied.

    (5)   Recalculate the allowance.

    (6)   Compare to the receivables ledger to ensure that all relevant balances have been included.

    (7)   Check that none of the balances in the specific allowance have been included in the calculation, by review.

    (8)   Consider whether last year's allowance was reasonable in the light of events since last year's audit.

    (9)   Consider the results of any customer's circularisation undertaken. Customers may recognise the debt which will imply that they intend to make payment. If they acknowledge the debt it may be worth asking the client to contact them to agree on a payment timetable.

    (10)   Calculate ratios concerning debtor days and provision as a percentage of debt. They should be comparable to the previous year.

    (11)   Enquire whether the allowance has been considered and approved by the directors.

(ii) *Consider subsequent events*

    (1)   Test a sample of the balances in the receivables ledger to see if any cash has been received since the year end.

    (2)   Enquire of the credit controller as to whether any cash has been received on these accounts since the year end.

(c) **Specific allowance**

(i)   Obtain a list of the bad debts.

(ii)   Check that the list has been correctly totalled.

(iii)   Discuss the debt with the credit controller to ascertain why these are considered bad.

(iv)   Review the correspondence with the customer to ascertain whether the customer intends to pay or not.

(v)   If there is no correspondence, consider why. If the client has not chased the debt, it suggests that they expect to receive the money.

(vi)   Check cash receipts after date to ensure that the debt is still outstanding.

(vii)   Scrutinise lists of companies going into receivership up to the date of signing to ensure none of them are customers of the company.

(viii)   Ask the company solicitors whether they have started legal proceedings against any receivables against which allowances have been made.

(ix)   If they have, review correspondence with solicitor or inquire of solicitor the likelihood of the debt being recovered.

(x)   Ascertain whether the customer is 'on stop'. If not, enquire why the company is still trading with the customer. It may be because the debt is not really bad.

(xi)   Scrutinise board minutes since the balance sheet date to ascertain whether any subsequent events require the provision to be changed.

(xii)   Review credit notes issued since the balance sheet date and consider if any of them mean that the provision should be changed.

(xiii) Ensure that the allowance has been scrutinised and authorised by the directors.

46 Duckworth Computers

Text reference. Chapter 15

Top tips. The question specifically tells you to assume the recipient has no knowledge in part (a). You should ensure that you write your answer so that someone who knows nothing about auditing could audit the bank reconciliation.

Easy marks. Parts (b) and (c) should represent reasonably straightforward marks.

(a)   (i)   Audit procedures to verify bank reconciliation

Tests of details of balances

(1)   Confirm the bank balances per the client's working papers and general ledger to the bank letter on the file and the bank statements.

(2)   Check the receipts on the list of receipts to the bank statement for October, to ascertain if the outstanding deposits on the bank reconciliation are the only ones that are outstanding. Check that any deposits on the bank statement which are not on the list of receipts for October were listed as reconciling items on the September bank reconciliation.

(3)   Check the payments on the list of payments to the bank statement for October, to ascertain if the unpresented cheques on the bank reconciliation are the only ones that are outstanding. Check that any cheques on the bank statement which are not on the list of payments for October were listed as reconciling items on the September bank reconciliation.

(4)   Check that any reconciling item on the September bank reconciliation that is still outstanding is included on the October bank reconciliation.

(5)   Verify reconciling items on the October bank reconciliation.

•   Trace the outstanding deposits and cheques on the reconciliation to November bank statements to ensure that they clear the bank in reasonable time.

•   Agree the returned cheque to the entries on the bank statement for correctness.

•   Agree that the bank charges on the reconciliation statement agree to the bank statement and that they are the only such charge that has not been included in the cashbook.

(6)   List all the items that are still outstanding from the bank reconciliation at the end of the audit and put the list on the report to partner section of the file, for his attention.

(ii)   **Audit objectives**

(Numbers in this answer refer to the number of the points in part (i).)

(1)   This is to agree the correctness of the bank balance.
(2)   This is to test the completeness of the bank reconciliation.
(3)   This is to test the completeness of the bank reconciliation.
(4)   This is to test the completeness of the bank reconciliation.
(5)   This is to verify the existence of the reconciling items on the bank reconciliation.

(b) **Reliability of bank statements**

Bank statements are **third party evidence** as they are issued by the bank

However, the bank sends them to the client so they are **not third party evidence received directly from the third party.** This means that there is scope for the client to adjust them in some way if he wants to deceive the auditor.

It is rare for such a fraud to occur but the auditor should be **aware of the possibility of such evidence tampering** and treat the evidence accordingly.

Should the auditor have grounds to fear that the evidence will be tampered with, he **could request bank statements directly from the bank**. The client would have to give his permission for this.

(c) (i) **Auditing around the computer**

This is where the auditor audits the information input to a computer and audits the output of the computer but does not audit the computer processing of the information.

Auditing through the computer

This is where as well as auditing input and output, the auditor checks the processing routines and program controls of the computer as well.

(ii) **Situations where it is inappropriate to audit around the computer**

In general terms the inappropriateness of auditing around the computer increases with the **complexity of the computer program.**

Specifically, it is inappropriate to audit around the computer when the **computer generates totals for which no detailed analysis can be obtained.** It is also inappropriate in the absence of control totals and audit trails.

It is also inappropriate to audit around the computer where the **use of CAATs could reduce control risk and the level of substantive procedures significantly,** or substantive procedures could be done more efficiently by the use of CAATs. This is likely to be the case where a significant amount of use is made of the computer by the business and valuable information is contained within it.

47 Cash audit

Text reference. Chapter 15

Top tips. This question has a number of small parts, each of which is straightforward. You should be able to put together an answer to this question that gains you a high mark. Probably the worst thing that can happen on this question is that you allocate your time badly, and don't give yourself an opportunity to finish collecting the easy marks available for this question, or fail to answer other questions properly because you overran on the straightforward one. Don't fall into this trap. Allocate your time to each part of this question and be strict with yourself if you start to run over. Remember to state your points simply, and in a fashion that makes the marker's life easier. For example, in part (a), it would be appropriate to use bullet points to set out your points.

Easy marks. These are available for part (c) which is based on rote learning.

Examiner's comments. Generally reasonably well answered. Common mistakes included confusing audit objectives and control objectives, stating that the auditor would only need to count cash at shops near the office and confusion regarding the matters that would be confirmed in a bank letter.

Marking scheme

			Marks
(a)	Errors and misappropriations – cash		
	(i)	Receipts Up to 1 mark per point to maximum of	2
	(ii)	Payments Up to 1.5 marks per point to maximum of	3
	(iii)	Interest and charges Up to 2 marks	2
(b)	Principal audit objectives Up to 2 marks per point to max of		8
(c)	Why auditors seek bank confirmations – matters confirmed Up to 1 mark per point to a maximum of		$\frac{5}{20}$

(a) **Errors and misappropriations**

(i) *Receipts paid into bank accounts*

- The money could be **stolen** before it is banked. This will be easier if it is cash, but even cheques could be fraudulently diverted to personal accounts.

- If the bank records are not reconciled to the company's records, receipts could be **incorrectly entered** into the company's records.

(ii) *Payments made out of bank accounts*

- Payments could be **misappropriated** if cheques are signed with no backing documentation, as they could be fraudulently made out to members of staff or other third parties.

- Similarly, if there is no backing documentation reviewed when cheques are made out, non-business expenses could be paid for by the company.

- If payments are not recorded properly in the company records, suppliers may be paid more than once for an invoice, as the company will have no control over what payments have been made. Alternatively, suppliers may not be paid at all, and this could lead to **operational problems**.

(iii) *Interest and charges debited and credited to bank accounts*

- If the company does not record items debited or credited directly to their bank account, the amounts in their own records will be incorrect.

- Also, banks sometimes make mistakes in the amount of interest they credit to your account or the charges they take out. If the company does not check these, it could lose money.

(b) **Audit of cash**

The key audit objectives in the audit of cash are to verify the assertions of **existence**, **completeness/valuation**, **rights and obligations**, and **occurrence**.

Existence

The auditors will verify existence by carrying out cash counts. They will not necessarily need to carry out counts in every store. However, they should rotate the stores which they visit on an annual basis, and should not simply visit certain stores close to their offices because it is easy to do so.

This will involve checking that the cash in the tills equates with the cash records. Any items such as 'IOUs' should be investigated thoroughly. Unless staff have made purchases, it is extremely unlikely that the auditors should find IOUs in a shop.

Completeness and valuation

It will be important to ascertain that there is no unrecorded cash. Cash records at head office and at the stores must be reconciled. There should also be attention paid to the cut-off between cash at stores and head office at the year end, so that no cash is missed 'in transit'.

Rights

The auditors must ensure that the company has rights in the cash. This will be particularly relevant to cheques (are they made out to the company?) and the credit card vouchers (none are to third parties).

Occurrence

Lastly, the auditors must check that the cash transactions relate to the relevant year. The auditors should carry out a review of cheques in the till and ensure that they are dated prior to the year end. They should also check credit card vouchers.

(c) **Bank letters**

The auditors request confirmations from the bank to provide **third party evidence** about the **existence** and **valuation** of bank balances.

Details requested usually include:

- Details of all accounts held at the year end date
- The balance on each of the accounts at that date
- Details of any guarantees or security from the client
- Details of any facilities the bank extends to the client (eg overdraft)
- Whether the bank is aware the client has any other banking relationships

The bank may also confirm that it holds title deeds on behalf of the client. The auditor might want access to these as part of his non-current asset testing.

48 Liabilities

Text reference. Chapter 14

Top tips. This question looks at audit evidence in relation to a number of liabilities and provisions. As with all evidence questions it is important that you try to think about the key risks associated with the balance for example, completeness or valuation, and then ensure that the audit work which you suggest tackles those aspects. Also think about how you phrase each point. Vague descriptions of audit evidence will not score many marks.

Easy marks. Although there are no easy marks as such in this question it is still a question which you should be confident of passing. Avoid overcomplicating matters and make sure you get the basic point down. For example the overdraft can be agreed to the bank statement, the loan can be agreed to a bank letter.

Examiner's comments. Students should avoid repetition by considering making a single reference to parts of the answer that are relevant to more than one section. Credit is only given once where the same point is mentioned a number of times. To score marks, evidence had to be specific. Disclosure issues were highlighted by the question and credit was given for specific reference to the relevant accounting standard. If a tabular format of answer is adopted repetition should be avoided.

Marking scheme

		Marks
(a)	Company A	
	(i) 10 year bank loan and bank overdraft Up to 1 mark per point to a maximum of	5
	(ii) Expense accruals Up to 1 mark per point to a maximum of	4
	(iii) Trade payables and purchase accruals Up to 1 mark per point to a maximum of	6
(b)	Company B Up to 1.5 marks per point to a maximum of	5
		20

(a) **Audit procedures** (assuming all balances are material to the accounts)

(i) *10 year bank loan and overdraft.*

- The reply to the year end bank letter should be reviewed. This should provide confirmation of the **existence** of the loan. It will also confirm details of any interest paid and any capital repayments.

- The bank letter should also be reviewed to determine whether the loan is **secured**, and if so, which assets provide security. Correspondence with the bank should be reviewed to determine the extent to which any covenants restrict the use of these assets.

- Minutes of board meetings should be reviewed to confirm that the loan has been **authorised**.

- Analytical review should be performed on the **loan interest charge** in the income statement. This could be performed on a reasonableness test basis.

- A check should be performed on the **split of the loan liability between current and long term liabilities**. This should comply with the relevant legislation. Disclosure of liabilities due after more than five years is required in the notes to the accounts together with details of any security.

- The **overdraft balance** should be confirmed to the year end bank letter and bank statement. A **bank reconciliation** should be prepared/reviewed to establish the validity of any reconciling items.

- An analysis of current liabilities should be obtained to confirm that the **overdraft is disclosed** as part of the current liabilities total.

(ii) *Expense accruals*

- A **breakdown of the accruals total** should be obtained and the casting checked. A comparison should be made between those expenses accrued for in the current period and the previous period in order to establish completeness. Any variations should be investigated.

BPP
LEARNING MEDIA

- Further analytical review procedures would involve comparing the amounts accrued for individual expenses in comparison to previous years and budgets. Again any discrepancies would be investigated.

- The **basis of the calculation** of a sample of accruals should be reviewed. This may involve checking to documentation eg previous utility bills, as well as assessing any assumptions made.

- Where possible a sample of accruals should be agreed to subsequent invoices/bills received after the year end and/or payments made.

- A check should be made that the accruals balance is disclosed as part of current liabilities (unless any are due after more than one year).

(iii) *Trade payables and purchase accruals*

The nature and extent of the work to be performed in this area would depend on the initial assessment of risk at the planning stage and the evidence based on the tests of controls. However, the following types of procedures would normally be performed:

- Select a sample of payables from the payables ledger and obtain **direct confirmation** from the supplier, having sought the authorisation of the client.

- Any **differences** between the balance recorded by the client and those recorded by the supplier should be **reconciled and investigated**. Follow up procedures should be performed where there is no response.

  (Although this technique can provide useful audit evidence it is not always possible to carry it out. It may be that the client does not wish to co-operate or perhaps previous experience has shown that few suppliers respond. If this is the case alternative procedures should be performed.)

- Obtain any month end statements from key suppliers and perform a **reconciliation** of the balance. Where there are any disputes review any legal correspondence to assess the likely outcome.

- An **aged payables listing** should be obtained and any old outstanding balances should be investigated. Analytical review should be performed by comparing the current level of payables with prior periods and fluctuations investigated.

- For a sample of payables confirm their accuracy by tracing the balances back through the system from their entry in the nominal ledger to the initial supporting documentation.

- Obtain a schedule of purchase accruals and cast. Agree to supplier invoices received after the year end.

- Perform **cut-off procedures**. Check from goods received notes with serial numbers before the year-end to ensure that invoices are either posted to the payables ledger prior to the year-end or are included on the schedule of accruals. Review the schedule of accruals to the movements in inventories to determine that none relate to items received after the year-end.

(b) **Provisions for warranty claims**

Matters to consider:

- This is a high risk aspect of the audit as it is dependent upon the **judgement of the directors**.

- If the directors' judgement has proved reliable in the past the risk of error decreases, if they have proved unreliable the risk of error increases.

- Whether the item meets the definition of a provision as defined in IAS 37.

- In particular there must be a present obligation leading to a probable outflow of resources. This will depend on the specific terms although it is likely that a claim under warranty would meet the definition.

- Whether the **basis for the calculation of the provision** is reasonable in the light of prior experience and consistent with previous years.

- The extent to which any provisions created in previous years have been under or overprovided. Any subsequent adjustment can be used as a means of manipulating the recognition of profits.

- Whether the company has any **insurance** which would mitigate the effects of any claims under warranty.

- The existence and reasons behind any current claims.

- This would help to establish whether the current provision is adequate and depending on the reason for any claims may indicate a need to consider the valuation of inventories held.

Evidence

- Review the **terms of the warranty** to establish that the company does have an obligation to compensate and under which circumstances.

- Obtain a **calculation of the provision**. Check for mathematical accuracy and discuss the basis with the directors to assess whether it is a reasonable and consistently applied method.

- Compare the level of provision with **previous years** and assess the accuracy of previous provisions by contrast to actual claims made.

- Obtain copies of any **insurance policies** to establish the possibility of any losses being covered.

- Review any **legal correspondence** to determine the reasons for and the status of any ongoing claims.

- Review the **level of claims** being made after the year-end.

49 Question with helping hand: Boulder

Text reference. Chapter 14

Top tips. Part (a) of this question basically involves straight rote learning. The financial statement assertions from ISA 500 are core knowledge. It is important to write a sentence for each point – as the requirement asks you to 'List and describe'. If you just list out the terms, you are unlikely to pass this part.

Part (b) was more difficult. 14 marks is a high allocation for audit procedures on payroll, but if you read the scenario and question requirement carefully, there are quite a few clues on how to break down 'payroll' and generate enough distinct points.

- Avoid getting the two parts confused. Part (i) is looking at payroll balances in the balance sheet and part (ii) at payroll transactions in the income statement.

- Use the scenario to identify the different elements of payroll in this company – factory, both directly employed and agency staff, sales and admin staff as well as directors. There are also two different types of bonuses mentioned.

- Finally, take care over how you write the answer. Make sure that you given enough detail about each procedure that you are describing.

Easy marks. In part (a) there were some easy marks for knowing the financial statement assertions. This emphasises how important it is to have a good knowledge of the key ISAs.

In part (b) the easiest marks were probably those to be gained from good use of the clues in the question, for example the use of the clock cards should have given ideas for detailed substantive procedures and the information about the calculation of the bonuses should have suggested some specific analytical review procedures. **Examiner's comments.** Part (a) was relatively easy. Common errors included:

- Stating an assertion without stating what the assertion meant
- Listing comments that were not assertions eg *the balances must be materially correct*.

In part (b) some candidates were confused between the balance sheet and income statement split in this question. Many candidates provided an appropriate list of substantive tests using the scenario to give detail within the answer. There are two main areas of weakness: firstly the use of the term *check* as in *check the list of employees*. This was simply not precise enough to show what substantive test was being explained. The second weakness was lack of planning. Common errors included:

- Including **tests of controls** although the requirement clearly asked for **substantive procedures**.
- Lack of breadth in answers.

Marking scheme

		Marks
(a)	Six financial statement assertions Up to 1 mark per point to a maximum of	6
(b)	Substantive audit procedures	
	(i) Payroll balances in balance sheet, Boulder Up to 1 mark per point to a maximum of	10
	(ii) Payroll transactions in the income statement, Boulder Up to 1 mark per point to a maximum of	4

Note. Some flexibility can be used in marking for the allocation of marks between (b)(i) and (ii). There is some crossover.

$\underline{20}$

(a) **Financial statement assertions**

(i) Occurrence – the transactions or events that have been recorded genuinely occurred during the accounting period.

(iii) Valuation – assets and liabilities have been included in the financial statements at appropriate amounts.

(iii) Rights and obligations – the entity holds or controls the right to assets and liabilities are obligations of the entity.

(iv) Existence – assets and liabilities recognised on the balance sheet genuinely exist as at the balance sheet date.

(v) Classification – transactions and events have been recorded in the correct accounts.

(vi) Accuracy – amounts and other data relating to recorded transactions and events have been recorded appropriately.

(Cut-off is another assertion mentioned in the ISA but only SIX were required by the question.)

(b) **Substantive audit procedures on payroll balances**

    (i)   The balances relating to payroll in Boulder are likely to be:

- Unpaid wages and salaries
- Accrued bonuses for sales staff and directors
- Liabilities for tax and national insurance
- Unpaid amounts due to the agency relating to the temporary factory staff

All of these amounts included in the balance sheet should be tested as follows:

- Agree the balance sheet figures to supporting schedules and check the schedules for arithmetical accuracy

- The individual amounts on the supporting schedules should be agreed to the trial balance

- Agree the balance sheet figures to payments after the balance sheet date

    (ii)   Agree the unpaid wages and salaries to the latest payroll calculations before the year-end

    (iii)   Agree the totals due in respect of tax and national insurance to the latest payroll summary prior to the year end and review the amounts for reasonableness as a proportion of the total gross wages and salaries. This should be compared with previous months and explanations obtained for any unexpected variations.

    (iv)   A sample of the tax and national insurance calculations should be reperformed.

    (v)   Correspondence with the tax authority should be inspected for any evidence of further amounts due to them.

    (vi)   The terms of the sales staff bonus should be agreed to their contract of employment and the calculation reperformed. The figure used for the final quarter's sales should be agreed to audit work performed on sales.

    (vii)   The terms of the directors' bonus should be agreed to their contract of employment and the calculation reperformed. If the payment of this bonus requires special approval by the board or shareholders, inspect documentary evidence of this approval to verify that a liability exists at the year-end.

    (viii)   The amount due to the agency should be agreed to:

- The documents signed by factory supervisors confirming the amount of work done
- The agreement with the agency

    (ix)   If the amount is material a confirmation request could be sent to the agency to confirm the amount due to them.

Substantive audit procedures on payroll transactions

    (i)   Analytical procedures should be performed as follows:

- Total factory wage cost (including agency staff) should be measured as a proportion of sales each month

- Total sales salaries and bonuses should be measured as a proportion of sales each month

- Administrative salaries per employee should be calculated for each month

Any unexpected variation should be investigated by enquiries of management and corroborative evidence obtained for their explanations.

    (ii)   For a sample of payroll expense entries, test as follows:

- Agree total expense to weekly/monthly payroll summaries

     –   For a sample of individual pay records the calculation of basic pay should be checked verifying the number of hours worked to the clock card and the hourly rate to that approved by management for factory workers and to contracts for administrative and sales staff.

(iii)   The disclosure of directors' emoluments should be checked against statutory requirements.

(iv)   The classification of payroll expenses between the income statement headings should be compared to the prior year's audited financial statements to check consistency.

50 Newthorpe

Text references. Chapters 13 and 14

Top tips. In (a)(i) and (iii) note that you should have checked the completeness of the client's schedules, a test that would not be necessary here for inventory in (a)(ii) because of the satisfactory results of the inventory counting. You should have considered separately in (a)(i) and (ii) inventory and non-current assets that had been sold, and inventory and non-current assets that had not been sold.

It is important whether the company has acknowledged any liability, and also whether any reimbursement may be obtained. Our answer draws a distinction between the costs of the legal action and potential damages. It may well be that the costs need to be accrued, as they are virtually certain to be incurred. By contrast liability for damages needs to be disclosed but not accrued, since it is possible but not virtually certain that the company will incur the liability.

You needed to indicate giving an example or two how the auditors could check the likely sales value of non-current assets to be sold, but you would not have needed to go into the level of detail we have about each category of non-current asset.

Easy marks. There are relatively few easy marks in this question, part (b)(i) being the most straightforward but only worth three marks. To pass the question you need to take a step by step approach to avoid getting bogged down in the information. Break the question down so for example in part (a)(i) think about the NRV of plant and equipment and inventories separately. Also remember that you are looking at estimates. Think about how these figures have been calculated by management.

(a)   (i)   **Procedures (should be weighted towards high-value items)**

Plant and equipment

(1)   **Check** that the **non-current assets register** can be **reconciled** with the **accounting records** to ensure it is complete.

(2)   **Check** a sample of **non-current assets** in the non-current asset register to the **client's schedule** to ensure that the client's schedule is **complete.**

(3)   For items that are shown as sold, **check** the **value** of the **sales proceeds** to **supporting documentation,** checking that title has been transferred, the sales price and date of completion. Confirm payment to cash book.

(4)   For items that have yet to be sold **obtain evidence** of likely **sales prices** and **review correspondence** with possible buyers to assess likelihood of items being sold. Sales/scrap values are likely to be low. Any expensive, specialised machinery may be hard to sell. **Use trade press** to **check sales/scrap values** considering age, condition etc.

(5)   **Check** whether any **costs of disposal** will be **significant** (will the assets have to be moved piece-by-piece, or are transportation costs significant).

Inventories

(1) **Check** the **selling prices** of **inventories sold since the year-end** to **sales invoices** and **cash book.** If a number of different items have been sold at the same time, check whether the basis of allocation of sales proceeds appears to be reasonable.

(2) **Assess** the **reasonableness** of **management estimates** of realisable value of inventories that has not yet been sold by **reviewing sales before** the **year-end, comparing** the **values** with **inventories** that has been **sold since** the year-end and considering **offers** made which have not yet been finalised.

(3) For unsold inventories, **assess** reasonableness of **provisions for selling expenses** by comparison of selling expenses with inventories sold.

(4) **Review** the **records of inventory counting** for any items noted as **damaged, obsolete** or **slow-moving** and confirm that the realisable value of these items is appropriate (in most cases it is likely to be zero).

(5) **Discuss** with management any **significant disagreements** in estimates of net realisable value, and how inventory where there is little recent evidence of sales value was valued.

(ii) **Procedures**

(1) **Check** that **employees** who appear on the **payroll** when the factory was shut either **appear** on the **schedule** of **redundancy payments** or on the **payroll** of **another factory**.

(2) **Check** that **employees** who appear on the **schedule of redundancy payments** were **employed** by the **factory** that has **shut** by **examining pre-closure payrolls**.

(3) **Check** that **redundancy pay** has been **calculated correctly** by checking whether employees have received their **statutory** or **contractual** entitlement.

(4) **Check** that the **figures used** in the **calculation** of **redundancy pay** are **correct**. For employees whose redundancy package is based on service and salary, **check** details of **service** to **personnel records** and **final salary** to the **last payroll**. For employees whose redundancy payment is based on their service contract, confirm details to service contract.

(5) **Check schedule of redundancy payments** to **cash book** to confirm that payments have been made as indicated on the schedule.

(6) For **redundancy payments** that are **in dispute, review correspondence** and **obtain legal advice** about the likely outcome.

(b) (i) IAS 37 states that a provision should be recognised in the accounts if:

(1) An entity has a **present obligation** (legal or constructive) as a result of a past event

(2) A **transfer** of **economic benefits** will **probably** be **required** to settle the obligation

(3) A **reliable estimate** can be made of the amount of the obligation.

Under IAS 37 contingent losses should not be recognised. They should however be disclosed unless the prospect of settlement is remote. The entity should disclose:

(1) The **nature** of the liability

(2) An estimate of its **financial effect**

(3) The **uncertainties** relating to any possible payments

(4) The likelihood of any **re-imbursement**.

(ii) **Tests to determine likelihood and amount of damages**

(1) **Review** the director's **service contract** and **ascertain** the **maximum amount** to which he would be entitled and the **provisions** in the service contract that would **prevent** him making a **claim**, in particular those relating to grounds for justifiable dismissal.

(2) **Review** the results of the **disciplinary hearing. Consider** whether the company has acted in accordance with **employment legislation** and its **internal rules,** the **evidence** presented by the **company** and the defence made by the **director.**

(3) **Review correspondence** relating to the case and **determine** whether the **company** has **acknowledged** any **liability** to the director that would mean that an amount for compensation should be accrued in accordance with IAS 37.

(4) **Review correspondence** with the company's **solicitors** and **obtain legal advice**, either from the company's solicitors or another firm, about the likelihood of the claim succeeding.

(5) **Review** correspondence and contact the company's solicitors about the likely **costs** of the case.

(6) **Consider** the **likelihood** of **costs** and **compensation** being **reimbursed** by **reviewing** the company's **insurance arrangements** and contacting the insurance company.

(7) **Consider** the **amounts** that should be **accrued** and the **disclosures** that should be made in the accounts. Legal costs should be accrued, but compensation payments should only be accrued if the company has admitted liability or legal advice indicates that the company's chances of success are very poor. However the claim should be disclosed unless legal advice indicates that the director's chance of success appears to be remote.

51 Crighton-Ward

Text reference. Chapter 18

Top tips. Make sure you read each of the requirements carefully in this question. In part (b), you can break the question down further into two parts for five marks each – take each of the issues in turn and deal with them separately. Note that the requirements in parts (a), (b) and (c) are either to 'discuss' or 'explain', so make sure you do this and that your answers aren't simply a list of bullet points.

Easy marks. In this question the easiest marks were in the factual parts (a) and (c). In these parts a reasonable knowledge of the basic principles of ISA 580 *Management representations* would have brought you close to full marks, taking the pressure off in the significantly harder 'application' requirement.

Examiner's comments. In part (a) most candidates took the correct approach, explaining purposes such as provision of audit evidence and confirmation of responsibilities. A significant number of incorrect approaches were taken, such as:

- Explaining a letter of weakness
- Explaining the process of obtaining a representation letter
- Providing a list of contents of the letter

Part (b) allowed candidates to apply their knowledge of representation letters. Many candidates were confused as to when a representation letter point was needed. Well-prepared candidates recognised the need for a representation letter point regarding the legal liability due to the lack of other evidence and included a convincing paragraph to include in the letter. The issue of depreciation was dismissed because of the evidence provided in the scenario.

Part (c) allowed candidates to demonstrate their knowledge of procedures for obtaining a representation letter and the actions necessary if the procedure breaks down. Some candidates explained the process of discussion with directors through to qualification, and even resignation. Other focused on the auditor modifying the audit report. While modification was an option, emphasising this area above others severely limited the marks that could be awarded. A minority assumed that the letter was not required and detailed other audit procedures that could be used. Given that audit work was complete, obtaining sufficient evidence from other sources appeared to be unlikely.

Marking scheme

		Marks
(a)	Representations – one mark per relevant point to a maximum of	
(b)	One mark per relevant point	
	Lion's roar	
	Lack of supporting evidence	1
	Amount material	1
	Claim not justified and reason	1
	Treatment in financial statements (alternative provide allow)	1
	Draft paragraph for representation letter – maximum of	2
	Depreciation	
	Have sufficient evidence	1
	Examples of evidence and effect on depreciation charge (1 mark each)	1
	Example of evidence 2	1
	Matter not therefore crucial	1
	Auditor must provide audit evidence to support 'feelings'	1
	Maximum marks	**10**
(c)	Key points 1 for each point	
	Meet with directors	1
	Possible amendments to letter	1
	Issue – potential qualification	1
	Reason for qualification	1
	Issue – reliance on subsequent representation letter	1
	Could resign if situation serious enough	1
	Maximum marks	**5**
	Total	**20**

(a) The purpose of a management representation letter is to improve the reliability of audit evidence when the auditor wants to place some reliance on oral representations from management. This is appropriate only when it relates to a matter that is material to the financial statements and:

  (i) The matter is subjective

  (ii) Knowledge of the facts is confined to management

  (iii) The auditor cannot reasonably expect to obtain sufficient evidence from other sources

The management representation letter is not a substitute for other evidence and any contradictions between the representations and other evidence must be investigated.

The management representation letter also serves the purpose of obtaining a formal acknowledgement from management of their responsibility for:

  (i) Preparing and approving true and fair financial statements

  (ii) Making the estimates and judgements within the financial statements and selecting the accounting policies

(b)   **Lion's Roar**

The amount of the claim being made against Crighton-Ward is material being 53% of profit before tax.

None of the other evidence that auditors might expect to help them assess the likelihood of the company having to pay out in respect of the claim is available here. The solicitors cannot determine the liability and there appears to have been no settlement or any further negotiations after the balance sheet date.

In the circumstances the auditors will have to place some reliance on the directors' viewpoint as they have the best understanding of the circumstances relating to the normal expectations of the vehicles in their very specialised line of business.

For these reasons this matter should be included in the management representation letter.

A suitable paragraph would be:

'A customer has lodged a claim for $4m against the company. The directors are of the opinion that the claim is not justified and it is not likely that the company will have to make a payment. For this reason no provision has been made for the amount but it has been disclosed as a contingent liability. No similar claims have been received or are expected to be received.'

Depreciation

It appears that sufficient evidence has been obtained in respect of the depreciation charge. The method is consistent with prior years and with other companies in the sector. In addition there are no significant gains or losses on disposals, which also indicates that there is no material over or under depreciation. It appears that the matter is not critical to the financial instruments.

As the only worry over the depreciation is the 'feeling' of an apparently inexperienced audit senior, and no suggestion of a lack of the evidence that would normally be expected, it would not be necessary or appropriate to include this matter in the representation letter.

(c)   In response to the directors' refusal to sign the letter of representation the auditor should:

(i)   Discuss with the directors the reasons for their refusal and remind them that the need for a letter of representation was notified to them in the engagement letter

(ii)   Discuss whether there is any alternative form of words that the directors would be prepared to sign and that would still meet the needs of the auditor

(iii) If the directors continue to refuse to sign the letter, the auditor should request this decision to be formally minuted by the board

(iv)   The failure to provide the representations is likely to amount to a limitation on the scope of the audit so the auditor should consider the implications for the auditor's report. It appears that this should be qualified on the grounds of a material limitation on scope, using the words 'Except for..'

(v)   Discuss the matter with the audit committee

(vi)   Question the directors' integrity and review audit conclusions

(vii) Consider whether the position is untenable and resignation is the only option

52 Jayne

Text reference. Chapter 15

Top tips. This is a fairly straightforward question on audit evidence in relation to bank balances. In part (a) (ii), note the requirement to explain the audit assertions that are and are not supported by the examples of external confirmations provided in part (a) (i). In part (b) (i), again note the requirement to explain the procedures for obtaining a bank report for audit purposes – it isn't enough to simply produce a list of bullet points.

Easy marks. These are available in part (a) of the question for listing examples of external confirmations and in part (b) for explaining the procedures for obtaining a bank report for audit.

ACCA examiner's answer. The examiner's answer to this question is included at the back of this Kit.

Marking scheme

			Marks
(a)	(i)	0.5 for each relevant source of evidence	
		Accounts receivable letter	0.5
		Solicitor letter	0.5
		Bank confirmation letter	0.5
		Inventory held at third party	0.5
		Accounts payable letter	0.5
		Other relevant letters	0.5
		Maximum marks	**2**
	(ii)	Two marks for each type of audit evidence	
		One mark for stating assertion supported and one for stating assertion not supported	
		0.5 for valid assertion and 0.5 for explanation	
		Accounts receivable letter	2
		Solicitor letter	2
		Bank confirmation letter	2
		Inventory held at third party	2
		Accounts payable letter	2
		Other relevant letters	2
		Maximum marks	**8**
(b)	(i)	Award one mark for each well explained point. Allow 0.5 for simply stating the appropriate area	
		Ensure bank letter required	1
		Produce letter in accordance local regulations	1
		Client authorises disclosure	1
		Send to bank – before end of accounting period	1
		Bank complete and send to auditor	1
		Audit procedures	1
		Bank balances to accounts	1
		Loans disclosure	1
		Maximum marks	**5**

			Marks
(ii)	Substantive procedures – 0.5 per procedure		
	Trial balance		0.5
	Agree bank balance to computer system		0.5
	Agree bank balance to financial statements		0.5
	Bank reconciliation		0.5
	Obtain copy		0.5
	Cast		0.5
	Agree to TB		0.5
	Agree to bank statement		0.5
	Lodgements		0.5
	Unpresented credits		0.5
	Other relevant procedures (each)		0.5
	Maximum marks		**5**
Total			**20**

(a) (i) External confirmations

– Bank letter for bank balances
– Accounts receivable confirmation
– Accounts payable confirmation
– Solicitor's letter for opinion on legal case outcome
– Inventory held by third parties

(**Note**. Only four are required.)

(ii) *Bank letter*

This provides audit evidence on the **existence** of bank accounts held by the company as confirmation is received directly from the bank.

It may not provide audit evidence of **completeness** because it will not provide evidence of bank accounts held at other banks.

Accounts receivable confirmation

This provides audit evidence of the **existence** of a receivable at the year-end because a reply is received from each customer who has been circularised.

It does not provide audit evidence of the **valuation** of the receivable at the year-end – confirmation of the debt by the customer does not guarantee that it will be paid.

Accounts payable confirmation

This provides audit evidence of the **existence** of a payable at the year-end because a reply is received from each supplier who has been contacted.

It does not provide audit evidence of the **completeness** of accounts payables at the year-end, since there may be liabilities in existence that have not been recorded by the client and could not have been selected in the sample.

Solicitor's letter

This provides audit evidence of the **existence** of legal claims at the year-end.

It does not provide audit evidence of the **valuation** of claims at the year-end because of the uncertainty involved and the level of judgement required to make an assessment of the likely outcome.

Inventory held by third parties

This provides audit evidence of the **existence** of inventory held because a confirmation is received from the third party.

It does not provide evidence of the **valuation** of the inventory at the year-end, as it will not indicate the condition and saleability of the inventory.

(b)   (i)   **Procedures for bank reports**

–   The bank requires explicit written authority from the client to disclose the information requested.

–   The auditor's request must refer to the client's letter of authority and the date of this. Alternatively it may be countersigned by the client or accompanied by a specific letter of authority. For joint accounts, letters of authority signed by all parties are required.

–   The request is sent by the auditor and should aim to reach the branch manager at least two weeks in advance of the client's year-end and should state both the year-end and the previous year-end.

–   The bank will complete the letter and send it back directly to the auditor.

Audit procedures to be carried out on a bank report

–   Agree the balances per the bank letter to the client's bank reconciliations and the balance per the financial statements.

–   Agree the interest charges to the interest amount in the financial statements and ledger.

–   Agree any outstanding loan amounts to the liabilities figure in the accounts and check that all required disclosures have been made.

(ii)   **Substantive procedures on bank balances**

–   Check arithmetic of bank reconciliations.

–   Agree the balance per the bank accounts to the bank reconciliation and to the financial statements and the ledger.

–   Trace outstanding cheques per the bank reconciliation to the cash book and to after-date bank statements.

–   Agree any uncleared lodgements to after-date bank statements.

–   Obtain explanations for any large or unusual items not cleared at the time of the audit.

–   Compare cash book and bank statements in detail for the last month of the year and check items outstanding at the reconciliation date to bank statements after the year-end.

–   Confirm that uncleared bankings have been paid in prior to the year-end date by examination of paying-in slips.

53 FireFly Tennis Club

Text references. Chapters 12, 14 and 17

Top tips. This is a fairly straightforward question on audit work to undertake on income and expenditure, however you need to bear in mind that the entity being audited is a not-for-profit organisation so remember the particular issues associated with such bodies. Use the information in the scenario to help you generate ideas for your answers. Part (c) should be fairly straightforward if you can apply your knowledge of the audits of not-for-profit organisations but remember that the question is asking you to discuss the issues so you need to produce a logical, coherent answer to score well in this part.

Easy marks. You should be able to score reasonably well in parts (a) and (b) of this question on the audit work to perform on income and expenditure, provided that you make good use of the information in the scenario and that the audit work you describe is as specific as possible.

ACCA examiner's answer. The examiner's answer to this question is included at the back of this Kit.

Marking scheme

		Marks
(a)	Income – one mark per relevant point	
	All income	
	Paying-in slips to bank statements	1
	Paying-in slips to cash book confirm amounts agree	1
	Analysis correct in cash book	1
	Cast cash book	1
	Agree totals per cash book to the financial statements	1
	Membership fees	
	Compare list of members to determine how many members 2005	1
	Analytical review of subscriptions – overall process	1
	AR – calculating approximate fee income	1
	Agree subscriptions to FS accounting for differences	1
	Court hire fees	
	Obtain list of court hire fees/calculate for week hire fee	1
	Confirm hire fee to paying-in slip – account for differences	1
	Other relevant tests	1
	Maximum marks	**10**
(b)	Key points one for each point	
	Expenditure analysis back to cash book	1
	Cast cash book	1
	Cash book to purchase invoice – amounts and analysis in CB	1
	Expenditure *bona fide* the club	1
	Investigate any other expenditure	1
	Other relevant points	1
	Maximum marks	**5**

	Marks
(c) Key points one for each point	
Lack of segregation of duties	1
Lack of authorisation controls	1
Cost	1
Management override	1
Use of volunteers – lack of training	1
Lack of profit motivation	1
Other relevant points (each)	1
Maximum marks	5
Total	**20**

(a) **Audit work on completeness of income**

– Compare current year income for both membership fees and court hire to the prior year figures to confirm the reasonableness of the amounts. Investigate any large variances (eg greater than 10%) by enquiry of the treasurer.

– Carry out a proof in total on membership fees by taking the annual membership fees and the number of members in the year. Membership fees are $200 per year. New members joining during the year pay 50% of the total fees. There were 50 new members and 430 at the start of the year. Therefore, membership fee income should be (430 x 90% x 200) + (50 x 50% x 200) = $82,400.

– Agree membership fee income to the financial statements to ensure it has been disclosed correctly.

– Agree court hire fee income to the financial statements to ensure it has been disclosed correctly.

– Review the list of court hire in the club house for court hire during the year and calculate the expected income from court hire by multiplying this by $5. Compare this to the income from court hire in the cash book, bank paying-in slips and financial statements and seek explanations for any differences by enquiry of the treasurer.

– Compare the list of bankings for membership fees prepared by the secretary to the cash book and to the paying-in slips to ensure amounts reconcile.

– Review paying-in slips for the analysis between court hire fees and membership fees and agree these to the analysis in the financial statements.

– Agree amounts on paying-in slips to the amounts in the cash book to ensure accuracy and completeness of recording. Also check these to the amounts on the bank statements.

(b) **Audit procedures on completeness and accuracy of expenditure**

– For a sample of expenditure invoices during the year, check the details to confirm that the expenditure is *bona fide* for the club, i.e. that it relates to court maintenance, power costs for floodlights, or tennis balls for championships.

– Reconcile the debit card statements to the cash book and receipts and to the financial statements. Investigate any discrepancies and seek explanations for them from the treasurer.

– Review the analysis in the accounts for each expenditure type, selecting a sample of payments from the cash book and tracing back to the invoice and to the financial statements to check that the analysis is correct.

– Perform an analytical procedure on expenditure by comparing the amounts for the current year to the prior year for each of the three types of expenditure to confirm whether it appears reasonable. For any large variances (say, greater than 10%), investigate further to obtain satisfactory explanations.

(c)   Internal control testing has limited value when auditing not-for-profit entities such as the Firefly Tennis Club because of the lack of segregation of duties due to the small number of staff, who may or may not be qualified. In the case of the tennis club, there appear to be two members of staff responsible for running the club and preparing the accounts – the treasurer and the club secretary.

Another issue is that the majority of the income may be in the form of cash. At Firefly Tennis Club, all income is cash-based and the controls over this appear to be weak, for example, non-members leave court hire fees in a cash box. This is open to theft and misappropriation by users or by staff.

There is also a lack of authorisation controls in place. For example, the treasurer pays for all expenditure items using the club's debit card but there is no system in place for another person to review and authorise the purpose of the expenditure.

In such a small organisation, it may not be possible to implement a system of internal control because of the very small number of staff and also because of the cost involved in setting up such a system.

54 Walsh

Text references. Chapters 10 and 11

Top tips. In part (a), don't just explain what CAATs are – read the question requirement carefully - you have to provide examples from the company in the question scenario to demonstrate the advantages of using CAATs in an audit. Part (b) should be very straightforward as the requirement is to list examples of audit tests to perform on the wages system. In part (c) again, you need to explain the benefits and drawbacks of using test data but applying your knowledge to the company in the question scenario.

Easy marks. Easy marks are available in part (b) of this question where you are asked to list audit tests to perform on the wages system.

ACCA examiner's answer. The examiner's answer to this question is included at the back of this Kit.

Marking scheme

		Marks
(a)	Award one mark for explaining the use of CAAT and one mark for application to Walsh	
	Testing programmed controls	2
	Test larger number of items	2
	Test actual accounting records	2
	Cost	2
	Other relevant points	2
	Maximum marks	**8**
(b)	Audit tests – one mark per test	
	Recalculation of net pay	1
	Usual items – zero wages payments	1
	Unreasonable items – large payments	1
	Violation system rules – amendment of data	1
	New analysis – analytical review of wages	1
	Completeness checks – all employees clocked in and out	1
	Other relevant tests	1
	Maximum marks	**6**

		Marks
(c)	Use of audit test data – one mark per point	
	Data submitted by auditor	1
	Live and dead testing	1
	Create dummy employee in Walsh	1
	Check accuracy of processing of wages	1
	Problem – damage client computer	1
	Problem – remove auditor data	1
	Problem – cost	1
	Other relevant tests	1
	Maximum marks	**6**
Total		**20**

(a) There are two main types of computer assisted audit technique (CAAT) – audit software and test data. Audit software involves the use of computer programs by the auditor to process data of audit significance from the entity's accounting system. Test data is entering data into an entity's computer system and comparing the results with predetermined results.

The benefits of CAATs include the ability to test program controls as well as general internal controls associated with the system. For example, in the case of Walsh Co's wages system, one of the controls in the system is the generation of a report if overtime over 10% of standard hours is done.

CAATs allow auditors to test a greater number of items more quickly and accurately. In the case of Walsh Co, CAATs can be used to test a sample of wage and deduction calculations to provide evidence that these are being correctly calculated by the system.

CAATs enable the auditor to test transactions electronically rather than paper records of transactions.

CAATs can be cost-effective in the long-term, provided the client does not change its systems. In the case of Walsh Co, the wages system has just been implemented so this is likely to remain in place for a few years.

(b) Examples of audit tests to perform on Walsh Co's wages system using audit software.

– Analytical review of wages by carrying out a proof in total test of wages cost for the year.

– Looking for unusual amounts such as large payments or negative amounts by analysing the transaction data for wages in the year.

– Recalculation of pay and deductions for a sample of employees to confirm that the system is calculating amounts correctly.

– Selecting a sample from the data file for wages to perform detailed substantive testing.

– Checking access to the system to ensure that only authorised personnel, such as the financial accountant, have access.

– Testing for completeness to confirm that an electronic record exists for all employees who have clocked in and out.

(c) Test data is a type of CAAT which involves entering data into the entity's computer system and comparing the results obtained with predetermined results.

Using test data should help in the audit of Walsh Co's wages system because it could be used to test specific controls in the system, such as password access to the system, which should be controlled so that only authorised personnel have access to it. It can also be used to test the control in place for the report produced when overtime greater than 10% of standard hours is done.

One of the main problems with the use of test data as an audit technique is that any resulting corruption of data files has to be corrected. This can be difficult with real-time systems which often have built-in controls to ensure that data entered cannot be easily removed without leaving a mark.

Another problem is that test data only tests the operation of the system at a single point of time and auditors are only testing controls in the programs being run and controls they know about.

55 Audit confirmations

Text references. Chapters 12, 13 and 18

Top tips. With this question it is important that you adopt a structured approach. Notice that as well as there being three sources of evidence to deal with, you are asked to discuss three specific aspects of each of these: audit evidence, practical difficulties and alternative evidence. Also bear in mind that in some instances the correct answer may be to identify that there are no alternative sources of evidence!

Easy marks. This is a demanding question with few easy marks as such. The key is to take a step by step approach.

Examiners comments. As with previous papers candidates found management representations difficult. Students need to master this topic.

Marking scheme

		Marks
(a)	Management representations Up to 1 mark per point to a maximum of	3
(b)	Direct confirmation of receivables Up to 1 mark per point to a maximum of	4
(c)	Confirmation of inventory held by third parties Up to 1 mark per point to a maximum of	3 10

(a) **Management representations**

Audit evidence

An auditor will seek written management representations on matters where sufficient, reliable audit evidence does not exist. The representations are normally made in the form of a letter from the directors which covers both general and specific matters.

General matters include:

• Acknowledgement of **directors' responsibilities** for the preparation of the financial statements

• Confirmation that all **books and records have been made available** to the auditor

• There have been **no events since the balance sheet date** which necessitate revision of the financial statements

Specific matters normally relate to aspects which are judgemental in nature or where knowledge of the issue is confined to management. For example, the directors could be asked to confirm their assessment of the likely outcome of legal proceedings or to confirm the completeness of disclosures regarding related party transactions.

It is important, however, that **the auditor does not use this evidence as a substitute** for other independent evidence which would normally be available. The auditor should also confirm that the representations are **consistent with other sources of evidence**.

Practical difficulties

The directors may not be willing to sign the letter of representation. This may not simply be because they wish to be uncooperative but may be due to genuine concerns about their ability to confirm the matters stated. If agreement cannot be reached (for example by revising the wording of the letter) the auditor will need to consider the impact that this will have on the audit report. It is likely that the report will have to be qualified on the grounds of limitation on scope due to lack of evidence.

Alternative evidence

Normally there would not be any alternative sources of evidence as management representations should only be sought where either other evidence is not available, or where the evidence is insufficient without representations for the auditor to form his opinion.

(b) **Direct confirmation of receivables**

Audit evidence

This provides evidence of the adequacy of the system of internal controls over sales and the accuracy of cut-off procedures. It also assists in confirming that balances are genuine, accurately stated and not in dispute. It does not, however, confirm that the balances are recoverable.

The method of requesting information from the debtor may be positive or negative. Weak internal controls, a suspicion of irregularities or the existence of book-keeping errors are an indication that the direct method should be adopted.

Practical difficulties

The circularisation is carried out by the client at the auditor's request. The client may refuse to do this outright or may refuse to contact certain customers.

Reply rates may be low and repeated follow up requests may be required. Where replies are received customers may make errors, particularly where they are asked to insert the outstanding amount rather than to simply confirm the balance provided.

Alternative evidence

This includes:

- Review of post year-end cash receipts

- Tracing of the individual invoices which make up the receivables balance to despatch notes and purchase contracts

- Where a reply is received but it does not agree with the balance held by the client the client should provide a reconciliation of the two balances. Any discrepancies or disputes should be investigated.

- Analytical review of the aged receivables listing with any significant variations investigated

(c) **Confirmation of inventories held by third parties**

Audit evidence

Confirmation of inventories held by third parties should provide evidence of the **existence and condition** of inventory where the auditor is unable to attend the inventory count.

Practical difficulties

The auditor will need to assess the extent to which he can rely on this evidence as part of his overall assessment of risk as the information could be incorrect due to error or fraud. This will depend on the nature and quality of the information provided together with any previous dealings which the auditor has had with this organisation.

Even where information is comprehensive and reliable it may be difficult to reconcile the amounts held by the third party and the client's records due to differences in terminology and measurement methods.

Alternative evidence

The auditor may test the controls over inventories to and from the third party but this is unlikely to be sufficient evidence on its own. Alternatively the third party's auditors may be able to provide the confirmation required.

Ultimately, however, if the balance is material and third party confirmations are not adequate the auditor will need to consider attending the inventory count.

56 ZPM

Text references. Chapters 5 and 11

Top tips. In this question, you need to think about the scope of work from both internal and external audit points of view. Also use the information in the scenario to help you, for example, it states that the company has 103 stores in eight different countries so it would be impossible for the external auditors to visit each one so this is an area where they could potentially place reliance on the work of internal audit.

Easy marks. These are available in part (a) of the question. Even if you aren't familiar with the detail of ISA 610, you should be able to score well on this part of the question.

Examiner's comments. In part (a), for five marks, candidates were asked to explain the factors that the external auditor will consider when evaluating and testing the work of the internal auditor but many candidates found this difficult. The main problem was in distinguishing between factors for reliance on internal audit and factors for reliance on the work of the internal auditor. ISA 610 provides lists for both of these activities (paragraphs 13 and 17), although there is potentially some overlap. Some candidates provided long lists of points, leaving the examiner to determine which were relevant whereas simply did not attempt the question at all.

Part (b) produced a wide standard of answers ranging from very good to very poor. Weaknesses included providing generic lists of the objectives of internal and external audit, repeating information from part (a) in part (b) (iii) and stating that internal audit or was responsible for the inventory count in part (b) (i). Few candidates actually mentioned key areas such as checking the efficiency of the procurement department, or the legal issues affecting the marketing department.

The overall standard for this question was quite poor, with only a minority of candidates obtaining a clear pass standard. As many candidates answered this question last, answers often became quite lengthy with candidates finding it extremely difficult to remain focused on the question requirement. Spending some time planning, identifying the points to make, and then making those points clearly and concisely would significantly improve the standard of the answers submitted.

Marking scheme

			Marks
(a)	One mark for each valid point		
	Training and proficiency	1	
	Work supervised and reviewed	1	
	Evidence available to support opinion	1	
	Conclusions reached are appropriate	1	
	Unusual matters correctly resolved	1	
	Maximum marks		**5**

Marks

(b)   Inventory count

(i)	Check of control system over counting inventory	1
	Examples of control system e.g. counting in teams	1
	Carrying out test counts	1
	Not relevant – carrying out counts by internal audit	0
(ii)	Ensure inventory materially correct in FS	1
	Attend inventory count to check control system/quantities	1
	Note ZPM focus on quantities + reason	1
(iii)	Rely on IA to test control systems – lack of staff and 103 stores	1
	Does not mean not carry out any work	1
	Review differences between IA and external auditor results	1

Procurement system

(i)	Company policies followed	1
	Example of policy – no specific ones required	1
(ii)	Purchases and payables figures correct in FS	1
	Control system for procurement working effectively	1
(iii)	External auditor rely on IA where work relevant for FS audit	1
	Work reduced only – still carry out some testing	1

Marketing

(i)	Aims such as ensuring information available	1
(ii)	External auditor not interested – not impact FS	1
(iii)	No reliance needed	1

	Maximum marks	**15**
Total		**20**

(a)   **Factors to consider when evaluating the work of the internal auditor**

- The work should be performed by internal audit staff who have adequate technical training and proficiency as internal auditors. This can be confirmed by checking that training programmes are in place and the qualifications of staff are adequate.

- The work of assistants should be properly supervised, reviewed and documented. This can be confirmed by reviewing internal audit working papers and procedure manuals.

- Sufficient and appropriate audit evidence should be obtained to be able to draw reasonable conclusions. This can be checked by reviewing internal audit working papers and reports.

- Conclusions reached should be appropriate and any reports prepared should be consistent with the results of work performed. Again this can be confirmed by reviewing working papers and reports.

- Any exceptions or unusual matters disclosed by the internal audit team should be properly resolved.

(b)   (i)   **Objectives of the internal auditor**

Year-End Inventory Count

The objective of the year-end inventory count is to ensure that the figure for inventories in the financial statements is materially correct. The internal auditors will review the control system over inventory counting and ensure that all inventory is counted as well as performing test counts themselves to check the accuracy of the counting.

Procurement System

The objective of the internal auditor is to ensure that the procurement system is operating in accordance with company guidelines. For example, they will undertake work to ensure that all purchases are authorised, quantity discounts are received and goods received are documented and recorded appropriately.

Marketing Department

The objective of the internal auditor is to review the work of the marketing department to ensure that the operations of this department are managed effectively and efficiently. The internal auditor may also review the effectiveness of the information systems in the marketing department.

(ii) **Objectives of the external auditor**

Year-End Inventory Count

The objective of the external auditor is to determine whether inventory is materially correct in the year-end financial statements. Inventory should be valued appropriately at the lower of cost and net realisable value in accordance with accounting standards and legislation. In the case of ZPM the main risk appears to be inaccurate counting of inventory as some of it consists of lots of small items. The external auditor will attend the inventory count to check whether the quantities and condition of inventory are correctly recorded.

Procurement System

The objective of the external auditor is to determine whether payables and purchases in the financial statements are materially correct. If the testing allows the external auditor to conclude that the controls over procurement are operating effectively, this will form part of the evidence that purchases and payables are recorded completely and accurately, e.g. in the correct year of account.

Marketing Department

This may not be reviewed by the external auditor as it does not impact on the financial statements and its costs are unlikely to be material to the accounts.

(iii) **Extent of reliance**

Year-End Inventory Count

The company has over a hundred stores in various countries, making it impossible for the external auditors to attend the inventory count in every one of these. The external auditors can place reliance on the work of the internal auditors in addition to their own attendance at a small sample of stock counts the year-end inventory counts. The external auditors will still have to review the work of internal audit to ensure that they can rely on the work undertaken. They should also compare their own results with those obtained by internal audit.

Procurement System

The external auditors may be able to rely on the work performed by internal audit on the controls over the procurement system as these are relevant to financial statement assertions such as completeness of liabilities. The external auditors will still have to carry out their own work on the system, although it will be reduced if they can place reliance on any of the work done by the internal auditors.

Marketing Department

It is unlikely that the work done by internal audit will be relied upon as the operations of the marketing department will not impact on the financial statements. However, external audit should review the internal audit report for any aspects that may impact on the financial statements such as advertising spend.

57 Strathfield

> **Text references.** Chapters 11 and 12
>
> **Top tips.** Part (a) should be reasonably straightforward, book learning. In part (b), there are nearly as many marks as there are categories of error. This implies a mark for each and means that if you do find the question difficult, you should try and state a simple reason for each part, rather than spending all the time on one error and not others. You should attempt a calculation in part (c), even if you have struggled with part (b), as doing a calculation based on your reasoning will gain you some marks, even if your reasoning is not exactly right.
>
> **Easy marks.** These are available in parts (a)(ii) and (iii). You need to be familiar with the different methods of sample selection and should be familiar with the characteristics of each one.

(a) **Risks associated with the financial statement assertions for receivables**

One of the main risks associated with receivables is in respect of **valuation**. There is a risk of receivables and hence sales being overstated in the financial statements if they are over-valued. For example, if a customer has gone into liquidation before his debt has been settled, it may be very unlikely that the company will recover the debt and unless it is written-off, the accounts will be overstated. Any provision for bad and doubtful amounts should therefore represent a reliable estimate of the difference between gross receivables and their realisable value.

Incorrect **cut-off** is another issue with respect to sales and receivables because the entity may record the following year's sales in the current period or goods returned in the current period are not recorded as such, for example.

Classification is another important assertion for receivables, that is, that receivables are properly identified and disclosed in the balance sheet. This could be a risk area where amounts have been factored, for example.

(b) **Sample selection**

(i) *Aspects of Sarah's approach which are inconsistent with sampling*

A key criterion of sampling is that all items in the population could have been picked. In **not selecting accounts <$100 or government accounts**, Sarah has not taken the right approach.

Her choosing the **ten highest accounts** is not really sampling either. The choice of those accounts was not random, haphazard or statistical.

(ii) *Alternative means of sampling material balances*

Sarah could **stratify the sample**. This would involve splitting the sample into sub-populations. She could do this on the basis of size, or alphabetically, for example. In this instance, size would be logical because it is a relevant factor as a high proportion of the value of receivables is likely to be in a small proportion of receivables.

If she did this on the basis of size, then she would be able to 100% test the material balances and then sample (by one of the methods above – random, haphazard or statistical) in the other populations.

Sarah could use **monetary unit sampling**. This identifies individual $s as the units, giving $s within higher value balances a greater chance of selection. Each $ is regarded as being in error proportionately to the error in the account balance of which it forms a part.

(iii) *Comparison of methods of sample selection*

- **Random**. This is where a sample is chosen on standard basis, such as mathematical tables.

- **Systematic**. This is where a sample is chosen by selecting the nth one when reading through the list of receivables or the ledger in order.

- **Haphazard**. This is where there is no method of any kind to the sample selection.

While haphazard to the layman appears to be random selection, this is not the case. The first two forms of sample selection are more mathematical than the last one. Haphazard is far more prone to bias than the other two as it can be influenced by such factors as ease of selection.

(c) **Qualitative aspects of differences**

Debts where confirmations have not been received are potentially uncollectable, if the client has moved without giving a forwarding address. They could be included in a projection of population error. However, given that such situations are unlikely to be representative of the sample, rather they are likely to be unique (in a similar way to disputes, below), they could be referred into a test for old or doubtful debts and an allowance probably made.

Cut -off differences. These errors only occur by their nature in a specific region of the trade payables balance, ie invoices received adjacent to the year end. It would not be appropriate to include them in a projection of total sample error. They should be referred into a cut off test and adjusted for as appropriate.

Invoicing errors. These are errors which could occur in any part of the sample. It is therefore justifiable to include them in an estimation of population error. As the amount of error in each item would increase with the size of the item, the ratio method of projecting the error should be used.

Invoices posted to the wrong customer accounts. This is a control error, rather than a substantive one. The value of the sample/balance is not affected by such an error. It should not be included in a projection of total error.

Disputed invoices. These are not necessarily errors and disputes are likely to be unique. The company may have issued credit notes against disputed amounts in the subsequent period. The auditor should assess the impact of any after date credit note on the year end balance. Any matter so dealt with should not be included in a projection of total error. However, disputed matters not settled in this way, are isolated but may be symptomatic, therefore they should be included in a projection of error.

In conclusion, the invoicing errors and any of the latter category of disputed invoices should be included in a projection of total population error. The other differences should all point to further audit tests and should be dealt with separately.

(d) **Projected error**

The projected error would be based on the invoicing errors using the ratio method.

The ratio method uses the formula:

$$\text{Most likely error in population} = \text{Error found in sample} \times \frac{\text{Population value}}{\text{Sample value}}$$

The material amounts selected for sampling should be excluded from the population value when the error is calculated.

The total value of the error is: invoicing, $600, disputed invoices, $1,500, total, $2,100.

Thus:

	$
Error in sample	2,100
Population value (2,350,000 – 205,000)	2,145,000
Sample value	265,450
Projected error	16,969

(e) **Computer-assisted audit techniques**

Sarah could use computer-assisted audit techniques (CAATs) in her work on receivables to some extent. For example, she could use CAATs to help her in her sample selection for balances to confirm by circularisation because the population and sample size required are both large. She could also use CAATs to select receivables over a certain age and therefore test them to make an assessment of their recoverability. Sarah could use CAATs to select customer accounts where the total balance is negative or zero so that these are not neglected in her sample.

She could also use CAATs to perform calculations and comparisons for analytical procedures, such as comparisons to prior year and budget and aged analysis to look at the pattern from year-to-year. She could use CAATs to reperform calculations such as totalling the sales ledger.

All these uses would assist in increasing the efficiency of the audit of receivables but the extent of their use will depend on the entity's systems.

58 LALD

Text references. Chapters 4, 18 and 19

Top tips. This question had some rather complicated points in it that you may not have seen in other questions, such as the section about the non-payment of an amount of sales tax. It is important not to get too bogged down in any one part of a question like this. If you had little to say about the sales tax point it's best to move on to the other sections and aim to pass by having some sort of attempt at all parts of the question.

Easy marks. Part (c) had the only really easy marks here. The basic legal procedures for removal of auditors are not often examined but when they are it is usually, like this, a straightforward test of knowledge.

Examiner's comments. This question was answered reasonably well. Weak answers focused on auditing the sales system and depreciation without reference to the errors found. In part (c), the professional etiquette on a change in auditor was not enough to give a full enough answer.

Marking scheme

		Marks
(a)	**Audit procedures – underpayment of sales tax. One mark per point**	
	Discuss with head of accounting department	1
	Perform additional tests	1
	Determine amount of underpaying	1
	Discuss with directors	1
	Note in management letter	1
	Breach of law	1
	Ask for response from directors	1
	Audit any further amount paid	1
	Provision for late payment	1
	Other relevant points	1
	Maximum marks	7

		Marks
(b)	**1 mark for each value procedure**	
	Review working papers	1
	Determine extent of error	1
	Calculate new provision	1
	Material difference?	1
	Discuss with management	1
	Discuss with directors	1
	Management letter	1
	Potential need for qualification	1
	Other relevant points (each)	1
	Maximum marks	7
(c)	**1 mark per relevant point**	
	Notice to company – as shareholders – ask for removal	1
	Send to company within 28 days of meeting	1
	Write to members– with agenda – before meeting	1
	Send copy of auditor representations to members	1
	Attend meeting – organise votes	1
	Auditor remover – statement of circumstances	1
	Appoint new auditor	1
	Other relevant points	1
	Maximum marks	6

(a) **Additional procedures re the underpayment of sales tax**

- Discuss with management how the payment was missed in order to assess whether it was indeed an 'accidental' error. If there are indications that it was deliberate it might cast doubt on the integrity of management and have implications for other areas of the audit.

- Enquire as to when the payment will be made.

- Review the cashbook for the post balance sheet period to identify if the payment has been made.

- Obtain an analysis of creditors as at 30 September 2005 and identify whether a liability has been recognised for the unpaid sales tax. Also determine whether a liability has been recognised for any penalty that may become due as a result of the late payment.

- Agree the liability to any sales tax return that has been prepared for the quarter ended 31 August 2005.

- Review any correspondence between LALD and the tax authorities.

- Include details of the non-payment of sales tax in the management letter, drawing the directors' attention to the fact that this is a breach of law.

- Consider reporting the matter to the tax authorities.

(b) **Additional procedures re the under-provision of depreciation**

- Review the working papers prepared so far to assess whether the depreciation does appear to be understated.

- Carry out further substantive testing to determine the amount of the error. This could involve:

    - Analytical procedures such as proof in total calculations performed separately for each sub-class of plant and machinery at the appropriate rate.

    - Reperforming calculations of the depreciation charge on a sample (or extending the sample already tested) of individual assets from each sub class.

- If errors are found in the sample these should be extrapolated to the population to assess if the total understatement is material.

- Irrespective of materiality, the error should be mentioned in the management letter, pointing out what weakness in systems allowed it to happen, such as lack of review of depreciation rates as input to the fixed asset accounting system or lack of checking of year end manual journal adjustments.

- If the error is material, management should be asked to amend the financial statements and if they refuse this will lead to a qualification of the audit opinion on the grounds of disagreement.

(c)   **Procedures to remove auditors**

Note. This answer is based on UK law. In this International paper, no specific legal framework is implied, so answers under a different framework, or with less detail, would also be acceptable.

- The directors, as such, do not have the power to remove auditors. This power rests with shareholders, so the directors could only take this course of action if they were also shareholders or could persuade other shareholders to take steps to remove the auditors.

- (In their capacity as shareholders) they must send notice to the company asking for an extraordinary general meeting to be convened to consider a resolution to remove the auditors. This notice must be sent 28 days ahead of the meeting.

- (In their capacity as directors) they must send notice of this meeting and resolution to the shareholders and to the auditors.

- The auditors have a right to make written representations to the shareholders and the directors must send these to the members. The only exception to this is if the directors go to court and it is held that the representations are defamatory.

- The directors must allow the auditors to attend the extraordinary general meeting and speak to the shareholders.

- The resolution requires a majority vote of the shareholders.

- If the resolution is passed the directors must obtain a statement of circumstances form the auditors and deposit this along with the notice of the auditor's removal at Companies House within 14 days of the resolution being passed.

59 Question with helping hand: Sheraton

Text reference. Chapter 18

Top tips. This question required fairly detailed accounting knowledge of IAS 10 and IAS 37. This is a popular topic with the examiner so you need to ensure that you are familiar with these accounting standards. Note that the question wants you to focus on events after the balance sheet date. Do not waste time in your answer talking about general planning matters.

Easy marks. This question is tricky if your knowledge of IAS 10 and IAS 37 is sketchy. However part (a) is more straightforward as it concentrates on the audit aspects. Remember there are two key audit issues – (i) have all relevant events been identified, (ii) have all those identified been dealt with correctly.

(a)   **Detailed procedures for incorporation in audit plan**

(i)   Ensure that all staff are fully briefed on the requirements of the accounting standard IAS 10 and the related standard IAS 37 *Provisions, contingent liabilities and contingent assets.*

(ii) Ensure that the following procedures are included in the audit plan.

    (1) Discuss with management the steps taken to identify and act upon subsequent events in preparing the financial statements.

    (2) Examine all financial records for the period between the balance sheet date and the date of the audit report, with special reference to:

- Cash book for payments indicating liabilities at the balance sheet date
- Receivables' records for subsequent payment, issue of credit notes
- Files of correspondence with customers
- Accounts payable records and unpaid invoice files for unrecorded liabilities
- Sales at special prices, indicating need for inventory write-downs
- Journal entries
- Interim management accounts
- Areas requiring special attention as high risk areas
- Minutes of directors' meetings

    (3) Ensure that all large or unusual items, or significant variations, are allocated to the correct period and properly recorded.

(iii) Confirm that the letter of representation covers events after the balance sheet date.

(iv) Confirm that the going concern review includes consideration of the impact of subsequent events.

(v) Confirm that the effect of subsequent events on contingencies is considered.

(vi) Consider the materiality of subsequent events identified by auditors of subsidiary and associated companies.

(vii) Ensure that the possible effect of events between the date of the audit report and the date of the annual general meeting are considered, where such events come to the notice of the auditors.

(viii) Discuss the situation with the internal auditors (if any).

(ix) Discuss any matters that may arise as a result of the tests with the management to assess what further action is necessary.

(b) **Types of event and accounting treatment**

Events after the balance sheet date:

(i) Adjusting events
(ii) Non-adjusting events

Adjusting events are events after the balance sheet date which provide **additional evidence** of **conditions existing** at the balance sheet date. Financial statements should reflect all material adjusting events.

Non-adjusting events are events after the balance sheet date which concern conditions which **do not exist** at the balance sheet date. Material non-adjusting events should be disclosed by note to the financial statements, unless they cast doubt on the going concern status of the company, in which case the financial statements should be amended. Any note should explain the nature of the event, an estimate of its pre-tax effect and the taxation implications.

60 OilRakers

Text reference. Chapter 18

Top tips. This is quite a technical question testing your knowledge of subsequent events both from the accounting and the auditing perspective. This was an optional question in the exam so sensible question selection would be important. If you are comfortable with this technical area you can pick up excellent marks. If your knowledge is less precise another question may be a better bet.

Part (a) asks for procedures that can be used to identify subsequent events. Here knowledge of ISA 560 would be extremely useful as this contains a list of procedures. Alternatively you could generate your own list by thinking about the sources of evidence eg discussion with management, board minutes, legal documents.

Part (b) (i) tests your knowledge of IAS 10. Again it is essentially a technical question. Remember, an adjusting event is one which provides more information about a condition existing at the balance sheet date. Adjusting events should be adjusted for. Non-adjusting events should be disclosed if they are significant to the understanding of the financial statements.

Part (b) (ii) is probably the trickiest part and relies on your knowledge of the auditor's responsibilities for subsequent events at different points in time. The key technical point to remember is that the auditor has a responsibility to perform procedures which will identify subsequent events up to the date that the audit report is signed. After this time he has no responsibility but if matters are brought to his attention he must consider the need for the accounts to be revised and for a new audit report to be issued.

Easy marks. These are available in parts (a) and (b)(i). Notice that these account for 11 out of a total of 20 marks so if you score well on these sections you are well on the way to passing the question overall.

Examiner's comments. Lots of candidates answered this question well. Part (a) was answered well although a minority of answers focused on explaining the accounting treatment of post balance sheet events, which was not required. In part (b), the following points arose:

- Stating that the company would no longer be a going concern as a result of the bad debt
- Stating that the fire was an adjusting event rather than non-adjusting
- Stating that the auditor was responsible for amending the financial statements, rather than the directors

Marking scheme

		Marks
(a)	**Audit procedures – one mark for each of the following (or 0.5 where the point is made briefly)**	
	Reviewing management procedures	1
	Reviewing minutes of meetings	1
	Interim accounts and cash flow forecasts	1
	Lawyers	1
	Going concern assumption	1
	Maximum marks	**5**
(b)	**Asking management for information – 0.5 for each of**	
	New borrowing commitments	0.5
	Asset sales	0.5
	New shares or debentures	0.5
	Assets destroyed or impounded	0.5
	Unusual accounting adjustments	0.5
	Any other valid point	0.5
	Allow other relevant points	1

Marks

Maximum 5 marks per section

Bankrupt debtor

Adjusting event + reason	2
Audit responsible for detecting	1
Procedures include	
External evidence – receiver letter	1
Internal evidence	1
Audit accounting adjustment	1

Chemical spill

Non-adjusting event but disclose + reason	2
Audit responsibility for detecting – actually management	1
Procedures include	
Info on chemical spill	1
Discuss accounting treatment/disclosure note	1
Letter of representation	1
Amend audit report – emphasis of matter para	1

Destruction of oil well

Non-adjusting event but disclose + reason	2
Audit responsibility for detecting	1
Procedures include	
Evidence for destruction	1
Check directors' actions – contact members?	1
FS amended – audit amendment reissue report	1
FS not amended – lawyer advice	1
Maximum marks	**15**

(a)   **Audit procedures**

Reviewing procedures management has established to ensure that subsequent events are identified.

Reading minutes of board minutes and any minutes of meetings with shareholders.

Reading the latest available interim financial statements, budgets, cash flow forecasts and other related management reports.

Reviewing correspondence with solicitors regarding any litigation or legal claims.

Making inquiries of management as to whether events have occurred which might affect the financial statements. These inquiries would include:

- Updates on any ongoing issues already identified
- Whether new commitments, borrowings or guarantees have been entered into
- Whether sales or acquisitions of assets have occurred or are planned
- Whether the issue of new shares or debentures has been made or is planned
- Whether any assets have been destroyed eg by fire
- Whether there have been any developments regarding risk areas and contingencies
- Whether there are any events which call into question going concern

(b)   (i)   **Three events: IAS 10**

15 August 20X5

The bankruptcy of the major customer is an adjusting event after the balance sheet date. It provides additional information concerning the recoverability of the debt at the balance sheet date and as it represents 11% of receivables is likely to be material to the financial statements. An adjustment should be made in the financial statements reducing the receivables balance and profits.

1 November 20X5

The accidental release of the chemicals is a non-adjusting event. It occurred after the balance sheet date and does not provide further information about conditions at the year end. On this basis the adjustment made is not necessary. However the impact of the leak is likely to be significant as the company may incur penalties or fines due to the environmental damage. Disclosure of the event and an estimate of the financial effect should be made.

30 November 20X5

The fire at the well is a non-adjusting event. It occurred after the balance sheet date and does not relate to conditions which existed at the year end. Although there will be a loss of production and reduction in profits there is no indication that this is significant enough to call into question going concern. Disclosure should be made of the events surrounding the fire and an estimate of the financial effect.

(ii) **Auditor's responsibility and audit procedures**

15 August 20X5

The bankruptcy of the major customer takes place after the year end but before the audit report is signed. In accordance with ISA 560 the auditor should perform audit procedures designed to obtain appropriate evidence that all events up to the date of the auditor's report that may require adjustment of, or disclosure in, the financial statements have been identified.

These procedures would include the following:

- Confirming the details of the bankruptcy to documents received by OilRakers from the liquidator.

- Agreeing the balance outstanding to the confirmation received from the customer as part of the audit of receivables. If this is not available agree the outstanding balance to pre year-end invoices.

- Checking that the adjustment has been made correctly in the financial statements ie receivables are reduced in the balance sheet and profits in the income statement.

- Confirming in the letter of representation that there are no further amounts due from this customer.

1 November 20X5

This event takes place after the audit report has been signed but before the financial statements have been issued. After the date of the audit report the auditor does not have any responsibility to perform audit procedures or make inquiries. However in this case as the auditor has been made aware of the chemical spill the situation should be discussed with management and an appropriate course of action decided.

Audit procedures would be as follows:

- Confirm the details included in the disclosure notes in the accounts by discussing the situation with management, looking at press reports and any other records which are available. Assess the adequacy of the disclosure in compliance with IAS 10.

- Check that no adjustment has been made in the accounts in respect of the spill.

- Review correspondence with legal experts regarding any liability for environmental damage.

- Obtain a revised version of the letter of representation confirming that there are no other events which should be brought to the auditors' attention.

- As the financial statements have been amended after the auditor's report has been signed a new audit report would need to be issued. This should be dated no earlier than the date of the revised financial statements. The revised report should include an emphasis of matter paragraph highlighting the events which are disclosed in the notes to the accounts.

30 November 20X5

The fire at the oil well takes place after the financial statements have been issued. The auditor has no obligation at all to make any inquiries regarding such financial statements by this date. When, as in this case, the auditor becomes aware of a fact which would have had an impact on the audit report, the auditor should consider whether the financial statements need revision, should discuss the matter with management and decide on the appropriate course of action.

Procedures would be as follows:

- Clarify the facts by discussion with management, reading minutes of board meetings and any reports submitted by experts on site.

- Check insurance documents to confirm that the damage caused to the well and any consequential damage eg environmental, is covered. Assess the basis on which the ten month time period has been calculated for drilling the new well to determine whether it is reasonable. Both of these factors may affect the viability of the business which should be assessed.

- Determine how management intend to deal with the issue. If the accounts are to be revised review the steps taken by management to ensure that anyone who had received the previously issued financial statements is informed of the situation.

- Issue a revised audit report including an emphasis of matter paragraph highlighting the disclosure in the accounts.

- If management does not revise the financial statements and the auditor considers that revision is necessary, consider the means by which recipients of the initial financial statements can be contacted. Before any further action is taken legal advice should be sought.

61 Mowbray Computers

Text references. Chapters 18 and 19

Top tips. This is a straightforward question, if you have a reasonable knowledge of ISA 570 and ISA 700. For part (a) ISA 570 is particularly useful as it does include a list of factors indicating going concern problems. However, if you are not familiar with this you should be able to come up with a reasonable answer by using a little common sense. You would not have needed to mention all the points we have to gain full marks in (a).

Easy marks. You should expect to score well in part (a).

(a)   Companies usually fail because of liquidity problems: either the bank calls in the loan or overdraft, or other lenders (eg debenture holders) call in a receiver or liquidator. The liquidity problems are usually related to profitability and other problems.

Profitability problems

(i)   **Recurring losses/low profits**. This means that non-current assets cannot be purchased and working capital is not funded for inflation or expansion, ie losses produce liquidity problems.

(ii)   **Recession** in the economy/industry, reducing profits as sales prices fall.

(iii)   **Loss of customer(s),** particularly where the company has one major customer or only a few large customers. It may take time to gain new ones.

(iv)   **Loss of supplier**. The product(s) may not be available from another source or only at a much higher price.

(v) **Rapid technological change** makes the company's products (or even production processes) redundant and out of date (fashion may have an impact here).

(vi) **Funding** for research and development is not available, so new products cannot be developed.

(vii) **Foreign competition** with lower labour costs and more advanced technology may make cheaper products and take market share.

(viii) **Currency movements** ($ vs other currencies) may adversely affect both importers and exporters. Prices may be forced up or margins reduced.

(ix) **Low interest cover** indicates that the company is only just covering interest costs, leaving little for distribution or reinvestment. Any increase in gearing (ie more loans) would exacerbate the problem.

Liquidity problems

(i) A (large) **bank overdraft**, always fully utilised, or even exceeded on a regular basis.

(ii) **High gearing**. In general terms borrowers (particularly banks) will be concerned if gearing is greater than 1, particularly if it is increasing, although the industry norms should be taken into account.

(iii) **High levels** of inventories (hard to sell? obsolete? overvalued?); high levels of receivables (increased risk of bad debts); and high levels of payables (paying suppliers slowly, exceeding credit limits).

(iv) **Overtrading** problems, where working capital is not sufficient to deal with rapid increases in sales (because profits have yet to be taken) and so the increases in working capital and non-current assets must be funded by borrowings.

(v) **New non-current assets** are purchased before sufficient sales and profits have been generated to pay for them. In particular, the acquisition of non-current assets under leases may indicate a lack of resources.

(vi) **Factoring of debts** often indicates liquidity problems, although it may decrease borrowings.

(b) (i) Where such uncertainty exists which is adequately accounted for and disclosed in the financial statements, ISA 570 *Going concern* requires that an **emphasis of matter paragraph** be included in the audit report.

This paragraph appears after the opinion paragraph and will start as follows.

'Without qualifying our opinion, we draw attention to note X in the financial statements ......

It will then go on to explain the circumstances, ie the recession and strong competition and the resulting fall in sales and gross profit margin, and state that the accounts have been prepared on a going concern basis, and refer to the note which deals with this issue. The paragraph is likely to add that the business's continuation depends on increased profitability etc, and the support of the company's bank and payables.

(ii) ISA 701 *Modifications to the Independent Auditor's Report* requires that where adequate disclosure is not given in the financial statements it is necessary to decide whether the effect is so material or pervasive that the financial statements as a whole are misleading. Where this is so, as in the case of Mowbray Computers, an **adverse opinion** should be given. The opinion paragraph will be titled 'Adverse opinion'. It will explain the circumstances, ie the recession and strong competition and the resulting fall in sales and gross profit leading to questions about the validity of the going concern basis. It will go on to state that because of the failure to disclose the going concern problems the financial statements do not give a true and fair view.

62 Audit reports

Text reference. Chapter 19

Top tips. This is a reasonably straightforward question and is one where you should be able to score well. Don't be put off by the fact that it looks at the format of the internal audit report. Particularly in part (a) by using a bit of common sense you should be able to come up with a good answer.

Easy marks. There are plenty of achievable marks in this question given a little thought and planning. Part (b) is particularly straightforward as you should feel confident that you can list out the basic content of the audit report.

Examiner's comments. This was generally well answered, although some candidates submitted scruffy and sloppy answers which did not score well.

Marking scheme

		Marks
(a)	Information in internal audit reports Up to 1 mark per point to a maximum of	4
(b)	Contents of external audit reports Up to $\frac{1}{2}$ mark per point to a maximum of	2
(c)	Differences – internal and external audit reports Up to 2 marks per point to a maximum of	$\frac{4}{10}$

(a) **Categories of information**

(i) *Cover page*

This would include a title, a date, the name of the author of the report and a distribution list.

(ii) *Executive summary*

This would include:

- Background to the assignment
- Objectives of the assignment
- Major outcomes of the work
- Key risks identified
- Key action points
- Summary of the work left to do

(iii) *The main report contents*

This would include:

- Details of audit tests carried out and their findings
- A full list of action points and who has responsibility for carrying them out
- Future time-scales
- Costs

(iv) *Appendices*

These would include detailed schedules and summaries which form the basis of the conclusions in the report.

(b) **Contents of the external audit report**

In accordance with ISA 700 *The independent auditor's report on a complete set of general purpose financial statements* the following are the basic elements of the external audit report:

(i)   Title
(ii) Addressee
(iii) Introductory paragraph identifying the financial statements audited
(iv) A statement of management's responsibility for the financial statements
(v)   A statement of the auditor's responsibility
(vi) Opinion paragraph containing an expression of opinion on the financial statements
(vii) Any other reporting responsibilities and conclusion
(viii) Date of the report
(ix) Auditor's address
(x)   Auditor's signature

(c) **Differences**

(i)   The format and content of the external audit report is governed by **legislation and auditing standards**. There is no standard format for an internal audit report. It depends on the requirements of management and the approach chosen by the individual internal auditor.

(ii) The requirement to issue an external audit report comes from **company law**. The internal audit report is produced as a result of the management's decision to commission certain projects and reviews.

(iii) The main aim of the external audit report is to **express an opinion** as to whether the financial statements give a true and fair view. It does not aim to give a detailed account of the work performed or to offer solutions for problems identified. The internal audit report is normally expected to be an assessment of the work completed. It will therefore summarise results, conclusions and action points.

(iv) The external audit report is normally **addressed to the shareholders** and is a published document available to a wide range of users. As a result of this it is a highly regulated document. The internal audit report is for internal purposes only. The content can therefore be tailored more specifically to the needs of the individual business and management team.

63 Question with helping hand: Corsco

Text references. Chapters 18 and 19

Top tips. This question considers the issue of going concern and the potential impact on the audit report. This is primarily a technical question so the key will be to use your knowledge of ISA 570 and ISA 700/701. You do need to adopt a thorough approach, so for example in part (b) you need to consider **all** the possible scenarios where going concern might be called into question. Parts (c) and (d) are slightly trickier. For part (c) do not jump to conclusions but make sure you read all the information and weigh it up. Also remember that qualified opinions are issued relatively infrequently. In part (d) you need to think as practically as possible. Notice that you are asked to consider the difficulties which would be faced by both Corsco and the auditors.

Easy marks. There are no easy marks as such in this question although if you have a good knowledge of ISA 570 all the marks available are equally achievable. Parts (a) and (b) are slightly more straightforward as they do not involve application but you do need to give a reasonably detailed answer to score well.

Marking scheme

		Marks
(a)	External auditor responsibilities – going concern Up to 1 mark per point to a maximum of	5
(b)	Possible audit reports and circumstances Up to 1.5 marks per point to a maximum of	5
(c)	Report issued to Corsco Up to 2 marks per point to a maximum of	4
(d)	Difficulties associated with reporting on going concern Up to 1.5 marks per point to a maximum of	6 20

(a) **External auditor's responsibilities and the work that the auditor should perform in relation to going concern**

(i) *Responsibilities*

According to ISA 570 the auditor should consider:

- Whether the **management's assumption** that the business is a going concern as reflected in the preparation of the financial statements is appropriate.

- Whether there are **material uncertainties** about the company's ability to continue which should be disclosed in the financial statements.

- Whether **disclosures are adequate** regarding going concern such that the financial statements give a true and fair view.

- Whether there are **any circumstances**, current or future, which might affect the ability of the company to continue for the foreseeable future.

(ii) *Audit work*

- As part of the overall risk assessment the auditor should consider whether there are any events or conditions and related business risks which may cast significant doubt on the company's ability to continue.

- The auditor should evaluate the process by which management has assessed the viability of the company. The auditor should make enquiries of those charged with governance and examine supporting documentation such as cash flow forecasts and budgets.

- The auditor should consider whether the period used by management to assess the viability of the company is sufficient. If the period covers less than twelve months from the balance sheet date the auditor should ask management to extend the period to twelve months from the balance sheet date.

- The auditor should evaluate the assumptions used by management and determine whether they seem reasonable in the light of other known facts.

- The auditor should inquire of management as to its knowledge of events or conditions and related business risks beyond the period of assessment used by management that may cast doubt on the viability of the company.

- Where events or conditions have been identified which may cast significant doubt on the entity's ability to continue as a going concern the auditor should review management's plans for future actions and gather sufficient appropriate audit evidence to confirm whether a material uncertainty exists. This will include:

  - Analysing and discussing the cash flow and interim financial statements

  - Reviewing the terms of debentures and loan agreements

  - Reading minutes of the meetings of shareholders and directors for reference to financing difficulties

  - Inquiring of the company's lawyers regarding litigation and claims

  - Assessing the possibility of raising additional funds

  - Reviewing events after the period end

- The auditor should seek written representations from management regarding its plans for future action.

(b) **Audit reports**

(i) Where the use of the going concern assumption is appropriate but a material uncertainty exists, provided that the auditor agrees with the basis of preparation of the accounts and the situation is adequately disclosed, an **unqualified opinion** is issued. The audit report is modified however by the inclusion of an **emphasis of matter paragraph** highlighting the uncertainty to the user and referring them to the details in the disclosure note.

(ii) Where the material uncertainty exists but the situation is not adequately disclosed the opinion should be **qualified on the grounds of disagreement** with the level of disclosure. Depending on the specific circumstances this may be an 'except for' or adverse opinion.

(iii) If in the auditor's judgement the company will not be able to continue as a going concern and the financial statements have been prepared on a going concern basis the auditor should express **an adverse opinion**.

(iv) If the auditors are unable to form an opinion due to a limitation on scope they should issue **an 'except for' qualified opinion or a disclaimer**.

(v) If management is unwilling to extend its assessment where the period considered is less than twelve months from the balance sheet date the auditor should consider **the need to modify** the report as a result of the limitation on the scope of his work.

(c) **Report issued to Corsco**

Although the company is obviously experiencing some difficulties the evidence provided does not suggest that the business will cease to trade in the near future. The company has net assets and still appears to have options available to it in order to resolve its problems. The fact that the company has taken steps to restructure its finance and has been able to do so is also a positive sign.

On the basis that the situation is no worse than in previous years and that no reference has been made to going concern in the past it would not seem appropriate to refer to it this year. An unmodified audit report would be issued.

(d)   **Difficulties**

If the audit report mentions a going concern problem it is likely that Corsco will find it difficult to raise finance and customers and suppliers may be more cautious to do business with them. It is often said that it becomes a 'self-fulfilling prophecy' although this should not dissuade the auditor from modifying his report if he feels there is genuine need.

The relationship between the auditor and the management of Corsco could become very strained particularly where the management of Corsco genuinely believe that no reference is required. This is particularly difficult as the matter is essentially one of judgement and will rarely be cut and dried. In extreme circumstances the auditors may lose the audit and fees from associated work.

As there has been no reference to going concern in the past to refer to it this year would suggest that the situation has deteriorated further (which contradicts the evidence) or that previous reports were not correct. This is a particularly contentious issue as there is ongoing public concern about the role of the auditor in warning shareholders about matters which will affect the value of their investment.

64 Theta

> **Text references.** Chapters 18 and 19
>
> **Top tips.** This question examines your knowledge of ISA 701 and if you are familiar with the basics of audit report qualifications you should be able to score well.
>
> In part (a) think about the practicalities of the situation. Does this give rise to a disagreement or a limitation on scope? Are the effects material or pervasive? Does it affect any implied opinions?
>
> Part (b) is then really a question of writing down the thought processes you went through to come to your conclusions in part (a). Be as precise as possible and refer your answer to the scenario where you can.
>
> In (c) you must be able to distinguish clearly the different types of audit opinion.
>
> **Easy marks.** These are available in part (c). You must be familiar with the different forms of audit opinion.

(a)   The situation described would give rise to a limitation in the scope of the auditor's work. Therefore the standard **basis of opinion** paragraph would be amended as follows.

(i)   In the auditor's responsibilities paragraph we would state that we conducted our audit in accordance with relevant standards but would make reference to the explanatory paragraph (see point (ii)).

(ii)   We would include an explanatory paragraph stating that, as a majority of the company's books and records were destroyed by fire, the **evidence** available to us was **limited**. In this case it would be **difficult to quantify** the financial impact.

(iii)   Our audit **opinion** would be a **disclaimer** on the grounds that the impact is material and **pervasive**. We would have to state that due to the **limitation** in **scope** of our work we were **unable to form an opinion** regarding the truth and fairness of the information.

We would also have to report that we had **not obtained all the information and explanations** which we considered necessary, and that we were **unable to determine** whether **proper accounting records** had been **maintained**.

These points would be included in an additional paragraph after the opinion paragraph.

(b)   A lack of accounting records results in a **limitation in scope**; the auditors cannot obtain all the evidence which they would normally expect to collect and will therefore have difficulty in forming an opinion.

This **limitation** may be **material or pervasive**. In this situation it would seem more likely that a disclaimer would be appropriate as the destruction of the records will have had a fundamental impact on most of the balances rather than on one particular item.

I am also assuming that destruction of the information is such that it is not possible to obtain any other satisfactory information to support the estimates made by the accountant.

The work that we have been able to do has been inconclusive.

(c)   (i)   The auditor may qualify the audit report due to **disagreement** with any of the following:

- Non-compliance with Accounting Standards

- Disagreement due to known facts

- Inadequate disclosure by the directors of significant uncertainties and/or the assumptions made

If the disagreement is material but does not render the accounts as a whole meaningless an **'except for'** qualification would be used. The opinion would state that the accounts give a true and fair view overall apart from this one specific item.

The opinion paragraph would be headed up as qualified on these grounds and would include an explanation of the disagreement.

(ii)   A **disclaimer** by contrast would arise due to a limitation in the scope of the auditors' work which has such a severe impact that the auditors are not able to form an opinion on the truth and fairness of the accounts at all. The audit opinion would be headed up as a disclaimer.

(iii)   An **adverse opinion** would be given where a **disagreement** is not just material as in (i) but has such an impact on the **accounts** that they are rendered **meaningless** as a whole. The basis for such disagreements are listed in part (i). Here the audit opinion would be headed up as an adverse opinion and would state that the accounts do **not give a true and fair view**.

65 Hood Enterprises

Text reference. Chapter 19

Top tips. Parts (a) and (c) of this question should be reasonably straightforward as you should be familiar with directors' and auditors' responsibilities and with the difference between positive and negative assurance. In part (b), take a methodical approach and look at each sentence in turn.

Easy marks. Part (a) tests very basic knowledge so should have been reasonably easy. Part (b) was harder but there should have been a few easy marks for spotting some of the more obvious differences from what you will have seen in standard audit reports in your study material.

Examiner's comments. Part (a) focused on a relatively small area of knowledge. Candidates need to focus points on the published financial statements. This section was well answered. The main weaknesses occurred where candidates provided a list of duties of the directors that were not directly related to the financial statements.

The overall standard in part (b) was unsatisfactory. The main reason for this appeared to be the requirement word 'explain'. Most candidates managed to identify some of the errors in the report but answers contained very little explanation of why the point was an error. A minority of answers simply stated the contents of a normal unmodified report, which did not meet the question heading.

The overall standard in part (c) was high with most candidates correctly explaining positive and negative assurance and providing at least one benefit of negative assurance.

		Marks
(a)	**Duties re financial statements**	
	Allow 1 mark for director responsibilities, and 1 for auditor responsibilities	
	Preparation of financial statements	2
	Fraud and error	2
	Disclosure	2
	Going concern	2
	Similar relevant points – each point	2
	Maximum marks	**6**
(b)	**Auditors' reports**	
	Up to 2 marks per relevant point	
	Use of term Auditing Standards	2
	Limitation on use of judgements and estimates	2
	Time limitation	2
	FS free from material error	2
	Directors' responsibilities	2
	Reference to annual report	2
	Allow other relevant points	2
	Maximum marks	**10**
(c)	**Audit reports**	
	One mark per point	
	Meaning of positive assurance	1
	Meaning of negative assurance	1
	Advantages of negative assurance	
	Some comfort provided	1
	Credibility	1
	Cost effective	1
	Allow other relevant points	1
	Maximum marks	**4**
	Total	**20**

(a)   **Preparation of financial statements**

The directors have a legal responsibility to prepare financial statements giving a true and fair view. This implies that they have been prepared in accordance with the relevant IASs and IFRSs.

The auditor's duty is to carry out an audit (according to the International Standards on Auditing) and to give an opinion on whether a true and fair view is given. In doing this they will have to consider whether the relevant accounting standards have been properly followed.

Estimates and judgements and accounting policies

The directors have the responsibility for making the estimates and judgements underlying the financial statements and for selecting the appropriate accounting policies.

The auditor's responsibility is to assess the appropriateness of the directors' judgements and to modify the audit opinion in the case of any material disagreement.

Fraud and error

The directors have a duty to prevent and detect fraud and error. This is a duty they owe to the shareholders and there is no 'materiality' threshold attached to their duty.

The auditors' responsibility (under ISA 240) is to assess the risk of material errors arising from fraud in the financial statements and to design audit procedures to give reasonable assurance of detecting any such material errors. The auditor has a responsibility to qualify the audit opinion if there any unamended material errors arising from fraud in the financial statements. Any frauds detected or suspected by the auditor should be reported to management and in certain circumstances, for example, where required by law (e.g. money laundering), or where the public interest is involved, to external authorities.

Disclosure

The directors are responsible for disclosing all information required by law and accounting standards.

The auditor's responsibility is to review whether all the disclosure rules have been followed and whether the overall disclosure is adequate. There are certain pieces of information, which, if not disclosed by the directors, must be disclosed by the auditor in his report. Examples of this are related party transactions and transactions with directors.

Going concern

The directors are responsible for assessing whether it is appropriate to treat the business as a going concern. In doing this they should look at forecasts and predictions for at least twelve months from the balance sheet date. They should also disclose any significant uncertainties over the going concern status of the company.

The auditors' responsibility is to consider whether there are any indicators of going concern problems in the company, and assess the forecasts made by directors and decide whether the correct accounting basis has been used and whether there is adequate disclosure of significant uncertainties.

The auditor must modify the report if:

(i)   The directors have considered a period of less than twelve months from the balance sheet date (this will be a limitation on the scope of the audit)

(ii)   The directors have used the going concern basis when the auditor believes that its use is not appropriate (this will be a disagreement, and probably an adverse opinion)

(iii)   The auditor agrees with the basis chosen by the directors but feels that the disclosures are inadequate (this will be a disagreement, probably an 'except for' opinion)

(iv)   The auditor agrees with the chosen basis, and that the disclosures are adequate but there are uncertainties over the going concern status of the company. In this case the opinion will be unqualified but an emphasis of matter paragraph will be added.

(b)   **Errors in the report extract**

'In accordance with Auditing Standards'

The report should specify exactly which auditing standards have been used so that there is no risk that readers misunderstand how the audit has been done. It should specify that the audit has been performed in accordance with **International Standards on Auditing**.

*'Assessment of **all** the estimates'*

The standard wording in ISA 700 is '***significant** estimates...*'. It is inappropriate to imply that the auditor has considered every estimate made by management. This is unlikely to be true because auditors do not look at every single transaction and item in the financial statements; it is the duty of the auditor to give assurance only on whether the financial statements are free from material misstatement.

'Given the time available'

This phrase is inappropriate because it implies that the auditor has not had time to obtain all the evidence that is needed. The auditor is expected to obtain sufficient evidence on which to base conclusions. The auditor should have planned the audit so as to obtain sufficient evidence in the time available.

'Confirm'

This word should not be used because it implies a greater degree of certainty than is possible based on normal audit procedures. The certainty implied by the word *'confirm'* may expose the auditor to negligence claims if it turns out that there are any material errors in the financial statements. A more accurate description of the level of assurance given by an audit is 'reasonable assurance'.

'No liability for errors can be accepted by the auditor'

This disclaimer at first might appear to be useful in protecting the auditor against liability. However, the view of the ACCA is that general disclaimers should not be included in audit reports, as their use would tend to devalue the audit opinion.

'The directors are wholly responsible for the accuracy of the financial statements'

This statement should not appear in the basis of opinion section of the report, as this should describe how the *auditor* has arrived at his conclusion. Details of the directors' responsibilities should appear in an earlier section of the report that outlines the respective responsibilities of directors and auditors.

'Presentation of information in the company's annual report'

The auditor's legal responsibilities relate to the financial statements, which comprise the primary statements plus the supporting notes. They do not extend to any other information, for example a chairman's statement, or 5-year summary. To make this clear, this phrase should refer only to the financial statements.

Under ISA 720 *Other information in documents continuing audited financial statements* the auditor has a duty to read the other information to identify whether there are any inconsistencies with the financial statements or anything that is misleading. It would be appropriate to mention this responsibility.

(c) Positive assurance is the form of words used in a report where the auditor has obtained sufficient evidence to feel confident to give reasonable assurance that the information is free from material error. A normal audit opinion takes this form, i.e. ' In our opinion the financial statements give a true and fair view'.

Negative assurance is the form of words used where the auditor has obtained a lower level of evidence and can therefore give only a lower level of assurance. A review of a forecast would be an appropriate example of when this would be used. The auditor cannot be as confident about forward-looking information, based on the directors' assumptions.

A negative assurance opinion would be worded perhaps as ' nothing has come to our attention to suggest that the information is not based on reasonable assumptions...'

The advantages of the negative assurance would be:

- The bank will be able to place more reliance on the forecast as it has been subject to review by an independent professional. The level of comfort given will be less than that of an audit but forecast information cannot be verified to the same degree as historical information so the negative assurance is the best that could be expected in the circumstances.

- Negative assurance requires a lower level of work than a full scope audit so will be cheaper for the company.

ANSWERS

Mock Exams

ACCA

Paper F8

Audit and Assurance (International)

Mock Examination 1

Question Paper	
Time allowed	
Reading and Planning Writing	**15 minutes** **3 hours**
ALL FIVE questions are compulsory and MUST be attempted	
During reading and planning time only the question paper may be annotated	

DO NOT OPEN THIS PAPER UNTIL YOU ARE READY TO START UNDER EXAMINATION CONDITIONS

ALL FIVE questions are compulsory and MUST be attempted

Question 1

Viswa is a company that provides call centre services for a variety of organisations. It operates in a medium sized city and your firm is the largest audit firm in the city. Viswa is owned and run by two entrepreneurs with experience in this sector and has been in existence for five years. It is expanding rapidly in terms of its client base, the number of staff it employs and its profits. It is now 15 June 20X4 and you have been approached to perform the audit for the year ending 30 June 20X4. Your firm has not audited this company before. Viswa has had three different firms of auditors since its incorporation.

Viswa's directors have indicated to you informally that the reason they wish to change auditors is because of a disagreement about certain disclosures in the financial statements in the previous year. The directors consider that the disagreement is a trivial matter and have indicated that the company accountant will be able to provide you with the details once the audit has commenced. Your firm has explained that before accepting the appointment, there are various matters to be considered within the firm and other procedures to be undertaken, some of which will require the co-operation of the directors. Your firm has other clients that operate call centres. The directors have asked your firm to commence the audit immediately because audited accounts are needed by the bank by 30 July 20X4. Your firm is very busy at this time of year.

Required

(a) Describe the matters to consider within your firm and the other procedures that must be undertaken before accepting the appointment as auditor to Viswa. **(10 marks)**

(b) Explain why it would be inappropriate to commence the audit before consideration of the matters and the procedures referred to in (a) above have been completed. **(6 marks)**

(c) Explain the purpose of an engagement letter and list its contents. **(6 marks)**

(d) Briefly describe some of the audit risks that will be associated with the audit of Viswa, explaining why they are risks. **(8 marks)**

(Total = 30 marks)

Question 2

Towards the end of an audit, it is common for the auditor to seek a letter of representation (written representations) from the management of the client company.

Required

(a) Explain why auditors seek letters of representation. **(2 marks)**

(b) List the matters commonly included in the letter of representation. **(3 marks)**

(c) Explain why management is sometimes unwilling to sign a letter of representation and describe the actions an external auditor can take if management refuses to sign a letter of representation. **(5 marks)**

(Total = 10 marks)

Question 3

Professional ethics are relevant to both external auditors and internal auditors.

You work for a medium-sized firm of Chartered Certified Accountants with seven offices and 150 employees. Your firm has been asked to tender for the provision of statutory audit and other services to Billington Travel, a private company providing discounted package holiday services in the Mediterranean. The company is growing fast and would represent a substantial amount of fee income for your firm. The finance director has explained to you that the company would like the successful firm to provide a number of different services. These include the statutory audit and assistance with the preparation of the financial statements. The company is also struggling with a new computer system and the finance director considers that a systems review by your firm may be helpful. Your firm does not have much experience in the travel sector.

Required

(a)   Explain why it is necessary for external auditors to be, and be seen to be, independent of their audit clients.

(3 marks)

(b)   With reference to the ACCA's *Code of Ethics and Conduct*, describe the ethical matters that should be considered in deciding on whether your firm should tender for:

(i)   The statutory audit of Billington Travel   **(4 marks)**
(ii)   The provision of other services to Billington Travel   **(4 marks)**

You are a student Chartered Certified Accountant and you are one of four assistant internal auditors in a large manufacturing company. You report to the chief internal auditor. You have been working on the review of the payables system and you have discovered what you consider to be several serious deficiencies in the structure and operation of the system. You have reported these matters in writing to the chief internal auditor but you are aware that none of these matters have been covered in his final report on the system which is due to be presented to management.

Required

(c)   List the actions you might take in these circumstances.   **(6 marks)**
(d)   Explain the dangers of doing nothing in these circumstances.   **(3 marks)**

(Total = 20 marks)

Question 4

You are the auditor of Fitta Co, whose principal activity is fitting out shops, hotels and restaurants. The company employs 180 weekly-paid employees and all employees are paid by direct transfer into their bank accounts.

Hours worked are recorded on timesheets which are completed by the site and workshop supervisors and submitted to Michelle, the payroll clerk, in the personnel department. Michelle checks the timesheets for completeness and to satisfy herself that they have been signed by the appropriate supervisor.

Michelle accesses the payroll system using a password which is known only to her and Carla, an accounts clerk, who covers for leave of absence. She then enters the hours worked, split between basic and overtime, into a computer and the program calculates the gross and net pay.

A printout of the current period's payroll is generated, detailing for each employee, hours paid, split between basic and overtime, gross pay, deductions, net pay, employer's tax and totals thereof. Michelle checks the hours paid on the computer printout to the timesheets and, if necessary, re-runs the payroll incorporating any amendments, and a printout of the revised payroll is obtained. The following reports are then generated:

Summary: Cumulative details to date per employee

Payslips: Details of gross pay, deductions and net pay

Autopay list: Bank sort code, account number and net pay per employee, and total net pay.

The managing director, Mr Grimshaw, reviews the autopay list before Michelle uses a different password to transmit the details via direct transfer to the company's bank. Two days later a printout, listing bank and net pay details per employee together with the net pay total, is received from the bank and Michelle files it in date order.

On completion of payroll processing Michelle copies the payroll details onto a floppy disk which is stored in the fireproof safe in Mr Grimshaw's office.

Details of starters, leavers and amendments to employee details are recorded on standard forms by the site and workshop supervisors and passed to Michelle for input to the system. After updating the standing data, she obtains a printout and checks the details to the standard form which is filed with the personnel record of the respective employee.

Each month Michelle posts the weekly summaries to the nominal ledger accounts. She also extracts the tax details from the weekly payroll summaries and records the monthly figures on the taxation authorities payslip. The finance director, Mrs Duckworth, reviews the monthly figures for tax and prepares a cheque for the appropriate amount.

Required

(a)   Identify the objectives of exercising internal controls in a wages system and discuss the extent to which the procedures exercised by Fitta achieve these objectives.   **(10 marks)**

(b)   Describe the procedures which would strengthen Fitta's wages system.   **(10 marks)**

(Total = 20 marks)

Question 5

Your firm is the external auditor to two companies. One is a hotel, Tourex, the other is a food wholesaler, Pudco, that supplies the hotel. Both companies have the same year-end. Just before that year-end, a large number of guests became ill at a wedding reception at the hotel, possibly as a result of food poisoning.

The guests have taken legal action against the hotel and the hotel has taken action against the food wholesaler. Neither the hotel nor the food wholesaler have admitted liability. The hotel is negotiating out-of court settlements with the ill guests, the food wholesaler is negotiating an out-of-court settlement with the hotel. At the balance sheet date, the public health authorities have not completed their investigations.

Lawyers for both the hotel and the food wholesaler say informally that negotiations are 'going well' but refuse to confirm this in writing. The amounts involved are material to the financial statements of both companies.

Required

(a)   Describe how ACCA's *Code of Ethics and Conduct* applies to this situation and explain how the external auditors should manage this conflict of interest. **(6 marks)**

(b)   Outline the main requirements of IAS 37 *Provisions, contingent liabilities and contingent assets* and apply them to this case. **(7 marks)**

(c)   Assuming that your firm continues with the audit of both companies, for each company describe the difficulties you foresee in obtaining sufficient audit evidence for potential provisions, contingent liabilities and contingent assets, and describe how this could affect your audit reports on their financial statements. **(7 marks)**

(Total = 20 marks)

Answers

DO NOT TURN THIS PAGE UNTIL YOU HAVE
COMPLETED THE MOCK EXAM

A plan of attack

If this were the real Audit and Assurance exam and you had been told to turn over and begin, what would be going through your mind?

An important thing to say (while there is still time) is that it is vital to have a good breadth of knowledge of the syllabus because all the questions are compulsory. However, don't panic. Below we provide guidance on how to approach the exam.

Approaching the paper

Use your 15 minutes of reading time usefully, to look through the questions, particularly Question 1, to get a feel for what is required and to become familiar with the question scenarios.

Since all the questions in this paper are compulsory, it is vital that you attempt them all to increase your chances of passing. For example, don't run over time on Question 2 and then find that you don't have enough time for the remaining questions.

Question 1 is a 30 mark case-study style question on audit acceptance procedures and audit risks associated with the engagement. You must stick to time for this question as a whole and for each of the individual parts. Use the information in the scenario to help you and give you clues. For example, it states that the directors want the audit to be complete by a certain date so this will add to the audit risk.

Question 2 will always be a knowledge-based 10 mark question. You should be able to score well therefore. Look at the requirements of the question and the mark allocation carefully. For example, in part (b), you need to 'list' the matters included in the letter of representation, so make sure you do – don't be tempted to write down everything you know about letters of representation.

Question 3 is on ethics and professional matters. Again the question is split into several parts so take each in turn and don't run over time. There are lost of clues in the scenario so you should be able to generate enough points to score well. In part (b), use lots of sub-headings as this will give your answer more structure. Again, pay careful attention to the requirements for each part – 'list', 'explain' and so forth – these give you an idea of what your answer should look like.

Question 4 is a question on weaknesses in a payroll system. There is lots of information in the scenario so you need to work carefully through this first. A good way to set out your answer would be in a tabular format – in this way you can link the objectives to the potential improvements to the system. In this question, it is vital that you understand the difference between control objectives and the controls themselves. You need to set out your answer so that you are focussing on control objectives.

Question 5 is about events occurring after the balance sheet date and the potential impact on the audit report. You need to be sure of your financial reporting knowledge here, but there are also ethical and professional issues to address in this question so don't forget about those.

Forget about it!

And don't worry if you found the paper difficult. More than likely other candidates will too. If this were the real thing you would need to forget the exam the minute you left the exam hall and think about the next one. Or, if it is the last one, celebrate!

Question 1

Text references. Chapters 4 and 6

Top tips. This question looks at the procedures a firm should follow before taking on a new client. As such it should be a scenario that you feel reasonably well prepared for. Remember in broad terms that factors might include legal, ethical and practical considerations. In part (a) you are asked to describe matters to consider and other procedures that must be taken. The key here is to plan, as certain points could be mentioned under either heading. For example you could state that the level of fees is a matter you would consider. You could also say that discussion of fee levels with management is a procedure you would perform. You will not pick up marks for mentioning the same point twice. Mention it once and do not be too concerned about which point appears under which heading.

In part (b) notice that the structure of the question gives you the approach to take to the answer. Go back to the matters and procedures you have listed in part (a) and ask yourself why this was important. Try not to simply repeat the same point from part (a) again but explain its relevance, drawing on the specifics of the scenario as much as possible.

In part (d), use the clues in the scenario to help you to plan your answer. For example, it is a new client, there is a tight reporting deadline, potential lack of integrity of management etc.

Easy marks. These are available in part (c) of the question. You should be familiar with the basic purpose and content of the letter of engagement as set down in ISA 210 *Terms of audit engagements*. However you need to answer both parts of the requirement (ie purpose and content). A list of contents alone will not pick up full marks.

Examiner's comments. Answers to part (a) tended to be very long although this did not necessarily detract from the number of marks scored. Many answers showed a lack of planning and poor structure resulting in the repetition of points. Common errors included a failure to make a connection between the point made and the scenario and discussing procedures that would apply after appointment such as deciding methods of testing.

In part (b) most candidates correctly focused attention on ethical issues and problems of not providing an appropriate level of service. Common errors included repeating the points from part (a) without additional explanation and a failure to consider the scenario.

Part (c) was generally well answered.

Marking scheme

		Marks
(a)	Internal matters and other procedures before appointment Up to 1 mark per point to a maximum of *Note.* There are many more details that could be provided for the 'professional etiquette' letter – credit may be given for these but not more than a maximum of 5 marks for internal matters	10
(b)	Starting the audit Up to 1 mark per point to a maximum of	6
(c)	Engagement letter Up to 1 mark per point to a maximum of	6
(d)	Audit risks Upto $1\frac{1}{2}$ marks per well explained point to a maximum of	$\frac{8}{30}$

(a) **Matters to consider and other procedures before accepting appointment**

(i) *Matters to consider*

- The **risk** associated with the audit. The fact that the company has had three different auditors in five years increases the risk associated with accepting the appointment. It suggests that disputes are commonplace and are not necessarily as trivial as the directors have suggested.

- The size of the **fee** which the firm will be able to charge and whether this will lead to other work.

- Whether the firm has **staff available** with the relevant **expertise** who can perform the work to the required timescale. As the firm has other clients in this field it is likely that staff will have the relevant experience. However the firm may not have sufficient resources available as this is a particularly busy time of year.

- Whether there are any **conflicts of interest**. This is a potential problem as the firm has other clients that operate call centres. The firm needs to assess the extent of any risk and its ability to put suitable safeguards in place.

- Whether there are any other **ethical reasons** why the firm should not accept appointment. For example there may be independence issues if there is a close relationship or other connection between partners and staff and the directors.

(ii) *Other procedures*

- Seek the permission of the directors to obtain the details of the disagreement from the company accountant.

- Make independent enquiries if the directors are not personally known.

- Seek the permission of the directors to contact the outgoing auditors to confirm whether there are any matters that they should be aware of in making their decision as to whether they should accept the appointment or not. If permission is refused the appointment should not be accepted.

- Request the directors to notify the outgoing auditors of their possible appointment and to give the outgoing auditors permission to communicate with them. If this request is refused the appointment should not be accepted.

- Contact the outgoing auditors in writing, asking them to confirm the details of any matters relevant to their appointment. If there are no such matters this should also be confirmed.

- Review the communications received from the outgoing auditors and assess the impact of any matters noted.

- Discuss a more detailed timetable of events and the basis of the firm's fees.

- Obtain credit checks.

(b) **It would be inappropriate to commence the audit before consideration of the matters and procedures referred to above because:**

- **Audit risk needs to be managed**. Where there are significant questions over the integrity of management in their dealings with the auditors the firm may conclude that audit risk cannot be managed at an acceptable level and that therefore the appointment should not be accepted.

- The auditor will weigh up the fee that can be charged as the work would normally only be accepted on the basis that it would make **commercial sense** to do so.

- It is an **ethical requirement** that the work should be performed competently. This will not be the case if resources are insufficient or staff inexperienced. The firm would also want to reduce the risk of being sued for negligence.

- It is an ethical requirement to consider the effect of any conflicts of interest and the existence of any independence issues. The firm would be **in breach** of the ACCA's *Code of Ethics and Conduct* if it failed to do so. It may also find that other clients may object if they believe that a conflict exists between themselves and Viswa.

- The incoming auditors need to be able to evaluate **the integrity** of management. Communicating with the previous auditors is an important part of that process as well as any other independent enquiries which can be made.

- It is important that the auditor is fully aware of the expectations of the client so that he can assess his ability to satisfy these. An outline timetable of events aids this process.

- The audit firm is a commercial enterprise. It is important that the client is aware of the basis and size of the fee. This reduces the risk of subsequent disputes over payment.

(c) **Purpose and content of the engagement letter**

Purpose

The engagement letter should define clearly the extent of the **auditors' responsibilities** and so minimise the possibility of any **misunderstanding** between the client and the auditors. In this way it helps to reduce the expectation gap. It acts as a **contract** between the two parties and provides **written confirmation** of the auditors' acceptance of the appointment, the scope of the audit, the form of their report and the scope of any non-audit services.

Content

The form and content of the letter of engagement may vary for each client, but they would generally include reference to the following:

- The objective of the audit

- Management's responsibility for the financial statements

- The applicable financial reporting framework

- The scope of the audit (including reference to applicable legislation, regulations or pronouncements of professional bodies to which the auditor adheres)

- The form of any reports or other communication of results of the engagement

- The fact that because of the test nature and inherent limitations of an audit, together with the inherent limitations of any accounting and internal control system, there is an unavoidable risk that some material misstatement may remain undiscovered

- Unrestricted access to records, documentation and other information requested in connection with the audit

- Basis on which fees are computed and billing arrangements

(d) **Audit risks associated with the audit of Viswa**

Viswa is rapidly expanding

The company is rapidly expanding. Rapid growth can lead to overtrading which in turn can result in the company going into liquidation as it cannot continue to finance itself. Ultimately this impacts on whether the company can continue as a going concern.

Integrity of directors

The previous auditors were dismissed on the basis of disagreements with the two directors. In fact, Viswa has had three different auditors since its incorporation five years ago. This may mean that the directors are prepared to bully the auditors to do as they wish and calls into question their integrity.

Tight reporting deadline for audit

The directors want the firm to start the audit immediately as audited accounts are required by the bank a month after the year-end. This increases the detection risk of the audit as the audit firm will be under time pressure and will also lack evidence of events occurring after the balance sheet date.

Reliance on financial statements by the bank

The directors of Viswa are meeting with the bank and will want to present a healthy set of accounts to them, in order to secure more borrowing for instance. This increases the risk that figures in the accounts are manipulated and hence misstated. There will also be increased risk of error in figures that are subjective such as provisions.

New audit client

Viswa will be a new audit client for the firm and although it does have other call centre companies in its portfolio, this increases the detection risk of the audit as the firm has had no previous experience of the company. This means it will be more difficult to identify areas of risk.

Question 2

Text reference. Chapter 18

Top tips. This question is quite structured so take each part in turn and deal with it, noting the mark allocation against each one and ensuring that you spend the appropriate time on each section of the question. Note the requirements in parts (a) and (d) to 'explain why' – this means that your answer should not just consist of a list of bullet points but that you must develop each point more fully. This question assumes a good knowledge of ISA 580 *Management representations* so make sure you are familiar with this area of the syllabus as it could come up in scenario-based questions about audit evidence or in a knowledge-based context, as in this case.

Easy marks. The requirements for this question are not difficult however so with sound technical knowledge you should be able to pick up good marks in part (a) and (b).

Examiner's comments. There were few good answers to this question with many candidates confusing this with the engagement letter or letter of weakness. Many thought that where the letter of representation could not be obtained the answer was to obtain other evidence. This demonstrated a failure to realise that by its very nature the letter of representation covers matters where there is little alternative evidence.

Marking scheme

		Marks
(a)	Letter of representation Up to 1 mark per point to maximum of	2
(b)	Common categories of matter included in the letter of representation ½ mark per point to maximum of	3
(c)	Management unwilling to sign and action if management refuses to sign Up to 1.5 marks per point to maximum of	5
		10

(a)   **Letters of representation**

During an audit many representations are made to the auditor, usually in response to specific queries. Where the auditor considers that other **sufficient appropriate evidence is not expected to exist,** written confirmation is sought. This might include instances for example where knowledge of the facts is confined to management or where the matter is principally one of judgement. This reduces the possibility of misunderstandings arising.

Management representations should not however, be a substitute for other independent evidence.

The letter may also be used to obtain confirmations regarding more general matters. These are listed in points (i) – (iii) below.

(b)   **Matters commonly included**

(i)   Acknowledgement of directors' responsibility for the preparation and approval of the financial statements

(ii)   Confirmation that the transactions of the company have been recorded in the books and records and that all of these have been made available to the auditor

(iii) Opinion as to the expected outcome of any legal claims

(iv) Assumptions used in respect of tax treatments

(v)   Confirmation as to the existence or otherwise of related party transactions

(vi) That there have been no events since the balance sheet date which require revision of the accounts

(c)   **Actions**

(i)   In some instances the directors may be unwilling to sign the letter. This may be because they genuinely feel unable to confirm some of the information included. Alternatively it may be that they have not been entirely open with the auditor about some of the information provided and whilst they are willing to make statements orally, they are less prepared to confirm them in writing.

(ii)   If the directors refuse to sign, the auditor should **discuss** the matter with the directors to determine the reason and attempt to come to a compromise which is acceptable to all.

If this is unsuccessful the auditor could **send a letter** setting out his understanding and ask for management confirmation. If management does not reply, the auditor should follow up to ascertain that his understanding is correct.

If this is still unsuccessful and the required representations cannot be obtained the auditor will need to consider the impact on the audit report of this limitation in scope. The auditor will need to consider whether the **audit opinion** will be qualified or a disclaimer issued.

Question 3

Text reference. Chapter 5

Top tips. This question examines ethics from the point of view of the external and internal auditors. You may find the second part of the question more difficult. Try to think logically, and apply what you know. As has been said a number of times already in this kit, it is important to be comfortable with internal audit issues. Remember, you are likely to be awarded a mark for each valid point you make. So, in part (a), three bullet pointed (relevant) reasons will be sufficient to obtain your marks. Apply this logic to each part you attempt.

Easy marks. These can be found in parts (a) and (b) of the question. Make sure you can explain the basic principle of independence. Application of the ACCA's *Code of Ethics and Conduct* is also a popular exam topic.

Marking scheme

			Marks
(a)	Independence of auditors		
	Up to 1 mark per point to maximum of		3
(b)	Ethical matters		
	(i) Audit of Billington Travel		
	Skill and resources	2	
	Level of fee income	1	
	Conflict of interest	1	
			4
	(ii) Other services	2	
	Independence	1	
	Skill and resources	1	
	Level of fee income		4
(c)	Actions to take		
	Up to 1 mark per point to a maximum of		6
(d)	Risks of doing nothing		
	Up to 1 mark per point to a maximum of		3
			20

(a) **External auditor independence**

There are several reasons why external auditors need to be, and be seen to be independent.

(i)   Auditors are required to give an **impartial view** as to whether accounts show a true and fair view to the owners of the company. They must be independent of management to do this.

(ii)   The professional body, ACCA requires that firms are independent and may discipline firms that do not follow **ethical guidance**.

(iii) **Legislation** in many countries requires auditors to be independent of their clients.

(b) **Ethical matters**

(i)   *Statutory audit considerations*

When deciding if the firm should tender for the statutory audit of Billington Travel, the ethical matters to consider are:

- Whether the firm has the **necessary skill** to undertake the audit. They do not have very much experience in the travel sector.

- Whether the level of the **fee income** (for the audit itself, and then combined with any other services undertaken), would make Billington's fees above 15% of total income.

   This would mean that the level of fees was higher than what is recommended by the ethical guide and would imply that the firm would not be sufficiently independent of the client to take the work.

- Whether undertaking the audit of Billington would cause a conflict of interest to arise with another client. This is unlikely, given their lack of experience in the travel sector.

- They must ensure that they have the staff available at the appropriate time to do the audit if their tender is successful.

(ii)   *Other services considerations*

When deciding whether to tender to provide services other than audit to Billington Travel, the ethical matters to consider are:

- Whether the provision of services other than the audit will affect their **independence** to do the audit.

  This can be viewed in fee terms, and whether the other work will require them to make any management decisions, or review their own work. Preparing the accounts for a small private company is allowed by the ethical rules, if the directors accept responsibility for the accounting records.

  The firms will have to put some safeguards in place, however. They should ensure, where possible, that different staff prepare and audit the accounts. They should also discover why the client does not have the necessary skill to put together accounts and consider giving them assistance in this area.

- Whether they have **necessary skills** to undertake the work.

  A one-off review of a computer system should not affect independence. No management decisions would be made for the client. This could be seen as a systems review, adding value to the service of the auditor. It will also assist them to gain knowledge of the business to undertake the audit.

  However, if they do not possess enough IT knowledge to do an appropriate review, they should not tender for the work.

- As noted above, whether the **additional fee income** will affect the independence of the firm to do the audit.

Internal audit issues

(c)   **Actions to take**

The following actions are available to an internal auditor, in the order in which they are available.

- Discuss the problem with **other internal auditors** at the same level.

  Discussing the problem might reveal that the deficiency is not as serious as was feared. It might show alternative safeguards which counter-act the perceived deficiency and reveal that the senior internal auditor is right not to include it in the report.

  Discussion may also reveal that this problem is not isolated and that other staff at the same level may believe that there are other problems.

- Discuss the problem again with the **chief internal auditor**.

  It may be that the chief internal auditor has misunderstood the point being made or that the exclusion of the issue was an oversight. It may be possible for the chief internal auditor to be convinced of the problem. He might then amend his report.

- Make **notes** of the discussions.

  If the internal auditor cannot convince the chief internal auditor of the issue and feels that the system still has serious deficiencies, he will have to take his issue up with someone at a higher level in the organisation.

BPP
LEARNING MEDIA

It is therefore a good idea that he makes notes of all the discussions that he has had with the chief internal auditor on the issue, so that he can make his point fairly to those in authority over the chief internal auditor.

- Approach **senior management**

  Who exactly the senior management are will depend on the organisation. Often, organisations large enough to have a significant internal audit department will have an audit committee and such a problem might best be shared with a member of this committee.

  As members of audit committees are non-executive directors, they may show less bias towards the system than the chief internal auditor.

- **Further action**

  The concern is one internal to the organisation, so assuming that the issue does not involve any illegal activity (unlikely), no question of reporting to third parties arises.

  However, if the external auditors were later to seek to use internal audit's work, the internal auditor would be within his bounds to make his comments and concerns available to them as it is his duty as an employee of the company to give them explanations required for their audit.

(d) **Dangers of doing nothing**

A student chartered certified accountant is bound by the ethical code of the ACCA whichever sector he is working in. **Professional ethics** require accountants to be pro-active about such issues as this one. Ignoring this problem could result in the chief internal auditor perpetrating a fraud, for example.

In serious cases, doing nothing in a situation like this might result in the student being **disciplined by ACCA**.

In regard to the ongoing job prospects of the student accountant, if the problem later emerges, the blame for not discovering or reporting the problem may be laid with him. This will not look good on his **employment** record and might even lead to the **loss of his job**, should the systems fail to operate properly and problems arise.

Question 4

Text references. Chapters 9 and 10

Top tips. In this question you need to discuss the extent to which the company has achieved the control objectives of a wages system and then make recommendations for any improvements. The best way to set your answer out therefore would be in a tabular format, so that objectives and recommendations are linked together. This gives your answer much more structure. There are lots of clues in the question scenario so make sure you go through this carefully first and spend some time planning before launching straight into your answer. Look at the mark allocation and work out how many points roughly you need to raise to score well. Make sure your recommendations for improvement are sensible and pertinent to this company – in real-life you would be trying to add value to the client as a result of your audit work.

Easy marks. There aren't easy marks as such in this question but by careful consideration of the information in the scenario, together with your knowledge of controls, you should be able to pick up marks by your discussion points and sensible recommendations.

Marking scheme

		Marks
(a)	Objectives in the payroll system	
	Correct employees paid	2
	Paid the correct amount	2
	Ensure the deductions calculated correctly	2
	Correct accounting for the cost and deductions	2
	No fraud or error	2
	Maximum 2 points for each objective must be adequately explained	10
(c)	1 mark per sensible correction of a weakness identified in section (a)	
	Restricted to a maximum	10
		20

(a)	(b)
Objective: To ensure the right employees are paid.	

Achieved?	Improvements
Amounts are paid directly into bank accounts via direct transfer, and this eliminates any cash mishandling problems.	Mr Grimshaw should perform the transmission of data by using a password known only to him and the review should cover the areas mentioned.
The autopay list is reviewed before transmission although it is not clear what for.	
Unusual amounts, employees, duplicate sort codes may not be identified.	
Mr Grimshaw reviews the list before Michelle transmits the details to the bank. This gives Michelle the opportunity to change the details before transmission.	Mr Grimshaw should also receive the printout from the bank, review to ensure accuracy of transmission, initial the form as evidence of review and then pass to Michelle for filing.

Objective: To ensure genuine employees only are paid and are paid correctly for all work done.	

Achieved?	Improvements
Michelle reviews the timesheets for completeness which should ensure they are all received.	
Michelle ensures that the appropriate supervisor has authorised the hours worked.	
However she then enters the details and is the only one to check that the hours have been entered correctly. This could result in errors of numbers of hours processed.	An independent review using total hours and sample of employees should be performed after input to the system. Batch control totals may be sued to ensure completeness and accuracy of input.
Michelle does not appear to perform any review for reasonableness of the timesheets to ensure number of hours claimed are feasible.	A review of all timesheets independent of supervisors should be performed to ensure reasonableness of hours claimed.
	Total number of hours of overtime claimed should be reviewed for reasonableness.
	Reconciliation of basic hours claimed should be performed each week by an independent person (from Michelle and supervisor).

(a)	(b)
Objective: To ensure that net pay and deductions are calculated correctly.	

Achieved?	Improvements
Amendments to be made to personnel records are detailed on a standard form by supervisors.	Amendment forms should be pre-numbered and breaks in the sequence should be investigated promptly.
There does not seem to be any check of completeness or accuracy of processing.	Printout obtained by Michelle should be reviewed by employee or supervisor or accountant as appropriate to check accuracy.
Michelle appears to have access to standing data and can therefore make unauthorised changes.	Master file changes should be made only by Mr Grimshaw who should periodically check sample of payslips for details back to source documentation.

Objective: To ensure that accounting for cost and deductions is accurate in the financial statement and in returns sent to the taxation authority.	

Achieved?	Improvements
Cumulative details are stored on disc in a safe ensuring that returns can be filed even if data is last from the system.	Storage of the floppy disks could be more secure off-site (eg bank deposit box).
Mrs Duckworth reviews the monthly figures for tax and should identify any obvious errors.	The review could be more thorough and encompass all deductions with calculations of estimated costs and monthly reviews performed to identify fluctuations.

Objective: To ensure duties are adequately segregated.	

Achieved?	Improvements
There is very little segregation of duties with Michelle performing most tasks.	More appropriate segregation has been noted above but generally more use of other personnel staff would achieve this objective.

Question 5

Text references. Chapters 4, 8 and 19

Top tips. The key with this question is to ensure that you apply your knowledge to the situation described. With part (a) and (b) in particular there is a danger that you could write everything you know about the ACCA's *Code of Ethics and Conduct* and IAS 37. Marks will be awarded for this (see below) but it is important that you show how the theory relates to the scenario.

In part (c) don't be afraid of suggesting more than one form of audit report. Where circumstances are uncertain there is likely to be a range of possible outcomes which will potentially affect the audit report issued.

Easy marks. The majority of the easy marks can be found in parts (a) and (b) of the question. In part (a) you can score well by demonstrating a basic knowledge of the ACCA's *Code of Ethics and Conduct*. In part (b) you are asked to outline the requirements of IAS 37. This is an opportunity to score marks for rote learned knowledge albeit Financial Reporting. The key is to use the definitions of a provision, contingent liability and contingent asset as a starting point.

> **Examiner's comments.** Parts (a) and (c) were generally well answered.
>
> In part (b) many candidates demonstrated a lack of basic understanding of IAS 37. Candidates must realise that provisions are provided for in the accounts but that contingent liabilities and contingent assets are disclosed at most.
>
> Accounting standards are examinable for Paper F8 and must be learnt. (Those examinable in detail at this level are those examinable for Paper F3.)

Marking scheme

		Marks
(a)	Managing conflicts of interest Up to 1.5 marks per point to a maximum of	6
(b)	Main requirement of IAS 37 Up to 1.5 marks per point to a maximum of (No more than 4 marks for the requirements of IAS 37)	7
(c)	Sufficient audit evidence and audit reports Up to 1.5 marks per point to a maximum of	7 20

(a) **Conflict of interest**

(i) The ACCA's *Code of Ethics and Conduct* states that on the face of it there is **nothing improper** in firms having two or more clients whose interests may be in conflict, provided that the work that the firm undertakes is not itself likely to be the subject of the dispute. In the case of Tourex and Pudco the conflict has arisen as the result of food poisoning which is in no way related to the work of the auditors. On this basis there is no reason why the auditors should not continue to act for both parties.

(ii) The Code states that the firm's work should be managed so as to avoid the interests of one client adversely affecting those of another. This could be achieved by the auditors of Tourex and Pudco by putting adequate **safeguards** in place.

(iii) The audit firm should **notify** Tourex and Pudco that they are acting for both and ask for consent to continue. Tourex and/or Pudco may decide to seek alternative representation although if the audits have already commenced this may be difficult.

(iv) The impact of the potential conflict of interest would be reduced if **different engagement partners** were appointed and different staff made up the audit team. It may be possible to use teams from different offices of the same firm.

(v) Depending on the size of the audit firm it may have specific procedures and monitoring in place to prevent confidential information being passed on. This is sometimes referred to as a '**Chinese wall**'.

(b) **IAS 37**

Requirement

IAS 37 states that a provision is a **liability of uncertain timing or amount**. It should be recognised as a liability when:

- An entity has a **present obligation** (legal or constructive) as a result of a past event
- It is **probable** that a transfer of economic benefits will be required to settle the obligation
- A **reliable estimate** can be made of the obligation

Application

In this case it appears that both Tourex and Pudco have an **obligation** to compensate for the food poisoning. As the talks are out-of-court this seems to be a constructive rather than a legal obligation. As negotiations are on-going it seems more likely than not (ie probable) that both companies will have to pay some compensation. If a reliable estimate of the amounts involved can be made then the accounts of both Tourex and Pudco would include a provision. However as lawyers for both the hotel and the food wholesaler refuse to confirm the state of affairs in writing there may not be sufficient evidence to support an estimate of the obligation. If this is the case no provision would be included.

Requirement

IAS 37 defines a contingent liability as:

- A **possible obligation** that arises from past events and whose existence will be confirmed only by the occurrence or non-occurrence of one or more uncertain future events not wholly within the entity's control; or

- A **present obligation** that arises from past events but is not recognised because:

  - It is **not probable** that a transfer of economic benefits will be required to settle the obligation; or

  - The amount of the obligation **cannot be measured with sufficient reliability**.

Contingent liabilities should **not be recognised** in the financial statements but they should be **disclosed**. Required disclosures are:

- A brief description of the nature of the contingent liability
- An estimate of the financial effect
- An indication of the uncertainties which exist
- The possibility of any reimbursement

Application

If it is not probable that Tourex and/or Pudco will be required to pay compensation or if it is not possible to estimate the amounts involved a contingent liability should be disclosed in the accounts as described above.

Tourex and Pudco would also need the consider the need for a contingent liability in respect of any fines that they may incur as a result of the public health authority investigations.

Requirement

A contingent asset is a **possible asset** that arises from past events and whose existence will be confirmed by the occurrence or non-occurrence of one or more uncertain future events not wholly within the entity's control. A contingent asset **must not be recognised**. Only when realisation of the related economic benefits is **virtually certain** should recognition take place (ie when it is no longer contingent.)

Disclosure is required in the accounts if it is **probable** that economic benefit will be realised. A brief description should be provided along with an estimate of its likely financial effect.

Application

Tourex has a potential contingent asset in respect of its counter claim against the food wholesaler. The treatment will depend on the likelihood of the claim being successful. At this stage it would not be reasonable to conclude that receipt of payment from Pudco is virtually certain therefore an asset would not be recorded. If sufficient evidence is available to confirm that receipt is probable then the contingent asset should be disclosed as described above.

Requirement

IAS 37 states that where some or all of the expenditure needed to settle a provision may be expected to be recovered from a third party the reimbursement should be recognised only when it is **virtually certain** that it will be received. The reimbursement should be treated as a separate asset and the amount recognised should not exceed the liability to which it relates. The provision and the reimbursement may be **netted off** in the income statement.

Application

It is possible that Tourex and/or Pudco have insurance to cover them in these circumstances. Only if the success of any insurance claim is virtually certain should an asset be recognised. If success is probable the reimbursement should be disclosed as a contingent asset, otherwise no reference to this should be made.

(c)   **Difficulties and audit report implications**

Difficulties

The main problem is going to be the **availability of evidence** regarding the outcome of the litigation and the public health authority inspection and the amounts which are involved. This affects the decision as to whether or not provisions need to be recognised or contingent assets and liabilities need to be disclosed. The lack of evidence is caused by the following:

The out-of-court settlements are still on-going

- The lawyers have refused to confirm the state of affairs in writing. Informal oral representations are less reliable than written evidence.

- The public health authority investigation is not complete. This could result in fines being incurred or if severe breaches of regulations are identified could lead to the businesses being shut down.

Audit report implications

- The lawyers refusal to provide written evidence could constitute a **limitation on scope**. Unless alternative evidence is available the audit opinion would be qualified 'except for'.

  (In the light of this possibility the lawyers may be persuaded to provide the evidence required.)

- The outcome of the various legal proceedings constitute a significant uncertainty as resolution is dependent upon circumstances outside the control of the companies involved and the amounts are material to the accounts. Provided that all the evidence expected to be available supports the treatment adopted by management the opinion would not be qualified but the report would be modified by an emphasis of matter paragraph highlighting the situation for the readers.

- If there is an indication that the public health authority inspection could lead to the closure of either business significant doubts could surround the issue of going concern. Provided that the auditors agree with the treatment of this situation and the level of disclosure provided by management the matter would also be referred to as an emphasis of matter without qualifying the audit opinion.

ACCA

Paper F8

Audit and Assurance (International)

Mock Examination 2

Question Paper	
Time allowed	
Reading and Planning Writing	**15 minutes** **3 hours**
ALL FIVE questions are compulsory and MUST be attempted	
During reading and planning time only the question paper may be annotated	

DO NOT OPEN THIS PAPER UNTIL YOU ARE READY TO START UNDER EXAMINATION CONDITIONS

ACCA

Paper F8

Audit and Assurance

(International)

Mock Examination 2

Question Paper		
Time allowed		
Reading and Planning		15 minutes
Writing		3 hours

All FIVE questions are compulsory and MUST be attempted.

During reading and planning time only the question paper may be annotated.

DO NOT OPEN THIS PAPER UNTIL YOU ARE READY TO START UNDER
EXAMINATION CONDITIONS

ALL FIVE questions are compulsory and MUST be attempted

Question 1

Fizzipop manufactures and distributes soft drinks. Its inventories are controlled using a real-time system which provides accurate records of quantities and costs of inventories held at any point in time. This system is known within the company as the 'Stockpop' system and it is integrated with the purchases and sales system. Fizzipop has an internal audit department whose activities encompass inventories.

No year-end inventory count takes place. Inventories are held in several large warehouses where non-stop production takes place.

Your firm is the external auditor to Fizzipop and you have been asked to perform the audit of inventories. Inventories include finished goods and raw materials (water, sugar, sweeteners, carbonating materials, flavourings, cans, bottles, bottle tops, fastenings and packaging materials).

Your firm, which has several offices, wishes to rely on the 'Stockpop' system to provide the basis of the figure to be included in the financial statements for inventories. Your firm does not wish to ask the company to conduct a year-end inventory count.

Required

(a)   Describe the principle audit risks associated with the financial statement assertions relating to inventory.

(4 marks)

(b)   Describe the audit tests that you would perform on the 'Stockpop' system during the year in order to determine whether to rely on it as a basis for the raw materials and finished goods figures to be included in the financial statements. **(12 marks)**

Note. You are not required to deal with work in progress.

(c)   Describe the audit tests you would perform on the records held by Fizzipop at the year-end to ensure that raw materials and finished goods are fairly stated in the financial statements. **(10 marks)**

(d)   Explain the factors you should consider before placing reliance on the work undertaken by internal audit on the inventory at Fizzipop. **(4 marks)**

(Total = 30 marks)

Question 2

There are similarities and differences between the responsibilities of internal and external auditors. Both internal and external auditors have responsibilities relating to the prevention, detection and reporting of fraud, for example, but their responsibilities are not the same. Both internal and external audit are part of an organisation's overall corporate governance arrangements. Sometimes, the responsibilities of internal auditors are outsourced to external organisations.

Required

(a) Explain the difference between the responsibilities of internal auditors and external auditors for the prevention, detection and reporting of fraud and error. **(5 marks)**

(b) Outline the issues that should be considered when an organisation decides to outsource the internal audit function. **(5 marks)**

(Total = 10 marks)

Question 3

You have been presented with the following draft financial information about Hivex, a very successful company that develops and licences specialist computer software and hardware. Its non-current assets mainly consist of property, computer hardware and investments, and there have been additions to these during the year. The company is experiencing increasing competition from rival companies, most of which specialise in hardware or software, but not both. There is pressure to advertise and to cut prices.

You are the audit manager. You are planning the audit and are conducting a preliminary analytical review and associated risk analysis for this client for the year ended 31 May 20X3. You have been provided with a summarised draft income statement which has been produced very quickly and certain accounting ratios and percentages. You have been informed that the company accounts for research and development costs in accordance with IAS 38 *Intangible assets*.

INCOME STATEMENT

	Year ended 31 May	
	20X3	20X2
	$'000	$'000
Revenue	15,206	13,524
Cost of sales	3,009	3,007
Gross Profit	12,197	10,517
Distribution costs	3,006	1,996
Administrative expenses	994	1,768
Selling expenses	3,002	274
Profit from operations	5,195	6,479
Net interest receivable	995	395
Profit before tax	6,190	6,874
Income tax expense	3,104	1,452
Net profit	3,086	5,422
Retained profits	1,617	3,983
Dividends paid	$1,469,000	$1,439,000

Accounting ratios and percentages

Earnings per share	0·43	1·04
Performance ratios include the following:		
Gross margin	0·80	0·78
Expenses as a percentage of revenue:		
Distribution costs	0·20	0·15
Administrative expenses	0·07	0·13
Selling expenses	0·20	0·02
Operating profit	0·34	0·48

Required

(a)   Using the information above, comment briefly on the performance of the company for the two years.

(8 marks)

(b)   Use your answer to part (a) to identify the areas that are subject to increased audit risk and describe the further audit work you would perform in response to those risks. **(12 marks)**

(Total = 20 marks)

Question 4

You are an audit manager in an audit firm with ten offices and 250 staff. Your firm is the auditor of Calva, a chain of supermarkets. Your firm has been the auditor of this client for many years.

All of the planning work and tests of controls have been completed for Calva for the year ended 31 December 2003. Staff are still working on substantive procedures. The company operates a continuous inventory checking system with good records and you have tested this system and will be relying on the records for the year-end figure.

The company is intending to invest a substantial amount in opening new stores during the next year and it has been negotiating with both banks and property companies in relation to leases.

Required

(a)   Describe the objectives of the following and how these objectives will be met in the audit of Calva:

      (i)   Overall review of financial statements;   **(4 marks)**

      (ii)   Review of working papers.   **(6 marks)**

(b)   Describe the:

      (i)   Auditor's responsibilities with regard to subsequent events;   **(6 marks)**

      (ii)   Procedures that should be applied during the subsequent events review at Calva.   **(4 marks)**

(Total = 20 marks)

Question 5

Homes'r'Us is a large listed construction company based in the north of the country, whose activities encompass housebuilding and development. Its annual revenue is $550 million and profit before tax is $70 million.

You are the audit senior involved with the audit of Homes'r'Us for the year ended 31 December 20X7. The following matters have come to your attention during the review stage of the audit in April 20X8.

(i)   Customer going into liquidation

      One of Homes'r'Us' major commercial customers has gone into liquidation shortly after the year-end. As at the year-end, the customer owed the company $7.5 million.

(ii)   Claim for unfair dismissal

      One of the company's construction workers, Basil Evans, was dismissed in November 20X7 after turning up to work under the influence of alcohol. In December 20X7, Mr Evans began a case against the company for unfair dismissal. Lawyers for the company have advised that it will be highly unlikely that he will be successful in his claim.

(iii)   In March 20X8 a fire was started by vandals at one of the company's ten storage depots, destroying $1 million worth of building materials.

Required

For each of the three events at Homes'r'Us mentioned above:

(a)   Describe the additional audit procedures you will carry out.   **(7 marks)**

(b)   State whether the accounts will need to be amended and explain your reasoning.   **(7 marks)**

(c)   Discuss the potential impact on the audit report, fully explaining your answers.   **(6 marks)**

(Total = 20 marks)

Answers

DO NOT TURN THIS PAGE UNTIL YOU HAVE
COMPLETED THE MOCK EXAM

A plan of attack

If this were the real Audit and Assurance exam and you had been told to turn over and begin, what would be going through your mind?

An important thing to say (while there is still time) is that it is vital to have a good breadth of knowledge of the syllabus because all the questions are compulsory. However, don't panic. Below we provide guidance on how to approach the exam.

Approaching the paper

Use your 15 minutes of reading time usefully, to look through the questions, particularly Question 1, to get a feel for what is required and to become familiar with the question scenarios.

Since all the questions in this paper are compulsory, it is vital that you attempt them all in order to increase your chances of passing. For example, don't run over time on Question 2 and then find that you don't have enough time for the remaining questions.

Question 1 is a 30 mark case-study style question on audit procedures on inventory. You must stick to time for this question as a whole and for each of the individual parts. Use the information in the scenario to help you and give you clues.

Question 2 will always be a knowledge-based 10 mark question. You should be able to score well therefore. Look at the requirement of the question and the mark allocation carefully. For example, in part (b), you need to outline the issues to consider for outsourcing, so make sure you do – don't be tempted to write down everything you know about outsourcing in general.

Question 3 is a scenario-based question on audit risk using analytical procedures. Don't be daunted by all the figures. Go through them line-by-line and note down areas that you could comment on. Your answer to part (a) should help you with part (b) but note the two requirements in part (b) – to identify the risk areas and to describe the audit work you would do.

Question 4 is on the review stage of the audit. The question has been broken down into four parts, so take each in turn and deal with it. In parts (a) and (b) (ii) remember to relate your answer to the company in the scenario – don't just produce a general answer on audit review and subsequent events.

Question 5 is on subsequent events and their potential impact on the audit report. There are three situations in this question so take each in turn, making sure you take materiality and accounting treatment into consideration.

Forget about it!

And don't worry if you found the paper difficult. More than likely other candidates will too. If this were the real thing you would need to forget the exam the minute you left the exam hall and think about the next one. Or, if it is the last one, celebrate!

Question 1

Text reference. Chapter 13

Top tips. The key to this question is to appreciate that the scenario deals with the issue of a perpetual inventory system. Remember that in this case there is no year end count to determine inventory quantities but inventory records are maintained instead. When you think about the tests that you would perform in part (a) think about what will affect the accuracy of the inventory records. What you are really being asked for are tests of controls with the emphasis on confirming the **quantity** of inventory. Your tests need to consider the accuracy with which movements in inventory are recorded (ie sales and purchases) and whether the regular counts which are performed will pick up any discrepancies between book records and actual inventory. In part (b) which considers the year end tests, assuming that you can rely on the system to provide the correct figure for the quantity of inventory the other main issue will be valuation. Here you can use your basic knowledge of IAS 2 to provide you with ideas. Note that in part (b) you are being asked for substantive procedures with the emphasis on valuation.

Easy marks. Easy marks are available in parts (a) and (b). The other parts are quite demanding so don't run over time.

Examiner's comments. The distinction between tests to be carried out during the year and at the year end seemed to confuse students. Many did not appreciate the need for inventory checks to be carried out during the year and described year end counts in spite of the fact that the question said these were not performed. Where candidates explained how the real-time inventory system would be agreed to physical inventory in part (a) they obtained high marks.

Common errors in part (b) included:

- Explaining valuation tests which would have been appropriate for the year end
- Providing extensive details of general controls over the writing of the computer program which was not the main focus of the question.

Answers to part (c) were of a higher standard. Most were aware of the relevant accounting standard and then applied this to tests to confirm cost and net realisable value. Some good comments were made regarding the storage of soft drinks showing that candidates were attempting to use the scenario.

Common errors in part (c) included:

- Explaining year-end inventory counts
- Explaining tests on the payables system which, whilst affected by inventory movements, was not the focus of the question.

Marking scheme

		Marks
(a)	Risk associated with inventory	4
(b)	Audit tests on 'Stockpop' system during the year Up to 1.5 marks per point to a maximum of	12
(c)	Audit tests on records at year-end Up to 1.5 marks per point to a maximum of	10
(d)	Factors to consider to rely on internal audit work Upto 1 mark per point to a maximum of	_4_
		30

BPP
LEARNING MEDIA

(a) **Principal risks associated with the financial statement assertions for inventory**

One of the risks associated with inventory is its appropriate **valuation**. Inventory should be valued at the lower of cost and net realisable value per IAS 2 *Inventories*. Inventory can be a material figure in the financial statements of many entities, particularly manufacturing companies, and therefore appropriate valuation of inventory is very important, particularly for obsolete and slow-moving items. The valuation can also be a matter of judgement and this increases the risk associated with inventory.

Inventory in the balance sheet must **exist** - this is another key assertion. Inventory can be subject to theft and misappropriation, and is often held at more than one location, and so controls to safeguard it are very important.

Cut-off is another key issue for inventory. All purchases, transfers and sales of inventory must be recorded in the correct accounting period as again inventory can be a material figure for many companies. Incorrect cut-off can result in misstatements in the financial statements at the year-end and this can be of particular concern where inventory is material. Auditors therefore need to consider whether the management of the entity being audited have implemented adequate cut-off procedures to ensure that movements into and out of inventory are properly identified and reflected in the accounting records and ultimately in the financial statements.

(b) **Audit tests during the year**

The key issues during the year will be to confirm that the system forms a sound basis for recording the **quantity** of inventory and that unit costs are recorded accurately. As a result the following tests will be performed:

- Discuss with management the procedures for inventory checking during the year to ensure that all items are **counted at least once**.

- Obtain a **copy of the inventory count instructions** and review them to establish whether procedures are adequate and will result in reliable information.

- A sample of counts would be **observed** during the year. The sample would be selected on the basis of warehouses where material inventory balances are held and those where the risk of error is increased. The procedures would be observed to ensure that they comply with the instructions. Staff from other offices may be asked to visit warehouses local to them.

- **Test counts** would be performed and the results traced through the sales and purchases system.

- Any reports produced by internal audit regarding the procedures adopted at the inventory count and the 'Stockpop' system design would be **reviewed** and their **conclusions evaluated** (providing that it is appropriate to place any reliance on internal audit).

- For a sample of goods received and goods despatched I would **trace the entries** through the 'Stockpop' system. These transactions would also be checked to the purchases and sales system to ensure that costs are correctly recorded.

- Review all **exception reports** and confirm that exceptions have been dealt with and any necessary adjustments made.

- As the validity of the inventory balance is dependent on the system it may be appropriate to consider the use of **CAATs**. For example test data could be used to confirm the controls over the incorrect input of unit cost data.

(c) **Audit tests at the year-end**

Obtain a breakdown of the inventory quantity and costs and agree these figures to the figures produced by the 'Stockpop' system.

Discuss with management any recent problems experienced with the system particularly those occurring between the last count attended by the auditors and the year end. Confirm the action taken by management to resolve any problems.

Compare inventory levels with those of the previous year and discuss any significant differences with management.

Perform cut-off tests. Despatch notes and goods received notes before and after the year end should be traced to the sales and purchases account to ensure that they have been accounted for in the correct period. Entries in the sales and purchases accounts should also be agreed back to source documentation

Obtain schedule of inventory valuation and confirm it is in accordance with IAS 2 *Inventories* ie at the lower of cost and net realisable value.

For raw materials check a sample of items to suppliers invoices.

For finished goods review and test the system for identifying slow-moving and out of date products. The company should be able to provide information showing the ageing of inventory by reference to sell by dates.

Review the basis for any adjustment made by management for slow-moving/obsolete items. Compare the level of adjustment with previous years and discuss with management.

Review quantities of products sold after the year end to determine that year end inventory has or will be realised.

(d)   **Factors to consider before relying on the work of internal audit**

- Whether the work has been performed by staff with adequate technical training and proficiency as internal auditors

- Whether the work of internal audit assistants has been properly supervised, reviewed and documented

- Whether sufficient, appropriate audit evidence has been obtained in order for reasonable conclusions to be drawn

- Whether the conclusions reached are appropriate

- Whether any report produced is consistent with the results of work undertaken

- Whether any exceptions or unusual matters identified and disclosed have been adequately resolved

Question 2

Text references. Chapters 1 and 5

Top tips. This question covers corporate governance and the role of the internal auditor. It also covers another important issue, fraud, and the role of both internal and external auditors in relation to it. It is important in this question that you do not get the timing wrong. This is critical on this question of the paper, especially, as it is very tempting to write down everything you know about fraud and outsourcing.

Easy marks. This question is wholly knowledge-based so should be straightforward, proving your knowledge is sound. As stated above, make sure you stick to the time allocation so that lack of time does not affect your performance in subsequent questions.

Examiner's comments. Parts (a) and (b) were generally answered well, although many candidates spent far too long on part (a) at the expense of the rest of the paper.

Marking scheme

Marks

(a) Prevention, detection and reporting of fraud and error
1.5 marks per point to maximum of

5

(b) Outsourced internal audit issues
1 mark per point to maximum of

5
10

(a) **Prevention, detection and reporting of fraud and error**

External auditors

Prevention and detection

The external auditors are bound by the requirements of ISA 240. This requires that auditors recognise that **fraud and error may materially affect the financial statements** and design procedures to ensure that the risk is minimised. The auditors have no specific requirement to prevent or detect fraud. However, they should plan and perform the audit with an attitude of **professional scepticism**, recognising that circumstances may exist that cause the financial statements to be materially misstated. By conducting the audit in accordance with ISAs the auditor obtains reasonable assurance that the financial statements are free from material misstatement caused by fraud or error. However, due to the nature of fraud the risk of not detecting fraud is higher than the risk of not detecting error.

Reporting

ISA 240 also sets out the requirements in relation to reporting fraud. If auditors suspect or detect a fraud, they should **report it to those charged with governance**, unless the fraud necessitates immediate reporting to a **third party**.

The matter should only be referred to in the audit report if the report is qualified on those grounds. It may also be that the matter is one which needs reporting to a relevant authority in the public interest. If the auditors feel that this is so, they should seek **legal advice** before taking any action, and request that the entity reports itself. If the directors refuse to make any disclosure in these circumstances, the auditors should make the disclosure themselves.

Internal auditors

Prevention and detection

It is likely that the internal auditors will have a role both in the prevention and detection of fraud. Indirectly, they play a role in their involvement with the **internal controls** of a business, which are set up to limit risks to the company, one of which is fraud. Directly, they may be engaged by the directors to carry out tests when a fraud is suspected, or routinely to discourage such activity.

However, if a serious fraud was suspected, a company might bring in **external experts**, such as forensic accountants or the police, to carry out investigations.

Reporting

If internal auditors discovered issues which made them suspect fraud, they would **report it immediately** to their superiors, who would report to those charged with governance. In the event that an internal auditor suspected top level fraud, he might make disclosure to the relevant authority in the public interest.

(b) **Outsourcing internal audit**

There are various matters to consider:

(i) A major matter to consider is **cost**. It is possible that a fee to a service provider might be lower than the fixed cost of maintaining an internal department. This must be assessed.

(ii) **Independence**. A key aim of an internal audit department is to provide an objective look at the company's operations. An external provider will be more independent.

(iii) **Understanding of the business**. Conversely, however, an external provider is likely to have less knowledge of the business and its staff, particularly at the outset of the relationship.

(iv) Another important matter is **control**. When an internal audit department is truly internal, the directors have control over what work is carried out. To an extent, they may be able to still control what work is done under the terms of their contract with the service provider, but the control over day to day work will inevitably be less. On the other hand, however, an external team may be able to see the bigger picture, and provide an excellent service the directors might not have envisaged.

(v) **Change issues**. When considering outsourcing a department, the firm will obviously have to consider carefully what happens to the staff previously involved in that department, particularly in the current employment law climate.

(vi) **Choice**. There is much choice of service provider on the market, and the company will have to ensure that it purchases the correct blend of skill, qualification, value and service.

Question 3

Text references. Chapters 6 and 7

Top tips. This question looks much more daunting than it actually is. In part (a) you are asked to assess the performance of a company based on information provided. The key is not to panic but to work systematically through the information noting the key changes. Use the ratios provided but don't be afraid to do your own basic calculations, for example calculating the % rise in revenue. Try to avoid simply stating that figures have gone up or down. Instead you should be evaluating the situation ie is this good or bad, is there any information in the question which might explain this change, is this in line with expectations? These are the sorts of questions which you need to be asking.

Part (b) then asks you to identify the risk areas and to describe the audit work you would perform. Note that the emphasis is on the audit work rather than risk. The examiner is expecting you to identify the areas which need more attention but is not looking for a detailed explanation of the risk itself.

Easy marks. In this question it is probably fair to say that there are no easy marks. That does not mean that you are not capable of passing the question but you do need to think carefully about your approach. In part (a) the examiner is looking for comment supported by basic calculations, ie an appraisal of the situation set out by the income statement.

In part (b) the most effective way to pick up marks is to target the right areas for further work. One way to achieve this is to ensure that you use your results in part (a) to provide the structure for part (b) of your answer.

Examiner's comments. Most candidates made a good attempt at analysing the performance of the company but too many made basic calculation errors. A common mistake was to approach the question from the point of view of a management consultant rather than an auditor. Many candidates ignored the audit work requirement in part (b) and provided business advice instead. Whilst many of the suggestions were valid they did not score marks as this was not the requirement of the question. Those who did address the audit work often used vague and unspecific terms for example, 'further testing should be undertaken'. Candidates also showed a basic lack of understanding in key areas. Too many stated that they would perform substantive procedures on tests of controls and thought that earnings per share was calculated using retained earnings as the numerator. Also note that costs are often 'misposted' (but rarely 'misappropriated').

Marking scheme

		Marks
(a)	Performance Up to 1 mark per point to a maximum of	8
(b)	Higher risk areas and audit procedures Up to 1.5 marks per point to a maximum of	<u>12</u> <u>20</u>

(a) **Performance**

(i) Revenue and gross profit have both **increased significantly**, revenue by 12% and gross profit by 16%. In addition the gross profit margin has increased from 78% to 80% which seems high. These figures indicate **strong performance** but could also be the result of errors particularly in the light of the fact that we are told that the information has been produced quickly. This issue will affect all of the figures in the draft income statement.

(ii) Operating profit has **fallen** by 20% as compared to the previous year and the operating profit margin has fallen from 48% to 34%. This appears to be due to the **increase in distribution and selling expenses**.

(iii) Distribution costs **have increased** by over 50% and represent 20% of revenue as compared to 15% of revenue last year. This could be the result of a significant **change in sales mix** (hardware is likely to be comparatively more expensive to distribute than software) or **inefficiencies**. Alternatively costs may not have been allocated on a consistent basis between distribution costs and administrative expenses.

(iv) Selling expenses have **increased** substantially now representing 20% of revenue. This could be explained by the **need to increase advertising**.

(v) The increase in distribution and selling costs has been slightly offset by a decrease in administrative expenses of 43%. This could be the result of misclassification of expenses or effective economies. Overall it **does not have a significant impact** on the results.

(vi) Net interest receivable has increased by 151%. This has slightly offset the effects of the increased operating expenses on profit before tax, however profit before tax still represents a fall of nearly 10%.

(vii) Net profit has **fallen** by 43% largely due to the **significant increase in the income tax expense**. In spite of this dividend payments have seen a slight increase.

(viii) Without additional information it is not possible to explain fully the fall in the EPS ratio. It will have been affected by the fall in profits but it may also have been affected by a change in the number of shares.

(b)   **Risks areas and further work**

Revenue	• Obtain a breakdown of sales on a monthly basis and discuss significant fluctuations with management. Any explanations should be corroborated. • Check the accounting policy for revenue recognition particularly in respect of software licences to ensure that it has been applied consistently and in accordance with accounting standards. • Perform tests of controls on controls over the processing of sales orders and invoicing. Sample sizes should reflect the increased risk. • For a sample of sales transactions perform substantive procedures tracing the transaction from the initial order to the posting in the ledgers. The sample size would be affected by the results of the tests of controls. • Check cut-off at the year end to ensure that revenue has only been recognised in relation to sales genuinely made in the accounting period.
Gross margin	• The gross margin of 80% seems high in spite of the nature of the business. Obtain industry information to establish an industry average. • Compare the gross profit margin on a quarterly basis and compare with the results of the previous year. Discuss the reasons behind significant variations with management. • Obtain a breakdown of costs included in cost of sales and compare with previous year to establish any change in the way that costs have been allocated to the expense categories. • Check the basis on which costs have been capitalised as development costs. Those which do not meet the conditions of IAS 38 *Intangible assets* should be expensed. • For a sample of expenses trace the transaction from source documentation to posting in the accounts. • Agree opening inventory to previous years accounts. The balance sheet audit should provide evidence regarding the quantity and valuation of closing inventory. In particular cut-off should be confirmed to ensure that it is in line with sales cut-off.
Operating expenses	• Obtain a breakdown of distribution costs, administrative expenses and selling costs. Compare the nature of the expenditure with that included in the previous year to highlight any misclassification. • Compare monthly levels of expenditure with previous year and obtain explanations for any significant changes. • Review the impact of depreciation on the operating expenses figures. Obtain a schedule of non-current assets and recalculate depreciation charged based on the company's policy. Confirm that this is consistent and reasonable in the light of the nature of the asset. • Perform tests of controls on controls over the processing of expenses from initiation of the transaction to posting in the ledgers. • For a sample of expenses trace the transaction from its source eg invoice to its recording in the ledgers. • Review expenses incurred after the year end to ensure that all expenses relating to the current period have been correctly accrued for.

Interest	• Obtain an analysis of interest payable/receivable.
Tax	• Obtain a copy of the tax calculation to establish why it has increased so significantly. Discuss the calculation with management and confirm any explanations. • Obtain and review any correspondence with the tax authorities.
Dividends	• Discuss the rationale behind the dividend payment with management, particularly regarding sustainability. • Confirm that the payment of the dividend is minuted. • Check that the payment does not breach legislation regarding distributable profits.
Earnings per share	• Confirm the basis on which the calculation has been performed. If additional shares have been issued confirm that the legal procedures have been complied with and establish the purpose of the share issue. • Reperform the EPS calculation.

Question 4

Text reference. Chapter 18

Top tips. This is an example of a question which is easy if you know the answer! In other words if you have a good understanding of ISA 560 it is very straightforward but if you don't it will be a struggle. This type of question serves as a reminder that for this paper there is often no substitute for simply learning the basics of the auditing standards.

Easy marks. Overall this is a reasonably straight forward question. Easy marks are available particularly in part (b) but this depends on a sound knowledge of ISA 560.

Examiner's comments. This was essentially a knowledge based question. Those who were familiar with the material scored well. Those who were not performed badly.

Marking scheme

			Marks
(a)	(i)	Objectives and how they are met: overall review of financial statements Up to 2 marks per point to a maximum of	4
	(ii)	Objectives and how they are met: review of working papers Up to 2 marks per point to a maximum of	6
(b)	(i)	Responsibilities Up to 2 marks per point to a maximum of	6
	(ii)	Subsequent events review procedures Up to 2 marks per point to a maximum of	4
			20

(a) **Objectives and how they are met**

(i) *Overall review of the financial statements*

The objective of the review of financial statements in conjunction with the conclusions drawn from other audit evidence obtained is to provide a **reasonable basis** on which to form the audit opinion. Due to the skill involved in making this assessment this review would normally be carried out by the engagement partner or senior manager.

The auditor should consider whether the information presented in the financial statements is **in accordance with local/national statutory requirements**. This will vary depending on whether the company is listed or not. This work would normally be performed by the completion of a checklist.

The auditor should consider whether the **accounting policies** employed are in accordance with accounting standards, properly disclosed, consistently applied and appropriate to the company. This can be confirmed by performing a review of the accounting policies adopted, comparing them with previous years and discussing any changes with management. In the case of Calva there is no information to suggest that any changes have been made.

The auditors should consider whether the financial statements are **consistent** with their knowledge of the company's business and with the results of other audit procedures. In the audit of Calva this can be achieved by:

- Assessing whether analytical procedures applied when completing the audit confirm that information is consistent

- Whether the presentation adopted in the financial statements may have been unduly influenced by the directors' desire to present matters in a more favourable light

- Assessing the potential impact of the aggregate of uncorrected misstatements identified in the course of the audit.

(ii) *Review of working papers*

The objectives of the review of working papers is to ensure that:

- The work has been **properly planned** and **executed**

- **Key issues** have been identified and that **sufficient evidence** has been obtained particularly in risk areas.

- **Outstanding matters** are highlighted and that conclusions drawn are supported by facts.

In the audit of Calva this can be achieved as follows:

All working papers should be reviewed by a member of the audit team who is senior to the individual who has performed the work. Audit seniors will review the work of audit juniors, and audit managers will review the work of audit seniors. This type of review would normally take place as the audit progresses to ensure that the work performed is of good quality and to deal with any issues as they arise.

The review would normally be evidenced by a signature or initial. Review comments or follow up procedures would be noted. These are often written in red to highlight them. Significant matters would be referred to the engagement partner.

The extent of the review will depend on the materiality of the balances involved and the associated risk. In the case of Calva, a supermarket, these are likely to be non-current assets, cash and inventory. These would normally be reviewed in detail by the audit manager.

At the end of the audit the engagement partner would perform a final file review. This is less detailed than the audit manager review but concentrates on key risk areas and outstanding matters. It is essential that these are resolved satisfactorily before the audit opinion is issued and that there is documentary evidence of the partner's conclusions.

(b)   (i)   **Auditor's responsibilities with regard to subsequent events**

- The auditor is required by ISA 560 to perform procedures designed to obtain sufficient appropriate audit evidence that all events **up to the date of the auditor's report** that may require adjustment or disclosure have been identified.

- The auditors do not have any obligation to perform procedures or make enquiries regarding the financial statements **after the date of the report**.

- If after the date of the auditor's report but before the financial statements are issued the auditor becomes aware of a fact that might materially affect the financial statements, the auditor should consider the need to amend the accounts, should discuss the matter with management and should take appropriate action.

- If the financial statements are amended the auditors should extend their procedures to the date of their new report which should be dated the day it is signed.

- The auditor cannot insist that financial statements are amended. It is up to the management to make this decision. If the auditor believes that amendment is required but management refuse to do so the auditor should express a qualified opinion or an adverse opinion provided the audit report has not already been released. If the audit report has been issued to the company the auditor should take steps to prevent it from being circulated and seek legal advice.

- If facts are discovered after the financial statements have been issued the auditor would need to consider the need for these to be revised and for a new audit report to be issued.

(ii)   **Procedures**

- The auditors would consider the procedures by which management identify subsequent events.

- The auditors would read board minutes of meetings held after the year end for evidence of substantial transactions taking place shortly after the balance sheet date for example entering into commitments for new leases.

- The auditors would review the latest accounting records and financial information including cash flow forecasts and budgets. They would also review any post year end correspondence with the bank and property companies to assess the impact of the outcome of the negotiations.

- The auditors would make enquiries of management particularly regarding new borrowings or issues of shares and debentures which may have been necessary in order to finance the expansion plan.

Question 5

Text reference. Chapters 18 and 19

Top tips. This question looks at events occurring during the review stage of the audit. There are three events so take each in turn and deal with it separately. Use sub-headings in your answer so that you address each of the requirements in the question – audit procedures, accounting treatment and effect on audit report. You need to be familiar with your financial reporting knowledge on events after the balance sheet date and on provisions. You have to explain the effect on the audit report, if any. Make sure your explanations are succinct and to the point.

Easy marks. These are available in the part of the requirement on audit procedures, but make sure the procedures you describe are specific and well-explained, otherwise you won't score well.

		Marks
(i)	Customer going into liquidation	
	Upto 2 marks for additional audit procedures	2
	Explanation of any amendments to accounts	2
	Impact on the audit report	3
		7
(ii)	Unfair dismissal	
	Upto 2 marks for additional audit procedures	2
	Explanation of any amendments to accounts	2
	Impact on the audit report	3
		7
(iii)	Fire	
	Upto 2 marks for additional audit procedures	2
	Explanation of any amendments to accounts	2
	Impact on the audit report	2
		6
		20

(i) **Customer going into liquidation**

Audit procedures

- Assess the likelihood of recovery of this amount by discussion with the directors of Homes'r'Us

- Confirm the amount of the amount outstanding as at the year-end by inspection of the receivables ledger and correspondence with the customer

- Review any correspondence between the company and the customer to assess the likelihood of recovery of any amounts

- Obtain a management representation point regarding the amount outstanding from the customer from the directors of Homes'r'Us

- Confirm the details of the bankruptcy to documents received by Homes'r'Us from the liquidator

Impact on accounts

The financial statements will need to be amended as this is an example of an adjusting event after the balance sheet date. It provides additional information concerning the recoverability of the debt at the balance sheet date.

Revenue, profit and net assets will all be overstated by $7.5 million if the accounts are not adjusted. The amount represents 10.7% of profit before tax and 1.4% of revenue so is clearly material.

An adjustment is required in the financial statements to reduce the receivables balance and profits.

Effect on audit report

The effect of the matter on the financial statements is clearly material. If the adjustments required are made, then there would be no effect on the audit report.

If the directors refused to make the adjustment required, the financial statements would be qualified on the basis of a disagreement with management and an 'except for' opinion would be issued, as the matter is material but not pervasive.

(ii)   **Claim for unfair dismissal**

Audit procedures

- Discuss the case for unfair dismissal with the directors of Homes'r'Us to find out background of case, date when claim was lodged and assessment of success

- Review lawyer's correspondence regarding this case as it may have an impact for next year's audit

- Review any press reports in the local or national papers about this claim against the company

- Review minutes of board meetings regarding this case and any other claim cases against the company

- Obtain a management representation letter point on this matter from the directors of Homes'r'Us

Impact on accounts

A provision for this claim is not required since the requirements for recognising a provision under IAS 37 *Provisions, contingent liabilities and contingent assets* are not met. Under IAS 37, a provision should be recognised when there is a present obligation as a result of a past event, it is probable that a transfer of economic benefits will be required to settle it and a reliable estimate can be made.

In this case, it appears unlikely that Mr Evans will be successful in his claim and so no provision should be recognised in the financial statements for the year ended 31 December 20X7.

Disclosure of a contingent liability is also unlikely to be required since the possibility of any transfer in settlement appears to be remote.

Effect on audit report

There would be no effect on the audit report as a result of this matter as no amendment would be required to the financial statements. An unqualified report on the financial statements could therefore be issued.

(iii)   **Fire**

Audit procedures

- Discuss fire with management of Homes'r'Us to clarify facts of the situation
- Read minutes of board meetings and any reports submitted by insurers
- Review insurance documents to confirm that damage cause by the fire is covered

Impact on accounts

The fire at the storage depot is a non-adjusting event after the balance sheet date – it does not relate to conditions which existed at the year-end. It is unlikely that the fire is significant enough to impact on the going concern of the company. Disclosure of the event surrounding the fire should be made, together with an estimate of the financial effect.

Effect on audit report

Provided that adequate disclosure has been made of the event and its financial impact, there would be no need to qualify the financial statements as a result of this incident. An emphasis of matter paragraph drawing attention to this issue is probably not likely to be required, provided adequate disclosure has been made in the notes to the financial statements.

ACCA

Paper F8

Audit and Assurance (International)

Mock Examination 3

Question Paper	
Time allowed	
Reading and Planning Writing	**15 minutes** **3 hours**
ALL FIVE questions are compulsory and MUST be attempted	
During reading and planning time only the question paper may be annotated	

DO NOT OPEN THIS PAPER UNTIL YOU ARE READY TO START UNDER EXAMINATION CONDITIONS

ALL FIVE questions are compulsory and MUST be answered

Question 1

Westra Co assembles mobile telephones in a large factory. Each telephone contains up to 100 different parts, with each part being obtained from one of 50 authorised suppliers.

Like many companies, Westra's accounting systems are partly manual and partly computerised. In overview the systems include:

(i)   Design software

(ii) A computerised database of suppliers (bespoke system written in-house at Westra)

(iii) A manual system for recording goods inwards and transferring information to the accounts department

(iv) A computerised creditors' ledger maintained in the accounts department (purchased off-the-shelf and used with no program amendments)

(v)   Online payment to suppliers, also in the accounts department

(vi) A computerised nominal ledger which is updated by the payables ledger

Mobile telephones are assembled in batches of 10,000 to 50,000 telephones. When a batch is scheduled for production, a list of parts is produced by the design software and sent, electronically, to the ordering department. Staff in the ordering department use this list to place orders with authorised suppliers. Orders can only be sent to suppliers on the suppliers' database. Orders are sent using electronic data interchange (EDI) and confirmed by each supplier using the same system. The list of parts and orders are retained on the computer in an 'orders placed' file, which is kept in date sequence.

Parts are delivered to the goods inwards department at Westra. All deliveries are checked against the orders placed file before being accepted. A hand-written pre-numbered goods received note (GRN) is raised in the goods inwards department showing details of the goods received with a cross-reference to the date of the order. The top copy of the GRN is sent to the accounts department and the second copy retained in the goods inwards department. The orders placed file is updated with the GRN number to show that the parts have been received.

Paper invoices are sent by all suppliers following dispatch of goods. Invoices are sent to the accounts department, where they are stamped with a unique ascending number. Invoice details are matched to the GRN, which is then attached to the invoice. Invoice details are then entered into the computerised payables ledger. The invoice is signed by the accounts clerk to confirm entry into the payables ledger. Invoices are then retained in a temporary file in number order while awaiting payment.

After 30 days, the payables ledger automatically generates a computerised list of payments to be made, which is sent electronically to the chief accountant. The chief accountant compares this list to the invoices, signs each invoice to indicate approval for payment, and then forwards the electronic payments list to the accounts assistant. The assistant uses online banking to pay the suppliers. The electronic payments list is filed in month order on the computer.

Required

(a)   List the substantive audit procedures you should perform to confirm the assertions of completeness, occurrence and cut-off for purchases in the financial statements of Westra Co. For each procedure, explain the purpose of that procedure.   **(12 marks)**

(b)   List the audit procedures you should perform on the trade payables balance in Westra Co's financial statements. For each procedure, explain the purpose of that procedure.   **(8 marks)**

(c)   Describe the control procedures that should be in place over the standing data on the trade payables master file in Westra Co's computer system.   **(5 marks)**

301

(d)   Discuss the extent to which computer-assisted audit techniques might be used in your audit of purchases and payables at Westra Co.   **(5 marks)**

(Total = 30 marks)

Question 2

(a)   ISA 210 *Terms of audit engagements* explains the content and use of engagement letters.

Required

State SIX items that could be included in an engagement letter.   **(3 marks)**

(b)   ISA 500 *Audit evidence* explains types of audit evidence that the auditor can obtain.

Required

State, and briefly explain, four types of audit evidence that can be obtained by the auditor. (4 marks)

(c)   ISA 700 *The independent auditor's report on a complete set of general purpose financial statements* explains the form and content of audit reports.

Required

State three ways in which an auditor's report may be modified and briefly explain the use of each modification.   **(3 marks)**

(Total = 10 marks)

Question 3

You are the audit manager in the audit firm of Dark & Co. One of your audit clients is NorthCee Co, a company specialising in the manufacture and supply of sporting equipment. NorthCee have been an audit client for five years and you have been audit manager for the past three years while the audit partner has remained unchanged.

You are now planning the audit for the year ending 31 December 2007. Following an initial meeting with the directors of NorthCee, you have obtained the following information.

(i)   NorthCee is attempting to obtain a listing on a recognised stock exchange. The directors have established an audit committee, as required by corporate governance regulations, although no further action has been taken in this respect. Information on the listing is not yet public knowledge.

(ii)   You have been asked to continue to prepare the company's financial statements as in previous years.

(iii) As the company's auditors, NorthCee would like you and the audit partner to attend an evening reception in a hotel, where NorthCee will present their listing arrangements to banks and existing major shareholders.

(iv)   NorthCee has indicated that the fee for taxation services rendered in the year to 31 December 2005 will be paid as soon as the taxation authorities have agreed the company's taxation liability. You have been advising NorthCee regarding the legality of certain items as "allowable" for taxation purposes and the taxation authority is disputing these items.

Finally, you have just acquired about 5% of NorthCee's share capital as an inheritance on the death of a distant relative.

Required

(a)   Identify, and explain the relevance of, any factors which may threaten the independence of Dark & Co's audit of NorthCee Co's financial statements for the year ending 31 December 2007. Briefly explain how each threat should be managed.   **(10 marks)**

(b)   Explain the actions that the board of directors of NorthCee Co must take in order to meet corporate governance requirements for the listing of NorthCee Co.   **(6 marks)**

(c)   Explain why your audit firm will need to communicate with NorthCee Co's audit committee for this and future audits.   **(4 marks)**

(Total = 20 marks)

Question 4

SouthLea Co is a construction company (building houses, offices and hotels) employing a large number of workers on various construction sites. The internal audit department of SouthLea Co is currently reviewing cash wages systems within the company.

The following information is available concerning the wages systems:

(i)   Hours worked are recorded using a clocking in/out system. On arriving for work and at the end of each days work, each worker enters their unique employee number on a keypad.

(ii)   Workers on each site are controlled by a foreman. The foreman has a record of all employee numbers and can issue temporary numbers for new employees.

(iii)   Any overtime is calculated by the computerised wages system and added to the standard pay.

(iv)   The two staff in the wages department make amendments to the computerised wages system in respect of employee holidays, illness, as well as setting up and maintaining all employee records.

(v)   The computerised wages system calculates deductions from gross pay, such as employee taxes, and net pay. Finally a list of net cash payments for each employee is produced.

(vi)   Cash is delivered to the wages office by secure courier.

(vii)   The two staff place cash into wages packets for each employee along with a handwritten note of gross pay, deductions and net pay. The packets are given to the foreman for distribution to the individual employees.

Required

(a)   (i)   Identify and explain weaknesses in SouthLea Co's system of internal control over the wages system that could lead to mis-statements in the financial statements;

        (ii)   For each weakness, suggest an internal control to overcome that weakness.   **(8 marks)**

(b)   Compare the responsibilities of the external and internal auditors to detect fraud.   **(6 marks)**

The computer system in the wages department needs to be replaced. The replacement will be carried out under the control of a specialist external consultant.

Required

(c)   Explain the factors that should be taken into consideration when appointing an external consultant.

(6 marks)

(Total = 20 marks)

Question 5

EastVale Co manufactures a range of dairy products (for example, milk, yoghurt and cheese) in one factory. Products are stored in a nearby warehouse (which is rented by EastVale) before being sold to 350 supermarkets located within 200 kilometres of EastVale's factory. The products are perishable with an average shelf life of eight days. EastVale's financial statements year-end is 31 July.

It is four months since the year-end at your audit client of EastVale and the annual audit of EastVale is almost complete, but the auditor's report has not been signed.

The following events have just come to your attention. Both events occurred in late November.

(a)   A fire in the warehouse rented by the company has destroyed 60% of the stock held for resale.

(b)   A batch of cheese produced by EastVale was found to contain some chemical impurities. Over 300 consumers have complained about food poisoning after eating the cheese. 115 supermarkets have stopped purchasing EastVale's products and another 85 are considering whether to stop purchasing from EastVale. Lawyers acting on behalf of the consumers are now presenting a substantial claim for damages against EastVale.

Required

In respect of EACH of the events at EastVale Co mentioned above:

(i)   Describe the additional audit procedures you will carry out;   **(8 marks)**

(ii)   State, with reasons, whether or not the financial statements for the year-end require amendment; and

(6 marks)

(iii)   Discuss whether or not the audit report should be modified.   **(6 marks)**

Note. The total marks will be split equally between each event.

(Total = 20 marks)

Answers

DO NOT TURN THIS PAGE UNTIL YOU HAVE
COMPLETED THE MOCK EXAM

A plan of attack

If this were the real Audit and Assurance exam and you had been told to turn over and begin, what would be going through your mind?

An important thing to say (while there is still time) is that it is vital to have a good breadth of knowledge of the syllabus because all the questions are compulsory. However, don't panic. Below we provide guidance on how to approach the exam.

Approaching the answer

Use your 15 minutes of reading time usefully, to look through the questions, particularly Question 1, to get a feel for what is required and to become familiar with the question scenarios.

Since all the questions in this paper are compulsory, it is vital that you attempt them all in order to increase your chances of passing. For example, don't run over time on Question 2 and then find that you don't have enough time for the remaining questions.

Question 1 is the 30 mark case-study question, typical of what you will find in the real exam. The scenario is quite long so make sure you have used your reading time well to familiarise yourself with it and make some notes on key issues. The key to success in this question is to stay focussed, don't run over time and answer the questions set. In part (a), notice the requirement to 'list' – you could break this part down further into the three assertions, for fair marks each, to make it more manageable and less overwhelming. Make sure you also explain the reason for doing each test – this applies to part (b) as well.

Question 2 is a straightforward knowledge-based question on engagement letters, audit evidence and audit reports. You only have 18 minutes to answer this question, so about six minutes for each part. Don't be tempted to write down everything you know about each of these areas – stay focused and just answer the question set – unnecessary irrelevancies wont score you any marks and will waste time.

Question 3 is on ethical issues and corporate governance. Use the clues in the scenario to help you produce a relevant, focused answer. Note that part (a) ahs two sub-requirements – you need to explain how to mitigate the threats you have identified.

Question 4 is on the wages system of a company. For part (a), a good way of presenting your answer would be in a tabular format – this means you can link the weaknesses and recommended controls together. In this way, you present a structured answer. Parts (b) and (c) should be straightforward but you must explain your points fully to score well.

Question 5 is on events after the balance sheet date and their potential impact on the audit report. There are two scenarios in the question so each is worth 10 marks. Remember to consider materiality and accounting treatment in your answer.

Forget about it!

And don't worry if you found the paper difficult. More than likely other candidates will too. If this were the real thing you would need to forget the exam the minute you left the exam hall and think about the next one. Or, if it is the last one, celebrate!

Question 1

Text references. Chapters 10, 11 and 14

Top tips. This 30 mark question is split into four parts so it is very important that you spend the appropriate amount of time on each part – do not get bogged down in one part and then find out that you do not have enough time to answer the other parts of the question

In parts (a) and (b), you can score one mark for each audit procedure and one mark for explaining the purpose of that audit procedure, therefore half the marks available are for your explanations. Make sure that you do explain the reasons fully. An appropriate way of setting out your answer for those two parts would be in a table format. Such a format ensures that you link each audit procedure to an explanation

In part (c), you are asked to 'describe' control procedures over the trade payables master file. This means that, again, you need to explain the control procedure fully – you will not score the full marks available if you do not do this

In part (d), you are asked to discuss how CAATs can be used in the audit of payables at this client. Although you need to understand what CAATs are and how they can be used, it is very important that you apply your knowledge to this particular scenario. A general answer on CAATs will not score well unless it is relevant to the circumstances in this question

Easy marks. This is a challenging question and there are no easy marks as such. However by using the information in the scenario, you should be able to score relatively well in parts (a) and (c), provided you explain your answers as required by the requirements.

ACCA examiner's answer. The examiner's answer to this question is included at the back of this Kit.

Marking scheme

Marks

(a) Audit procedures – purchases 12 marks. 1 for procedure and 1 for the reason. Limit to 5 marks in each category where stated briefly without full detail.

Audit procedure	Reason for procedure
Parts to GRN	Check completeness
Parts no GRN number	System error or cut-off error
GRN to computer	Parts received were ordered – occurrence
GRN agree to invoice	Completeness of recording
Review unmatched GRN file	Completeness of recording of liabilities
Paid invoice – GRN attached	Confirms invoice in PDB
Invoice details to payables ledger	Completeness and accuracy of recording
Review unmatched invoices file	Indicate understatement of liability (lack of completeness)
Payables ledger to purchase invoice	Liability belongs to Westra
Payables ledger to payments list	Liability properly discharged – payments complete
Payment list entries to invoice	Payment made for bona fide liability
Payments list to bank statement	Confirms payment to supplier
Bank statement entry to payments list	Confirms payment relates to Westra
GRN cut-off testing	Accuracy of cut-off
Maximum marks	

12

Marks

(b) **Audit procedures – payables**, 8 marks. 1 for procedure and 1 for reason. Limit to 0.5 mark in each category where stated briefly without full detail.

Audit procedure	Reason for procedure
Obtain and cast list of payables	Ensure that the list is accurate
Total of payables to the general ledger and financial statements	Confirm that the total has been accurately recorded
Analytical procedures	Indicates problems with the accuracy and completeness of payables
Agree payables to supplier statements	Confirm balance due from Westra
Supplier statement reconciliation	Liabilities exist and belong to Westra
Reconcile invoices	Confirms completeness and cut-off assertions
Reconcile payments	Payment to correct supplier
Review ledger old unpaid invoices	Credits O/S or going concern indicator
After date credit notes	Payables not overstated
FS categorization payables	Classification objective
Maximum marks	

8

(c) **Controls over standing data**, 5 marks. 1 mark for explaining each control. 0.5 for poor/limited explanation.

Amendments authorised
How authorised (form or access control)
Reject deletion where outstanding balance
Keep record of amendments
Review list of suppliers – unauthorised amendments
Update supplier list on computer regularly
Review computer control log
Review list of suppliers – unauthorised additions
Other relevant points (each)
Maximum marks

5

(d) **Use of CAATs**
Review computer control log
Identify old / obsolete – computer may already do this
Test data – online payments system
Use of CAATs – limited – lack of computer system integration
Need to assess computer controls prior to use of CAATs
Not cost effective – bespoke systems
Limited use of CAATs in suppliers ledger
Other relevant points (each)
Maximum marks

5

(a)   Substantive procedures

Completeness

Audit procedure	Purpose
Perform analytical procedures on purchases, e.g. comparison to the prior year on a month-by-month basis, ratio of purchases to payables, gross profit % etc and investigate any significant fluctuations	To provide assurance on the completeness of amounts recorded in the accounts and to highlight any areas of concern for further investigation
For a sample of supplier invoices, trace amounts to the GRN, order and payables ledger	To confirm completeness of recording of purchases
Inspect the unmatched GRNs file and seek explanations for any old unmatched items and trace these to the year-end accruals listing	To provide assurance on completeness as these should be included in the year-end accrual
For a sample of amounts on the ledger, agree to the computerised payments list to verify the amount and supplier	To provide assurance that the payment list is complete and accurate

Occurrence

Audit procedure	Purpose
For a sample of amounts in the payables ledger, trace these to the invoice and other supporting documentation such as GRNs	To provide assurance on the occurrence assertion
For a sample of GRNs, agree back to the original order details	To provide assurance on occurrence
For a sample of payees on the computerised payments list, agree amounts back to the supporting documentation such as invoices and GRNs	To provide assurance that payment has been made for a *bona fide* liability of the company
For a sample of payments made after the year-end, trace back to the computerised payments list	To provide assurance that payment relates to the company
For a sample of payees on the computerised payments list, trace payment to post year-end bank statements	To confirm that payment was made to authorised suppliers of the company

Cut-off

Audit procedure	Purpose
For a sample of GRNs dated shortly before and after the year-end, agree that the amounts on invoices are posted to the correct financial year	To ensure that amounts are included in the correct financial period
Review the schedule of accruals and agree to GRNs, checking the date of receipt of goods to ensure that goods received after the year-end are not included	To ensure that amounts are included in the correct financial period
Inspect outstanding orders on the 'orders placed' file for any orders completed but not yet invoiced	To ensure that amounts are included in the correct financial period

(b)   Audit procedures on trade payables

Audit procedure	Purpose
Cast the list of payables balances from the ledger at the year-end	To provide assurance that the list is complete and accurate
Reconcile the payables list from the payables ledger to the general ledger and accounts	To provide assurance that the figures are complete and accurate and correctly reflected in the financial statements
Perform analytical procedures on trade payables, comparing balance to prior year and investigating any significant fluctuations	To provide assurance on completeness and accuracy and to highlight areas of concern
For a sample of balances, trace amount to supporting supplier statements	To confirm the existence and accuracy of the amount outstanding at the year-end
Test cut-off by taking a sample of GRNs either side of the year-end and checking that amounts are included on the payables ledger for goods received before the year-end	To ensure that amounts are included in the correct financial period
Review disclosure of payables in the draft financial statements	To ensure that payables have been disclosed appropriately in the balance sheet and notes as either current or long-term liabilities

(c)   Control procedures over standing data on trade payables master file

- Access to the trade payables master file is limited only to authorised staff

- Amendments to standing data can only be made by authorised staff and all amendments must be authorised prior to input

- Access to the file is controlled by logins and passwords and passwords must be prompted to be changed regularly (say, every 90 days)

- Computer log is reviewed regularly by IT department to check for any unauthorised access or attempts to access the trade payables master file

- The list of suppliers should be reviewed regularly by a senior manager and those no longer used should be removed from the system

(d)   Use of CAATs in audit of Westra

CAATs could be used in the audit of purchases and payables at Westra in a number of ways.

For example, audit software could be used to generate a sample of ledger balances to be agreed to supplier statements. CAATs could also be used to reperform the cost of the total on the file to ensure the file is a complete record of transactions. CAATs can also be used to perform ratio calculations for analytical procedures on the purchases and payables data. Test data could be used to undertake some controls testing on the trade payables master file, such as on data access and payments to suppliers.

However, generally for this audit, the use of CAATs is somewhat limited as the company uses a mixture of manual and computerised systems, and where computerised systems are used, they are not fully integrated with each other.

Question 2

Text references. Chapters 4, 8 and 19

Top tips. This is a straightforward knowledge-based question for 10 marks on various aspects of the F8 syllabus. Make sure therefore that you do not run over time on this question – be specific and answer the question set.

In part (a), you are asked to state six items that could be included in an engagement letter. Bullet points for this question would be appropriate as there are three marks available so you could expect half a mark for each item. You therefore certainly will not have time to go into detail about the purpose of an engagement letter or ISA 210 *Terms of audit engagements* – these are not required and will not score you any marks.

In parts (b) and (c), you are asked for brief explanations. Note that in part (b) you are asked for four types of audit evidence and in part (c) you are asked for three types of audit report modification. Giving more than the required number is a waste of your time and giving less than the required number will ensure you lose the straightforward marks available in this question.

Easy marks. This is a straightforward knowledge-based question on three areas of the syllabus. If your knowledge is sound, you will be able to score very well in this question.

ACCA examiner's answer. The examiner's answer to this question is included at the back of this Kit.

Marking scheme

		Marks
(a)	Contents of an engagement letter – 3 marks. 0.5 mark per point.	
	Objective of the audit of the financial statements	0.5
	Management's responsibility for the financial statements	0.5
	The scope of the audit with reference to appropriate legislation	0.5
	The form of any report or other communication of the results of the engagement	0.5
	The auditor may not discover all material errors	0.5
	Provision of access to the auditor of all relevant books and records	0.5
	Arrangements for planning the audit	0.5
	Agreement of management to provide a representation letter	0.5
	Request that the client confirms in writing the terms of engagement	0.5
	Description of any letters or reports to be issued to the client	0.5
	Basis of fee calculation and billing arrangements	0.5
	Maximum marks	**3**
(b)	Types of audit evidence – 4 marks: 0.5 only for stating the type and 0.5 for explanation.	
	Maximum 2 marks for simply providing a list of types of evidence.	
	Inspection	1
	Observation	1
	Inquiry	1
	Confirmation	1
	Recalculation	1
	Reperformance	1
	Analytical procedures	1
	Maximum marks	**4**

BPP
LEARNING MEDIA

	Marks
(c) Modification of audit reports. 3 marks. 0.5 for the type of report and 0.5 for explanation.	
Emphasis of matter paragraph	1
Qualification – limitation in scope	1
Qualification – disagreement	1
Maximum marks	**3**

(a) The following items would be included in the engagement letter:

- Objective of the financial statements

- Management's responsibility for the financial statements

- Scope of the audit

- Form of any reports or other communication of results from the engagement

- A statement that due to the test nature and inherent limitations of the audit and internal control, there is a risk that some material misstatements may remain undetected

- Unrestricted access to records and documentation requested for the audit

- Arrangements regarding planning and performance of the audit

- Expectation of receiving written management representations on specific matters

- Request for client to confirm the terms of the engagement by acknowledging receipt of the letter

- Basis on which fees are calculated and any billing arrangements

- Description of any letters or reports the auditor expects to issue to the client

(*Note*. Only six were required.)

(b) Audit evidence that can be obtained by the auditor is described below:

Inspection

Inspection can encompass examining records, documents or assets. Looking at records and documents provides different levels of reliability depending on their nature and source. Inspection of assets can provide good evidence of existence but not of rights and obligations or valuation.

Observation

This consists of looking at a process or procedure being performed. An example would be observation of inventory counting.

Inquiry

Inquiry consists of seeking information from knowledgeable individuals, both from within and outside the organisation being audited. It can encompass both formal written inquiries or informal oral inquiries.

Confirmation

This is the process of obtaining a representation of information or of an existing condition from a third party, for example, a bank confirmation.

Recalculation

Recalculation is checking the mathematical accuracy of documents or records.

Reperformance

This is the auditor's independent execution of procedures or controls that were originally performed as part of the organisation's internal control, either manually or using CAATs.

Analytical procedures

Analytical procedures consist of evaluations of financial information made by a study of plausible relationships among both financial and non-financial data.

(*Note*. Only four were required.)

(c)   Modified audit reports

Qualification due to limitation on scope

The financial statements can be qualified due to a limitation on the scope of the auditor's work so that insufficient audit evidence is obtained on a material matter. The opinion will be expressed as being 'except for' the effects of the matter that the qualification relates to. Where the matter is so material and pervasive that the auditor is unable to express an opinion on the financial statements, a disclaimer of opinion will be expressed.

Qualification due to disagreement

The financial statements can be qualified due to a disagreement with management on a material matter. The opinion will be expressed as being 'except for' the effects of the matter that the qualification relates to. Where the matter is so material and pervasive that the financial statements are misleading, an adverse opinion will be expressed.

Emphasis of matter

An explanatory paragraph is added to the audit report to highlight a matter such as a significant uncertainty affecting the financial statements which is also included in the notes to the accounts. The emphasis of matter paragraph does not affect the audit opinion on the financial statements.

Question 3

Text references. Chapters 3 and 4

Top tips. This is a 20-mark question on ethical issues and corporate governance considerations for a listed company, both important areas of the syllabus.

Part (a) is worth 10 marks for identifying and explaining the independence issues, but make sure you also explain how each threat could be managed – this is specifically asked for in the requirement. The best way to approach this part of the question is to go through the scenario carefully and methodically, noting down the issues as you go on and then developing them further. You can give more structure to your answer and make it 'marker-friendly' by using a sub-heading for each factor.

In parts (b) and (c) you need to apply your knowledge of a recognised code of corporate governance, such as the Combined Code, to the scenario in the question. You must explain your answers fully, not merely produce a list of points. In part (b), each action is worth one mark so make sure that you provide a sufficiently detailed answer to this part of the question. Similarly, in part (c), you need to submit four well explained points to score maximum marks.

Easy marks. The more straightforward marks are available in part (b) of this question but make sure you explain the actions, rather than just list them, in order to achieve maximum marks.

ACCA examiner's answer. The examiner's answer to this question is included at the back of this kit.

Marking scheme

	Marks
(a) Audit risks 10 marks. 0.5 for identifying risk area, 1 for explanation of risk and 1 for stating how to resolve. Maximum 2.5 for each area.	
Rotation of audit partner	
Preparation of financial statements	
Attendance at social event	
Unpaid taxation fee	
Inheritance	
Other relevant points (each)	
Maximum marks	**10**
(b) Meeting corporate governance requirements, 6 marks. 1 mark for each point.	
Chief executive officer (CEO)/chairman split	1
Appoint NED	1
NED with financial experience	1
NEDs to sub-committees of board	1
Internal audit	1
Internal control system	1
Contact institutional shareholders	1
Financial report information	1
Other relevant points (each)	1
Maximum marks	**6**
(c) Communication with audit committee, 4 marks. 1 each point.	
Independence from board	1
Time to review audit work	1
Check auditor recommendations implemented	1
Review work of internal auditor (efficiency, etc.)	1
Other relevant points (each)	1
Maximum marks	**4**

(a) **Threats to independence**

Same audit partner and long-standing audit client

NorthCee has been a client of Dark for five years, during which time the audit partner has remained the same. This gives rise to a familiarity threat.

The threat can be mitigated by rotating the audit partner. ACCA's *Code of ethics* and conduct states that for listed companies, the engagement partner should be rotated after no more than five years and should not return until a period of five years has passed. Therefore, although NorthCee is not yet listed, the firm could consider this. It could also ensure that an independent internal quality review of the audit work is undertaken.

Preparation of financial statements

The firm has been asked to continue to prepare the financial statements for the company, as well as carry out the audit. This gives rise to a self-review threat, as there could be a perception that the firm will not apply sufficient professional scepticism to its own work.

This threat can be mitigated by having separate teams for each engagement so that auditor independence is still retained. The other option would be for Dark to decline the engagement to prepare the financial statements.

Attendance at evening reception

The audit partner and audit manager have been asked to attend an evening reception where NorthCee will present its listing arrangements to banks and existing shareholders. This gives rise to a familiarity threat, as the acceptance of the hospitality could lead to a closer relationship with client management and a risk of placing too much trust in their representations.

This threat can be reduced by the firm declining the invitation to attend the reception.

Overdue taxation fees

Dark has provided taxation services to NorthCee which is generally considered not to pose a self-review threat. However, there are overdue fees which can be considered as a loan to the client and therefore poses a self-interest threat. There could be a perception that the firm would be reluctant to qualify its opinion in the face of the risk of not receiving the overdue fees.

This threat can be mitigated by firstly discussing the overdue fees with the senior management of NorthCee and, as a last resort, considering resigning if they are not paid.

Inheritance of share capital

The audit manager has inherited 5% of NorthCee's share capital as a result of a death in the family. This poses a self-interest threat and ACCA guidance states that a member of the assurance team should not hold a direct financial interest in a client.

This threat would therefore be mitigated by the audit manager declaring the interest to the firm and then disposing of the shares straightaway. An alternative would be to move the audit manager to another client.

(b) **Actions required to meet corporate governance requirements**

The company should appoint a Chairman and Chief Executive for its board of directors and these must be different people with clear divisions of responsibility so that no one individual has unfettered powers of decision.

The company should appoint a mixture of executive and non-executive directors for the board. The ratio of non-executive directors to executive directors should be the same so that no individual or small group of individuals can dominate the board's decision taking.

The company should set up an internal audit department which can review its internal controls and report findings to the audit committee.

The company should establish remuneration and nomination committees. The nomination committee should consist of a majority of non-executive directors and the remuneration committee should have at least three non-executive directors.

There should be a terms of reference document established to set out the scope of the audit committee.

The company should set up procedures and policies to establish a sound system of internal control.

(c) **Communication with audit committee**

Dark must communicate with NorthCee's audit committee for this and future audits so that the external auditors are reporting their findings and recommendations to a set of people which consists of an independent element (in the form of the non-executive directors).

The audit committee also provides a means for the external auditors to communicate with the company and raise issues of concern.

The audit committee will have more time to examine the external auditors' reports and recommendations and this provides comfort that recommendations and other matters are being considered and reviewed.

The audit committee provides a forum for Dark in the event of any disputes with the management of NorthCee.

Question 4

Text references. Chapters 9, 10 and 11

Top tips. In part (a), there are eight marks available for identifying the control weaknesses and suggesting controls to overcome them. The best way to present your answer is in a columnar format because this allows you to link each weakness with a recommendation. Make sure you explain the weaknesses you have identified fully, as required by the question. Go through the scenario carefully, noting down potential areas of weakness as you do so. Part (b) is a straightforward question on the respective responsibilities of external and internal auditors for the detection of fraud. Part (c) is also a straightforward question on the use of an external consultant. First identify the factors to consider – these can form the sub-headings for your answer – and then explain those factors in more detail.

Easy marks. Easy marks can be achieved in parts (b) and (c) of this question on fraud responsibilities and the factors to consider when appointing an external consultant.

ACCA examiner's answer. The examiner's answer to this question is included at the back of this kit.

Marking scheme

Marks

(a) Control weaknesses and recommendations. 8 marks. 1 for explanation of weakness and 1 for internal control recommendation. Maximum 2 per weakness/recommendation.

Control weakness	Recommendation
Employees can be paid for work not done.	
No check hours actually worked	Authorise hours worked on computer
Fraudulent input employee number	Reconcile computer to actual employees
Fake or dummy employees can be put onto the payroll.	
Foreman setup	Check employees against personnel records
Wages office staff setup	List of employees reviewed for accuracy
Gross pay inflated by wages department staff.	
Add extra hours work done	List amendments to payroll produced
Other valid points	
Maximum marks	8

(b) Fraud and External/Internal audit. 6 marks. 1 for internal audit work and 1 for external audit. Maximum 2 per point

Main reason for audit work
Materiality
Identification of fraud
Other relevant points
Maximum marks 6

	Marks
(c) Use of expert. 6 marks. 1 mark per valid point.	
Qualification	1
Experience	1
References	1
Project management skills	1
Access to information	1
Acceptance by other staff	1
Other relevant points (each)	1
Maximum marks	**6**

(a)   **Wages system – weaknesses and recommended controls**

(i) Weakness	(ii) Internal control recommendation
The foreman is in a position to set up fictitious employees onto the wages system as he has authority to issue temporary employee numbers. This would allow him to collect cash wages for such bogus employees.	The issue of new employee numbers should be authorised by a manager and supported by employee contract letters etc.
The two wages clerks are responsible for the set up and maintenance of all employee records. They could therefore, in collusion, set up bogus employees and collect cash wages from them.	The list of personnel should be matched with the payroll by a manager and all new employee records should be authorised before being set up on the system.
The wages clerks are responsible for making amendments to holidays and illness etc. They could make unauthorised amendments which affect individual staff members' pay.	Any amendments to standing data on the wages system should be done by an authorised manager so that unauthorised amendments are not made. A log of amendments should be regularly reviewed.
The computer system calculates gross pay and any deductions but these are hand-written by the wages clerks for the staff pay packets, so errors could be made and incorrect wages issued.	A payslip should be generated by the computer system and including in the wage packet to reduce the chance of errors in deductions and gross pay being made.
The computer automatically calculates gross pay and deductions, however there is no check to ensure the calculations are accurate.	One of the wages clerks should check the gross pay and deductions for a sample of employees to gain assurance that the computer is calculating amounts correctly.
The foreman distributes cash wages to the employees. He could therefore misappropriate any wages not claimed.	The distribution of wages should be overseen by another manager. Any unclaimed wages should be noted on a form and returned to the wages department.

(b)   **Responsibilities for the detection of fraud**

External auditors

It is not the responsibility of the external auditors to detect fraud within a client. This responsibility lies with the management and those charged with governance.

ISA 240 *The auditor's responsibility to consider fraud in an audit of financial statements* sets out guidance in this area. It states that the auditor should maintain an attitude of professional scepticism throughout the audit, consider the potential for management override of controls and recognise that audit procedures that are effective in detecting error may not be appropriate in detecting fraud due to the nature of fraud.

As part of the audit planning process, the audit team should discuss the susceptibility of the client's financial statements to material misstatement by fraud.

Internal auditors

Responsibility for the prevention and detection of fraud lies with the management and those charged with governance at the client. To this end, management should place a strong emphasis on fraud prevention and fraud deterrence.

Internal audit can help in this regard because its aim is to review the internal control systems of the company to ensure they are effective and efficient. Part of this review could involve detailed work to ensure that fraud was not occurring. The internal audit department could also be required to undertake special projects to investigate suspected instances of fraud.

(c) **Factors to consider when appointing an external consultant:**

Qualifications

The professional qualifications of the consultant should be considered. He should be appropriately qualified to carry out the work required.

Experience

The technical experience of the consultant should be considered as he should be sufficiently experienced to undertake the assignment. He should also be familiar with the system being implemented.

Cost and service

The company should consider the cost to be incurred for replacing the wages system. It should also consider what the cost includes, for example, whether it includes a servicing agreement.

Availability

The company should consider whether the consultant will be available post-implementation to assist with any teething problems and other issues that might arise.

Training

The company should consider whether staff who will be using the new system will require training in order to be able to use the new package.

References and background

The company should consider who the consultant works for or whether he works alone and details of his previous clients and work.

Question 5

> **Text references.** Chapters 18 and 19
>
> **Top tips.** This question tests your knowledge and application of audit reviews and reports. It's also important that you remember your financial reporting studies to apply to the two events that occur after the balance sheet date. The best way to present your answer is to take each event in turn and answer the three requirements. This allows you to break the question down into more manageable chunks and gives more structure to your answers. Make sure that in (i), your answer is as specific as possible. In (ii), you must support your answer with good explanations. In (iii), you must justify your answer in order to score well.
>
> **Easy marks.** There aren't easy marks as such in this question but if you take each situation in turn, and answer each of the requirements, you should be able to score reasonably well.
>
> **ACCA examiner's answer.** The examiner's answer to this question is included at the back of this Kit.

Marking scheme

		Marks

(a) **Fire at warehouse**

(i) Audit procedures. 5 marks for fire 1 per well-explained point

	Marks
Discuss the matter with the directors	1
Letter of representation point	1
Schedule of inventory destroyed – reasonable?	1
Insurance	1
Going concern status of company	1
Other relevant points (each)	1
Maximum marks	**4**

(ii) Amendment to financial statements 2 marks – 1 per well-explained point

	Marks
Disclosure in FS – unlikely with reason	1
No amendment to B/S etc	1
Other relevant points	1
Maximum marks	**3**

(iii) Modification of audit report 3 marks – 1 per well-explained point

Modification of report

	Marks
Going concern status?	1
Inadequate disclosure by directors	1
Other relevant points (each)	1
Maximum marks	**3**

(b) **Batch of cheese**

(i) Audit procedures 5 marks for fire 1 per well-explained point

	Marks
Discuss with directors	1
Copy of damages claim	1
Legal advice	1
Press reports (or other third party) on cheese	1
Going concern?	1
Other relevant points (each)	1
Maximum marks	**4**

(ii) Disclosure of event 2 marks – 1 per well-explained point

	Marks
Disclosure event – because significant impact	1
No adjustment	1
Going concern issue – reputation	1
May result in amendment to FS	1
Other relevant points (each)	1
Maximum marks	**3**

(iii) Modification of audit report – 3 marks – 1 per well-explained point

	Marks
Preparation of FS breakup basis	1
Prepared going concern basis – emphasis of matter to note this	1
Prepared going concern – but in doubt – emphasis of matter to not this	1
Prepared going concern and disagree – qualify report	1
Maximum marks	**3**

BPP
LEARNING MEDIA

(a) **Fire in warehouse**

(i) *Additional audit procedures*

- Discuss with management of EastVale to establish the date of the fire and exactly what happened

- Estimate the value of the inventory that was destroyed in the fire

- Inspect the insurance policy of the company to check that the company is covered adequately for the loss incurred and review any correspondence regarding this

- Discuss with the directors of EastVale whether the company can continue as a going concern given the high level of inventory that was destroyed in the fire

- Obtain written representations from management regarding the going concern status of the company

(ii) *Impact on financial statements*

As the fire is a non-adjusting event after the balance sheet date, providing the going concern basis is still appropriate no amendments are required to the financial statements for the financial year being audited. However, disclosure of the event is required by IAS 10 *Events after the balance sheet date* as the event is likely to be material. This disclosure should include the nature of the event and an estimate of its financial effect.

(iii) *Impact on audit report*

Providing the directors have properly disclosed the event the audit opinion would not be qualified as this is a non-adjusting event after the balance sheet date and does not provide evidence of conditions that existed at the balance sheet date. However, an emphasis of matter paragraph could be included in the audit report to highlight the matter and draw it to the attention of users of the financial statements.

(b) **Cheese**

(i) *Additional audit procedures*

- Review legal correspondence regarding the claim to establish the amount of the claim

- Discuss the case with EastVale's solicitors to assess the likely outcome of the claim

- Review press reports regarding food poisoning to assess impact on the business

- Discuss the case with the directors, including their assessment of its impact on the going concern status of EastVale

- Obtain written management representations from the directors on the going concern status of the company

(ii) *Impact on financial statements*

This is a non-adjusting event after the balance sheet date. However, given its nature it should be disclosed in a note to the financial statements. If it impacts on the going concern status of the company, then the accounts would have to be prepared on a different basis and disclosures in accordance with IAS 8 *Accounting policies, changes in accounting estimates and errors* would be required.

(iii)   *Impact on audit report*

If the directors consider that as a result of the food poisoning reports the company cannot continue as a going concern and they produce the accounts on a break-up basis, then the audit report would not be qualified but would include an emphasis of matter paragraph to draw attention to users of this matter.

If the accounts are prepared on the assumption that the company is a going concern but the auditors do not agree with this then the audit report would be modified with an adverse opinion on the financial statements.

ACCA
Examiner's answers

December 2006 question	Kit question reference
1	26
2	15
3	52
4	53
5	54

1 (a) Risk assessment procedures

(i) The main purpose of risk assessment procedures is to help the auditor obtain an understanding of the audit client.

The procedures will provide audit evidence relating to the auditor's risk assessment of a material misstatement in the client's financial statements.

The auditor will also obtain initial evidence regarding the classes of transactions at the client and the operating effectiveness of the client's internal controls.

Finally, the auditor may identify risks in other areas such as being associated with a particular client or not being able to follow ethical guidelines of ACCA.

(ii) The auditor may obtain evidence from:

– Inquiries of management and others connected with the entity such as external legal counsel or valuation experts

– Analytical procedures including ratio analysis to obtain high level data on the client

– Observation of entity activities and inspection of documents, etc.

(b) Provide the range of services required – small firm

Serenity requires an enhanced range of services this year including review of and implementation of additional control systems. This service provides the following risks:

Skills necessary

Mal & Co must check whether they can provide these services. Mal & Co is only a seven partner firm and so the company must ensure it has the necessary staff and skills to undertake this work.

Self-review threat

There is a self-review threat. If Mal & Co are to implement new control systems then they may also be auditing those systems as part of the statutory audit. Mal & Co must ensure different staff implement and audit the systems. Preferably different departments in the firm should undertake the work. If insufficient staff are available then Mal & Co must refuse the additional systems work.

Acceptance of non-audit work

There is a possibility that Mal & Co will be breaching ethical or statutory guidelines by accepting the work. In some countries such as the USA, audit firms are barred from undertaking any other work for a client. Mal & Co must ensure this is not the case in their country.

Fee income

Acceptance of additional work will result in additional fee income for Mal & Co. ACCA's Code of Ethics and Conduct states that the amount of fee income derived from any one client should not exceed 15% for non public companies. Mal & Co will need to ensure that total fee income from Serenity does not breach these guidelines.

Client growth

Serenity is growing quickly. The company has poor internal controls providing high risk of financial misstatement. Mal & Co will need to ensure sufficient staff of appropriate experience are available and that enough time is allocated to the audit to complete all audit procedures.

Internal audit

Client expectations regarding the use of internal audit may be difficult to meet. As a new department, it will take time for the internal auditors to understand the systems at Serenity and produce any useful reports. Expectation of reduced fee will have to be managed carefully and checks made to ensure the auditor does not limit work because of fee pressure.

Association threat

Serenity are producing a new mobile telephone. The legal status of the telephone is currently uncertain; it may be illegal. Mal & Co need to determine the likelihood that the telephone is illegal. The audit firm may not wish to be associated with a company producing illegal products.

Advocacy threat

Mal & Co may be asked to provide evidence to support Serenity regarding the mobile telephone development. This will result in an advocacy threat – with the audit firm seen to be supporting the client's interests. Mal & Co must determine exactly what information is required, and if necessary refuse to provide information.

Report on cash flow

The mobile telephone application also requires a report on Serenity's cash flow forecast. This increases audit risk due to the nature of the forecast (in the future) and the danger of issuing an incorrect report. Serenity must determine exactly what type of report is required (positive or negative) and ensure they have the time and staff with the necessary skills to provide the service.

Possible going concern

It is not clear whether failure to obtain the new mobile telephone licence will result in Serenity no longer being a going concern. Mal & Co will need to review the cash flow forecasts closely to determine the company's status in the future.

(c) The term negative assurance means that the auditor has carried out work on the cash flow but that the accuracy of the forecast cannot be confirmed. The auditor will report that the cash flow appears to be reasonable, but not that it shows a true and fair view. The auditor is therefore not confirming that the cash flow is correct, rather that there is nothing to indicate it is incorrect.

This type of report is appropriate for a forecast because it relates to the future. It is therefore not possible to state that the forecast is materially correct in terms of truth and fairness because the forecast has not been tested against the future. The actual results are therefore uncertain. It may not be correct simply because future conditions do not agree with those under which the forecast was prepared.

2 (a) Purpose of three Es

A value for money audit is concerned with obtaining the best possible combination of services for the least resources. It is therefore the pursuit of 'Economy', 'Efficiency' and 'Effectiveness' – sometimes referred to as the three 'Es'.

Economy relates to least cost. The systems in an organisation should operate at a minimum cost associated with an acceptable level of risk.

Efficiency relates to the best use of resources. The goals and objectives of an organisation should be accomplished accurately and on a timely basis with the least use of resources.

Effectiveness provides assurance that organisational objectives will be achieved.

(b) (i) Internal control weaknesses and recommendations

Internal control weakness	Recommendation
Transfer of information from purchase requisition to order form Details of the goods to be ordered are transferred onto the order form after the chief buyer has authorised the initial order requisition. This means that there is no check on the transfer of order information onto the form; clerks could easily make an error or even complete an order form for which there is no valid requisition.	The order form should be signed for authority to purchase and to show that details have been agreed to the requisition.
Purchase requisition The purchase requisition is destroyed after goods have been ordered. This means that there is no audit trail to show who ordered the goods or whether the order form has been completed correctly.	The requisition should be filed in the ordering department as audit evidence of goods being ordered.
Order form Only the original and one copy of the order form are available – one is sent to the supplier and the second to accounts. This means that there is no record of goods ordered in the ordering department. There are risks that goods could be ordered twice and that late deliveries cannot be identified and queried with suppliers.	The order document is in three copies, with the additional copy being kept in the ordering department.
No copy order to goods inwards department A copy of the order form is not available in the goods inwards department. This means that the department does not know what goods to expect and may therefore receive goods that the organisation has not ordered.	A copy of the order is sent to goods inwards. Deliveries are only accepted where they relate to an authorised order.

Internal control weakness	Recommendation
Goods Received Notes (GRNs) filed in order of goods reference number	
GRNs are filed in order of the reference numbers for the goods being ordered. Filing GRNs in this way provides an internal control weakness because a numeric sequence check on the completeness of the filing system cannot be performed. GRNs may be missing meaning that the organisation cannot necessarily prove that goods have been received.	GRNs are filed in numeric sequence.

(ii) Additional weaknesses

Issue efficiency – orders authorised by the chief buyer

All orders are signed by the chief buyer. While this provides good control over the ordering process, the chief buyer does not necessarily need to authorise all orders; orders below a certain limit could be authorised by a junior buyer. This allows the chief buyer more time to concentrate on larger orders and monitor the running of the department.

Issue economy – individual items ordered – no economy of scale

Ordering clerks place orders for goods from each individual order received. However, orders can relate to the same items being ordered from different departments. Orders based on each order do not take into account any volume discounts obtainable from combining orders.

Orders should be combined on a daily or even weekly basis to obtain appropriate economies.

Issue efficiency – routing of GRN

The top copy of the GRN is sent to the accounts department via the ordering department. There does not appear to be any reason for sending the GRN via the ordering department; sending the GRN via this department delays the process of checking the GRN to the order.

To provide an earlier check on whether goods received relate to *bona fide* orders either goods should be checked to the copy order in the goods inwards department, or a copy of the GRN sent directly to accounts.

Issue efficiency – filing GRNs in part number order

This filing system may hinder retrieving a GRN. This gives rise to an efficiency problem that in most situations the GRN number will be known (for example, as a cross reference from the invoice) rather than individual part numbers. Filing in GRN number order will help find GRNs quicker.

3 (a) (i) Four examples of external confirmations are:

- – Accounts receivable letter
- – Solicitor letter
- – Bank report letter
- – Inventory held by third parties.

(ii) *Note one example of each assertion only required.*

Accounts receivable letter

This letter provides evidence of the existence of the receivable when a reply is returned from that receivable direct to the auditor.

The letter provides evidence on cut-off because sales or cash receipts recorded in the incorrect accounting period will have to be reconciled to the balance provided by the receivable.

The letter does not provide evidence of completeness of the receivables balance because receivables may not query balances which are understated.

The letter does not provide evidence of the valuation of the receivables balance because the receivable cannot be expected to list all outstanding balances and confirmation of the debt does not mean it will be paid.

Solicitor letter

A solicitor letter provides evidence as to the existence of claims at the period end as the solicitor will confirm specific claims.

However, the letter does not necessarily confirm the valuation of claims due to uncertainty about the future or the completeness of any legal claims as solicitors do not normally provide a list of all claims – they prefer to comment only on claims they are actually asked about.

Bank report letter

A bank confirmation letter provides good evidence on the existence of the company's bank accounts as the bank has confirmed this information in writing.

A bank letter cannot necessarily be relied on to provide complete or accurate information. Most banks place a disclaimer on the letter of 'errors and omissions excepted' indicating that the auditor must review this evidence against other cash and bank evidence obtained.

Inventory held by third parties

A letter from the third party holding the inventory will provide evidence of the existence of that inventory because the third party has confirmed this in writing.

However, the letter does not provide evidence regarding the valuation of the inventory; confirming something exists does not necessarily mean it is in good condition.

(b) (i) Procedure for obtaining a bank letter

The auditor should consider if a bank letter is required. For the audit of Jayne Co the letter is required as the company has significant cash transactions and a loan from the bank.

The auditor will produce a confirmation letter in accordance with local audit regulations and practices.

The letter will be sent to the client to sign and authorise disclosure and then it will be forwarded on to Jayne's bank. Alternatively, the client may already have provided a standard authority for the bank to respond to a bank letter each year. In this case separate authority would not be required.

Ideally the letter should be sent before the end of the accounting period to enable the bank to complete it on a timely basis e.g. at the year-end.

The bank will complete the letter and send it back directly to the auditor.

Audit procedures on the bank letter include:

– Agree the balances for each bank account to the relevant bank reconciliation and the year end balance in the financial statements.
– Agree total interest charges on the letter to the interest expense account in the general ledger.
– For any details of loans, ensure repayment terms are correctly disclosed in the financial statements between current and non-current liabilities.

(ii) Substantive procedures for the audit of bank balances.

(1) Obtain a copy of the year end trial balance.

Agree the bank balance on the trial balance to

– the year end bank balance on the computer system, and
– the balance on the financial statements.

(2) Obtain a copy of Jayne Co's bank reconciliation.

– Cast the reconciliation
– Agree the bank balance to the trial balance.
– Agree the bank statement balance to the year end bank statement.
– Agree any unpresented lodgements to the bank statement after the end of the year
– Agree any unpresented cheques or similar expenses to the cash book before the end of the year and the bank statements after the end of the year.

4 (a) Audit tests for completeness of income

All income

For a sample of paying-in slips during the year, trace amount banked to the bank statements agreeing the total banked.

Agree the total per the paying-in slip to the cash book to confirm that the total has been correctly recorded in the cash book.

Confirm that the analysis on the bank paying-in slips is correctly recorded between membership fees and court hire in the cash book.

Cast the cash book to confirm total income for the year.

Agree total income received and the analysis of membership fees and court hire to the financial statements.

Membership fees

Compare the list of members as at 1 October 2004 to 1 October 2005 to determine how many members did not renew their membership during the year. This is normally approximately 10%.

Confirm total membership fees are correct by analytical review. Membership income should be:

430 members less 10% = 387
387 * $200 = $77,400
50 new members at 50% fee = 50 * $100 = $5,000
Total fee income $82,400

Agree the membership fee income to the financial statements. If the amount is materially different enquire of the treasurer why this is the case.

Court hire fees

Obtain the list of court hires from the clubhouse.

For a number of weeks, determine how many hours courts were hired for. Agree this time to the bank paying-in slip (hours * $5 should equal the amount banked).

Ask the secretary to explain any differences in amounts banked.

(b) Audit tests on expenditure

Audit tests focus on ensuring that recorded expenditure is accurate and *bona fide* to the activities of the club.

Agree analysis of expenditure from financial statements back to the cash book ensuring amounts agree.

Cast the cash book to ensure accuracy of the different expenditure figures.

For a sample of items in the cash book, agree to purchase invoice ensuring that the amounts are correctly recorded in the cash book and the analysis is correct. Similarly agree entries in the cash book back to the invoice checking analysis and amount are correctly recorded.

For each invoice selected above, ensure that the expenditure relates to the club (e.g. is for court maintenance, power costs or tennis balls).

For any other expenditure, enquire with club treasurer why the expenditure was incurred. Ensure appropriate authorisation is available on the invoice or from club committee minutes.

(c) Limitation of internal control testing

Internal control testing is limited in relatively small audits such as FireFly Tennis Club for the following reasons:

There is a **lack of segregation of duties**. The club has only a limited number of staff in responsible positions. This means segregation of duties between, for example, authorising of purchase invoices and paying them, is not possible.

Lack of authorisation controls. In small organisations, the senior officials tend to be the people 'authorising' transactions and also carrying them out. For example, the treasurer effectively authorises purchase invoices by paying for them rather than a senior official signing the invoice and a more junior clerk paying the invoice.

Cost. Establishing an internal control system can be expensive. A small club cannot afford the expense of employing sufficient staff to provide a complete segregation of duties.

Management override. Even if there was an internal control system in place, senior officials are in a position to override that system. For example, the club treasurer could pay for his own expenses using the club debit card.

5 (a) Sampling risk

Sampling risk is the possibility that the auditor's conclusion, based on a sample, may be different from the conclusion reached if the entire population were subjected to the audit procedure.

Examples of sampling risk are that a material error does not exist, when in fact it does and that a material error does exist when in fact there is no material error. Both of these situations will lead to an incorrect audit opinion.

Sampling risk is controlled by the audit firm ensuring that it is using a statistically valid method of selecting items from a population.

Non-sampling risk

Non-sampling risk arises from any factor that causes an auditor to reach an incorrect conclusion that is not related to the size of the sample.

Examples of non-sampling risk include the use of inappropriate procedures, misinterpretation of evidence or the auditor simply 'missing' an error.

Non-sampling risk is controlled by providing appropriate training for staff so they know which audit techniques to use and will recognise an error when one occurs.

(b) The audit manager suggests checking all invoices, effectively ignoring any statistical sampling. Audit tests will be applied to all of the sales invoices. This approach is appropriate for the audit of Tam because:

- The population is relatively small and it is likely to be quicker to test all the items than spend time constructing a sample.
- All the transactions are not large (about 0·2% of revenue) but could be considered material in their own right. As all the transactions are material, then they all need to be tested.

The audit senior suggests using statistical sampling. This will mean selecting a limited number of sales invoices from the population using a non-biased selection method such as random numbers and then applying audit tests to those invoices only. This approach may be appropriate because:

- The population consists of similar items (i.e. it is homogeneous) and there are no indications of the control system failing or changing during the year. There is the query about how long it will take to determine and produce a sample, which may make statistical sampling inappropriate in this situation.

The audit junior suggests using 'random' sampling, which means that the auditor will manually choose which invoices to look at. The approach therefore involves an element of bias. While this approach appears to save time, it is not appropriate because:

- The sample selected will be chosen 'randomly' but on the whim of the auditor. Human nature will tend to avoid difficult items for testing.

- Also, as invoices will not have been chosen using statistical sampling, no valid conclusion can be drawn from the results of the test. If an error is found it will be difficult extrapolating that error on to the population.

(c) Information is material if its omission or misstatement could influence the economic decisions of users taken on the basis of the financial statements.

Materiality depends on the size of the item or error judged in the particular circumstances of its omission or misstatement.

It is important that the auditors of Tam ensure that the financial statements are free from material error for the following reasons:

- There is a legal requirement to audit financial statements and present an opinion on those financial statements. If the auditors do not detect a material error then their opinion on the financial statements could be incorrect

- There are only two owner/directors who will be the initial users of the financial statements. While the owners/directors maintain the accounting records, the directors will want to know if there are material errors resulting from any mistakes they may have made; the auditor has a responsibility to the members to ensure that the financial statements are materially correct

- There are also other users of the financial statements who will include the taxation authorities and the bank who have made a loan to the company. They will want to see 'true and fair' accounts. The auditors must therefore ensure that the financial statements are free from material misstatement to avoid any legal liability to third parties if they audit the financial statements negligently.

6 (a) Use of Computer-Assisted Audit Techniques (CAATs)

Testing programmed controls

Reliance on CAATs will force the auditor to rely on programmed controls during an audit; in fact using CAATs may be the only way to test controls within a computer system. Use of the CAAT enables the auditor to meet the auditing standard requirement of obtaining appropriate audit evidence.

For example, in Walsh Co, an overtime report is generated by the computer, although this can also be overridden by the accountant. Test data can be used to check that the overtime report is being created correctly and audit software can monitor that only the accountant's password can be used to override the overtime payment.

Test larger number of items

Using CAATs enables the auditor to test a larger number of items quickly and accurately, meeting the auditing standard requirement of obtaining sufficient audit evidence.

Using audit software, the auditor can check the deduction and net pay calculations of a significant proportion of wages calculations – or all of them if necessary. Checking each calculation manually would take a long time.

Test actual accounting records

Using CAATs enables the auditor to test the actual accounting records (the electronic version) rather then relying on printouts or other copies of the data. It is always appropriate for the auditor to test original documentation where possible.

In the case of Walsh, the actual wages will be tested rather than any paper copies.

Cost

After initial set-up costs, using CAATs is likely to be cost effective; the same audit software programs can be run each year as long as the client does not change the accounting systems.

In Walsh Co, the system has just been implemented. Hopefully the wages system will be used for a number of years, making the use of CAATs cost-effective for the audit firm.

(b) Examples of the use of audit software

Calculation checks: For example, re-calculation of net pay for a number of employees to ensure the mathematical calculation is correct.

Reviewing the list of employees paid each week/month and printing a list of employees, who have not be been paid, for further investigation.

Detecting unreasonable items: Reviewing the list of net wages for large or negative payments.

Detecting violation of system rules: For example, where other people besides the accountant have been overriding overtime payments or employees amending their own gross wages.

Conducting new analysis as part of the analytical review of wages. For example, calculating total wages for the year from the number of employees and average wages paid.

Completeness checks – ensuring there is an electronic record of all employees who 'clocked in' for a day's work and 'clocked out' again.

(c) Audit test data consists of data submitted by the auditor for processing on the client's computer-based accounting systems. The data can be processed during a normal processing run (a 'live' testing situation) or in a special run outside of the normal processing cycle (a 'dead' testing situation).

In Walsh, the auditor can create a 'dummy employee' record on the wages master file, and then use a magnetic card to mimic that employee working a certain number of hours in the company over the course of, for example, one week.

Knowing how many hours has been input into the wages system; the auditor can calculate the expected net pay and then compare this to the actual net pay produced by the computer system.

If the amounts agree then this provides appropriate audit evidence of the accuracy of recording and processing of the wages software.

The problems of using this audit technique include:

The possibility that the client's computer system will be damaged by the testing being undertaken by the auditor. For example, by errors being caused by entering data that the client's software cannot process.

The need to reverse or remove any transactions input by the auditor. The transactions may be incorrectly or incompletely removed leaving dummy data in the client's live computer system.

Use of test data can be expensive – the auditor needs to ensure that the benefit gained from the test outweighs the expense. In this situation, it will take a long time to input employee details and there may be more efficient audit tests available.

Pilot Paper F8 (INT)   **Answers**
Audit and Assurance (International)

Tutorial note: Some answers are longer than could be expected from candidates sitting this examination. The answers may also include more points than would be necessary to obtain full marks in the examination. This is to provide examples of valid points that could be made.

1   (a)   Audit procedures – purchases

Audit procedure	Reason for procedure
Obtain a sample of list of parts documents from the computer. Trace individual parts to the goods received note (GRN).	Checks the *completeness* of recording of liabilities.
For entries in the list of parts where no GRN number has been entered, enquire with goods inwards staff why there is no GRN. Document reasons obtained.	Checks that goods have not been received but details not recorded. Possible *cut-off* error where goods have been received but GRN not raised.
Obtain a sample of GRNs. Agree details to the list of parts document on the computer.	Ensures that the parts received had been ordered by Westra, giving evidence for the *occurrence* assertion.
For a sample of GRNs from the goods inwards department, trace to the invoice held in the accounts department.	Ensures the *completeness* of recording of liabilities. GRNs with no matching invoice indicate a liability has been incurred. Unmatched GRNs should be included in the payables accrual. Note this test will be difficult because there is no cross reference maintained of the GRN to the invoice.
Review file of unmatched GRNs, investigate reasons for any old (more than one week) items.	Ensures the *completeness* of recording of liabilities. Unmatched items prior to the year end should be included in the payables accrual.
Obtain a sample of paid invoices. Ensure that the GRN is attached.	Confirms that the invoice should be included in the payables ledger, meeting the *completeness* assertion.
For the sample of invoices, check details into the computerised payables ledger, ensuring the correct account has been updated and the invoice amount is accurate.	Confirms the *completeness* of recording of payables invoices in the ledger.
Obtain the unmatched invoices file. Investigate old items obtaining reason for GRN not being received / invoice not being processed.	Unmatched items at the year end could indicate unrecorded liabilities. Ensure included in the payables accrual if the goods had been received pre-year end.
For a sample of entries from the payables ledger, agree details back to the purchase invoice.	Ensures that the liability does belong to Westra, meeting the *occurrence* assertion.
For the sample of entries on the payables ledger, agree to the electronic payments list confirming that the supplier name and amount is correct.	Ensures that the liability has been properly discharged by Westra and that the payments list is therefore *complete*.
For a sample of entries on each electronic payments list, agree details to the purchase invoice.	Ensures that the payment has been made for a liability incurred by Westra, meeting the *occurrence* assertion.
For the sample of entries in the electronic payments list, agree details to the bank statement.	Shows that the payment was actually made to that supplier.
Obtain the bank statements. Trace a sample of payments to the electronic payments list.	Confirms that the payment made does relate to Westra, confirming the *occurrence* assertion.
For a sample of GRNs in the week pre- and post- year-end, trace to the supporting invoice and entry in the payables ledger, ensuring recorded in the correct accounting year.	Confirms the accuracy of *cut-off* in the financial statements.

Tutorial note. This answer follows the structure of the scenario provided in the question. An alternative and valid format would be to use the assertions as main headings and to make points under each heading.

(b)   Audit procedures – payables

Audit procedure	Reason for procedure
Obtain a list of payables balances from the computerised payables ledger as at Westra's year end. Cast the list.	To ensure that the list is accurate and that the total is represented by the individual balances (completeness assertion).
Agree the total of payables to the general ledger and financial statements.	To confirm that the total has been accurately recorded and that the balance in the financial statements is represented by valid payables (occurrence assertion).
Perform analytical procedures on the list of payables. Determine reasons for any unusual changes in the total balance or individual payables in the list.	Provides initial indication of the accuracy and completeness of the list of payables.
For a sample of payables on the list, agree to supplier statements at the year-end.	Confirms that the payables balance is due from Westra meeting the occurrence assertion.
Reconcile supplier statement balances to the payables ledger.	Ensures that the liabilities exist and belong to Westra at the year-end.
For invoices on the statements not in the ledger, agree to invoices entered after the year-end. Check the date of goods receipt per the GRN attached to the invoice. Where goods received pre-year end agree invoice to the payables accrual.	Ensures that all liabilities were recorded at the year end, meeting the completeness and cut-off assertions.
For payments not included in the supplier statements, agree to the next month-end statement ensuring that the payment has been recorded.	Ensures that payments have been made to the correct supplier.
Review the payables ledger for old unpaid invoices. Enquire of the chief accountant the reason for non-payment.	Non-payment may be indicative of goods being returned for credit indicating that the payables figure may be overstated. Alternatively, taking additional credit from payables may be a going concern indicator.
Review credit notes received post-year end ensuring that where they relate to pre-year end purchases that the payables accrual has been reduced.	Ensures that payables are not over-stated at the year-end. Large credit notes may also be an indication of overstating payables deliberately to reduce profit.
Ensure that payables have been included in the financial statements under the heading of current liabilities.	Confirm the correct classification of payables in the financial statements.

(c)   **Controls over standing data**

Controls include:

–   Any amendment (addition, amendment or deletion) to the payables ledger should be authorised by a responsible official, for example, the chief accountant.

–   Authorisation can be by a manual form being signed or by the chief accountant having restricted access password to amend the standing data.

–   The computer should reject deletion of a supplier account where there is an outstanding balance (debit or credit).

–   A record of amendments made to the payables ledger should be maintained within the ledger and reviewed on a regular basis by the chief accountant to ensure that the changes are bona fide.

–   The chief accountant should review the list of suppliers on a regular basis (perhaps every four to six months) and delete those which are no longer used.

–   A comparison should be made regularly (perhaps every month) between the authorised list of suppliers on the computerised list of suppliers and the payables ledger. Any new supplier on the list of suppliers should be added to the payables ledger in preparation for payment.

–   A review of the computer control log regarding access to the payables standing data should be made on a regular basis and any unauthorised access identified and changes made under that access identified and if necessary reversed.

      –   A list of suppliers should be printed out occasionally (about every three months) and kept in a secure location in the chief accountant's office. The chief accountant should then compare this list with the computerised list in three months time and account for any unauthorised additions.

(d) Use of CAATs

Audit software may be used to identify old/obsolete balances in some of Westra's systems eg outstanding deliveries and payments not being made to suppliers. However, the usefulness of the testing is limited and it is possible that the computer system already provides similar controls.

Test data input by the auditor would be useful in checking the online payments system, perhaps by setting up some "dummy" accounts and ensuring that payments are sent to the correct suppliers. Other controls over payments such as access controls are more likely to be tested manually by the auditor.

Use of Computer-Assisted Audit Techniques (CAATs) may be limited in Westra due to the lack of integration of computer systems. For example, the suppliers' database is not connected to the payables ledger, limiting the use of test data to check transactions all the way through the purchases/payables system.

There is no indication provided in the scenario regarding the extent and effectiveness of computer controls. Controls would have to be identified and assessed for reliability prior to reliance being placed.

Given that some of Westra's systems are bespoke, then it may not be cost effective to use CAATs given the time required to write specific test data or program audit software to use Westra's data.

Use of CAATs in the suppliers' database may not be effective given that the database does not input directly into any financial accounting system. Testing GRNs to purchase invoice to ledgers, etc will provide greater assurance of the completeness and accuracy of purchases than testing the suppliers' database.

2   Engagement letter

(a) Contents of an engagement letter

–   Objective of the audit of the financial statements
–   Management's responsibility for the financial statements
–   The scope of the audit with reference to appropriate legislation
–   The form of any report or other communication of the results of the engagement
–   The auditor may not discover all material errors
–   Provision of access to the auditor of all relevant books and records
–   Arrangements for planning the audit
–   Agreement of management to provide a representation letter
–   Request that the client confirms in writing the terms of engagement
–   Description of any letters or reports to be issued to the client
–   Basis of fee calculation and billing arrangements.

(b) Types of audit evidence

–   Inspection – examination of records or documents in whatever form eg manual computerised, external or internal.

–   Observation – looking at the processes or procedures being carried out by others.

–   Inquiry – seeking information from knowledgeable persons, both financial or non-financial, either within or outside the entity being audited.

–   Confirmation – the process of obtaining a representation of an existing condition from a third party eg a receivables letter.

–   Recalculation – checking the mathematical accuracy of documents or records.

–   Reperformance – this is the auditor's independent execution of procedures or controls that were originally performed as part of the entity's internal control system.

–   Analytical procedures – evaluation of financial information made by a study of plausible relationships among both financial and non-financial data.

(c)   Modification of audit reports

Emphasis of matter paragraph. Used where the auditor wishes to draw attention to an important item in the financial statements.

Qualification – limitation in scope. Used where the audit cannot obtain sufficient evidence regarding an item in the financial statements.

Qualification – disagreement. Used where the auditor disagrees concerning the amount or disclosure of an item in the financial statements.

3   (a)   Threats to independence

Rotation of audit partner

NorthCee Co have had the same audit partner for the last five years. An audit partner's independence may be impaired where that position is retained for more than five years for a listed company. The reason being that the partner has become too close to the directors and staff in the firm and this may impair his judgement on the financial statements. However, NorthCee is currently not listed so this requirement does not apply.

As NorthCee is now being listed, Dark & Co should rotate the audit partner this year to avoid any familiarity threat. However, given that NorthCee was not a listed company up to this audit, may imply that the partner could continue this year, but would be recommended to be rotated before the 2008 audit.

Preparation of financial statements

Apparently Dark have been preparing NorthCee's financial statements as well as carrying out the audit in previous years. While this may not have been an independence issue in the past, it is likely to be now as in many jurisdictions auditors may not provide other services to their audit clients, especially listed client. Preparing financial statements as well as auditing them would provide Dark with a self-review threat, that is they may not see any errors, or want to report errors in material that they have previously prepared.

Dark should therefore decline from preparation of NorthCee's financial statements.

Attendance at social event

Attending the social event with respect to the new listing may be inappropriate as Dark may be seen as supporting NorthCee in this venture. There is an advocacy threat to independence. Support for a client may imply that the audit firm are "too close" to that client and may therefore lose their independent view regarding the audit. There is also a familiarity threat.

Dark should therefore politely decline the dinner invitation, clearly stating their reasons.

Unpaid taxation fee

The unpaid fee in respect of taxation services could be construed as a loan to the audit client. Audit firms should not make loans to or receive loans from audit clients. An outstanding loan will affect independence as closure of the loan may be seen as more important than providing an appropriate audit opinion.

Dark need to discuss the situation with NorthCee again, suggesting that a payment on account could be made to show that the whole fee will be paid. Alternatively, audit work on the 2007 financial statements can be delayed until the taxation fee is paid.

Inheritance

Under ACCA's Code of Ethics and Conduct, audit partners may not hold beneficial shares in a client company. This provision includes audit staff where they are involved in the audit. The independence issue is simply that the shareholder (the auditor in this case) may be more interested in the value of the shares than providing a "correct "opinion on the financial statements.

The shares should be disposed of as soon as possible. However, given the inside knowledge of the listing, disposal now, or delaying disposal a few days to obtain a better price may be considered "insider dealing". It may be better that the audit manager resigns from the audit immediately to limit any real or potential independence problems. Professional advice may be needed on when to sell the shares.

(b)   Meeting corporate governance requirements

Currently, the only action that the directors appear to have taken is to establish an audit committee. Given that NorthCee is going to be listed on a recognised stock exchange, then there are other corporate governance requirements to be met. These requirements include:
–   Ensuring that the chairman and the company chief executive officer (CEO) are different people.
–   Appointing non-executive directors (NEDs) to the board of NorthCee. The number of NEDs should be the same as the number of executive directors less the chairman.
–   Ensuring that at least one NED has relevant financial experience.

- Appointing the NEDs to the audit committee, remuneration committee and possibly an appointments committee. The chairman will also have a seat on these committees.
- Establishing an internal audit department to review NorthCee's internal control systems and make reports to the audit committee.
- Ensure that NorthCee has an appropriate system of internal control and that the directors recognise their responsibilities for establishing and maintaining this system.
- Establishing procedures to maintain contact with institutional shareholders and any other major shareholders. The evening reception for shareholders could become a regular event in this respect.
- Checking that the annual financial report contains information on corporate governance required by the stock exchange (eg a report on how directors monitor the internal control systems).

(c) Communication with the audit committee

Under most systems of corporate governance, the external auditor's primary point of contact with a company is the audit committee. There are various reasons for this:

- Initially, to ensure that there is independence between the board of directors and the audit firm. The audit committee consists of non-executive directors (NEDs), who by definition are independent of the company and can therefore take an objective view of the audit report.

- The audit committee will have more time to review the audit report and other communications to the company from the auditor (eg management letters) than the board. The auditor should therefore benefit from their reports being reviewed carefully.

- The audit committee can ensure that any recommendations from the auditor are implemented. The audit committee has independent NEDs who can pressurise the board to taking action on auditor recommendations.

- The audit committee also has more time to review the effectiveness and efficiency of the work of the external auditor than the board. The committee can therefore make recommendations on the re-appointment of the auditor, or recommend a different firm if this would be appropriate.

4 (a) Control weaknesses and recommendations

Control weakness	Internal control recommendation
Employees can be paid for work not done. There appears to be no check to ensure that hours recorded in the computer system actually relate to hours worked.	A record of hours worked by each employee should be printed from the computerised wages system and signed by the site foreman to confirm that the hours are accurate.
There is no check to ensure that each employee inputs his/her employee number. One employee could input two numbers hiding the fact that one employee is absent.	The computerised wages system should print a list of employees present per the computer system during the day and the foreman should then sign this list to confirm it is accurate.
Fake or dummy employees can be put onto the payroll. The foreman can set up employee records for workers who do not exist. As payment is made automatically from the record of hours worked.	The wages office should check the list of employees against personnel records of authorised employees. Any new employees particularly should be verified in this way before payment is made.
The staff in the wages office could collude by setting up fake employee records in a similar way to the site foreman.	The list of employees on the payroll should be checked for accuracy by a person outside of the wages department, for example the personnel department or the chief accountant. The list of net payments should be signed by this person to show it is correct.
Gross pay inflated by wages department staff. The staff in the wages department could add extra hours to the records of some employees, and remove the net pay from the payment received from the courier prior to making up the pay packets.	The computerised payroll system should be programmed to produce a list of all amendments made to the payroll. This list should be reviewed by a responsible official outside of the wages department prior to wages being paid. Alternatively, the computerised payroll system should produce payslips for each employee showing the hours worked, gross and net pay etc. Employees should then check that the cash paid agrees to the net payment recorded on the payslip.

(b) Fraud and External/Internal audit

Guidance on the auditor's responsibility with respect to fraud can be found in ISA 240 *The Auditor's Responsibility to Consider Fraud in an Audit of Financial Statements*.

Main reason for audit work

The external auditor is primarily responsible for the audit opinion on the financial statements. The main focus of audit work is therefore to ensure that the financial statements show a true and fair view. The detection of fraud is therefore not the main focus of the external auditor's work.

The main focus of the work of the internal auditor is checking that the internal control systems in a company are working correctly. Part of that work may be to conduct detailed review of systems to ensure that fraud is not taking place.

Materiality

In reaching the audit opinion and performing audit work, the external auditor takes into account the concept of materiality. In other words, the external auditor is not responsible for checking all transactions. Audit procedures are planned to have a reasonable likelihood of identifying material fraud,

However, internal auditors may carry out a detailed review of transactions, effectively using a much lower materiality limit. It is more likely that internal auditors will detect fraud from their audit testing.

Identification of fraud

In situations where the external auditor does detect fraud, then the auditor will need to consider the implications for the entire audit. In other words, the external auditor has a responsibility to extend testing into other areas because the risk of providing an incorrect audit opinion will have increased.

Where internal auditors detect fraud, they may extend testing into other areas. However, audit work is more likely to focus on determining the extent of fraud and ensuring similar fraud has not occurred in other locations.

(c) Use of expert

Qualification

The consultant should have a relevant qualification to show ability to undertake the work. In this case being a member of a relevant computer society or the Institute of Internal Auditors would be appropriate.

Experience

The consultant should be able to show relevant experience from previous projects for example, upgrading or amending wages systems for other clients.

References

Hopefully the consultant will be able to provide references from previous employers showing capability to undertake the work.

Project management skills

The consultant should be able to display appropriate project management skills as managing a team will be an important element of the systems change work.

Access to information

The consultant will need access to important and sensitive information in SouthLea. The chief accountant must ensure that this information will be made available to third parties. The consultant will have to sign a confidentiality agreement.

Acceptance by other staff

Employing a consultant can be difficult as other internal audit staff may feel threatened or resentful that a consultant has been employed. The chief internal auditor must ensure that the reasons for employing the consultant are understood by members of the internal audit department.

5 (a) Fire at warehouse

(i) Audit procedures

- Discuss the matter with the directors checking whether the company has sufficient inventory to continue trading in the short term.

- Enquire that the directors are satisfied that the company can continue to trade in the longer term. Ask the directors to sign an additional letter of representation to this effect.

- Obtain a schedule showing the inventory destroyed and if possible check this is reasonable given past production records and inventory valuations.

- Enquire that the insurers have been informed. Review correspondence from the insurers confirming the amount of the insurance claim.

- Consider whether or not EastVale can continue as a going concern, given the loss of inventory and potential damage to the company's reputation if customer orders cannot be fulfilled.

(ii) Amendment to financial statements

- Enquire whether the directors have considered whether the event needs disclosure in the financial statements. Disclosure is unlikely given that the inventory was not in existence at the year-end and on the assumption that insurance is adequate to cover the loss.

- Amendment is not required as the fire did not affect any company property and the inventory would not have been in existence at the year end (inventory turn being very high).

(iii) Modification of audit report

- Consider modifying the audit report with an emphasis of matter paragraph to draw attention to the disclosure of the note on the fire in the financial statements.

- If the going concern status of EastVale is in doubt, then consider modifying the audit report with an emphasis of matter paragraph to this effect.

- If disclosure made by the directors is considered to be inadequate, then modify the audit report with an "except for" qualification.

(b) Batch of cheese

(i) Audit procedures

- Discuss the matter with the directors, determining specifically whether there was any fault in the production process.

- Obtain a copy of the damages claim and again discuss with the directors the effect on EastVale and the possibility of success of the claim.

- Obtain independent legal advice on the claim from EastVale's lawyers. Attempt to determine the extent of damages that may have to be paid.

- Review any press reports about the contaminated cheese. Consider the impact on the reputation of EastVale and whether the company can continue as a going concern.

- Discuss the going concern issue with the directors. Obtain an additional letter of representation on the directors' opinion of the going concern status of EastVale.

(ii) Amendment to financial statements

- The event should be disclosed in the financial statements in accordance with IAS 37 *Provisions, Contingent Liabilities and Contingent Assests* as it may have a significant impact on EastVale. Over two-thirds of EastVale's customers have either stopped purchasing products from the company or are considering taking this action.

- No adjustment is required for the event itself as it was not a condition at the balance sheet date.

- However, the event may become adjusting if company's reputation has been damaged and the amount of the legal claim is significant. In this situation the directors may decide that EastVale is no longer a going concern so the financial statements may have to be re-drafted on a break-up basis. This action complies with International Accounting Standard 8; the break-up basis is used where the directors have no realistic alternative but to liquidate the company.

(iii) Modification of audit report

Modification of the audit report depends on the director's actions above.

–   If the financial statements are prepared on a breakup basis, and the auditor agrees with that assessment, then a modified report can be issued with an emphasis of matter paragraph drawing attention to the accounting basis used.

–   However, if the financial statements are prepared on a going concern basis then the auditor should consider modifying the audit report with an emphasis of matter paragraph to draw attention to the disclosure of the note on the fire in the financial statements. This is providing that the auditor agrees that the going concern basis is appropriate.

–   If the going concern status of EastVale is in doubt, then consider modifying the audit report with an emphasis of matter paragraph to this effect, drawing attention to disclosure made by the directors.

–   If EastVale is not a going concern, and the financial statements have been prepared using this assumption, qualify the audit report with an adverse qualification stating that the company is not a going concern.

Review Form & Free Prize Draw – Paper F8 Audit and Assurance (International) (6/07)

All original review forms from the entire BPP range, completed with genuine comments, will be entered into one of two draws on 31 January 2008 and 31 July 2008. The names on the first four forms picked out on each occasion will be sent a cheque for £50.

Name: _____ **Address:** _____

_____

_____

How have you used this Kit?
(Tick one box only)

☐ Home study (book only)

☐ On a course: college _____

☐ With 'correspondence' package

☐ Other _____

Why did you decide to purchase this Kit?
(Tick one box only)

☐ Have used the complementary Study Text

☐ Have used other BPP products in the past

☐ Recommendation by friend/colleague

☐ Recommendation by a lecturer at college

☐ Saw advertising

☐ Other _____

During the past six months do you recall seeing/receiving any of the following?
(Tick as many boxes as are relevant)

☐ Our advertisement in *Student Accountant*

☐ Our advertisement in *Pass*

☐ Our advertisement in *PQ*

☐ Our brochure with a letter through the post

☐ Our website www.bpp.com

Which (if any) aspects of our advertising do you find useful?
(Tick as many boxes as are relevant)

☐ Prices and publication dates of new editions

☐ Information on product content

☐ Facility to order books off-the-page

☐ None of the above

Which BPP products have you used?

Text	☐	*Success CD*	☐	*Learn Online*	☐
Kit	☑	*i-Learn*	☐	*Home Study Package*	☐
Passcard	☐	*i-Pass*	☐	*Home Study PLUS*	☐

Your ratings, comments and suggestions would be appreciated on the following areas.

	Very useful	Useful	Not useful
Passing ACCA exams	☐	☐	☐
Passing F8	☐	☐	☐
Planning your question practice	☐	☐	☐
Questions	☐	☐	☐
Top Tips etc in answers	☐	☐	☐
Content and structure of answers	☐	☐	☐
'Plan of attack' in mock exams	☐	☐	☐
Mock exam answers			

Overall opinion of this Kit	Excellent ☐	Good ☐	Adequate ☐	Poor ☐

Do you intend to continue using BPP products?   Yes ☐   No ☐

The BPP author of this edition can be e-mailed at: jaitindergill@bpp.com

Please return this form to: Nick Weller, ACCA Publishing Manager, BPP Learning Media, FREEPOST, London, W12 8BR

Review Form & Free Prize Draw (continued)

TELL US WHAT YOU THINK

Please note any further comments and suggestions/errors below.

Free Prize Draw Rules

1   Closing date for 31 January 2008 draw is 31 December 2007. Closing date for 31 July 2008 draw is 30 June 2008.

2   Restricted to entries with UK and Eire addresses only. BPP employees, their families and business associates are excluded.

3   No purchase necessary. Entry forms are available upon request from BPP Learning Media. No more than one entry per title, per person. Draw restricted to persons aged 16 and over.

4   Winners will be notified by post and receive their cheques not later than 6 weeks after the relevant draw date.

5   The decision of the promoter in all matters is final and binding. No correspondence will be entered into.